ATE D

GRANT W. NEWTON, C.P.A., received his Ph.D. from New York University Graduate School of Business Administration. He is a member of the accounting faculty of the University of Alabama and formerly taught at the University of Bridgeport. Dr. Newton is an active participant in accounting continuing education instruction, specializing in the area of bankruptcy and insolvency.

BANKRUPTCY AND INSOLVENCY ACCOUNTING

Practice and Procedure

GRANT W. NEWTON, C.P.A.

THE RONALD PRESS COMPANY • NEW YORK

Library of Congress Catalog Card Number: 75–14948
PRINTED IN THE UNITED STATES OF AMERICA

To Lauren

Preface

This book is designed to provide a broad range of practical guidance for accountants, lawyers, bankruptcy trustees, referees, and creditors of business enterprises in financial straits.

The role of the independent accountant is viewed against a background of economic, legal, and management considerations, and the interdependence of the various interests involved is clearly delineated.

From informal adjustments made out of court through full court proceedings under Chapter XI jurisdiction, the book discusses alternative courses of action, working procedures, and statutory requirements applicable to the particular situation. The accountant is shown the type of information required by the debtor attorney for the bankruptcy petition and how to prepare operating statements to be filed with the court. He is aided in formulating a plan of arrangement that will gain acceptance by creditors and at the same time allow the client to operate his business successfully. The means by which the accountant can help the creditors' committee exercise adequate control over the debtor's activities are also described.

The bankruptcy and insolvency audit is explored in detail, with emphasis on the detection of irregularities and procedures to be performed if irregularities exist. The types of reports often required of the accountant are illustrated, and advice is offered on the special problems encountered in reporting on a company in financial difficulty. The reader is taken step by step through a typical bankruptcy audit including preparation of requisite forms and issuance of the audit report.

Taxes, which often impose undue hardship on the bankrupt during the administration period, are dealt with in a separate chapter. Instructions are given for tax minimization, filing returns, treatment of income during bankruptcy, and dealing with the varied tax planning and compliance problems peculiar to bankruptcy.

In addition to the coverage of practical procedure and statutory provisions, the book views the history of financial failure and surveys the proposed legislation for bankruptcy practice reform. It is hoped, therefore, that the work overall will serve the advancement of understanding and competence in this essential but neglected area of accounting.

GRANT W. NEWTON

September, 1975

Acknowledgments

Many individuals provided invaluable assistance during the writing of this book, particularly the members of the Committee on Development of a Manual of Bankruptcy and Insolvency Procedures of the New York Society of Certified Public Accountants who provided support, encouragement, and timely assistance on many occasions.

While it is not possible to recognize all of the persons to whom thanks are due, acknowledgment is gratefully given to Robert A. Adams and Dan E. Williams of Arthur Andersen & Co.; Bernard L. Augen, Louis Klein, Milton Mintzer, and Irving Rom of Clarence Rainess & Co.; Kermit Easton of S. D. Leidesdorf & Co.; Walter J. Henning of J. K. Lasser & Co.; Jerry Klein of Hertz, Herson & Co.; Joseph E. Lane, Jr. of The University of Alabama; Norman Martin and Jeremy Wiesen of New York University; Elliot Meisel of Roberts & Leinwander; Alexander E. Slater and Jerry Toder of Seidman & Seidman; Burton D. Strumpf of Ballon, Stoll & Itzler; and Edward A. Weinstein of Touche Ross & Co.

I am especially grateful to Dr. Lee J. Seidler, New York University, for introducing me to the area of bankruptcy accounting and for the many valuable suggestions he provided during the writing of the book.

I must thank Shirley Powell for the excellent job she did in typing the manuscript, and Sam W. Jackson, my graduate assistant, for his contributions. Finally, I express appreciation to my wife, Lauren, for her research assistance and her constant encouragement and patience.

It should be emphasized, however, that final responsibility for the views and information contained in this work is borne by the author alone.

G. W. N.

Contents

BANKRUPTCY AND INSOLVENCY ACCOUNTING

1

The Accountant's Role

in Perspective

1. Thousands of businesses fail each year in the United States and the number grew considerably in 1974, the first increase in seven years. The liabilities associated with these failures have escalated every year since 1968, representing a percentage increase of over 300 per cent. It has been estimated that one out of every five Americans has been involved in bankruptcy proceedings as a bankrupt or a creditor, or is acquainted with someone who has become bankrupt.[1]

2. At one time or another almost all accountants will find that one or more of their clients are experiencing some type of financial difficulty. Since accountants are often the first professional persons to realize that a financial problem exists, they are in a position to

---

[1] David T. Stanley *et al.*, *Bankruptcy: Problems, Process, Reform* (Washington, D. C.: The Brookings Institution, 1971), p. 1.

3

render very valuable services. Before accountants can give useful advice to a financially troubled client, they must be thoroughly familiar with the various alternatives available to the client and the ramifications of each.

3. The purpose of this book is to analyze in detail the accountant's role in bankruptcy and insolvency procedures, and to provide a practice guide which will assist accountants in rendering professional services in bankruptcy and insolvency proceedings. The book describes those aspects of bankruptcy and insolvency proceedings of which accountants must be aware, delineating their functions and duties and the procedures they must follow in the auditing inquiry and in the preparation of the various financial statements and reports that are required by the courts. It presents the accounting methods, procedures, and techniques that may be used and explains the applicability of generally accepted accounting principles (GAAP) and generally accepted auditing standards (GAAS) to bankruptcy and insolvency. Finally, it discusses the conflicts and problems in principles and practice.

4. It is hoped that this book will also benefit non-accountants such as referees, judges, receivers, and attorneys in clarifying the purposes, nature, and limitations of the services of the accountant. Although the primary effort in the development of the book has been directed to the accountant in an explanation of "how to do it" and in a discussion of the ethical problems and responsibilities involved, the coverage of the economic and legal aspects of bankruptcy and insolvency should be of value to other professionals involved in these proceedings.

SCOPE OF COVERAGE

5. The scope of the book is, deliberately, fairly broad. The various accounting procedures to be followed under each alternative remedy for business failure are analyzed in detail. To provide a complete and realistic description of the environment within which the accountant must work, the discussion incorporates the economics and the legal aspects of business bankruptcies.

6. The economics of insolvency proceedings is most important when considering the various causes of financial difficulties. Once the causes have been ascertained, the most appropriate remedy may then be determined. Economic considerations are also important

when analyzing what remedies have proven most successful in particular circumstances.

7. The legal aspects of bankruptcy permeate the entire book, for the Federal Bankruptcy Act establishes the framework within which anyone concerned with insolvency must work. As a result the Bankruptcy Act is explicitly cited in the descriptions of the petitions, forms, and schedules which must be filed; the alternatives and rights available to all parties involved, including the creditors; the requirements of the debtor; and the treatment of the various transactions and property of the debtor, both before and after the proceedings. Insolvency proceedings cannot be correctly handled unless everyone involved has a thorough understanding of the legal aspects of the case.

8. Only about 10 per cent of the bankruptcy petitions are filed by businesses. The majority of the balance are filed by wage earners; however, it is primarily the business bankruptcies which require the services of an accountant. As a result, the book is written for business bankruptcies. Although the emphasis is on incorporated businesses, the book is also applicable to partnerships and proprietaries since, with the exception of Chapter X, the remedies available are basically the same.

THE NEED FOR ACCOUNTANTS' SERVICES

9. The accountant may become a party to insolvency and bankruptcy proceedings while serving a client who is having financial problems. In an arrangement under Chapter XI of the Bankruptcy Act, the debtor, who remains in possession, has the right to retain an accountant to perform necessary accounting functions.

10. Reorganization of a corporation involves additional parties who may need the assistance of accountants. These include the attorneys, trustee, examiner, unsecured creditors, security holders, and stockholders.

11. In liquidation proceedings the accountant often assists in accounting for the distribution of the debtor's assets. If the liquidation proceedings are initiated involuntarily, the petitioning creditors will need the assistance of an accountant in establishing a case of insolvency, and the debtor will need an accountant's assistance in trying to prove a defense of solvency. An audit investigation may be required for specific purposes, such as by the

debtor to defend a turnover proceeding or by a third party to defend a suit by the trustee alleging a preferential transfer.[2]

12. The trustee in an insolvency proceeding most frequently finds it necessary to employ an accountant to audit the debtor's books, records, and transactions. A corporation's past transactions may need investigation to determine whether any assets have been concealed or removed or any preferences, fraudulent conveyances, or other voidable transactions committed. Often the debtor may have kept inadequate books and records, further complicating the situation.

13. Under Section 339(2) of the Bankruptcy Act the creditors' committee is permitted to employ such agents, attorneys, and accountants as may be necessary to assist it in the performance of its functions. Thus it may retain its own accountant to audit the debtor's books and records. The creditors' committee is expected to render an opinion on the plan of arrangement and to do so it must have knowledge of the debtor's acts and property. It must know the value of the debtor's assets in liquidation and the nature of the transactions entered into by the debtor before proceedings began. Since accountants are most qualified to establish these facts, they are often engaged to perform an investigatory audit so that the committee will be able to give an informed opinion on the plan.

14. The debtor's internal accounting staff is also actively involved in the proceedings. Staff members often provide information or advice which assists the debtor in selecting the appropriate remedy. They also provide the debtor's attorneys with the accounting information needed to file the bankruptcy petition.

"Accountants" Defined

15. It is not unusual to see several accountants involved in bankruptcy proceedings. There may be independent accountants for the debtor, internal accountants of a debtor company, independent accountants for the receiver or trustee, and independent accountants representing the creditors' committee. Many of the accounting functions may be performed by more than one accountant. For example, each of the accountants will want to determine

---

[2] Asa S. Herzog, "CPA's Role in Bankruptcy Proceeding," *The Journal of Accountancy*, Vol. 117 (January 1964), p. 59.

the underlying causes of failure. The term "accountants" is used here to refer to any accountant involved in the proceedings; where the service must be rendered by a particular accountant, the type of accountant is identified either in the text or at the beginning of the chapter.

TOPICAL OVERVIEW

Economic Causes of Business Failure

16. The first topic discussed, in Chapter 2, is the economic causes which lead to business failure. A knowledge of the common causes of financial trouble can often enable the accountant to identify a potential problem, and corrective action can be taken before the situation becomes too serious. Methods of detecting failure tendencies are also described.

Alternatives Available to a Financially Troubled Business

17. In order to effectively render services in bankruptcy and insolvency proceedings, the accountant must be familiar with the Federal Bankruptcy Act. Chapter 3 begins with a discussion of the history of the Act, and the provisions of the Act are described throughout Chapters 3 and 4.

18. The debtor's first alternatives are to locate new financing, to merge with another company, or to find some other basic solution to its situation, in order to avoid the necessity of discussing its problems with representatives of creditors. If none of these alternatives is possible, the debtor may be required to seek a remedy from creditors, either informally (out of court), or with the help of judicial proceedings. To insure that the reader is familiar with some of the alternatives available, they are briefly described in the paragraphs that follow. The alternatives are described in greater detail in Chapters 3 and 4.

Informal Arrangement with Creditors' Committee

19. The debtor may request a meeting with a few of the largest creditors and one or two representatives of the small claimants to effect an informal agreement. The function of such a

committee may be merely to investigate, consult, and give advice to the debtor, or it may involve actual supervision of the business or liquidation of the assets. The chief disadvantage of this remedy is that there is nothing binding those who dissent to the plan.

Informal Composition Settlement

20. An informal composition settlement, usually involving an extension of time, a pro rata settlement, or a combination of the two, may be requested by the debtor. The details of the plan are worked out between the debtor and creditors, the latter perhaps represented by a committee. Such extralegal proceedings are most successful when there are only a few creditors, adequate accounting records have been kept, and past relationships have been amicable.

Assignment for Benefit of Creditors (State Courts)

21. A remedy available through the state courts to a corporation in serious financial difficulties is an "assignment for the benefit of creditors." In this instance, the debtor voluntarily transfers title to its assets to an assignee who then liquidates them and distributes the proceeds among the creditors. Again, to be successful, it is necessary to have the consent of all the creditors or at least their agreement to refrain from taking action, because this procedure is an act of bankruptcy which then gives creditors the right to file an involuntary bankruptcy petition. Assignment for the benefit of creditors is an extreme remedy because it results in the cessation of the business.

22. Proceedings brought in the federal courts are governed by the Federal Bankruptcy Act. It will normally be necessary to resort to such formality when suits have already been filed against the debtor and its property is under garnishment or attachment.

Arrangements—Chapter XI Proceedings

23. Chapter XI of the Bankruptcy Act sets forth provisions for an arrangement with creditors, subject to court approval, with the corporation remaining in business and securing an extension of time, a pro rata settlement, or both. The petition must be voluntary; proceedings must be initiated by the debtor. This remedy is used primarily by small, individual businesses and corporations with few

stockholders, when the debtor is unable to secure sufficient creditor agreement for an informal composition settlement. Recently, many large companies have also found that the provisions of Chapter XI are more suitable for their needs than the formal reorganization proceedings under Chapter X of the Act. Chapter XI is most appropriate for those businesses which, given time, may be able to salvage their situation, gain financial stability, and avoid liquidation. With court confirmation of the plan, the debtor is discharged from all of its unsecured liabilities. Proceedings under Chapter XI are by far the most commonly used remedy when a company finds itself in financial difficulty. Because of the vast importance of this remedy, Chapter 4 of this book has been devoted entirely to a detailed discussion of Chapter XI proceedings.

Reorganization—Chapter X Proceedings

24. Proceedings under Chapter X of the Bankruptcy Act are aimed at a complete reorganization of the debtor corporation. Chapter X may not be used until it has been shown that adequate relief cannot be obtained under Chapter XI. To determine which method should be used, it is necessary to look at the "needs to be served." [3] It should first be determined whether the business is worth saving and will be able to operate profitably; if not, the corporation should be liquidated.

25. Chapter X is properly used when the stock or securities of the corporation are widely held and its creditors are diversely located so that their interests probably would not be protected by Chapter XI. Proceedings may be voluntarily or involuntarily initiated. Greater protection is afforded the creditors and minority shareholders under Chapter X when a recasting of the capital structure is necessary and there is a large number of public owners or a highly complex capital structure. Where secured debt becomes involved, in order to successfully rehabilitate the debtor, Chapter X will be necessary. Reorganization will allow the corporation to resume business in its new form without the burden of debt which existed prior to the proceedings.

26. There is much greater power under Chapter X for investigation and review. There will be new management in the

---

[3] Leon S. Forman, *Compositions, Bankruptcy, and Arrangements* (Philadelphia: The American Law Institute, 1971), p. 170.

form of a trustee and, generally, new accountants. These new managers and accountants sit in judgment on those leaving the business. As a result, Chapter X proceedings are most costly; however, they do provide for independent review as to the factors causing financial difficulty.

Straight Bankruptcy and Liquidation

27. Straight bankruptcy is used only when the corporation sees no hope of being able to operate successfully or to obtain the necessary creditor agreement. Under this alternative, the corporation is liquidated, the remaining assets are distributed to creditors after administrative expenses are paid, and the debtor is discharged from its liabilities. Chapters I through VII of the Bankruptcy Act contain the provisions for the liquidation of the bankrupt's estate.

28. The decision as to whether rehabilitation or liquidation is best also depends upon the amount to be realized from each alternative. The method resulting in the greatest return to the creditors and stockholders should be chosen. The amount to be received from liquidation depends on the resale value of the firm's assets minus the costs of dismantling and legal expenses. The value of the firm after rehabilitation must be determined (net of the costs of achieving the remedy). The alternative leading to the highest value should be followed.

29. Financially troubled debtors often attempt an informal settlement or liquidation out of court, but if it is unsuccessful they will then initiate proceedings under the Bankruptcy Act. Other debtors, especially those with a large number of creditors, may not try an out-of-court settlement but at the time they recognize continuance of the business under existing conditions is impossible, the bankruptcy petition will be filed.

30. Table 1–1 summarizes the most common alternatives available to the debtor in case the first course of action proves unsuccessful.

Retention of the Accountant and Fees

31. Accountants must be retained by order of the court before they can render services in bankruptcy proceedings for the receiver, trustee, or debtor-in-possession. For out-of-court settlement, the

TABLE 1-1. Schedule of Alternatives Available

Unsuccessful Action	Alternatives Available
Informal arrangement with creditors	Assignment for benefit of creditors (state court) Arrangement—Chapter XI Reorganization—Chapter X Straight Bankruptcy
Informal composition settlement	Assignment for benefit of creditors (state court) Arrangement—Chapter XI Reorganization—Chapter X Straight bankruptcy
Assignment for benefit of creditors (state court)	Straight bankruptcy
Arrangement—Chapter XI	Reorganization—Chapter X Straight bankruptcy
Reorganization—Chapter X	Straight bankruptcy

accountant obtains a signed engagement letter. Chapter 5 of the book describes and provides examples of the formal and informal retention procedures, and illustrates how independent accountants must clearly set forth the scope of their examination and not deviate from it. The chapter also enumerates the factors to consider in estimating fees and keeping time records, and describes the procedure for filing a petition for compensation.

Accounting Services

32. In addition to the usual accounting services performed for the debtor, the accountant provides information needed in the bankruptcy petition, prepares operating statements for the courts, and assists in formulating a plan of arrangement. Chapter 6 provides information concerning the nature of these services.

33. The creditors' committee often needs an accountant to assist them in protecting their interests and supervising the activities of the bankrupt. Some of the services rendered by the accountant, which are described in Chapter 7, include assisting the committee in exercising adequate control over the bankrupt's activities,

performing an investigation and audit of the operations of the business, and assisting the committee in evaluating the proposed plan of settlement or arrangement.

Auditing and Financial Reporting

34. Reporting on insolvent companies requires the application of audit procedures which vary somewhat from those used under normal circumstances. Emphasis in Chapter 8 is on audit procedures which differ from those used under normal conditions and on procedures which assist in the discovery of irregularities and fraud. Chapter 9 describes and illustrates some of the financial reports the accountant prepares in insolvency and bankruptcy proceedings, and describes the nature of the accountant's opinion associated with the reports.

Tax Aspects

35. Chapter 10 covers the statutory tax reporting and filing requirements and points out how proper tax planning can preserve and even enlarge the debtor's estate.

Bankruptcy Act of 1973

36. In 1970, Congress established a Commission to study the bankruptcy laws and make recommendations for improving the 1898 law as amended, which is still in effect. The Commission's recommendations, known as the "Bankruptcy Act of 1973" are now being considered by Congress. Chapter 11 of the text analyzes some of the key provisions of the proposed new law and compares these provisions with the current law.

RESPONSIBILITIES OF INDEPENDENT ACCOUNTANT

37. Independent accountants are aware that their responsibilities to clients often extend beyond merely auditing the books and giving an opinion on the financial statements. They frequently give management an opinion on the progress of the business, its future, and avenues of improvement, not only in the system of record keeping, but in the overall management of the enterprise. The

intensity of involvement required depends upon several factors, including an individual judgment to be made by the accountant.

38. Independent accountants also owe some degree of responsibility to third parties interested in their clients' affairs. This includes the duty to remain independent so that an unbiased opinion can be rendered. The accountant is also relied upon to reveal all those facts which might be relevant and important to other persons. This again involves judgment as to the level of disclosure which is appropriate. See Chapter 6, paragraphs 55–69.

39. The accountant's position and responsibilities as they relate to a client experiencing financial difficulties and to third parties interested in the proceedings will be considered in the remaining sections of this chapter.

Observation of Business Decline

40. The first and most crucial step in any situation involving a business in financial trouble is recognizing that a problem exists. This is important because corrective action should be taken as soon as possible, to halt any further deterioration in the firm's position.

41. Many people normally maintain close contact with a business—management, employees, lawyers, accountants, customers, competitors, suppliers, owners, and the government, to list only the most obvious ones. Few of these persons, however, would be in a position to recognize when the enterprise is headed for trouble. Normally this requires someone who intimately works with the financial data and is trained in analyzing such information. Usually only the financial managers of the business, such as the treasurer and controller, or the independent accountants employed by the firm have these qualifications.

42. Some independent accountants who conduct only an annual audit and do not maintain close contact with their client throughout the year are often of little assistance in recognizing a potential problem. However, in many small and medium-size businesses the accountants not only conduct the annual audit but review quarterly and monthly statements and render various types of advisory services. In these situations, the accountants are aware of what has been occurring in the major accounts and in the firm as a whole and, because of their education and experience in business

finances, they should be able to identify when an enterprise is headed for trouble and alert management to their suspicions. Thus, because of the nature of both the type of work they do and the ability they possess, accountants are in an excellent position to identify any tendencies to failure.

43. As an example, the independent accountants of a New York garment business had served as auditors for the company for many years. The company had been operative through successive generations of the same family for approximately 90 years. As a consequence of changing fashion styles, the company experienced a few consecutive years of operating losses. The accountants noticed that the company was not taking any action to correct the loss trend—the president, in fact, seemed incapable of reversing the situation. Although there was still some working capital and net worth which might have enabled the company to obtain credit and continue in business, the accountants suggested that the following actions be taken:

Discontinue placing orders for raw materials for the upcoming season, other than to permit completion of orders on hand.

Start terminating personnel in the areas of design, production, and administration.

Offer the plant facilities for sale.

Liquidate inventories in an orderly fashion.

Meet with creditors to explain the situation.

44. The accountants' suggestions were followed and the plants were sold, resulting in a settlement with creditors at 87.5¢ on the dollar. The stockholders received payment in full on a mortgage loan which they had made to the company. Had the accountants' suggestions not been followed, further substantial operating losses would most probably have been incurred; the creditors would have been fortunate to receive a distribution of 15 per cent; and it is doubtful that the mortgage loan would have been paid in full.

45. To be able to recognize a potential problem, accountants need to have an understanding of the definition of financial failure, the nature of insolvency, and the most common causes of financial difficulties. They must have a familiarity with the characteristics of

business decline, which include lower absolute sales and slower growth in sales, poorer cash flow and weak cash position, deteriorating net income, insufficient working capital, large incurrence of debt, and high operating costs and fixed expenses. These symptoms are normally found in the accounting records, and the accountant is most likely to be first to recognize them.

Responsibility to Client

46. At the very first suspicion of pending financial trouble, accountants have a duty to alert management to the situation, submit as much supporting information as is possible, describe the various alternatives available to reverse the deterioration, and advise on what avenue should be chosen as a remedy. All these measures are taken to implore the client to begin corrective action before the situation becomes more serious, and the accountant should be concerned with pointing out to the client ways of avoiding insolvency. The responsibility of the independent accountant where fraud is involved is described in Chapter 8.

47. Should the situation have become serious enough to warrant some type of remedy outside the usual business corrective measures, the accountant must make a thorough analysis to determine the most appropriate action to be taken (Chapter 2). This involves an investigation into the causes of financial difficulty and steps which will correct the trouble. The accountant must therefore be familiar with the various alternatives available and when they are most appropriate. This involvement by the accountant should aid the debtor in adopting the rehabilitation procedure most likely to be successful.

48. It is also the accountant's responsibility to know the procedures which are required under each alternative remedy. In an out-of-court settlement, this involves awareness of the methods which have proven successful in particular situations. For example, in an informal composition the accountant should know when it is best to have all creditors meet and under what circumstances only a representative group is more advisable. When formal proceedings are initiated, it is imperative that the accountant know what information is required on the petition and what schedules must be filed. Otherwise it would not be possible to converse with the

debtor's attorney, which could quite conceivably delay the settlement and cause further deterioration in the client's position.

49. Timing is very crucial in a situation involving insolvency. Should the accountant fail to alert the debtor to the situation and urge some action, the creditors might move first and attempt legally to seize the assets. Speed is also important if the debtor wishes to file voluntarily and remain in possession.

Advice on Selection of Attorneys

50. One of the first steps of a debtor faced with financial difficulties is the employment of legal counsel. When a company realizes that it will be unable to continue profitable operations or pay liabilities as they become due, it should quickly seek a lawyer to help effect a compromise or extension of the indebtedness. Since the independent accountant is often the first professional the client contacts concerning financial difficulties, the accountant is frequently asked for advice as to the selection of a special bankruptcy attorney.

51. There are many advantages to the accountant's involvement at this point. Frequently accountants are aware of those attorneys most familiar with insolvency cases, and can recommend someone with adequate experience and knowledge. By suggesting a lawyer of known reputation, the accountant is assured of working with someone in whom full confidence can be placed. It is imperative that the accountant and attorney be able to work well together. The accountant should be present at the meetings with the debtor and provide the counsel with an overall view of the bankrupt's financial condition and the events which preceded it, including the basic facts and information about the business, its history, and the causes of its present difficulties.

52. Because they are most familiar with the attorneys best qualified in this field and will be required to work with the lawyer chosen by the debtor, accountants have good reason to be involved in the selection process. However, the situation may give rise to questions concerning an accountant's independence because if an attorney is recommended more on the basis of friendship with the person than on qualifications, the accountant is not being fair to the client. The accountant must be very careful not to have a vested

interest in any attorney suggested. But disregarding this situation, the accountant is a logical person for the debtor to turn to for help in choosing legal counsel.

Other Steps To "Manage" the Proceedings

53. Accountants are often intimately involved in every aspect of a bankruptcy or insolvency case. They may "manage" the case from the initial discovery of financial trouble with suggestions as to the best remedy to seek, to any necessary alterations or modifications of the plan chosen, and finally to monitoring of the consummation of the proceedings. They maintain close contact with the creditors, working with their committee in an effort to find the most advantageous settlement for them. They then provide all the financial information concerning the debtor's progress and make sure all interested parties are aware of what is occurring. Possibly more than any other outside party, the accountant is responsible for the smooth and successful rehabilitation of the debtor. This is primarily because of a close involvement with all the interested parties, including the bankrupt, creditors, attorney, trustee, receiver, and governmental agencies.

2

Economic Causes of
Business Failures

1. Business failures have been with us as long as businesses have existed, and their end is not in sight. A failure may be in the form of a small retail store owner closing his door because he cannot pay his rent or it may be a large corporation that is forced to liquidate because of continuously mounting losses.

2. It is crucial for accountants to understand the material presented in this chapter because a knowledge of the common causes of financial troubles will enable accountants to identify a potential problem, alert management to their suspicions, and assist management in taking corrective action before the situation becomes too serious. Accountants can often point out to their clients ways of avoiding failure.

DEFINITION OF SUCCESSFUL AND
UNSUCCESSFUL BUSINESS

3. Terms indicative of financial difficulties are used indiscriminately in discussion and often fail to convey the legal or even the generally accepted meaning of the word.

4. *Failure* is defined by Webster as "the state or fact of being lacking or insufficient, 'falling short.' " While all businesses plan to be successful, not all of them accomplish their objective. The fact that many firms fail to achieve success is evidenced to some extent by the increasing number of businesses which discontinue operations each year. All of the businesses which were discontinued could not be defined as failures. No doubt several were discontinued because they were successful in that they had accomplished their objective.

5. Dun & Bradstreet has adopted the term failure to refer to those businesses which ceased operations following assignment or bankruptcy, ceased doing business with a loss to creditors, or were involved in court action such as reorganization or arrangement. The Department of Commerce discounted the reporting of new businesses and discounted business in 1962; however, for each year from 1940 to 1962 the number of failures reported by Dun & Bradstreet amounted to only 3 or 4 per cent of the total business discounted. Table 2-1 shows the number of failures for selected years as reported by Dun & Bradstreet. It should be pointed out that the failures only include the type of firms registered in Dun & Bradstreet's Reference Book. Specific types of businesses not included are financial enterprises, insurance and real estate companies, railroads, terminals, amusements, professionals, farmers, and many small single-owner services. A business would not have to be listed in the Reference Book to be included in the failure statistics provided it is engaged in a type of operation which is normally covered in the Reference Book.

6. A business is also known as a failure when it can no longer meet the legally enforceable demands of its creditors. If the debtor is unable to reach some type of an arrangement with the creditors, it may be necessary to file for relief under the provisions of the Bankruptcy Act. Under conditions where there is not only a certain

degree of lack of success but an official recognition of it, legal failure exists. Bankruptcy is the term most commonly used to refer to legal failure. "Bankruptcy" is also used to refer to an enterprise where the total liabilities exceed the fair value of the assets; however, when the term "bankruptcy" is used in this book it refers to the formal declaration by a firm in a federal court.

7. Table 2–1 also compares the Dun & Bradstreet failure record with the business bankruptcy petitions filed for the past several years. Since many firms that filed petitions with the bankruptcy court were not registered with Dun & Bradstreet, the number of business bankruptcy petitions filed is greater than the number of failures. The number of petitions filed in 1974 increased by 21 per cent to 23,253 cases while the number of failures increased by 6 per cent to 9,915 and for the first quarter of 1975 failures were up by 25 per cent.

CAUSES OF FINANCIAL DIFFICULTY

8. It is not easy to determine the exact cause or causes of financial difficulty in any individual case. Often it is the result of

TABLE 2-1. Comparison of Business Failures with
Business Bankruptcy Petitions Filed, 1963-73*

Year	Failure Record		Business Bankruptcy Petitions Filed	
	(1) Number	(2) Percentage of Change	(3) Number	(4) Percentage of Change
1963	14,374		16,302	
1964	13,501	− 6 %	16,510	1 %
1965	13,514	0.1	16,910	2.5
1966	13,061	− 3	16,430	− 3
1967	12,364	− 5	16,600	1
1968	9,636	−22	16,545	− 0.3
1969	9,154	− 5	15,430	− 7
1970	10,748	17	16,197	5
1971	10,326	− 4	19,103	18
1972	9,566	− 7	18,132	− 5
1973	9,345	− 2	19,787	8

*Calendar year was used for failures and fiscal year was used for bankruptcy petitions.

Sources: Column (1): The Business Failure Record 1973 (New York: Dun & Bradstreet, Inc., 1974), p. 2; column (3): United States District Courts, Bankruptcy Statistics (mimeographed).

TABLE 2-2. Causes of Business Failure—1973

Underlying Causes	Manufacturers	Wholesalers	Retailers	Construction	Commercial Services	All Concerns
Inexperience or incompetence:						
Lack of experience in the line	12.0%	11.4%	20.0%	12.8%	17.0%	16.4%
Lack of managerial experience	11.2	11.2	14.3	18.3	13.8	14.1
Unbalanced experience*	20.8	22.1	20.9	24.3	21.5	21.6
Incompetence	50.4	49.5	37.0	39.1	40.0	41.0
Total	94.4%	94.2%	92.2%	94.5%	92.3%	93.1%
Neglect	1.4%	2.2%	1.7%	1.6%	1.1%	1.6%
Fraud	0.8	1.6	1.4	1.6	0.8	1.3
Disaster	1.2	0.6	0.7	0.2	0	0.6
Reason unknown	2.2	1.4	4.0	2.1	5.8	3.4
Total	100.0%	100.0%	100.0%	100.0%	100.0%	100.0%
Number of failures	1,463	940	4,341	1,419	1,182	9,345
Average liabilities per failure	$545,106	$291,757	$154,994	$217,812	$207,240	$245,972

*Experience not well rounded in sales, finance, purchasing, and production on the part of the individual in case of proprietorship, or of two or more partners or officers constituting a management unit.

Source: The Business Failure Record, 1973 (New York: Dun & Bradstreet, Inc., 1974), p. 12.

several factors leading up to one event which immediately brings failure. A fundamental cause may not be at all obvious from the evidence at hand. Table 2–2, which is based on data prepared by Dun & Bradstreet, sets forth the causes of failure as observed by the creditors of the bankrupt firms. Different answers as to the fundamental causes would undoubtedly have been given if the bankrupt owners had been interviewed. A lack of capital would likely be high on the bankrupts' list of causes of failure, and incompetence would only rarely be admitted.

Size of Business Failures

9. Although the number of business failures has declined in recent years, the total liabilities associated with each failure have increased tremendously. Table 2–3 summarizes the failure trends since 1940, several of which are significant. First, the failure rate per 10,000 concerns decreased in 1973 to 36, which is the lowest rate since the early 1950's. In addition, the total number of failures

TABLE 2-3. Failure Trends Since 1940 (Selected Years)

Year	Number of Failures	Total Failure Liabilities ($000)	Failure Rate Per 10,000 Listed Concerns	Average Liability Per Failure
1940	13,619	$ 166,684	63	$ 12,239
1945	809	30,225	4	37,361
1950	9,162	248,283	34	27,099
1955	10,969	449,380	42	40,968
1960	15,445	933,630	57	60,772
1965	13,514	1,321,666	53	97,800
1966	13,061	1,385,659	52	106,091
1967	12,364	1,265,227	49	102,332
1968	9,636	940,996	39	97,654
1969	9,154	1,142,113	37	124,767
1970	10,748	1,887,754	44	175,638
1971	10,326	1,916,929	42	185,641
1972	9,566	2,000,244	38	209,099
1973	9,345	2,298,606	36	245,972

Source: The Business Failure Record, 1973 (New York: Dun & Bradstreet, Inc., 1974), p. 2.

continued to decline. The average liability per failure, however, has moved in the opposite direction. The average has increased to $245,972 in 1973 from only $97,654 in 1968. Part of this increase is due to the rise in prices which is reflected in larger asset and liability balances, but most of this change has been caused by a greater number of large companies having financial difficulties. Table 2–4, which presents the failure distribution by liability size, indicates the increased number of large companies that are having financial problems. The number of failures with liabilities in excess of $1,000,000 has increased from 155 in 1969 to 343 in 1973. Dun & Bradstreet reported that there were particularly large liabilities among failures of general merchandise retailers, general building contractors, business service enterprises, and textile and apparel manufacturers. For the first time, the number of failures with liabilities over $1,000,000 was greater than the number with liabilities under $5,000 as reported by Dun & Bradstreet. It remains to be seen whether the trend of large-company failures will continue.

TABLE 2-4. Failure Distribution by Liability Size, 1940-73 (Selected Years)

Year	Under $5,000		$5,000 to $25,000		$25,000 to $100,000		$100,000 to $1 Million		Over $1 Million	
	No.	%	No.	%	No.	%	No.	%	No.	%
1940	6,891	50.6	5,442	40.0	1,067	7.8	209	1.5	10	0.1
1945	270	33.4	343	42.4	146	18.0	45	5.6	5	0.6
1950	2,065	22.5	4,706	51.4	1,975	21.6	407	4.4	9	0.1
1955	1,785	16.3	5,412	49.3	2,916	26.6	820	7.5	36	0.3
1960	1,688	10.9	6,884	44.6	5,078	32.9	1,703	11.0	92	0.6
1965	1,007	7.5	5,067	37.5	5,266	39.0	2,005	14.8	169	1.2
1966	932	7.1	4,569	35.0	5,332	40.8	2,042	15.7	186	1.4
1967	814	6.6	4,434	35.9	4,896	39.6	2,045	16.5	175	1.4
1968	481	5.0	3,332	34.6	4,016	41.7	1,686	17.5	121	1.2
1969	416	4.6	3,000	32.8	3,776	41.2	1,807	19.7	155	1.7
1970	430	4.0	3,197	29.7	4,392	40.9	2,450	22.8	279	2.6
1971	392	3.8	2,806	27.2	4,413	42.7	2,423	23.5	292	2.8
1972	394	4.1	2,497	26.1	4,149	43.4	2,236	23.4	290	3.0
1973	285	3.0	2,434	26.1	3,908	41.8	2,375	25.4	343	3.7

Source: The Business Failure Record, 1973 (New York: Dun & Bradstreet, Inc., 1974), p. 7.

Geographic Distribution of Business Failures

10. During 1973, 12 per cent of the failures reported by Dun & Bradstreet occurred in New York City. This large percentage, which is consistent with prior years, is due in part to the large number of firms that have corporate offices in New York. Table 2–5

TABLE 2–5. Failures in 25 U.S. Cities,* 1972–73

City	1972 Number	1972 Liabilities ($000)	1973 Number	1973 Liabilities ($000)
New York, New York	1,256	$ 385,234	1,100	$ 445,031
Chicago, Illinois	111	38,682	147	27,907
Los Angeles, California	166	25,882	168	39.588
Philadelphia, Pennsylvania	105	27,953	114	22,994
Detroit, Michigan	151	77,420	127	29,817
Houston, Texas	243	37,259	151	57,129
Baltimore, Maryland	107	8,924	73	14,129
Dallas, Texas	89	48,264	79	20,928
Washington, D.C.	36	1,248	38	4,262
Cleveland, Ohio	59	7,114	33	22,484
Indianapolis, Indiana	22	3,923	17	2,105
Milwaukee, Wisconsin	52	6,302	51	7,297
San Francisco, California	58	15,452	95	23,790
San Diego, California	53	8,090	51	5,976
San Antonio, Texas	87	21,391	71	3,766
Boston, Massachusetts	32	11,379	36	67,858
Memphis, Tennessee	24	2,889	32	2,787
St. Louis, Missouri	29	2,115	20	4,458
New Orleans, Louisiana	25	4,042	23	2,319
Phoenix, Arizona	21	2,085	19	3,481
Columbus, Ohio	20	2,843	14	2,070
Seattle, Washington	23	1,733	23	13,233
Jacksonville, Florida	27	520	28	7,088
Pittsburgh, Pennsylvania	41	3,422	29	2,869
Denver, Colorado	26	4,925	22	3,905
Total, 25 cities	2,863	$ 749,091	2,561	$ 837,271
Balance of country	6,703	$1,251,153	6,784	$1,461,335
Total, United States	9,566	$2,000,244	9,345	$2,298,606

*These figures include city area only.

Source: The Business Failure Record, 1973 (New York: Dun & Bradstreet, Inc., 1974), p. 4.

summarizes the failures in 25 large cities in the United States for a two-year period. The nationwide total of failures has been decreasing during recent years and the number of failures in the 25 largest cities has generally increased; however, in 1973, the number of failures in these cities decreased 14 per cent while the number in the rest of the country increased 3 per cent. California, Oregon, and New York have the largest failure rate per 10,000 listed concerns.

Age of Business Failures

11. One of the most consistent bankruptcy statistics is the age at which companies fail. For the past twenty years the percentage of failures of companies which have been in business for five years or less has ranged only from 53.2 to 58.9 per cent. The percentage of failures of those in business between six and ten years has a range of less than 4 per cent since 1957. Table 2–6 shows the age of failures by industry for 1973. The retail industry has consistently had a larger percentage of failures in the first five years of operation than the other industries.

Business Failures and Economic Conditions

12. As would be expected, the number of business failures does increase as a result of a contraction of economic activity. The mild recessions of 1948–1949, 1953–1954, 1957–1958, 1960–1961, and 1969–1970 have all resulted in an increase in the number of business failures. The slowdown in economic activity which began in 1974 will also have its impact on the number of failures. For example, the number of business failures for January 1975 was 1,080 which represents an increase of approximately 35 per cent over the number for January 1974. Also, the SEC reviewed 117 bankruptcy petitions in fiscal 1974, but it estimated that it would process 1,225 in fiscal 1975 and 1,300 in fiscal 1976. During periods of expansion the failure rate has almost always decreased. It is very difficult to determine the impact of inflation on the number of failures. The number of failures decreased for the years 1971, 1972, and 1973 when the rate of inflation was the highest since the inflationary period following World War II. No doubt inflation does have an unfavorable effect on the operations of some firms but it tends to assist others.

TABLE 2-6. Age of Failed Businesses by Function—1973

Age in Years	Manufacturers	Wholesalers	Retailers	Construction	Commercial Services	All Concerns
One year or less	1.5%	0.9%	2.0%	0.8%	2.3%	1.7%
Two	10.8	11.0	17.0	11.4	12.5	13.9
Three	16.9	15.8	20.8	16.0	16.3	18.4
Total, three years or less	29.2	27.7	39.8	28.2	31.1	34.0
Four	10.7	12.2	13.2	13.2	15.1	12.9
Five	9.6	8.2	10.5	9.6	11.2	10.1
Total, five years or less	49.5	48.1	63.5	51.0	57.4	57.0
Six	7.8	7.4	6.3	8.0	8.8	7.2
Seven	5.0	5.7	5.0	6.3	6.2	5.4
Eight	4.1	3.7	3.9	4.5	4.1	4.0
Nine	2.5	2.6	2.7	5.0	2.7	3.0
Ten	2.7	4.5	2.5	3.2	2.0	2.8
Total, six–ten years	22.1	23.9	20.4	27.0	23.8	22.4
Over ten years	28.4	28.0	16.1	22.0	18.8	20.6
Total	100.0%	100.0%	100.0%	100.0%	100.0%	100.0%
Number of failures	1,463	940	4,341	1,419	1,182	9,345

Source: The Business Failure Record, 1973 (New York: Dun & Bradstreet, Inc., 1974), p. 10.

13. The causes of business failure are divisible into three categories: characteristics of the economic system, inside underlying causes, and outside immediate causes.

Characteristics of the Economic System

14. The economic structure within which a firm must exist acts as a cause of failure which originates outside the business itself and is not a result of acts of management. Management instead must accept the changes that occur in our economic system and attempt to adjust the firm's operations to meet these changes.

15. One characteristic of the American economic system is freedom of enterprise, meaning the absolute right of all individuals to engage in any business regardless of their personal qualifications. This permits the entry of people who lack experience and training in their chosen business and who are thus more susceptible to failure. Galbraith suggests that there are two parts to the economy. One is the small and traditional proprietors and the other consists of the world of the few hundred technically dynamic, massively capitalized, and highly organized corporations.[1] The smaller firms are the ones most susceptible to failure. The large firms can tolerate market uncertainty much better than the smaller firm. Galbraith further states, "Vertical integration, the control of prices and consumer demand and reciprocal absorption of market uncertainty by contracts between firms all favor the large enterprise." [2]

16. Frequently given as a cause of failure is intensity of competition; however, an efficient management is a tough foe for any competitor. Some new businesses do fail because of a lack of adequate ability, resources, and opportunity to successfully meet the existing competition. Also, established concerns may be unable to match the progressive activities of new and better qualified competition.[3]

17. Analogous to intense competition is the challenge offered by business changes and improvements and shifts in public demand. Companies that fail in the transition to modern methods of

[1] John Kenneth Galbraith, *The New Industrial State* (Boston: Houghton Mifflin Co., 1967), pp. 8–9.

[2] *Ibid.*, p. 32.

[3] H. N. Broom and J. G. Longenecker, *Small Business Management* (Cincinnati: Southwestern Publishing Co., 1971), pp. 86–87.

production and distribution, or are unable to adapt to new consumer wants, must ultimately go out of business.[4]

18. Business fluctuations are another characteristic of a free economic system such as ours. Adverse periods marked by maladjustment between production and consumption, significant unemployment, decline in sales, falling prices, and other disturbing factors will have some effect on the number of business failures. However, a temporary lull in business activities is not usually found to be a fundamental cause, although it does at least accelerate movement toward what is probably an inevitable failure.

19. The freedom of action which characterizes our society may result in actions by third persons which prove detrimental to a business firm. The demands of labor unions and organized actions by community and other special interest groups have in recent years contributed to the failure of some businesses. Government actions —for example, the enactment of new tax legislation, lowering or elimination of tariffs, wage and hour laws, court decisions, price regulations, and the like—occasionally result in the failure of some companies. As an example, several small manufacturers have been forced out of business because they were unable to meet the pollution standards established by the federal government.

Casualties

20. The causes of trouble occasionally may be entirely beyond the control of the business. Some of these causes are known as "acts of God" and this category is found in all societies regardless of their particular economic system. Included are such things as fires, earthquakes, explosions, floods, tornadoes, and hurricanes, all of which may certainly cause the downfall of some businesses.

21. Thus the parameters within which a business must function prove to be an important determinant of its success. The challenge to management is to meet and adapt to changing conditions in such a manner that they do not prove to be adverse. A company cannot change the environment; it must be able to use it to its benefit.

---

[4] Elvin F. Donaldson, John K. Pfahl, and Peter L. Mullins, *Corporate Finance*, 4th Ed. (New York: The Ronald Press Co., 1975), pp. 612–14.

Inside Underlying Causes

22. Internal causes of failure are those which could have been prevented by some action within the business, and often result from an incorrect past decision or the failure of management to take action when it was needed. Management must assume the responsibility for any business difficulties resulting from internal factors.

Overextension of Credit

23. One inside cause of failure is the tendency for businesses to overextend credit and subsequently become unable to collect from their debtors in time to pay their own liabilities. Manufacturers overextend credit to distributors so that they may increase their sales. Distributors, to be able to make payments to their manufacturers, must then overextend credit to their customers. These buyers must in turn continuously keep bidding lower and lower to be able to keep their equipment busy and meet their commitments. In this manner a chain of credit is developed, and if one link defaults there is trouble all the way down the line. The failure to establish adequate credit margins thus may result in business crises.

24. The obvious answer is to expand credit investigations and, possibly, restrict sales made on account. However, many businesses feel that their volume of sales will fall as a result, perhaps more than offsetting the credit losses they are now experiencing. But one unusual default could cause serious financial trouble for the firm and might have been avoided by a more careful credit policy. A manager's decision to indiscriminately grant credit means a risk of the company's own financial stability. Unusual credit losses may so greatly weaken the firm's financial structure that it is no longer able to continue operation.

Inefficient Management

25. Businesses often fail because of managers' lack of training, experience, ability, adaptation, or initiative. Indications of probable failure of an enterprise include management's inability in any of the

TABLE 2-7. Apparent Causes of Failure—1973

Evidence of Inexperience or Incompetence	Industry Group*					
	Manufacturers	Wholesalers	Retailers	Construction	Commercial Services	All Concerns
Inadequate sales	50.0%	47.7%	45.6%	35.2%	46.3%	45.0%
Heavy operating expenses	12.7	8.9	6.7	10.7	11.3	9.0
Receivables difficulties	16.1	17.0	3.5	15.5	6.2	9.0
Inventory difficulties	7.5	10.5	8.8	1.6	1.0	6.7
Excessive fixed assets	6.6	2.5	2.0	2.6	5.8	3.3
Poor location	0.5	1.1	5.8	1.6	3.5	3.6
Competitive weakness	15.4	18.7	21.7	25.4	20.4	20.8
Other	3.2	3.5	3.1	3.8	2.4	3.2

*Classification of failures is based on opinion of creditors and information in credit reports. Since some failures are attributed to a combination of apparent causes, percentages do not add up to the totals in Table 2-2.

Source: The Business Failure Record, 1973 (New York: Dun & Bradstreet, Inc., 1974), p. 13.

major functions of business, lack of educational training, and lack of experience in the particular line of business which is being pursued.[5] Inefficient management has been found to be the cause of the majority of business failures.

26. Included in this category is neglect on the part of managers to coordinate and effectively communicate with specialists. With the great complexity and vast specialization of business, complete harmony and cooperation becomes crucial. All management services must be integrated for maximum profitability. Often it has been found that a business failure could have been avoided by the proper application of effective managerial control tools.[6]

27. Dun & Bradstreet's analyses show that 93 per cent of business failures are due to management's incompetence and lack of experience. The incompetence and inexperience were evidenced to a large extent by management's inability to avoid conditions which resulted in inadequate sales and competitive weakness. Table 2–7 lists the apparent cause of failure which is, in fact, evidence of the incompetence and inexperience indicated in Table 2–2.

28. Every accountant interviewed in the course of preparing this book listed inefficient management as the number-one cause of business failures. Several other studies have also confirmed the analysis that deficient management is primarily responsible for the failure of businesses. The Bureau of Business Research of the University of Pittsburgh made a detailed study of ten unsuccessful manufacturing plants in western Pennsylvania between 1954 and 1956.[7] The firms that failed were contrasted with ten conspicuously successful firms to determine points of contrast that might explain the reasons for failure. These differences were as follows:

> The unsuccessful firms had very poor records and record-keeping procedures. One firm shipped $10,000 of oil burners to a customer who was bankrupt. The shipments continued over nine months, during which time no payments were received.

[5] Victor Sadd and Robert Williams, *Causes of Commercial Bankruptcies* (U. S. Department of Commerce, Domestic Commerce Series—No. 69, 1932), pp. 5–8, 16–32.

[6] Robert Beyer, "Profitability Accounting: The Challenge and the Opportunity," *Journal of Accountancy*, Vol. 117 (June 1964), pp. 33–35.

[7] A. M. Woodruff, *Causes of Failure*, undated pamphlet reporting address by Dr. Woodruff and distributed by the Small Business Administration in 1957. A summary of the results of this research is contained in Broom and Longenecker, pp. 85–86.

The successful firms spent time and money on product development while several unsuccessful firms ignored this need.

Several unsuccessful firms allowed themselves to go beyond the technical depth of their management.

Executives of unsuccessful firms neglected market analysis and selling.

Unsuccessful plants displayed a lack of organization and of efficient administrative practices.

The results of the analysis were summarized in the following statement:

> None of the failures studied occurred because the firm was small. They all occurred because of a very obvious, easily identified management error. The management error might have occurred because one man was saddled with too much, and didn't have time to devote to his various responsibilities, a situation indirectly associated with smallness, but in the last analysis, the failure was occasioned by a management error which could have been avoided.[8]

29. A common situation involves managers who are experts in their particular fields, such as engineering, but lack the simple tools necessary to run their finances or administer a going concern. In this instance it is often found that they fail to restrain salaries or benefits and are unable to maintain a close rapport with their accounting staff.[9] Effective and efficient management is partially dependent upon adequate accounting records which will reveal inefficiencies and act as a guide in formulating policies. Several of the accounting firms actively involved in bankruptcy audits have estimated that at least 90 per cent of the financially troubled businesses they examine have very inadequate accounting records. Although poor accounting information or records may not be the underlying cause of failure, their inadequacy does prevent the business from taking corrective action in many cases.

30. Inefficient management is often evidenced by its inability to avoid conditions which have resulted in the following:

[8] Woodruff, *ibid.*, p. 11.

[9] R. A. Donnelly, "Unhappy Ending? Chapters 10 and 11 of the Bankruptcy Act Don't Always Tell the Story," *Barron's*, July 12, 1971, p. 14.

Inadequate sales, which may be a result of poor location, an incompetent sales organization, poor promotion, or an inferior product or service. This obviously means that the firm will be unable to make a sufficient profit to stay in business.

Improper pricing. In relation to its costs the firm is charging too low a price, accepting either a loss on the item or very little profit.

Excessive overhead expenses and operating costs, and excessive interest charges on long-term debt. All these act as fixed charges against revenue, rather than varying with the volume of goods produced. This means that the firm's break-even point is high: it must sell a relatively large volume of goods before it begins earning a profit.

Overinvestment in fixed assets and inventories. Both types of investment tie up cash or other funds so that they are no longer available to management for meeting other obligations. As a company expands there is a need for greater investment in fixed assets. It becomes profitable for the company at the current production level to reduce labor costs by investing in additional equipment. If the company can continue to operate at this capacity, profits will continue; however, if production drops significantly the company is in a difficult position. Fixed assets are not used fully and as a result the depreciation charge against net income is unduly high for the level of production. These costs are committed and little can be done in the short run to affect their total. If the reduction in production is not temporary, action must be taken, very quickly, to eliminate some of the unprofitable divisions and dispose of their assets. Under some conditions, it may be best to liquidate the business. (See Chapter 1, paragraphs 43 and 44.) The objective thus becomes to have the optimum level of investment and maximum utilization.

Carrying a large amount of inventories results in excessive storage costs, such as warehouse rent and insurance coverage, and the risk of spoilage or obsolescence. Thus, in addition to tying up the use of funds, overinvestment in fixed assets or inventories may create unnecessary charges against income.

Insufficient working capital, including a weak cash position. Inadequate working capital is often the result of excessive current debt due to acquisition of fixed assets through the use of short-term credit; overexpansion of business without providing for adequate working capital; or deficient banking facilities, resulting in high cost of borrowing current funds. An unwise dividend policy may use up funds that are needed for operating the business. A weak working capital position, if not corrected, will eventually cause a delay in the firm's payment of debt.

Unbalanced capital structure, that is, an unfavorable ratio of debt to capital. If the amount of capital secured through bonds or similar long-term liabilities is relatively high, fixed charges against income will be large. This is advantageous when the firm is earning a healthy profit and the residual after-interest charges accrue to the owners. But where the business is experiencing financial difficulties, this interest burden acts to drag down earnings. Alternatively, a high percentage of capital, obtained through equity, has a high intrinsic cost to the firm because the owners demand a rate of return higher than the interest rate given on debt to compensate them for their risk. It must also be remembered that, to attract investors, earnings per share must be maintained.

Inadequate insurance coverage. For example, if a business is not compensated for such losses as fire and theft, it might very well be forced to close its doors.

Inadequate accounting methods and records. Management will not have the information it needs to identify problem areas and take preventive action.

31. The existence of any one of these factors may be an indication of potential trouble due to management's inability or inefficiency. The accountant is in an excellent position to discover any of these conditions and alert management to their existence and possible consequences.

Insufficient Capital

32. As previously mentioned, insufficient capital may be thought to be an inside cause of business failures. When business conditions are adverse and there is insufficient capital, the firm may be unable to pay operating costs and credit obligations as they mature. However, the real cause of difficulty is often not insufficient capital, but a lack of ability to effectively manage the capital which is available for use or to convert merchandise and receivables into cash with which to pay the firm's debts.

Dishonesty and Fraud: Planned Bankruptcies, Sham

33. Premeditated bankruptcy fraud has been found to be the cause of a small number of bankruptcies. The reasons for fraudulent bankruptcies include the desire of many credit grantors to maintain their sales volume at any cost, the neglect of creditors to investigate bankruptcy causes, and the ability of dishonest persons to utilize profitably the benefits of the bankruptcy courts without fear of prosecution.

Outside Immediate Causes

34. Normally the immediate action that leads to failure is not the fundamental reason for failure. Some of the outside immediate causes that are responsible for the inevitable end of the firm include threatened or actual suits, involuntary bankruptcy petitions, execution levies, tax levies, and set-offs by lending institutions.[10] Many companies delay the filing of the bankruptcy petition until they are forced to do so by their creditors in the form of a suit filed to collect an outstanding debt. Or, they may be forced into bankruptcy by an involuntary petition filed by the creditors. Banks have the right to set off money in their possession against a claim that is past due. If a company has a past-due note or installment payment, the bank may take funds on deposit in the firm's account to cover the debt owed the bank. Normally, banks will not take this type of action unless a business is very weak financially. Thus, set-offs and other creditors' actions may become the precipitating cause of bankruptcy.

STAGES OF FINANCIAL FAILURE

35. The general activity in firms which are failing includes lower sales, a slower growth in sales, poorer cash flow and net income positions, and large incurrence of debt. These factors combine to cause marked deterioration in the firm's solvency position. Unsuccessful firms also experience higher major operating costs, especially excessive overhead costs, than the average for

---

[10] David T. Stanley *et al.*, *Bankruptcy: Problems, Process, Reform* (Washington, D. C.: The Brookings Institution, 1971), p. 111.

similar successful firms. As the firm suffers losses and deteriorates toward failure, its asset size is reduced. Assets are not replaced as often as during more prosperous times and this with the cumulative losses further reduce the prospects for profitable operations.[11]

36. The stages of financial failure may be analyzed in four distinct phases: period of incubation, cash shortage, financial insolvency, and total insolvency. The time period associated with each stage will differ depending on many factors.

Period of Incubation

37. A business does not suddenly or unexpectedly become bankrupt. Any business concern having financial difficulty will pass through several transitional stages before it reaches the point where it is necessary to file a bankruptcy petition. An ailing business has been compared with an individual suffering at the start from a minor ailment, such as a common cold, which if not remedied, in due time could develop into a serious disease like pneumonia and result in death.[12] During the period of incubation one or even a number of unfavorable conditions are quietly developing without being recognizable immediately by outsiders or even by management. For example, a company whose major source of revenue came from steel fabrication work in connection with highway construction failed to take action two years previously, when it was obvious that interstate highway construction would be reduced in the company's market area. As a result the company was forced to file a petition in bankruptcy. Some of the types of developments which may be occurring in the incubation period are listed below:

Change in product demand

Continuing increase in overhead costs

Obsolete production methods

Increase in competition

Incompetent managers in key positions

Acquisition of unprofitable subsidiaries

---

[11] Edward I. Altman, "Financial Ratios, Discriminant Analysis and the Prediction of Corporate Bankruptcy," *Journal of Finance*, Vol. 23 (September 1968), pp. 590–97.

[12] Helene M. A. Ramanauskas, "How Close to Bankruptcy Are You?," *Woman CPA*, Vol. 28 (October 1966), p. 3.

Overexpansion without adequate working capital

Incompetent credit and collection department

Lack of adequate banking facilities

38. It is often in the incubation stage that an economic loss occurs, in that the return realized on assets falls below the firm's normal rate of return. It is at this stage of failure that management should give careful consideration to the cause. If the cause cannot be corrected, management must look for other alternatives. It is best for the company if the problem is detected at this stage, for several reasons. First, replanning is much more effective if initiated at this time. Second, the actions required to correct the causes of failure are not nearly so drastic as those required at later stages. Third, the public confidence is less likely to be impaired if corrective action is taken at this stage. This is critical because if public confidence is shaken, the charges for funds will increase and the firm will be in a position where would-be profitable projects must now be rejected.[13]

39. It is possible that, under certain conditions, the economic loss may not occur until the enterprise is in the second stage, experiencing a shortage of cash.

Cash Shortage

40. The business for the first time is unable to meet its current obligations and is in urgent need of cash, although it might have a comfortable excess of physical assets over liabilities and a satisfactory earning record. The problem is that the assets are not sufficiently liquid and the necessary capital is tied up in receivables and inventories.

Financial or Commercial Insolvency

41. In this third stage, the business is unable to procure through customary channels the funds required to meet its maturing and overdue obligations. Management will have to resort to more drastic measures such as calling in a business or financial specialist,

---

[13] Ernest Walker, *Essentials of Financial Management* (Englewood Cliffs, N. J.: Prentice-Hall, Inc., 1965), p. 202.

who is often a CPA, appointing a creditors' committee, or resorting to new financing techniques. However, there still exists a good possibility for survival and for future growth and prosperity if substantial infusions of new money and financing can be obtained.

Total Insolvency

42. At this point the business can no longer avoid the public confession of failure, and management's attempts to secure additional funds by financing generally prove unsuccessful. Total liabilities exceed the value of the firm's assets. The total insolvency becomes confirmed when legal steps, involuntary or voluntary, are taken by filing a petition under the Federal Bankruptcy Act.

DETECTION OF FAILURE TENDENCIES

43. Effective management cannot wait until the enterprise experiences total insolvency to take action, since at this final stage the remedies available are rather restricted. There are several tools that may be used to diagnose business failures, but they will not necessarily reveal the cause of failure. It is the cause which must be determined and corrected; it is not enough just to correct the symptoms. For example, a constantly inadequate cash position is an indication that financial problems are developing, but the problem is not solved by management's borrowing additional funds without determining the real cause for the shortage. However, if the cause of the shortage is ascertained and corrected, management can then raise the necessary cash and be reasonably certain that the future cash inflow will not be interrupted in such a manner as to create a similar problem.[14]

44. External and internal methods may be used to detect failure tendencies. The most common sources of external data are trade reports and statistics and economic indicators published by the federal government and by private organizations.

45. Many times, internal methods are simply an extension of the work done by accountants. During their audit investigation, the preparation of their reports, and the performance of other services

[14] *Ibid.*, p. 202.

accountants often become aware of what has been occurring in the major accounts and in the firm as a whole. Because of their training and experience in business finances, they often are able to identify when the enterprise is headed for trouble and alert management to these suspicions. Thus, because of the nature of both the type of work they are doing and the ability they possess, accountants are in an excellent position to identify any tendencies toward failure.

Trend Analysis

46. One of the most frequently used methods of examining data from within the firm is an analysis of the financial statements over a period of years so that trends may be noted. Using a certain year as base, a trend analysis of the important accounts is developed on a monthly or quarterly basis.[15] The balance sheet trends will generally reveal the following failure tendencies:

Weakening cash position

Insufficient working capital

Overinvestment in receivables or inventories

Overexpansion in fixed assets

Increasing bank loans and other current liabilities

Excessive funded debt and fixed liabilities

Overcapitalization

Subordination of loans to banks and creditors

47. The income account changes which may disclose additional failure tendencies are as follows:

Declining sales

Increasing operating costs and overhead

Excessive interest and other fixed expenses

Excessive dividends and withdrawals compared to earning records

Declining net profits and lower return on invested capital

Increased sales with reduced mark-ups

[15] See Louis P. Starkweather, "Corporate Failure, Recapitalizations, and Readjustments," in *Fundamentals of Investment Banking* (Englewood Cliffs, N. J.: Prentice-Hall, Inc., 1949), pp. 432–38, for a detailed example of trend analysis.

Analysis of Accounting Measures

48. In conjunction with the trend analysis, certain ratios or accounting measures are of benefit in indicating financial strength. The current and liquidity ratios are used to portray the firm's ability to meet current obligations. The efficiency in asset utilization is often determined by fixed asset turnover, inventory turnover, and accounts receivable turnover. The higher the turnover, the better the performance, since management will be able to operate with a relatively small commitment of funds.

49. The soundness of the relationship between borrowed funds and equity capital is set forth by certain equity ratios. The ratios of current liabilities, long-term liabilities, total liabilities, and owners' equity to total equity assist in appraising the ability of the business to survive times of stress and meet both its short-term and long-term obligations. There must be an adequate balance of debt and equity. When the interest of outsiders is increased, there is an advantage to the owners in that they get the benefit of a return on assets furnished by others. However, there is in this advantage an increased risk. By analyzing the equity structure and the interest expense, insight can be gained as to the relative size of the cushion of ownership funds creditors can rely on to absorb losses from the business. These losses may be the result of unprofitable operations or simply due to a decrease in the value of the assets owned by the business.[16] Profitability measures which relate net income to total assets, net assets, net sales, or owners' equity assist in appraising the adequacy of sales and operating profit. An analysis of the various measures and relationships for a given year may be of limited value, but when a comparison is made with prior years, trends can be observed which may be meaningful.

50. In a recent model designed by Altman,[17] five basic ratios were used in predicting corporate bankruptcy. The five ratios selected from an original list of twenty-two are as follows:

Working capital/Total assets
Retained earnings/Total assets

16 Ramanauskas, p. 12.
17 Edward I. Altman, "Corporate Bankruptcy Prediction and Its Implications for Commercial Loan Evaluation," *Journal of Commercial Bank Lending*, Vol. 53 (December 1970), pp. 10–19.

Earnings before interest and taxes/Total assets

Market value equity/Book value of total debt

Sales/Total assets

51. Based on the results of his research, Altman suggested that the bankruptcy prediction model is an accurate forecaster of failure up to two years prior to bankruptcy and that the accuracy diminishes substantially as the lead time increases. Table 2–8

TABLE 2-8. Five-Year Predictive Accuracy of the Multiple Discriminant Analysis Model (Initial Sample)

Years Prior to Bankruptcy	Hits	Misses	Percentage Correct
1st $n = 33$	31	2	96%
2nd $n = 32$	23	9	72
3rd $n = 29$	14	15	48
4th $n = 28$	8	20	29
5th $n = 25$	9	16	36

Source: Edward I. Altman, "Corporate Bankruptcy Prediction and Its Implications for Commercial Loan Evaluation," Journal of Commercial Bank Lending, Vol. 53 (December 1970), p. 18.

summarizes the predictive accuracy, using the model, of the initial sample of 33 manufacturing firms which filed petitions under Chapter X during the period 1946–1965. Each firm's financial statement was examined each year for five years prior to bankruptcy. The n value is less than 33 for the second to fifth years prior to bankruptcy because some of the firms in the sample were not in existence for five years before they went bankrupt.

52. Altman also selected a second sample of 33 firms which were solvent and still in existence in 1968. This sample was taken to test for the possibility of a Type II error. (A Type II error is the classification of a firm in the bankruptcy group when in fact it did not go bankrupt.) The Type II error from the sample was only 3 per cent.

53. These five ratios selected by Altman showed a deteriorating trend as bankruptcy approached and the most serious change in the majority of these ratios occurred between the third and second years prior to bankruptcy.

54. An analysis of accounting measures or predictions of

failure by Beaver indicates that the non-liquid asset measures predict failure better than the liquid asset measures. The evidence also indicates that failed firms tend to have lower, rather than higher, inventory balances as is often expected.[18]

Analysis of Management

55. Certain characteristics giving evidence of inefficient and ineffective management also serve as warning signals to potential trouble. Those concerned with the firm's viability should be on the alert if it is known that management lacks training or experience in basic business methods, such as interpreting financial data, managing funds, scheduling production and shipping, coordinating departmental activities, and any other management functions. In a common situation, a manager may be an expert in a technical field, such as designing, but have little managerial ability for directing the activities of the business.

56. Indications that management is ineffective and that trouble may result include the presence of any of the following: inefficient and inadequate information systems, disregard for operating and financial data which are supplied, lack of interest in maintaining an adequate sales volume, large fixed charges resulting from excessive overhead and operating expenses or large debt in the capital structure, or illogical pricing schemes. Other conditions pointing to inefficient management certainly are possible, and all such factors should alert those interested to the possible existence of later trouble.

Importance of Forecasts

57. The debtor's accountant can assist in the detection of financial failure tendencies by preparing, or in some cases reviewing, for management forecasts and projections of operations and cash flow for the next accounting period. These forecasts often highlight problems at a very early point in time, which permits corrective action to be taken. Forecasts, if prepared realistically, should answer these questions for management:

---

[18] William H. Beaver, "Financial Ratios as Predictors of Failure," in *Empirical Research in Accounting: Selected Studies 1966*, 1st University of Chicago Conference (May 1966), p. 121.

Can the profit objective be achieved?

What areas of costs and expenses will create a drag on profitability and should be watched?

Are financial resources adequate?

58. It is also important that interim financial statements be prepared, in a meaningful manner, and that the company have year-end certified audits.

Other Factors

59. The following events may also indicate to the accountant that financial difficulties are imminent:

Factoring or financing receivables, if they are normally handled on an open account basis

Compromise of the amount of accounts receivable for the purpose of receiving advance collections

Substitution of notes for open accounts payable

Allowing certain key creditors to obtain security interests in the assets

Inability of the firm to make timely deposits of trust funds such as employee withholding taxes

Death or departure of key personnel

Unfavorable purchase commitments

Lack of realization of material research and development costs

Change in accounting methods by client primarily designed to improve the financial statements

3

Nature of Bankruptcy and

Insolvency Proceedings

1. Any competent accountant who understands the scope and nature of bankruptcy and insolvency engagements is capable of representing a client in the proceedings. Part of the accountant's background must consist of some familiarity with the legal aspects

of bankruptcy. This chapter and the next provide the accountant with the legal background needed to effectively represent a client in various situations involving financial difficulties. The objective of this chapter is threefold: to describe the origin of our current bankruptcy law, to discuss the legal meaning of insolvency, and to set forth the various alternatives available to debtor and creditor when failure appears imminent.

HISTORICAL ORIGIN

2. In early times the proverb "He who cannot pay with his purse, pays with his skin" had a ruthlessly literal application. The law of ancient Rome (450 B.C.) declared that the borrower was *nexus* to his creditors, which meant that his own person was pledged for repayment of the loan. If the borrower failed to meet his obligation, the creditor could seize him. The creditor then publicly invited someone to come forth to pay the debt, and if no one did, the creditor killed or sold the debtor.[1] A number of Biblical references testify to the fact that one could be enslaved for the non-payment of debt. In 11 Kings 4: ". . . a certain woman of the wives of the sons of the prophets cried out to Elisha, 'Your servant my husband is dead, and you know that your servant feared the Lord; and the creditor has come to take my two children to be his slaves.'" Elisha said, "Go, borrow vessels at large for yourself from all your neighbors. . . ." From one jar of oil she filled all the vessels that had been borrowed. Elisha said to her, "Go, sell the oil and pay your debt, and you and your sons can live on the rest." In ancient Greece, under the criminal code of Draco (623 B.C.), indebtedness was classified with murders, sacrilege, and other capital crimes. Solon, during his reign, ordered that the debts which remained after an attempt at restitution should be forgiven, but that the debtor and his heirs had to forfeit their citizenship.[2]

3. The first English bankruptcy law, passed in 1542, was a law against the debtor. Only the creditor could, under certain conditions, initiate bankruptcy action and divide up the assets of the debtor. If there were liabilities that the debtor was unable to pay

[1] George Sullivan, *The Boom in Going Bust* (New York: The Macmillan Co., 1968), p. 25.
[2] *Ibid.*

with his assets, he was sent to prison. The 1542 law only applied to traders, but in 1570 it was amended to include merchants.[3] It was not until 1705 that the English law provided for discharge of the debtor from his debts.

United States

4. Physical punishment, imprisonment, and other similar practices, which were common in England and in some of the American Colonies and which were seen by many as being totally ineffective, influenced American lawmakers to see the need for a national bankruptcy law. However, it was not considered until a very late date in the proceedings of the Federal Convention. On August 29, 1787, Charles Pinckney of South Carolina moved to give the federal government the power to establish uniform laws on the subject of bankruptcy as a part of the Full Faith and Credit Clause (Article XVI). On September 1, 1787, John Rutledge recommended that in Article VII, relating to the Legislative Department, there be added after the power to establish uniform rule of naturalization a power "to establish uniform laws on the subject of bankruptcies." On September 3, 1787, this clause was adopted after very little debate. Only the State of Connecticut opposed the provision; its representative Roger Sherman objected to any power which would make it possible to punish individuals who were bankrupt by death. In the final draft the power to establish uniform bankruptcy laws was inserted after the provision to regulate commerce in Section 8 of Article I.[4]

5. The wording of the provision is: "Congress shall have the power . . . to establish . . . uniform laws on the subject of bankruptcies throughout the United States." Although the right was granted, the states were so opposed to it that national bankruptcy laws existed intermittently for only about seventeen years prior to 1900.[5] The meaning and scope of the term

[3] Louis Levinthal, "The Early History of Bankruptcy Law," *University of Pennsylvania Law Review*, Vol. 66 (1917–1918), p. 224n.

[4] Charles Warren, *Bankruptcies in United States History* (Cambridge, Mass.: Harvard University Press, 1935), pp. 4–5.

[5] Charles Gerstenberg, *Financial Organization and Management of Business* (Englewood Cliffs, N. J.: Prentice-Hall, Inc., 1959), p. 532.

"bankruptcy" as used by the framers of the Constitution is unclear. The English law in existence at the time this provision was added to the Constitution used the word "bankruptcy" as an involuntary proceeding applying only to traders. However, at this time, some states had laws which used the term to apply to all classes of persons and all forms of insolvency. The intent of the writers in using the term "bankruptcy" served as a focal point of debate each time a bankruptcy law was proposed for over a period of eighty years.

6. Under the authority granted, Congress passed three bankruptcy acts prior to 1898. The first act, passed in 1800 and repealed three years later, applied to traders, brokers, and merchants, and contained no provisions for voluntary bankruptcy. The first act was finally passed as a result of a financial crash brought about by overspeculation in real estate. Many rich and prominent traders were in prison because they were unable to pay their creditors. Robert Morris, the great financier of the Revolution, was in the Prune Street Jail in Philadelphia with liabilities of about $12,000,000. James Wilson, a Justice of the United States Supreme Court, just before his death went to North Carolina to avoid imprisonment for debts he owed in Pennsylvania.[6]

7. The first act by its terms was limited to five years, but it lasted only three due to several factors. First, there was the difficulty of travel to the distant and unpopular federal courts. Second, very small dividends were paid to creditors. One reason for this is that most of the debtors forced into bankruptcy were already in prison. Third, the act had been largely used by rich debtors, speculators, and in some cases by fraudulent debtors to obtain discharge from their debts.[7] Among the debtors who were released as a result of this act was Robert Morris.

8. The second act, passed in 1841, applied to all debtors, contained provisions for voluntary bankruptcy, and allowed a discharge of the unpaid balance remaining after all assets were distributed to creditors. The second act was not really given an opportunity to succeed. The bill was defeated in the House on August 17, 1841, by a vote of 110 to 97. Due to some maneuvering the bill was reconsidered the next morning and passed by a vote of

---

[6] Warren, p. 13.
[7] Ibid., pp. 19–20.

110 to 106. Opponents of the bill started working toward its repeal and the bill was revoked by a vote of 140 to 71 in the House and 32 to 13 in the Senate after it had lasted just over one year.

9. The financial problems created by the Civil War caused Congress to consider a third act which became law in 1867 and was repealed in 1878. This act marked the beginning of an attempt by Congress to permit the debtor to escape the stigma associated with bankruptcy by allowing a composition of his debts without being adjudicated a bankrupt.

10. The bankruptcy act now in force is the act passed in 1898, as amended. The act was thoroughly revised by the Bankruptcy Act of 1938, commonly known as the Chandler Act, which added to the basic law the chapter proceedings as they are known today. No doubt, the most profound of all developments in bankruptcy law must have been the passing of the Chandler Act which gave the courts the power to regulate the disposition of all debtors' estates—individuals as well as business, agriculture, railroads, municipalities, and real estate, whether in liquidation, rehabilitation, or reorganization. The most frequently used of the chapter proceedings created by the Chandler Act is Chapter XI, which was established to provide rehabilitation of the honest debtor with a maximum of speed and a minimum of cost.[8]

11. It is interesting to note how the economic philosophy of bankruptcy has changed over the past 400 years. The first laws in Great Britain and the United States were for the benefit of creditors only. Later they gave consideration to the debtor by allowing discharges. They also gave the debtor some protection against haphazard seizure by creditors; however, this provision became law primarily to protect the interest of other creditors. But it appears that very little consideration was given to the public in the United States until 1933 when Section 77 was added to the 1898 act granting railroads the right to reorganize.[9] The current bankruptcy law was intended not only to secure equality among creditors and to provide relief to the debtor by discharging him from his liabilities and allowing him to start a new economic life, but to benefit society at large.

[8] George Ashe, "Rehabilitation Under Chapter XI: Fact or Fiction," *Commercial Law Journal*, Vol. 72 (September 1967), p. 260.

[9] Gerstenberg, p. 532.

Insolvency and Bankruptcy Laws Today

12. The term "bankruptcy laws" is used only in reference to federal laws because of the power given to Congress to establish these laws in the United States Constitution. The term "insolvency laws" is used to refer to the enactments of the various states. Insolvency laws may be used as long as they do not conflict with the federal laws.

13. The Bankruptcy Act currently consists of fourteen chapters. The first seven deal with the basic structure of the bankruptcy system as well as setting forth all of the proceedings of straight bankruptcy. Chapter VIII deals with the reorganization of railroads and Chapter IX concerns the composition of debts of certain public authorities. Chapter X sets forth in great detail the rules for reorganizing corporations. Chapter XI deals with arrangement primarily for business debtors and by other persons who are not wage earners. Provisions for wage earners are described in Chapter XIII. Chapter XII covers debts that are secured by liens on real property and Chapter XIV deals with maritime liens. Chapters VIII, IX, XII, and XIV are used very infrequently and along with Chapter XIII are beyond the scope of this book.

CURRENT BANKRUPTCY STATISTICS

14. Table 3–1 summarizes by district the number of voluntary and involuntary bankruptcy cases commenced during the fiscal year ended June 30, 1974. Less than 0.6 per cent of all filings were involuntary. Only 152 voluntary petitions were filed under Chapter X during 1974, while 2,171 cases were commenced under Chapter XI. The percentage of Chapter X proceedings out of the total number of Chapter X and XI petitions filed has declined considerably. In 1960 there were 81 petitions filed under Chapter X and only 622 under Chapter XI for percentages of 11 and 89 respectively. This compares with 6 per cent Chapter X and 94 per cent Chapter XI filings in 1974.

15. The number of voluntary cases commenced during the fiscal year ended June 30, 1974, by occupation of the debtor, is shown in Table 3–2. Business cases comprise 10 per cent of the total petitions filed.

TABLE 3-1. Voluntary and Involuntary Cases Commenced* During the Fiscal Year Ended June 30, 1974, by Chapters of the Bankruptcy Act

Circuit or District †	Total	Voluntary						Involuntary		
		Total	Straight Bankruptcy	Chapter X	Chapter XI	Chapter XII	Chapter XIII	Total	Straight Bankruptcy	Chapter X
Total All Districts	189,513**	188,493	156,958	152	2,171	172	29,023	1,020	1,009	11
District of Columbia	127	124	114	—	1	—	9	3	3	—
First Circuit	4,217	4,085	2,705	3	290	—	1,087	132	129	3
Second Circuit	9,841	9,698	8,413	10	671	2	602	143	143	—
Third Circuit	4,210**	4,137	3,800	—	178	17	127	73	72	1
Fourth Circuit	9,745	9,684	7,399	25	45	—	2,215	61	58	3
Fifth Circuit	26,349**	26,180	17,499	40	276	10	8,354	169	169	—
Sixth Circuit	32,802	32,714	27,040	9	120	3	5,542	88	88	—
Seventh Circuit	24,574**	24,483	21,616	4	132	1	2,729	91	91	—
Eighth Circuit	15,656	15,608	13,673	9	80	52	1,794	48	48	—
Ninth Circuit	48,087	47,905	42,313	26	340	84	5,142	182	182	—
Tenth Circuit	13,905	13,875	12,386	26	38	3	1,422	30	26	4

*Cases commenced reflect initial filings, not subsequent transfers that may have occurred during the year from one Chapter of the Act to another.

†States or jurisdictions within each Circuit are as follows:

First Circuit: Maine, Massachusetts, New Hampshire, Rhode Island, Puerto Rico

Second Circuit: Connecticut, New York, Vermont

Third Circuit: Delaware, New Jersey, Pennsylvania, Virgin Islands

Fourth Circuit: Maryland, North Carolina, South Carolina, Virginia, West Virginia

Fifth Circuit: Alabama, Florida, Georgia, Louisiana, Mississippi, Texas

Sixth Circuit: Kentucky, Michigan, Ohio, Tennessee

Seventh Circuit: Illinois, Indiana, Wisconsin

Eighth Circuit: Arkansas, Iowa, Minnesota, Missouri, Nebraska, North Dakota, South Dakota

Ninth Circuit: Alaska, Arizona, California, Hawaii, Idaho, Montana, Nevada, Oregon, Washington, Guam

Tenth Circuit: Colorado, Kansas, New Mexico, Oklahoma, Utah, Wyoming

**These figures include the following type cases not reflected elsewhere: Pennsylvania—fifteen Section 77 cases; Florida—one Chapter IX case; Indiana—one Chapter IX case.

Source: United States District Courts.

TABLE 3-2. Voluntary Bankruptcy Cases Commenced During the Fiscal Year Ended June 30, 1974, by Occupation of Bankrupt or Debtor

Circuit or District*	Total Voluntary†	Business					Nonbusiness	
		Farmer	Professional	Merchant	Manufacturer	Others	Employee	Others
Total All Districts	188,493	308	1,582	5,317	710	11,870	141,877	26,829
District of Columbia	124	—	5	7	—	10	85	17
First Circuit	4,085	2	13	363	38	357	3,013	299
Second Circuit	9,698	27	155	699	128	967	6,012	1,710
Third Circuit	4,137	6	54	374	75	762	2,093	773
Fourth Circuit	9,684	8	58	228	29	434	7,906	1,021
Fifth Circuit	26,180	52	245	751	122	1,688	20,285	3,037
Sixth Circuit	32,714	33	150	456	80	1,112	27,834	3,049
Seventh Circuit	24,483	44	149	403	35	972	20,431	2,449
Eighth Circuit	15,608	52	99	391	47	844	11,849	2,326
Ninth Circuit	47,905	58	534	1,268	111	3,728	32,625	9,581
Tenth Circuit	13,875	26	120	377	45	996	9,744	2,567

* For a listing of the states or jurisdictions within each District, see Table 3-1.

† In fiscal year 1974, there were 1,020 involuntary bankruptcies filed, including 960 business cases and 60 non-business cases.

Source: United States District Courts.

THE NATURE OF INSOLVENCY

16. Accountants must know and understand the technical meaning of insolvency because they play a vital role in proving insolvency or solvency, as the case may be. The accountant may be retained by the bankrupt to prove solvency on a given date or by the creditors to establish that the debtor was insolvent on the date the petition was filed. The accountant is requested not only to establish insolvency, but to establish it as of a given date.

Types of Insolvency

17. Insolvency in the equity sense refers to the inability of the debtor to pay obligations as they mature. In this situation the test is the corporation's present ability to pay and the concern is primarily with equity for the protection of creditors.

18. The bankruptcy sense of insolvency is the definition contained in Section 1(19) of the Bankruptcy Act:

> A person shall be deemed insolvent within the provisions of this act whenever the aggregate of his property, exclusive of any property which he may have conveyed, transferred, concealed, removed, or permitted to be concealed or removed, with intent to defraud, hinder, or delay his creditors, shall not at fair valuation be sufficient in amount to pay his debts.

This is also referred to as legal insolvency or the balance sheet test.

19. Other definitions of insolvency have been devised to apply to special situations. The Uniform Fraudulent Conveyance and Transfer Act which was incorporated into the Bankruptcy Act uses a slightly different definition. Found in Section 67d(1)(d) of the Act and to be used only for the purposes of Section 67d regarding fraudulent transfers, it states that a person is "insolvent" when the present fair salable value of his property is less than the amount required to pay his debts.

20. The Uniform Commercial Code also contains a definition of insolvency in Section 1–201(23) which incorporates both the equity and the bankruptcy sense. A person is insolvent who either has ceased to pay his debts as they become due or is insolvent within the meaning of the Federal Bankruptcy Act. This definition is intended to be used for both the buyer's right to the delivery of

goods on the seller's insolvency, and the seller's remedy in the event of the buyer's insolvency.[10]

Equity Versus Bankruptcy Meanings of Insolvency

21. It is important to make a clear distinction between the equity and bankruptcy meanings of insolvency. Under the 1867 Bankruptcy Act, the equity test was used to determine insolvency. The balance sheet approach replaced the equity test in the 1898 Act. The test of insolvency is important because it is a necessary element in proving three of the six acts of bankruptcy.[11] In two of the acts—making or suffering a preferential transfer while insolvent, and failing to discharge a judgment lien while insolvent—the balance sheet approach is used to prove insolvency.[12] A third act—suffering or permitting the appointment of a receiver while insolvent—requires that the debtor be insolvent only in the equity sense; however, the balance sheet test as defined in Section 1(19) may be used as an alternative for the equity test.[13]

22. It is quite possible for a firm to be temporarily unable to meet its current obligations but also be legally solvent. If the equity test is used to determine insolvency, the firm with a temporary shortage of liquid assets will be at the mercy of its creditors, regardless of whether its total position shows an excess of assets over liabilities. On the other hand, a debtor may be insolvent in the bankruptcy sense, with liabilities greater than the fair value of its assets, but temporarily able to pay its currently maturing debts. In this situation creditors may also organize and initiate proceedings to protect their interests; however, they are often unaware of the company's insolvency.

23. Several problems arise in using the balance sheet test for determining insolvency. Should insolvency in the equity sense occur first, the delay in initiating proceedings will result in a greater wastage of the assets and diminution of the estate to be distributed to creditors. For an outsider to file a petition, there must be an

[10] Sydney Krause, "What Constitutes Insolvency," *Proceedings, 27th Institute on Federal Taxation* (New York University, 1969), pp. 1085–86.

[11] Bankruptcy Act, Sec. 3a(1–6).

[12] Thomas H. Burchfield, "Balance Sheet Test of Insolvency," *University of Pittsburgh Law Review*, Vol. 23 (October 1961), p. 6.

[13] *Ibid.*, pp. 6–7.

investigation of the internal financial condition of the debtor, and creditors will often lack the information necessary to initiate bankruptcy at the most apropos moment. The methods of valuing the debtor's assets are very subjective, a condition which gives a distorted picture of the debtor's net worth and an unpredictability regarding the proceedings. This further complicates the creditors' decision as to when or whether to initiate proceedings.[14]

Determination of Assets and Liabilities

24. The Bankruptcy Act requires that the fair value of the firm's assets exceed its liabilities for the firm to be considered solvent. Section 1(19) of the Act explicitly excludes any property the debtor may have conveyed, transferred, concealed, removed, or permitted to be concealed or removed, with intent to defraud, hinder, or delay its creditors from its assets. Intangible property such as trade names, patents, and property rights has often been included, although goodwill is normally deleted. The total assets used in the balance sheet test also include the debtor's exempt property, that is, the assets which are expressly excluded by law from the payment of debts. Section 6 of the Act permits the bankrupt to exempt the property from his estate which is allowed by the exemption laws of the state where the bankrupt is domiciled. The inclusion of exempt property may give rise to situations unfair to general creditors. The debtor may have ceased paying his current liabilities while he is legally solvent due to the inclusion of exempt property in his asset determination. His creditors may be prevented from action while he makes preferential payments or converts assets into property which will be exempt.[15]

25. The liabilities used in determining insolvency are defined in Section 1(14) of the Act. "Debt shall include any debt, demand, or claim provable in bankruptcy."

Valuation of Assets

26. The method of determining the fair value of assets may also give rise to controversy. Three approaches are generally found

[14] *Ibid.*, pp. 13–14.
[15] *Ibid.*, pp. 8–10.

in use by the courts. First and most common is the fair market value. Courts which use the fair value method have generally emphasized that it does not mean the amount which would be received for the assets at a forced sale. It also does not represent the value which could be received under ideal conditions during the normal course of business.[16] It is defined as "such a price as a capable and intelligent businessman could presently obtain for the property from a ready and willing buyer." [17] This definition does not give any insight into whether the courts assume the assets will be sold separately or as a unit.[18] Second is the use value of the assets to the debtor which is based on the future earning power of the business and assumes that the firm will continue to be operated by the debtor rather than being liquidated. The third approach is the value the assets are intrinsically worth under a hypothetical set of conditions. This value is used when the assets are not marketable or have little or no use value because the business is failing.[19]

Insolvency and Bankruptcy

27. The various definitions of insolvency assume importance in the different proceedings under the Bankruptcy Act. In Chapter XI arrangement proceedings, the petition must be voluntarily filed and the debtor must be insolvent in either the equity or bankruptcy sense. Reorganization, as provided for in Chapter X, may be voluntarily or involuntarily initiated, and also requires insolvency in one of the two alternatives. However, which situation governs is of supreme importance to stockholders. Should the corporation be insolvent in the bankruptcy sense, the shareholders will not be allowed to retain any interest in the reorganized corporation. On the other hand, the stockholders must be included in the plan of reorganization if the corporation is insolvent in the equity sense. To voluntarily begin liquidation under the Chandler Act, the debtor need not be insolvent in any manner. For creditors to begin liquidation proceedings against the debtor, insolvency in the bankruptcy sense is necessary for the filing of a petition after the commission of an act of bankruptcy. There are two exceptions to

[16] *Duncan v. Landis,* 106 Fed. 839, 1901.
[17] *Ouellette,* 98 F. Supp. 943, 1951.
[18] Burchfield, p. 12.
[19] *Ibid.,* pp. 11–13.

this: a general assignment for the benefit of creditors, or an admission in writing of the debtor's inability to pay its debts and its willingness to be adjudicated bankrupt.

28. As implied above, the term insolvency with its various meanings is not synonymous with bankruptcy. In Section 1(4) the Bankruptcy Act defines a bankrupt as a person against whom an involuntary petition or an application to revoke a discharge has been filed, or who has filed a voluntary petition, or who has been adjudged a bankrupt. Thus a firm may be insolvent but not involved in the legal proceedings necessary for it to be a bankrupt. And conversely, a remedy may be sought under the Bankruptcy Act for financial difficulties while the debtor is not insolvent.

ALTERNATIVES AVAILABLE TO A
FINANCIALLY TROUBLED BUSINESS

29. When a corporation finds itself heading toward serious financial difficulties and unable to obtain new financing or to solve the problem internally, it must seek a remedy vis-à-vis its creditors either informally (out of court) or with the help of judicial proceedings. Under either method, the debtor has several alternatives to choose from as to the particular way it will seek rehabilitation. The method selected depends upon the debtor's history, size, and future outlook, and upon the creditors' attitudes, types, and size of claims. This section of Chapter 3 contains a discussion of three of the most common alternatives selected: informal arrangement with creditors' committee, informal composition settlement, and reorganizations under Chapter X. Arrangements under Chapter XI, the fourth most common alternative, is the subject of Chapter 4. The debtor may also decide to liquidate the business by making an assignment for benefit of creditors or filing a petition for straight bankruptcy. These two liquidation alternatives are also described.

Committee Cases

30. Creditors' committees are often formed to effect a voluntary agreement between debtor and creditors made out of court. Where the number of creditors is large, formation of such

committees is necessary to obtain harmonious action and an acceptable plan. Essentially, the rules of law governing the duties and obligations of a creditors' committee, whether formed in or out of court, are the same.

Formation of Creditors' Committee

31. There is no set procedure to the formation of an unofficial committee. Typically, the debtor will request a meeting with its creditors, at which time the creditors will appoint a committee including four or five of the largest creditors and one or two representatives from the smaller creditors. It is advantageous if such creditors are those most friendly to the debtor. These meetings are often "arranged and conducted by adjustment bureaus associated with local credit managers associations or by trade association." [20]

Duties, Functions, and Procedures of Creditors' Committee

32. The creditors' committee is the liaison between creditor and debtors and is also the representative and bargaining agent for the creditors. Once a settlement has been arranged it is the responsibility of the committee to solicit acceptance by the creditors. Honesty and good faith are requirements in the performance of all committee functions. Committee members must recognize that their interests are the same as those of the other creditors; they must not allow their own interests to be brought into conflict with those of the body of creditors and must completely refrain from seeking personal gain.[21]

33. At the first meeting, the facts are presented in a general statement to the creditors and the adjusting bureau if one is involved. If it is judged that the case is capable of adjustment, a committee selected by the creditors will be established to make an exhaustive report. The committee will examine all the facts of the situation, including an evaluation of the assets and liabilities of the debtor. It will often request that the debtor's books be audited by

[20] Fred Weston, *Managerial Finance* (New York: Holt, Rinehart and Winston, Inc., 1962), p. 563.

[21] Chauncey Levy, "Creditors' Committees and Their Responsibilities," *Commercial Law Journal*, Vol. 74 (December 1969), p. 360.

an independent accountant. The committee will also investigate to see if there were fraudulent transfers, concealments, preferences, incorrect financial statements, or any type of questionable transactions. The creditors' committee must be sure it is dealing with an honest debtor. The facts collected are used in the formulation of a plan.

34. "In non-bankruptcy matters the functions of a committee have run the gamut from investigation, consultation, advice to supervision and liquidation." [22] All these functions include supervision of the activities of the debtor, ensuring that all possible steps are taken to collect and preserve the assets, guard against careless acts of the debtor, and receive information from creditors as to the conduct of the debtor. This generally amounts to the submission of business and financial affairs by the debtor to the control of the committee.

35. Under creditor committee management, an agreement is entered into between the debtor and the creditors, whereby control of the business is turned over to a committee of the creditors. The debtor in doing this normally executes an assignment for the benefit of creditors. This assignment is held in escrow by the committee. If it becomes necessary, the creditors can liquidate the debtor's assets or use the assignment as an act of bankruptcy. The directors and officers of the debtor corporation tender resignations which the committee holds in escrow. The stockholders often endorse all shares of stock in blank. These are also held in escrow by the committee. The committee can operate the business itself, bring in an outside business expert, or use a present officer of the company. Usually included in the agreement is a provision for existing creditors to grant extensions or subordinate their claims in return for new financing. New funds can then be obtained from banks and others to provide the company with working capital. Usually the internal organization of the company is not changed; alterations are made only as necessary to effect efficiency and economies in operation.

36. After the business has operated for a short time under the plan designed by the creditors' committee, those in charge of managing the company determine whether recovery under the new

[22] *Ibid.*, p. 359.

regime is possible, or whether reorganization or liquidation is necessary.[23] If recovery seems possible, the agreement normally continues for a given period of time or until the creditors' claims have been paid or adjusted out of the proceeds realized under the management of the committee. When reorganization appears necessary, the committee may assist management in designing a plan. If the only alternative is liquidation, the committee may supervise the process.

Success of Committee

37. In an informal agreement, where there is no provision binding on the minority of creditors to accept the will of the majority, the consent of the members of the committee must be obtained for the plan to work. "These methods of friendly adjustment out of court are feasible only where the debtor corporation and substantially all the creditors are disposed to take a cooperative and realistic attitude and to work harmoniously toward a solution of the problem." [24] Creditors' committees have had success in "prevailing upon creditors to withhold institution of actions or the prosecution of pending actions." [25] And if the firm does not begin to recover under the aegis of the committee, it can be liquidated.

38. The main advantages associated with creditors' committees as a means of rehabilitation is that they avoid unfavorable publicity and are less costly than legal proceedings. However, such committees have "no legal authority to set aside questionable claims and are powerless to prevent a dissatisfied creditor from throwing the company into receivership or bankruptcy." [26]

Assignment for the Benefit of Creditors (State Court)

39. Under an assignment for the benefit of creditors, the debtor voluntarily transfers title to all his assets to a trustee or assignee who then sells or otherwise liquidates the assets and

---

[23] Gerstenberg, p. 517.

[24] William J. Grange, *et al.*, *Manual for Corporation Officers* (New York: The Ronald Press Co., 1967), p. 340.

[25] Levy, p. 357.

[26] Weston, pp. 700–1.

distributes the proceeds among the creditors on a pro rata basis. An assignment provides an orderly method of liquidation and prevents the disruption of the business by individual creditors armed with attachments or executions acquired subsequent to the assignment. Most statutes uphold assignments as against the attack of particular creditors.

40. The board of directors usually has the power to make an assignment for the benefit of creditors when the corporation is insolvent. However, when a going concern sells a large share of its assets, such action must be approved by the stockholders.

Duties, Functions, and Procedures of Assignee

41. The debtor initiates the action by executing an instrument of assignment which is recorded in the county where executed. This recordation serves as notice to all third parties. Most statutes have no prohibition against the choice of the debtor's representative as the assignee. Thus the proceeding is of a quasi-judicial nature: the corporation may select anyone it prefers to act as the assignee, but the person chosen is subject to the control of the court.[27] Attorneys are generally selected as the assignee. The statutes in New York, as in many other states, are very comprehensive and contain detailed regulations covering the proceedings, which include specifications of the duties and powers of each assignee.[28] The assignee supervises the proceedings, including the sale of the assets and the distribution of the proceeds. This procedure results in a quick disposition of assets and avoids creditors' attaching claims to the assets or the debtor's wasteful use of the assets. But if the facts warrant a finding of misconduct or incompetence on the part of the debtor and/or assignee, the creditors could petition for a substitution of the assignee or file an involuntary petition in bankruptcy.

42. Assignees are trustees for all the creditors and will be held personally liable to the creditors if they fail to exercise the care and diligence required of trustees. To further insure the protection of the creditors, assignees must usually post a bond in an amount determined by the court. The duties of assignees generally include taking charge of, inventorying, and liquidating the assets transferred

[27] Grange *et al.*, p. 391.
[28] New York Debtor and Creditor Law, Sec. 2–24.

to them. Liquidation is usually done at a public sale, although a private sale may be held upon specific authorization by court order. Assignees also collect any money owed to the debtor, solicit additional claims, and distribute the proceeds from the liquidation to the creditors on a pro rata basis, giving preference to any claims which are legally entitled to priority, such as secured claims, taxes, and wages. Assignees then must have their accounts approved and their bond discharged by the court.

43. It may be advantageous to continue the business for a short period if it appears that the amount realized from liquidation will be greater if the business is phased out gradually rather than liquidated immediately. Also, if the necessary adjustments can be made to the operations so that there is a net cash inflow, the business may continue long enough to satisfy all, or at least a large percentage, of the creditors' claims. It will be necessary under these conditions for the assignee to obtain leave of the court (authorization); otherwise the assignee will be held personally liable for any losses which occur. Any profits earned accrue to the benefit of the creditors.

Discharge of Debts

44. State assignment laws do not discharge debts; thus, this remedy does not offer a means of cancelling the debts of the corporation. The creditors may receive their pro rata dividends and still have a valid claim against the debtor. Thus the debtor must still file a bankruptcy petition and obtain its discharge if it wants to be relieved from its debts. However, in the case of a corporation which is to be liquidated, since activities will be ended and the entity no longer in existence, the consideration of discharge is irrelevant. Although the debtor is not automatically discharged through the proceedings of an assignment, it may discharge itself by writing on the dividend check the necessary legal language to make the payment a complete discharge of the obligation. Essentially this is a statement that endorsement of the check represents full payment for the obligation.[29] As a practical matter this is not generally done since it is the assignee who issues the dividend checks.

[29] Weston, pp. 587–88.

45. In order for an assignment to be successful, consent of all the creditors must be obtained or at least they must refrain from filing an involuntary petition. An assignment is an act of bankruptcy which gives creditors the right to begin bankruptcy proceedings. In most states formal acceptance is not legally required and all creditors are not necessarily asked for their consent. However, if any three creditors opposed to the assignment desire to file a bankruptcy petition based upon the assignment as an act of bankruptcy, they are free to do so within four months after the assignment. In most states, if no creditor action is taken within four months, the assignment is then binding upon all creditors. Because it is a federal statute, the Bankruptcy Act is superior in authority to the state laws governing assignments. Therefore, when a petition in bankruptcy is filed, the assignee must surrender control and turn the assets over to the receiver or trustee in bankruptcy.[30] If the debtor is unable to obtain the support of the creditors, it should file a petition under the Bankruptcy Act because it will be impossible to arrange an assignment for the benefit of the creditors.

46. Assignments may also be used as a condition to continued negotiations, to become effective upon default of the debtor to the terms of the agreement, the failure of the debtor to negotiate fairly, or the happening of other events set forth in the assignment.[31] Thus an assignment is used as an "escrow document" where the collateral is deposited with the creditors' committee and in the event of a default by the debtor in making payments, the creditors can liquidate the debtor's assets through the assignment or use the assignment as an act of bankruptcy.[32]

Advantages

47. An assignment for the benefit of creditors has the advantage of being quicker, simpler, and less expensive than straight bankruptcy proceedings. It is simpler to initiate and less time-consuming to consummate. It is also preferred by debtors because

[30] Grange, *et al.*, pp. 391–92.

[31] Sydney Krause, "Insolvent Debtor Adjustments Under Relevant State Court Status as Against Proceedings Under the Bankruptcy Act," *The Business Lawyer*, Vol. 12 (January 1957), p. 189.

[32] Benjamin Weintraub, Harris Levin, and Eugene Sosnoff, "Assignment for the Benefit of Creditors and Competitive Systems for Liquidation of Insolvent Estates," *Cornell Law Quarterly*, Vol. 39 (1953–1954), pp. 4–6.

they are able to select their own liquidators. Under this procedure creditors usually receive a larger percentage of their claims because more time is available to find good buyers, a foreclosure sale is not necessary, and court and legal costs are greatly reduced.[33] An additional advantage to the debtor is that its self-image suffers less damage than if it were to experience the stigma associated with bankruptcy. Less publicity is involved and a future credit rating may suffer less. Assignments have also been successful in preserving assets for the benefit of creditors. If any creditor attempts to take action before any of the other creditors, the debtor may effect an assignment so that all the creditors will be treated equally. Under such circumstances a vindictive creditor does not have an advantage, because there is no property in the hands of a debtor on which a judgment must rest as a lien.[34]

Disadvantages

48. If certain preferences must be set aside or liens invalidated, bankruptcy is essential for the creditors. Some states do not allow any preferences and others have very limited provisions. Federal tax claims in insolvency proceedings are governed by Rev. Stat. s. 3466, 31 U.S.C. Sec. 191 where "debts due to the United States shall be first satisfied." If the claims are not satisfied, personal liability is imposed on the assignee.[35]

49. Satisfaction of federal tax claims is required only after administrative expenses are paid, but they do have priority over state and local taxes and wages.[36] In general, "the assignee's armory is rather weak compared with the trustee's arsenal." [37]

50. A disadvantage often cited for the debtor is the possibility of dissenting creditors or an inability to compel the creditors to assent to the assignment. This is found to be inconsequential in the case of a corporation, however, because following the realization of the assignment no assets will remain for such creditors to pursue.

[33] Elvin F. Donaldson, John K. Pfahl, and Peter L. Mullins, *Corporate Finance*, 4th Ed. (New York: The Ronald Press Co., 1975), p. 615.
[34] Gerstenberg, p. 516.
[35] 31 U.S.C. Sec. 192.
[36] *Kennebec Box Co. v. O. S. Richards Corp.*, 5 F.2d 951 (2d Cir. 1925).
[37] Richard A. Kaye, "Federal Taxes, Bankruptcy and Assignments for the Benefit of Creditors—A Comparison," *Commercial Law Journal*, Vol. 73 (March 1968), p. 78.

51. An assignment would be inappropriate in any case involving fraud and requiring intensive investigation. Such situations should be handled in the bankruptcy courts. It should also be realized that there are often major differences between the procedures under state court statutes and the Bankruptcy Act, and the various classes of creditors should be aware of the distinctions in the order of priority in state court assignments and bankruptcy.[38]

52. Even though an assignment is an act of bankruptcy and may be used by the creditors as the basis for a petition in involuntary bankruptcy, it is still commonly used, especially in the New York City area. Assignment is a less expensive but effective means of orderly liquidation in situations where there is no particular need for bankruptcy proceedings.

Informal Composition Settlement

53. An informal settlement effected between a debtor and his creditors is normally one of three possible types of agreement:

> *Moratorium*—an extension of time with eventual full payment in installments
>
> *Pro rata cash settlement*—payment on a proportional basis in cash in full settlement of claims
>
> *Combination*—payment of part of the debts in cash at the time of the settlement and agreement to make further installment payments[39]

54. Certain conditions are normally advantageous to a successful out-of-court agreement. The debtor company should be a good moral risk so that creditors may have some assurance it will be true to its word. The debtor should have the ability to recover from financial difficulties. General business conditions should be favorable to a recovery.[40]

Creditors' Committee

55. The debtor will request a meeting with its creditors, at which time a committee will be appointed. Ideally, the committee

[38] Krause, "Insolvent Debtor Adjustments . . . ," p. 188.
[39] John E. Mulder, "Rehabilitation of the Financially Distressed Small Business—Revisited," *The Practical Lawyer*, Vol. 11 (November 1965), p. 40.
[40] Weston, p. 564.

should consist of four or five of the largest creditors and one representative of the smaller creditors. A lot of unnecessary time wasted on deciding the size and composition of the committee would be saved at creditors' meetings if the committees were organized in this manner. However, regardless of whether a creditors' committee is being formed in an out-of-court situation or in straight bankruptcy or Chapter XI proceedings, there are no legal or rigid rules defining the manner in which a committee shall be formed. Although a smaller creditor will often serve on a committee, there are committees on which only the larger creditors serve either because of lack of interest on the part of the smaller creditors or because the larger creditors override the wishes of others. At this meeting the creditors will want to know whether the debtor can be rehabilitated and deserves to be rehabilitated, the financial history and structure of the business, whether there have been any great reductions in the inventory, and whether any large payments have been made recently to favorite creditors (Chapter 7). The committee will elect a chairman and legal counsel, and may retain an independent accountant to audit the debtor's books (Chapter 8).[41]

Requirements of Plan

56. A plan will be worked out between the creditors and debtor. The plan must provide that all costs of administration, secured claims, and priority claims, including taxes, wages, and rent, are adequately disposed of for the eventual protection of the unsecured creditors.[42] If the debtor's plan includes a cash down payment, in full or partial settlement, the payment should at least equal the probable dividend the creditors would receive in bankruptcy. It is not likely that creditors will accept under an agreement anything less than they would get in straight bankruptcy proceedings. See Chapter 6, paragraphs 20–24, 40–41.

Conditions of Agreement

57. When an agreement calls for future installment payments, the creditors may insist that these payments be secured, for

---

[41] Leon S. Forman, *Compositions, Bankruptcy, and Arrangements* (Philadelphia: The American Law Institute, 1971), pp. 10, 13.

[42] *Ibid.*, p. 13.

example, by notes or a mortgage on real estate.[43] The debtor may execute an assignment for the benefit of creditors to be held in escrow and to become effective only if the debtor defaults in performance of the plan. The creditors may require that their own accountant make frequent audits or supervise the operation of the business (Chapter 7, paragraphs 16–24). As an extreme, creditors may even require that they or a third party be allowed to operate the business during the period when the plan is to be carried out.[44]

58. After the creditors' committee approves a plan, it will notify all of the other creditors and recommend to them that they accept it. Even if a few creditors do not agree, the debtor should continue with the plan. Such creditors will eventually have to be paid in full, and the plan may even provide for full payment to small creditors, thus destroying "the nuisance value of the small claims." [45] When a plan is agreed upon, the debtor should "either make out the checks for the initial payment and turn them over to counsel for the creditors' committee, or deposit with such counsel the funds for that purpose." [46] The funds to be deposited by the debtor must usually be sufficient to pay priority claims, secured claims, and administrative costs.

Advantages and Disadvantages

59. The advantages of an informal composition settlement are those common to other out-of-court agreements: the proceedings are simple, informal, economical, and expeditious. Also, because court costs are avoided, dividends to creditors are usually larger.

60. The greater obstacle to successful rehabilitation under this remedy is that a settlement requires unanimous approval of all creditors. Legally two or more creditors may effect a composition agreement, but those not joining may force the debtor into bankruptcy.

61. Another disadvantage under an informal composition agreement is that the debtor remains in possession of its assets and they are thus subject to levy or attachment.

[43] Mulder, p. 44.
[44] Forman, p. 12.
[45] *Ibid.*, p. 15.
[46] *Ibid.*

62. The number of common-law compositions represents only a small percentage of settlements involving time payment extension plans.[47] The majority are arranged through proceedings under Chapter XI.

Reorganization Under Chapter X

63. Chapter X of the Bankruptcy Act contains the provisions for a plan of reorganization which, when confirmed by a majority of the creditors, will allow the corporation to operate in its new form without the debt which existed prior to proceedings. In contemplating reorganization, it must first be decided whether the business is really worth saving. This involves investigating the condition of the business and the causes of its present difficulties (Chapter 6, paragraphs 5–13, 22–24). If it is concluded that the business could not be operated profitably, the company should be liquidated.

64. Chapter X may be used for rehabilitation only when the debtor cannot obtain sufficient relief under Chapter XI.[48] Chapter X proceedings are used sparingly because they involve the rights of secured creditors and stockholders. This provision means that the judge in a Chapter X petition must make a preliminary finding that relief is not available under Chapter XI.[49]

65. The principal objectives of a Chapter X case are eliminating the factors which caused the financial difficulty and getting the business into such condition that it can operate successfully in the future and meet the expectations of those who take the firm's securities issued in reorganization. This usually involves one or more of the following adjustments:

Correcting any managerial defects, finding economies in the operation of the business, and assuring continued efficient management

Reducing fixed charges, such as the interest rate or the principal amount of bonds

Reducing floating debt and funding current or past-due debts into long-term obligations

Raising new capital and collecting new money

[47] Levy, p. 363.
[48] Bankruptcy Act, Sec. 321.
[49] *Ibid.*, Secs. 141, 146(2).

Filing of Petition

66. Chapter X proceedings may be initiated voluntarily by the corporation or involuntarily by outside parties. A voluntary petition may be filed as an initial move by the corporation, provided it can be adjudged a bankrupt under the Bankruptcy Act, or has already been adjudged a bankrupt, or has an involuntary bankruptcy petition pending against it.[50] An involuntary petition may be filed by an indenture trustee or three or more creditors who have unsecured claims against a corporation or its property totalling $5,000 or more.[51] Any petition may be contested by the corporation, a creditor, shareholder, or indenture trustee. If no bankruptcy proceeding is pending, the original petition is filed with the court in whose territorial jurisdiction the corporation has had its principal place of business or its principal assets for a longer portion of the preceding six months than in any other jurisdiction.[52] The court in which the petition is filed has exclusive jurisdiction of the debtor and his property wherever located.[53]

Stockholders' Rights

67. In determining the fair market value of the assets to be used in reorganization proceedings, the most important factor has become the earning capacity of the assets when taken as a whole. When determining solvency or insolvency and how the rule of absolute priority can be applied to the creditors' claims, the expected income to be earned from the assets during the period prior to reorganization, the actual proceedings themselves, and following the confirmation of a plan is capitalized at the rate normal to the industry.[54]

Insolvency and Stockholders' Rights

68. The determination of insolvency is important when considering the rights of stockholders in the proceedings. If the corporation is insolvent in the bankruptcy sense, the stockholders

[50] Grange *et al.*, p. 418.
[51] Bankruptcy Act, Sec. 126.
[52] *Ibid.*, Sec. 128.
[53] *Ibid.*, Sec. 111.
[54] Krause, "What Constitutes Insolvency," p. 1091.

will not be allowed to retain any interest in the reorganized corporation. Under these circumstances their acceptance of any plan is not required and they do not have to be protected under any plan. Also, no stockholder is permitted to file a suggested plan in the proceedings.[55]

Appointment and Duties of Trustee

69. Upon approval of the petition, if the debtor's liabilities exceed $250,000, it is mandatory that the court appoint one or more disinterested trustees. To be disinterested, the trustee cannot be:

A stockholder or creditor of the company, or

Within five years prior to filing the petition an underwriter of the company's securities, or

Within two years prior to the filing of the petition a director, officer, attorney, or employee of the company, or

Any other person who has a direct or indirect relationship with the company or underwriter and who might have an interest materially adverse to the interests of any class of creditors or shareholders.[56]

70. A few accountants have been appointed trustees; however, the majority are attorneys. To facilitate the operation of the business and the managing of the property during the reorganization, the judge may appoint as an additional trustee a person who is a director, officer, or employee of the debtor.[57]

71. If the debtor's total liabilities are less than $250,000, the court may at its discretion appoint a trustee or continue the debtor in possession and control of its property and business. When appointed, the trustee is in full charge. The trustee conducts an investigation, determines the facts, invites proposals from creditors and stockholders, and ultimately prepares the plan of reorganization. Where the debtor remains in possession, the debtor formulates the plan. In both cases, the role of the creditors and (in some instances) the shareholders and their representatives is limited to approval of the plan.

[55] Frederick J. R. Heebe, "Corporate Reorganization Under Chapter X of the Bankruptcy Act," *Loyola Law Review*, Vol. 16 (1969–1970), p. 30.

[56] Bankruptcy Act, Sec. 158.

[57] *Ibid.*, Secs. 156, 189.

72. The Bankruptcy Act requires that the first hearing be held between thirty and sixty days after the initial approval of the petition. This meeting is intended to provide for the initial confrontation between the parties involved.[58]

Plan of Reorganization

73. Section 170 of the Bankruptcy Act provides that where a debtor is continued in possession, a plan or plans may be filed within a time fixed by the judge, by the debtor, by any creditor or indenture trustee, by any stockholder, if the debtor is not found to be insolvent, and by the examiner, if so directed by the judge. Alternatively, where a trustee has been appointed, the trustee prepares and files the plan, and thereafter the judge may fix a time for hearing on the plan as proposed by the trustee or any amendments thereof or such other plans as may be proposed by the debtor or by any creditor or stockholder (Bankruptcy Act, Section 169). Certain steps are necessary in the formulation of the plan, regardless of who the author is. The causes of the failure should be determined, including a complete audit of the books for a period including several past years and a revision of certain items on the balance sheet (Chapter 8). Second, there should be a complete inspection of the physical plant, with an analysis of the existing facilities to determine whether they are adequate, and an overall analysis of the industry and its future potential. Finally, there must be a legal and financial analysis. The claims against the corporation, contracts, leases, tax structure, and any other legal matters should be examined and a plan for obtaining the necessary funds must be formulated.[59]

74. If the corporation is insolvent in the bankruptcy sense, the plan of reorganization does not have to make provision for the stockholders; otherwise they must be included in the plan. The plan must observe the "absolute priorities" rule: provide for the satisfaction of all of the first class of creditors before the second class can receive anything, and the satisfaction of the second class before the third class, and so on.[60] The priority of claims following the preferred group of administrative expenses, wages, taxes, etc., is

---

[58] Heebe, p. 32.
[59] Gerstenberg, p. 540.
[60] Heebe, p. 37.

determined essentially by the legal positions they occupy. The order of priority is (1) holders of trustee's certificates, (2) senior mortgage bondholders, (3) junior bondholders, (4) divisional or subsidiary company bondholders, (5) unsecured creditors without preference, (6) preferred stockholders, and (7) common stockholders.[61]

Provisions of Plan

75. The following are the requirements set forth in the Bankruptcy Act for the content of any plan of reorganization:

Shall include in respect to creditors generally or some class of them, secured or unsecured, and may include in respect to shareholders generally or some class of them, provisions altering or modifying their rights either through the issuance of new securities of any character or otherwise.

May deal with all or any part of the property of the debtor.

Shall provide for the payment of all costs and expenses of administration and other allowances which may be approved by the judge.

May provide for the rejection of any executory contract, except contracts in the public authority.

Shall specify what claims, if any, are to be paid in cash in full.

Shall specify the creditors or shareholders or any class of them not affected by the plan and the provisions, if any, with respect to them.

Shall provide, for any class of creditors that is affected by the two-thirds majority in amount required, adequate protection for the realization by them of the value of their claims against the property dealt with by the plan.

Shall provide, for any class of shareholders that is affected by the plan and does not accept the plan by the majority of the stock required, adequate protection for the realization by them of the value of their equity, if any, in the property of the debtor dealt with by the plan, provided the judge shall determine that the debtor is not insolvent.

May include provisions for the retirement of debt extended under the plan for more than five years by payments from a sinking fund, if secured, within the useful life of the security and if unsecured, within a reasonable time period not to exceed forty years.

Shall provide adequate means for the execution of the plan.

[61] Gerstenberg, p. 542.

Shall include provisions which are equitable and compatible with the interests of creditors and stockholders and consistent with public policy, with respect to the manner of selection of the persons who are to be directors, officers, or voting trustees, if any.

Shall provide for the inclusion in the charter of the debtor, or any corporation organized or to be organized for the purpose of carrying out the plan, provisions prohibiting the debtor or such corporation from issuing non-voting stock, providing for the fair and equitable distribution of voting power among such classes, and adequate provisions for the election of directors representing preferred class in the event of default in the payment of such dividends.

May include provisions for the settlement or adjustment of claims belonging to the debtor or to the estate; and shall provide as to such claims not settled or adjusted in the plan, for their retention and enforcement by the trustee or examiner appointed for that purpose.

May include any other appropriate provisions not inconsistent with the provisions of the Act.[62]

76. When the indebtedness of the debtor exceeds $3,000,000, the plan of reorganization must be submitted to the Securities and Exchange Commission for prior approval and report,[63] providing the company is a public corporation (Chapter 6, paragraphs 49–54).

Court Approval of the Plan

77. The plan must be approved by the judge before it is submitted to the creditors. If the court determines that the plan is fair, equitable, and feasible, and complies with the provisions of Section 216, it will enter an order approving the plan and set the time for acceptances. "Fair and equitable" means that each class of creditors and security holders is given its proper priority. This includes an examination of the legal and contractual rights of each party and may involve the following steps:

Estimate future sales

Estimate future earnings on those sales by analyzing operating conditions

Determine a capitalization rate to be applied to the future earnings

[62] Bankruptcy Act, Sec. 216.
[63] *Ibid.*, Sec. 172.

Obtain a value of the company's properties by applying the capitalization rate to the estimated future earnings

Provide for distribution to the claimants[64]

78. The requirement that a plan be feasible means that it places the corporation in such a position that it is not likely to approach failure again. One of the most important criteria in determining feasibility is that the fixed charges to be incurred by the corporation after reorganization be sufficiently covered by earnings. This may necessitate actions to improve the earning capabilities of the company, including:

Higher quality and more efficient management

More effective and efficient operations

Modernization of plant and equipment

Improvement in marketing, production, advertising, and other functions

Development of new products in areas where growth potential is greater[65]

Creditors' Acceptance

79. Once the court has approved the plan, it may be submitted to the creditors. Any solicitation of acceptances before the plan is approved by the judge, without the consent of the court, is forbidden and any acceptances so obtained are invalid.[66] When the debtor is insolvent, acceptance requires agreement by two-thirds in amount of claims filed and allowed in each class of creditors; the shareholders have no vote on the plan. For a solvent debtor, creditor agreement must be as for an insolvent debtor, but approval also requires agreement by holders of a majority of each class of stock.[67]

Confirmation of Plan

80. After acceptance, the judge confirms the plan. This binds the debtor corporation and all corporations issuing securities or

[64] Weston, p. 577.
[65] Ibid., p. 580.
[66] Bankruptcy Act, Sec. 176.
[67] Ibid., Sec. 179.

acquiring property under the plan, as well as all shareholders and creditors, to its terms and provisions. Under the direction of the judge, the plan is carried out with as much speed as possible.

Final Decree

81. Upon the consummation of the plan, the judge enters a final decree:

> Discharging the debtor from all its debts and liabilities and terminating all rights and interests of stockholders of the debtor, except as provided in the plan or in the order confirming the plan or in the order directing or authorizing the transfer or retention of property
>
> Discharging the trustee, if any
>
> Making such provisions by way of injunction or otherwise as may be equitable, and
>
> Closing the estate[68]

82. The corporation which emerges from reorganization proceedings may bear little resemblance to the business as it once was. Usually the company's internal structure, including its finances, is reorganized, an entirely new management is brought in, new capital is acquired, and an entirely different operating philosophy may be instituted. The corporation is now able to continue its operations free of the burdens that forced the reorganization.

Unsuccessful Proceedings

83. When it appears that the reorganization proceedings will not result in adequate rehabilitation, the judge should either dismiss the Chapter X petition or transfer the proceeding into straight bankruptcy. The following situations would normally call for such action:

> No plan is proposed within the time fixed by the judge.
>
> No plan proposed is approved by the judge.
>
> No plan which has been approved by the judge is accepted within the time fixed by him.
>
> Confirmation is refused or the confirmed plan is not consummated.[69]

---

[68] *Ibid.*, Sec. 228.
[69] Heebe, pp. 40–41.

Bankruptcy and Liquidation

84. The first seven chapters of the Bankruptcy Act, as amended in 1938, are concerned with the liquidation of a debtor in financial trouble and contain provisions for the adjudication of the debtor as a bankrupt, liquidation of the corporation, distribution of the estate to creditors, and discharge of the debtor from his liabilities. "It is the purpose of the Bankruptcy Act to convert the assets of the bankrupt into cash for distribution among creditors, and then to relieve the honest debtor from the weight of oppressive indebtedness and permit him to start afresh, free from the obligations and responsibilities that have resulted from business misfortunes." [70]

Filing the Petition

85. Any corporation may file a voluntary petition in bankruptcy except municipal, railroad, insurance, and banking corporations and building and loan associations. The corporation filing voluntarily need not be insolvent in either the bankruptcy or equity sense; the essential requirement is that the petitioner have debts. When the corporation is insolvent, shareholder approval or authorization to the filing of a petition is unnecessary; the board of directors has the power to initiate proceedings. The filing of a voluntary petition operates to automatically adjudge the corporation a bankrupt. Its property is then regarded as being in the custody of the court and "constitutes the assets of a trust for the benefit of the corporation's creditors." [71]

86. Under certain circumstances, an involuntary petition in bankruptcy may be filed against a corporation, excluding building and loan associations and municipal, railroad, insurance, and banking corporations.[72] The general rules applicable to the filing of an involuntary petition follow:

1. The alleged bankrupt corporation must owe debts totalling at least $1,000.[73]
2. The petition must be filed by either
   a. Three or more creditors having claims in the aggregate of $500
      or

[70] 1 Collier on Bankruptcy, 13th Ed., p. 6.
[71] Grange, *et al.*, pp. 398–99.
[72] Bankruptcy Act, Sec. 4a.
[73] *Ibid.*, Sec. 4b.

b. When there are fewer than 12 creditors, one creditor with a claim of at least $500.[74]

3. Within four months preceding the petition, the debtor must have committed at least one of six acts of bankruptcy:
    a. Concealment or fraudulent conveyance—hiding assets with the intent to defraud creditors, or a transfer of property to a third party without adequate consideration and with the intent to defraud creditors.
    b. Preferential transfer—while insolvent, transfer of the debtor's property to a creditor, giving that creditor a greater portion of his claim than other creditors would receive on liquidation.
    c. Legal lien or distraint—while insolvent, permit a creditor to obtain a lien on the debtor's property and not discharging that lien within thirty (30) days, or permit a landlord to distrain for non-payment of rent.
    d. Assignment—make a general assignment for the benefit of creditors.
    e. Appointment of a receiver or trustee—while insolvent, permit the appointment of a receiver or trustee to take charge of the debtor's property.
    f. Admission—admit in writing an inability to pay debts and willingness to be adjudged bankrupt.[75]

Preliminary Trial and Contest of the Petition

87. After the filing of an involuntary petition, a subpoena is issued and served upon the debtor with a copy of the petition. The alleged bankrupt must then answer giving all of its defenses and, if it so desires, denying any material allegation contained in the petition. The debtor or any of its creditors may contest the allegations of the petition and the court will subsequently try issues.[76] Before the trial, the judge may require any person to be examined before the court upon an application by any officer, bankrupt, or creditor.[77] Following the preliminary findings by the court, the judge either enters an adjudication that the debtor is a bankrupt or dismisses the petition.

[74] *Ibid.*, Sec. 59b.
[75] *Ibid.*, Sec. 3.
[76] *Ibid.*, Sec. 18.
[77] *Ibid.*, Sec. 21a.

88. The first duty of the bankrupt is to file a schedule of the assets and liabilities of the corporation, with the names, addresses, and amount due each of the creditors. A statement of the debtor's financial affairs must also be filed.

Appointment of Receiver

89. After the petition is filed, the court may appoint a receiver to take charge of the property of the corporation, care for and protect the assets of the estate, and protect the interests of the creditors. The receiver continues in the proceedings until the creditors meet and appoint a trustee or until the petition is dismissed. The court may choose to leave the debtor in possession of its assets, but they are technically in the custody of the court.

Appointment of Appraiser

90. The court is required to appoint an appraiser to appraise the property of the bankrupt and file a report. The value determined by the appraiser serves as a standard which can be used to determine the adequacy of the amount realized on the sale of the bankrupt's property. Real and personal property must be sold subject to the court when practicable; however, the Bankruptcy Act provides that it shall not be sold, without court approval, for less than 75 per cent of its appraised value.[78]

Administration

91. After adjudication comes the administration of the bankrupt's estate. The case is sent to a referee in bankruptcy (bankruptcy judge), who takes general charge of the proceedings.[79] The administration of the estate in bankruptcy will be considered in terms of the following: first creditors' meeting, proof and allowance of claims, election of trustee, liquidation of assets, final distribution and priority of claims, and discharge.

First Creditors' Meeting

92. The first meeting of creditors must be called by the bankruptcy judge not less than 10 nor more than 30 days after the

[78] Bankruptcy Act, Sec. 70f.
[79] Ibid., Sec. 22.

adjudication. At this meeting the creditors may examine the debtor with respect to the schedules and statement of affairs it has filed. They may also appoint a committee of three or more creditors to consult with, advise, and make recommendations to the trustee.

Proof and Allowance of Claims

93. A proof of claim is a statement, in writing and signed by the creditor, setting forth the claim justly owed by the bankrupt. The proof and allowance of claims is initiated by the filing of claims by creditors with the bankruptcy judge. This procedure is important because only the holders of claims which have been allowed may participate in the proceedings of creditors' meeting and receive dividends declared from the estate. Also, provable claims are discharged at the end of the proceedings. Security and priority claims are allowable only to the extent that the security held is insufficient to meet the claim. A claim is regarded as proved and allowed upon filing unless it is contested by the trustee or another creditor. Filing must be done within six months after the date set for the first meeting of creditors.[80]

94. Once a claim is allowed by court declaration, it is valid against any defense or objections that may be raised by the trustee or any creditor. Types of claims that are provable and, therefore, allowable include fixed liabilities which are absolutely owing, taxable costs when the bankrupt is plaintiff or defendant, debts based on open account or implied contract, judgments recovered after bankruptcy, workmen's compensation award, negligible claim, contingent debts and contingent contractual liabilities, and claims for anticipatory breach of executory contracts. Claims which are not provable include future alimony, secured claims, and priority claims.[81]

Election and Duties of Trustee

95. A trustee must be elected to act as the representative of the creditors and the agent of the court in administering the bankrupt estate. The trustee is elected by the creditors and must receive a majority in number and amount of all claims allowed and

[80] *Ibid.*, Sec. 57.
[81] Forman, pp. 66–73.

represented at the meeting.[82] Otherwise a trustee will be appointed by the court.[83]

96. The trustee is vested with title to the bankrupt's assets and one of the first duties is to collect the bankrupt's property.[84] The trustee may need to resort to turnover proceedings—actions to obtain property in the possession of the bankrupt or third parties, which they may refuse to deliver to the trustee. Reclamation proceedings may be filed by a third party which claims superior title or a lien to property which is in the trustee's possession.

97. The bankrupt has the right to exempt some of its property from the proceedings. The Bankruptcy Act follows the law of the state of the bankrupt's domicile in determining what portion of the assets should be exempt. However, to be granted an exemption, the bankrupt must make a proper and timely claim to it. It is then the duty of the trustee to determine what property is exempt. If on the eve of bankruptcy, the debtor converts non-exempt assets into exempt property, such an act will not in itself constitute fraud so as to deprive the bankrupt of its right to exemptions. But the exemptions will be refused if it can be shown that there was fraudulent intent in the transaction.[85]

98. Within sixty days after adjudication, the trustee is required to assume or reject any executory contracts when it seems likely that the estate will benefit from such action.[86]

99. Certain transfers made by the debtor may be voidable by the trustee, necessitating acquisition of the assets by the trustee for the benefit of the estate. These include:

Transfers which a creditor with a lien by legal or equitable proceedings could avoid under state law

Liens against the bankrupt's property obtained within four months of the filing if the bankrupt was insolvent at the time the lien was obtained

Fraudulent conveyances made within one year prior to filing

Preferential payments made within four months of bankruptcy[87]

[82] Bankruptcy Act, Sec. 56a.
[83] *Ibid.*, Sec. 44a.
[84] *Ibid.*, Sec. 70.
[85] *Ibid.*, Secs. 6, 47a(6).
[86] Forman, p. 90.
[87] *Ibid.*, pp. 91, 112.

100. Statutory liens which are valid in bankruptcy and not voidable by the trustee, even though they were obtained while the debtor was insolvent and within four months of the petition, include "employees, contractors, mechanics, or any other class of person, and liens of the states and Federal Government for taxes or debts." [88]

Liquidation of Assets

101. The trustee is responsible for the liquidation of the assets, selling the bankrupt's property under the supervision of the referee. The sale will not be confirmed by the court unless 75 per cent of the amount of the appraised value of the assets is received.[89]

102. It is also the trustee's duty to ensure that claimants are paid in the order of their priority. This priority, which is the same as that observed under arrangement and reorganization proceedings, with the inclusion of the various classes of shareholders, is as follows:

1. Administrative costs
2. Wages earned within three months of the petition not exceeding $600 per person
3. Costs to creditors resulting from the refusal, revocation, or setting aside of a discharge or a conviction of any person under the Bankruptcy Act
4. Taxes owed to the United States, a state, or municipal subdivision
5. Liabilities due any person which by state or federal law are entitled to priority, including secured creditors and rent owed to a landlord and accrued within three months prior to the bankruptcy
6. General or unsecured creditors
7. Preferred stock
8. Common stock[90]

103. After priority claims have been paid in full, assets are liquidated, and dividends are declared and paid pro rata to the general creditors. When the estate has been fully liquidated, the final meeting of the creditors is called. At this time, the last

---

[88] Forman, p. 118.
[89] Bankruptcy Act, Sec. 70f.
[90] *Ibid.*, Sec. 64.

dividend is declared and paid, and the trustee makes a final accounting and is discharged from further responsibility.[91]

Discharge

104. If the bankrupt wishes to be granted a discharge, he must file an application within six months after the adjudication. A discharge is rarely sought because the corporation generally goes out of business and a corporation may easily be formed if it is desired to begin operations again. However, if no objections to the discharge are filed, it must be granted as a matter of right.[92] The offenses which, when performed by the debtor, will bar him from discharge and the debts from which the debtor cannot be discharged *per se* are the same as under Chapter XI (Chapter 4, paragraphs 57–59).

[91] Grange *et al.*, p. 413.
[92] Forman, pp. 135–36.

4

Arrangement Proceedings

Under Chapter XI

1. Bankruptcy proceedings are generally the last resort for the debtor whose financial condition has deteriorated to the point where it is impossible to acquire additional funds. When the debtor finally agrees that bankruptcy proceedings are necessary, the liquidation value of the assets often represents only a small fraction of the debtor's total liabilities. If the business is liquidated, the creditors get only a small percentage of their claims. The debtor is discharged of its debts and is free to start over; however, the business is lost and so are all the assets. Normally, straight bankruptcy proceedings result in serious losses to the debtor, the

creditor, and the business community.[1] Arrangement proceedings were enacted in 1938 as a part of the Chandler Act to reduce these losses.

DEFINITION OF ARRANGEMENT

2. As defined in Section 306 of the Bankruptcy Act, an arrangement under Chapter XI is any plan of a debtor for settlement, satisfaction, or extension of the time of payment of unsecured debts, upon any terms.

3. Comprehensively, it is a "proceeding pursuant to which an embarrassed debtor, by arrangement with his creditors and subject to court approval, remains in business but secures either an extension of time for payment of his debts or pays them off on a pro rata basis, or both."[2] Upon agreement of the creditors and approval of the court, the debtor is discharged from debts and able to resume operations free from burdensome obligations. The purpose of this remedy is to allow the debtor to rehabilitate the business while continuing in operation.

4. Section 302 states that all those provisions of the Bankruptcy Act applicable to straight bankruptcy which are not inconsistent with Chapter XI apply also to arrangement proceedings. This includes provisions relating to priority claims, voidable preferences, voidable transfers, fraudulent conveyances, and voidable liens acquired by legal proceedings. The objective of this chapter is to describe in summary form the provisions of Chapter XI of the Bankruptcy Act.

PETITION UNDER CHAPTER XI

Filing the Petition

5. A petition filed under Chapter XI must be voluntary, that is, only the debtor may initiate the proceedings. To file, the debtor must be insolvent in either the bankruptcy or the equity sense.

---

[1] Leon S. Forman, *Compositions, Bankruptcy, and Arrangements* (Philadelphia: The American Law Institute, 1971), p. 162.

[2] *Ibid.*

6. Proceedings may be initiated in one of two ways. Pursuant to Section 321, a petition may be filed in a pending bankruptcy proceeding either before or after adjudication and whether brought voluntarily or involuntarily. This is often called a converter petition, and the debtor attempts to ward off bankruptcy while working out a successful plan. If no bankruptcy proceeding is pending, an original petition may be filed under Section 322. Official Forms Nos. 11–F2 and 11–F1 are used for petitions filed under Sections 321 and 322 respectively (see paragraphs 9 and 10).

7. In the petition the debtor must state that it is insolvent or unable to pay its debts as they mature, thus confessing insolvency in either the bankruptcy or the equity sense. The debtor must also set forth the provisions of the arrangement or allege that it intends to propose an arrangement.[3]

8. Accompanying the petition must be a statement of the debtor's executory contracts (Chapter 6, paragraph 9) and the schedules and statement of affairs (Chapter 9, paragraphs 5–32), if they have not been previously filed. Upon application by the debtor and for cause shown, the court may grant further time, not exceeding 15 days, for the filing of the above statements, provided the debtor includes with the petition a list of creditors and their addresses and a summary of its assets and liabilities. Bankruptcy Rule 11–11(b) provides that on application the court may grant up to 30 days for filing of schedules and statements. For an extension beyond the additional 30 days, cause must be shown and notice given to those persons directed by the court. With the filing of the petition, the debtor must pay the clerk any fees required by the Bankruptcy Act.[4] These include a fifty-dollar filing fee plus the local reporter fee. The debtor may, with proper application, pay the fees at a later date or in installments.

Information Included in Petition

9. Official Form No. 11–F1 is used for debtors who are filing an original petition under Chapter XI. In paragraph one of the form the debtor gives its address, and in paragraph two it states that

---

[3] Bankruptcy Act, Sec. 323.
[4] *Ibid.*, Sec. 324.

the principal place of business or residence was within the district for a longer portion of the preceding six months than in any other district. Paragraph three states that there is not another petition pending and paragraph four states that the debtor is qualified to petition and is entitled to the benefits of Chapter XI. In paragraph five, the debtor states that it is insolvent or unable to pay its debts as they mature. A list of the debtor's creditors and their addresses must be filed with this petition or the statements required by Bankruptcy Rule 11–11 must accompany the petition. Also, the debtor is required to complete Exhibit A which contains information about the amounts of the various types of liabilities outstanding, number of holders, number of common stock shares outstanding, total assets, and other general information. An example of Form No. 11–F1, including Exhibit A, is shown on pages 375–76, in Appendix A.

10. If a bankruptcy case under Chapter XII or XIII is pending, the debtor may file a petition which conforms to Form No. 11–F2. An example of this form also appears in Appendix A (pages 376–77).

Stay of Adjudication

11. The filing of a petition acts as a stay of any pending or subsequently instituted suit or proceeding to enforce any judgment against the debtor.[5] The same rule operates as a stay, upon filing of a petition, with respect to the commencement or continuation of any proceeding to enforce a lien against property in the custody of the bankruptcy court.[6] Unless terminated by the bankruptcy court, the stay lasts until the case is dismissed or the debtor is denied a discharge or until the collateral is transferred, abandoned, or of no further interest to the estate.[7]

12. To ensure that the correct remedy is used and that full consideration is given to creditors, the judge may dismiss the Chapter XI proceedings if, upon application by the Securities and Exchange Commission or any party in interest, it is found that proceedings should have been brought under Chapter X. Rather

[5] Bankruptcy Rule 11–44.
[6] *Ibid.*
[7] Bankruptcy Rule 11–44(b).

than dismissal, the petition may be amended to comply with the requirements of Chapter X.[8]

Timing of Petition

13. Since only a debtor may petition for an arrangement, a company may do so at the most advantageous time, usually before its creditors are aware of its intentions. At the same time the company may request appointment as debtor-in-possession. The creditors are caught by surprise and before they can take any type of action, the debtor has been allowed to retain possession of the business. Once appointed, it is very difficult to replace a debtor-in-possession with a receiver.

Jurisdiction, Powers, and Duties of the Court

14. Proceedings under Chapter XI are conducted under the exclusive jurisdiction of the court in which the debtor files the petition. This jurisdiction extends to the debtor's property, wherever located. In bankruptcy proceedings, jurisdiction is limited to the court's own district.[9] Furthermore, the jurisdiction, powers, and duties of the court are the same:

> When a petition is filed under Section 321 and a decree of adjudication has not been entered, as if a decree of adjudication had been entered in the bankruptcy proceedings when the petition under Chapter XI was filed; or
>
> When a petition is filed under Section 322, as if a voluntary petition for bankruptcy had been filed and a decree of adjudication had been entered at the time of the petition under Chapter XI.[10]

15. The court is expressly granted certain other powers when a petition for arrangement proceedings is filed. It may permit the rejection of any of the debtor's executory contracts, authorize the receiver, trustee, or debtor-in-possession to lease or sell any of the debtor's property, and, whenever required to fix a time for any purpose upon cause shown, extend such time.[11] The court may

[8] Bankruptcy Act, Sec. 328.
[9] *Ibid.*, Sec. 311.
[10] *Ibid.*, Sec. 312.
[11] *Ibid.*, Sec. 313.

enter a stay delaying any suits or the enforcement of any lien upon the debtor's property.[12] This provision halts such actions when immediate payment might hinder the successful completion of an arrangement. And finally, whenever notice is required to be given, the court is empowered to designate the time within which, the persons to whom, and the form and manner in which such notice is to be given.[13] Should it be necessary for the case to enter the appellate courts, the jurisdiction of such courts is the same as in a bankruptcy proceeding.[14]

Appointment of Referee (Bankruptcy Judge)

16. After the petition is filed by the debtor, the clerk refers the proceedings to a bankruptcy judge.[15] The judge is in complete control throughout the proceedings, and the debtor is required to file reports with the judge, including receipts, disbursements, and the amount of indebtedness incurred during the operation of the business and remaining unpaid. These reports are usually inadequate and misleading unless an accountant's services are employed in their formation.[16]

Operation of Business During Bankruptcy Proceedings

17. During the proceedings, the business may be operated by the debtor as debtor-in-possession, or a receiver may be appointed. When no receiver or trustee is appointed, the debtor continues in possession of its property and is accorded all the title and powers of a trustee appointed under the Bankruptcy Act. The debtor is subject to the control of the court at all times and to any limitations, restrictions, terms, and conditions designated by the court.[17]

18. Upon the application of any party in interest, the court may appoint a receiver of the debtor's property or continue the trustee in possession if one has been previously appointed in bankruptcy. The receiver may act merely as a custodian or be

[12] *Ibid.*, Sec. 314, and Bankruptcy Rule 11-44.
[13] *Ibid.*, Sec. 315.
[14] *Ibid.*, Sec. 316.
[15] *Ibid.*, Sec. 331.
[16] Stuart Hertzberg, "A Survey of Chapter XI With a Side Trip Through Chapter X," *Commercial Law Journal*, Vol. 77 (March 1972), p. 87.
[17] Bankruptcy Act, Sec. 342.

authorized to operate the business. Often, the receiver will supervise the existing management. Because the debtor has been unable to operate successfully, some courts prefer that a receiver be apponted just to supervise the existing management and to see that waste and mismanagement do not continue.[18] However, the appointment of a receiver is not mandatory, and receivers are frequently bypassed on the reasoning that their appointment only adds to the cost of administration. According to Ashe, experience has demonstrated that the cost to creditors is minimal in those districts where appointment of a receiver is the normal procedure.[19] The recently adopted Bankruptcy Rule 11–18(b) clearly provides that the debtor shall continue in possession, but that the bankruptcy judge may, on application of any party in interest, appoint a receiver to operate the business. The practice of some bankruptcy courts is to automatically appoint a receiver when the petition is filed, but this will probably cease as a result of this new Rule.

19. The court is also authorized, upon the application of any party in interest, to appoint an appraiser to prepare and file an inventory and appraisal of the property of the debtor.[20]

20. The determination of the powers and duties of the officers of the court and the rights, privileges, and duties of the debtor is dependent upon which section the petition is filed under. Where filed under Section 321, they are the same as if a decree of adjudication had been entered in bankruptcy proceedings at the time the petition was filed. Where filed under Section 322, they are the same as if a voluntary petition for adjudication in bankruptcy had been filed.[21]

21. Regardless of who is operating the business during the proceedings—the receiver, the trustee, or the debtor upon authorization by and subject to control of the court—that person is given the power to operate the business and manage the property of the debtor during such period, limited or indefinite, as the court may fix. During the operation or management, reports must be filed with the courts at intervals as designated by the court (Chapter 6,

---

[18] George Ashe, "Rehabilitation Under Chapter XI: Fact or Fiction," *Commercial Law Journal*, Vol. 72 (September 1967), pp. 261–62.

[19] *Ibid.*

[20] Bankruptcy Act, Sec. 333.

[21] *Ibid.*, Sec. 341.

paragraphs 16–19).[22] Normally these reports must include all receipts and their sources, disbursements and their purposes, and any liabilities incurred and still outstanding.

22. One of the first problems to be overcome by the receiver or debtor-in-possession is to obtain credit during the period of arrangement (Chapter 6, paragraphs 46–48). Existing creditors will at first refuse to grant additional credit. However, if creditors are notified immediately, most of them will "cooperate when informed that debts incurred during operation are expenses of administration, which are entitled to priority over claims which arose prior to the arrangement proceeding, and which will be paid prior to confirmation." [23] Should more capital be needed, the court may authorize the receiver, trustee, or debtor to issue certificates of indebtedness for such consideration as approved by the court and upon such terms and conditions, and with such security and priority in payment, as may be deemed equitable.[24] The certificate of indebtedness is a document issued by the debtor-in-possession or trustee upon the approval of the court for cash, property, or other consideration. To insure that the certificate of indebtedness will be paid at maturity by the debtor, the loan may be secured by the debtor's assets; however, the creditor's committee will scrutinize the operation very carefully if assets are pledged. Borrowing capital requires the filing of a petition with the court stating the reasons the loan is needed and obtaining a court order authorizing the transaction.[25] Normally these liabilities are given first priority along with administrative costs.[26]

First Meeting of Creditors

23. Bankruptcy Rule 11–25 requires that the court hold a first meeting of creditors not less than 20 nor more than 40 days after the petition is filed. With the notice of the meeting must be a copy of the proposed arrangement if one has been filed, a summary of the liabilities, and a summary of the appraisal if made, or a summary of

---

[22] *Ibid.*, Sec. 343.
[23] Hertzberg, p. 87.
[24] Bankruptcy Act, Sec. 344.
[25] Leslie W. Abramson (Ed.), *Basic Bankruptcy: Alternatives, Proceedings and Discharges* (Ann Arbor, Mich.: Institute of Continuing Legal Education, 1971), p. 114.
[26] Forman, p. 181.

the assets. If a copy of the proposed arrangement is not sent, Bankruptcy Rule 11–36(b) provides that the first meeting of creditors may be adjourned by the court from time to time, but when the proposed arrangement is filed, the court must mail notice of the next meeting with a copy of the proposed arrangement. The notice of the meeting may also include the time for filing an application to confirm the arrangement and the time for hearing on confirmation and objections.[27]

24. The bankruptcy judge is given specific functions to perform at the creditors' meeting. The judge presides over the meeting, receives proofs of claim and allows or disallows them, examines the debtor and other witnesses and permits their examination by others, and receives written acceptances of creditors on the proposed arrangement.[28]

25. An examination of the debtor is mandatory at the first meeting. Debtors are normally first examined by the bankruptcy judge, after which any other interested parties may question further. At this time creditors will usually question the schedule of assets and liabilities, proposed arrangement plan, and statement of affairs. Provisions are also made for the election of a committee by creditors and the nomination of a trustee who would thereafter qualify should it become necessary to subsequently administer the estate in bankruptcy.[29] However, if the proceedings were initiated by a converter petition and a trustee has already been appointed, the trustee would stay in office, remaining inactive unless otherwise authorized by the court or the arrangement proceedings fail. Under an original petition filed pursuant to Section 322, it is not customary to appoint a trustee.[30]

Creditors' Committee

26. A creditors' committee is selected by a vote of the creditors. It should be formed as soon as possible after filing by the debtor, preferably before the first meeting of creditors so that its designation can be approved at that meeting and it can subsequently have authority to speak for all of the creditors. Bankruptcy

[27] Bankruptcy Act, Sec. 335.
[28] *Ibid.*, Sec. 336, and Bankruptcy Rule 11–25(a)(2).
[29] Bankruptcy Act, Sec. 338.
[30] Forman, pp. 174–75.

Rule 11–27(a) provides that the creditors' committee may consist of at least three members but no more than eleven. It is most advantageous to include those creditors with the largest claims because their cooperation is necessary to a successful plan. At the meeting they will normally review and discuss the financial affairs of the debtor, question the debtor at length, and give an opinion as to the best course to be followed—rehabilitation or liquidation.

27. The creditors' committee has supervisory and control functions. Its duties are delineated in Section 339 of the Bankruptcy Act, as amended in 1967:

> Examine the conduct of the debtor's affairs and the causes of the insolvency or inability to pay debts as they mature.
>
> Ascertain whether the plan of arrangement is for the best interests of the creditors and is feasible.
>
> Negotiate with the debtor the terms of the arrangement and make recommendations to the creditors concerning the plan.
>
> Periodically report to the creditors on the progress of the pro ceedings.
>
> Collect acceptances of the plan and file them with the court.
>
> Perform any other services which may contribute to the confirmation of the agreement.

28. In addition, the committee is authorized to employ the necessary agents, attorneys, and accountants to assist it in the performance of its activities and the Bankruptcy Act provides for recovery of the expenses as a cost of administration.

29. By supervising the debtor's activities, the creditors' committee gains an intimate knowledge of the business and its operations. Active participation by the committee at all stages of the proceedings will help avoid complete domination by the debtor.

Creditors' Claims

30. The time for the filing of claims is set forth in Section 355 as amended in 1967. Any creditor must file his proof of claim before confirmation of the plan of arrangement except:

> If scheduled by the debtor, a claim may be filed within 30 days after the date of mailing notice of confirmation to creditors but shall not

be allowed for an amount in excess of that set forth in the debtor's schedules and

A claim arising from the rejection of an executory contract of the debtor may be filed within such time as the court may direct.

31. Confirmation of the plan does not have to wait for a filing of claims, but can be entirely independent, and may be on the sole basis of those claims that have been filed and the debtor's schedule.

32. These provisions are important because the court retains jurisdiction until the final allowance or disallowance of all claims affected by the arrangement which have been filed within the prescribed limitations as to time and amount but which have not been allowed or disallowed prior to confirmation.[31]

33. As elsewhere, the rights, duties, and liabilities of creditors and all other persons with respect to the debtor's property is governed by the section under which the petition is filed. With a converter petition, the rights, duties, and liabilities are the same as if a decree of adjudication had been entered in bankruptcy proceedings. With an original petition, they are the same as if a voluntary petition for adjudication in bankruptcy had been filed.[32]

34. When an executory contract is rejected under arrangement proceedings, any person injured by such rejection is accorded the status of a creditor. Furthermore, the claim for injury by a landlord from the rejection of an unexpired lease is explicitly made provable for rent not to exceed three years.[33]

Debts Allowed Under Chapter XI

35. Rehabilitation under Chapter XI affects only unsecured debts; secured claims are excluded from any plan. Those claims which are provable and granted priority are the same as provided for in straight bankruptcy.[34] Section 63(a) enumerates the debts which may be proved and allowed against the debtor's estate as follows:

[31] Bankruptcy Act, Sec. 369. See also Bankruptcy Rule 11–33.
[32] *Ibid.*, Sec. 352.
[33] *Ibid.*, Sec. 353.
[34] *Ibid.*, Sec. 63(a).

A fixed liability absolutely owing at the time of the filing of the petition

Costs taxable against a bankrupt who was at the time of filing the petition plaintiff in a cause of action which would pass to the trustee and which the trustee declines to prosecute after notice

A claim for taxable costs incurred in good faith by a creditor before the filing of the petition in an action to recover a probable debt

Debts based on open account or a contract, express or implied

Provable debts reduced to judgments after the filing of the petition and before the consideration of the bankrupt's application for a discharge

Workmen's compensation award where injury occurred prior to adjudication

The right to recover damages in any action for negligence instituted prior to and pending at the time of the filing of the petition

Contingent debts and contingent contractual liabilities

Claims for anticipatory breach of contracts, executory in whole or in part, including unexpired leases of real or personal property

Priority Claims

36. The rules of priority as found in the Bankruptcy Act apply only to the equity that remains after all secured claims have been satisfied. Priority claims must be adequately disposed of before the court will confirm a plan. Pursuant to Section 64 the satisfaction of claims in advance of the payment of dividends to creditors must occur in the following order:

1. The costs and expenses of administration
2. Wages not exceeding $600 per person which have been earned within three months of the filing of the petition
3. Costs and expenses incurred by creditors in the refusal, revocation, or setting aside of a discharge, or the conviction of any person or an offense under the Bankruptcy Act
4. Taxes legally due and owing by the bankrupt to the United States or any state or subdivision thereof which are not released by a discharge in bankruptcy
5. Debts other than for taxes owing to any person who by state or federal law is entitled to priority, including rent owed to a landlord and accrued within three months prior to filing

Federal Tax Claims

37. Federal tax claims which are unsecured have fourth priority, equal to that accorded state and local tax claims. Other federal claims enjoy only fifth priority.[35] A tax liability or claim is said to exist if a tax is due and not paid. However, such claim is unsecured and does not of itself subject the debtor's property to a tax lien. A tax lien arises if the District Director of Internal Revenue makes an assessment and demand for payment of the tax liability and the taxpayer fails or refuses to pay. The lien arises as of the date of the assessment, which occurs when the liability is recorded on the assessment list in the District Director's office. "A recorded federal tax lien in bankruptcy is superior to state and local tax claims although, insofar as personal property is concerned, it is subordinated to administration expenses and wage claims unless the lien was accompanied by possession." [36]

State Tax Claims

38. State tax claims which became legally due and owing more than three years before the petition are dischargeable as are other debts, they are denied the fourth priority normally given other debts, and they are expressly excluded from the fifth priority given federal claims other than taxes. They are allowable as claims on a par with general creditors. The exception to this is taxes which the debtor has collected or withheld from others, such as income taxes or employees' share of social security taxes. Such debts cannot be discharged, and priority is not lost regardless of how old the debt is.[37]

Subordination of Claims

39. Subordination of claims is intended to resolve equities as between creditors and seeks to determine whether there are extraordinary circumstances which indicate that certain creditors

[35] W. T. Plumb, Jr., "Federal Priority in Insolvency: Proposals for Reform," *Michigan Law Review*, Vol. 70 (November 1971), p. 37.
[36] Richard A. Kaye, "Federal Taxes, Bankruptcy and Assignments for the Benefit of Creditors—A Comparison," *Commercial Law Journal*, Vol. 73 (March 1968), p. 79.
[37] Plumb, pp. 43–44.

equitably are not entitled to share on a parity with others.[38] Situations in which the principles of subordination are most often applied include the following:

> Claims which result from transactions between the debtor and close relatives or favored insiders enjoying controlling positions
>
> Misconduct or misrepresentation by a creditor upon which others relied to their damage
>
> Creditor mismanagement of the debtor resulting in injury to other creditors
>
> Transactions between a corporate parent and a wholly controlled subsidiary
>
> Those claims wherein a guarantor or surety is denied the right to compete with those the guaranty is intended to protect[39]

40. Circumstances which bring subordination into play are described as follows: "Essentially there must exist an element of fraud, or moral turpitude, committed by the claimant, the commission of a breach of duty by virtue of which other creditors were deceived and suffered loss, or, because of circumstances involving the relationships existing between the claimant and the debtor, it would be manifestly unjust to allow the claimant to share equally with less favorably placed creditors." [40]

Preparation and Requirements of Plan of Arrangement

41. The court is empowered to divide the creditors into classes to effect the arrangement and its acceptance and to decide any controversies concerning the division.[41] This is most often done when there are many small creditors who might disrupt the plan. The small claimants may then be paid cash in full and the larger creditors given different percentages of their claims or deferred payments.[42]

---

[38] George Ashe, "Subordination of Claims—Equitable Principles Applied in Bankruptcy," *Commercial Law Journal*, Vol. 72 (April 1967), p. 91.

[39] *Ibid.*, p. 95.

[40] *Ibid.*, p. 92.

[41] Bankruptcy Act, Sec. 351.

[42] Abramson, p. 120.

Provisions of Plan

42. The plan of arrangement must be proposed by the debtor, with the creditors' committee acting in an advisory capacity only. There is no set pattern for the form a plan must take and the only requirement is that some provision be made for modifying or altering the rights of unsecured creditors generally, or of some class of them, upon any terms or for any consideration.[43] The plan may include provisions for:

> The treatment of unsecured debts on parity or the division of such debts into classes and the treatment of such classes in different ways or upon different terms
>
> The rejection of executory contracts
>
> Specific undertakings of the debtor during any period of extension
>
> The termination of any period of extension
>
> The continuation of the debtor's business with or without supervision or control by a receiver, creditors' committee, or otherwise
>
> The payment of debts incurred after the filing of the petition and during the pendency of the arrangement in priority over the debts affected by the arrangement
>
> The retention of jurisdiction by the court until provisions of the arrangement, after it has been confirmed, have been performed
>
> Any other provisions deemed appropriate and not inconsistent with Chapter XI [44]

43. In addition, if the plan contains provisions for installment payments, the creditors may require that it include a section requiring that the debtor grant a security interest on all its assets until all payments have been made and the plan has been successfully consummated.

44. It is usually best for the debtor to file the plan after the initial meeting with creditors. This is because it is necessary to appraise the assets and obtain their forced-sale price (Chapter 6, paragraph 21). Also, extensive negotiation must first be conducted with the creditors, who will usually require an audit of the books and a preliminary examination of the debtor (Chapter 8).

---

[43] Bankruptcy Act, Sec. 356.
[44] *Ibid.*, Sec. 357.

45. When drawing up the plan, it will be necessary for the debtor to determine the amount which the unsecured creditors would receive for the liquidation of the business in a straight bankruptcy proceeding. This will normally be the minimum settlement acceptable to such creditors in an agreement. This dividend is equal to the sum of the forced-sale value of assets, accounts receivable, cash, and prepaid items, minus priority claims, secured claims, and expenses of administration, divided by the total amount of unsecured claims.[45]

46. For a discussion of the accountant's role in the preparation of the plan of arrangement see Chapter 6, paragraphs 20–24, 40–41, and Chapter 7, paragraph 33.

Acceptance of Plan of Arrangement

47. After suitable investigation, normally including an independent audit (Chapter 8), if the creditors' committee has determined that the debtor's activities were in order and the plan proposed will result in greater realization to creditors than would result from liquidation, it will recommend that the plan be accepted by the creditors and the court. The plan may be accepted by the creditors or creditors' committee even before the petition is filed with the court, and the final plan is often the result of intense negotiations between the debtor or debtor's counsel and the creditors or their representatives (Chapter 7, paragraphs 5–13).

48. If the arrangement has not been accepted by all the creditors, an application for confirmation by the court may be filed when the plan has been accepted in writing by a majority in number and amount of those creditors filing claims. To be valid, the acceptance must be accompanied by a proof of claim, if not previously filed. If the plan provides for more than one class of creditors, it must be accepted by each class.

49. After the plan is accepted, at the first or adjourned meeting of the creditors, the judge or the referee must:

> Designate the person to act as the disbursing agent to distribute any consideration to be deposited by the debtor.
>
> Fix the time within which the debtor must deposit any consideration

[45] Hertzberg, p. 88.

to be distributed to the creditors, a sum equal to that necessary to pay all the debts which have priority and the costs and expenses of the proceedings.

Fix the time for the filing of the application to confirm the arrangement and for a hearing on the confirmation and any objections.[46]

50. After acceptance but prior to confirmation, the debtor may propose alterations or modifications to the plan. If the court finds that such proposals do not materially and adversely affect the interest of any creditor who has not agreed to them, it may enter an order that any creditor who accepted the arrangements be deemed to have accepted the plan as modified.[47] Ten days' notice of an adjourned or reopened meeting with a copy of the proposed alterations or modifications must be given all parties in interest.[48]

Confirmation by the Court

51. Once the plan has been accepted by the creditors, application is made to the court for a date for a hearing on confirmation, and notice is served upon the creditors. Creditors may be heard in opposition to confirmation and a hearing must be granted to those who object. They are usually the same creditors who have not approved the plan. The debtor uses Official Form No. 11–F18 in filing application for confirmation of the plan.

52. When all creditors affected accept a plan of arrangement, it is confirmed by the court as soon as the debtor has made the required deposit and the court is satisfied that the arrangement and its acceptance are in good faith and have not been made or procured by any means, promises, or acts forbidden by the Bankruptcy Act.[49]

53. Section 366 sets forth the conditions which must be satisfied for the court to confirm an arrangement:

All the provisions of Chapter XI must have been complied with.

The plan must be for the best interests of the creditors and be feasible.

[46] Bankruptcy Act, Sec. 337.
[47] *Ibid.*, Secs. 363–64.
[48] *Ibid.*, Sec. 365.
[49] *Ibid.*, Sec. 361.

The debtor must not have been guilty of any of the acts or failed to perform any of the duties which would bar him from a discharge.

The plan and its acceptances must be in good faith and not have been made or secured by any means, promises, or acts forbidden by the Bankruptcy Act.

54. Under the second requirement—that the plan must be in the best interests of the creditors—the creditors must receive at least as much under the arrangement as they would in liquidation. The plan is considered feasible if the debtor will have the capital to carry on its operations, will be able to make the payments called for by the plan, and will be financially rehabilitated.[50] Bad faith, under the fourth condition above, would include failure to disclose facts which are material to the decision as to whether the debtor's proposal should be confirmed, or any secret agreements made with creditors to accept the proposal for a distinct or additional consideration.[51]

55. Confirmation of the arrangement makes it binding upon the debtor, upon any person issuing securities or acquiring property under the plan, and upon all the creditors of the debtor, whether or not they are affected by the arrangement, have accepted it, or have filed their claims and had them scheduled or allowed. After confirmation, the money deposited for priority debts and the costs and expenses of administration is disbursed. Any consideration deposited is to be distributed and the rights provided for by the plan are to pass to the creditors affected by the arrangement, whose claims have been filed and allowed as prescribed. Normally, the case is then dismissed.[52] However, if called for by the arrangement, the court will retain jurisdiction.[53]

Discharge from Debts

56. Rehabilitation and liquidation proceedings are intended to relieve an honest debtor from the pressure of debts and allow a

---

[50] Forman, p. 188.

[51] Herbert U. Feibelman, "Which Shall It Be—Bankruptcy, an Arrangement or Corporate Reorganization?" *Commercial Law Journal*, Vol. 64 (January 1964), pp. 8–9.

[52] Bankruptcy Act, Sec. 367.

[53] *Ibid.*, Sec. 368.

chance to start again. To accomplish this, the Bankruptcy Act contains provisions for discharging or releasing debtors from debts and for stopping creditors from attempting to collect. In an arrangement, when the court confirms the plan, the effect is to discharge the debtor from all unsecured debts and liabilities provided for by the arrangement, except as otherwise provided in the arrangement or confirmation, and excluding debts not dischargeable under Section 17(a) of the Bankruptcy Act.[54] Official Form No. 11–F18 when signed by the bankruptcy judge serves as a discharge of all debts which are dischargeable.

Debts Excluded from Discharge

57. Those debts explicitly excluded from discharge by Section 17(a) of the Bankruptcy Act include:

> Taxes which became legally due and owing by the bankrupt to the United States or to any state or any subdivision thereof within three years preceding the bankruptcy. However, certain circumstances may prevent the discharge of a tax not covered by this provision, including the existence of a tax lien.
>
> Liabilities for obtaining money or property by false pretenses or false representations or willful and malicious conversion of the property of another.
>
> Debts which have not been scheduled in time for proof and allowance.
>
> Liabilities arising from fraud, embezzlement, misappropriation, or defalcation while acting as an officer or in a fiduciary capacity.
>
> Wages entitled to priority.
>
> Money of an employee held by his employer to retain performance as provided in an employment contract.
>
> Liabilities due for alimony support of wife or children, seduction of an unmarried female, breach of promise of marriage accompanied by seduction, or criminal conversation.
>
> Liabilities for willful and malicious injuries to the person or property of another.

[54] *Ibid.*, Sec. 371.

Acts Which Prevent a Discharge

58. Under Section 14(c) of the Bankruptcy Act, the debtor becomes barred from a discharge of debts if guilty of the following:

Committed an offense (e.g., concealment of assets, false oaths and claims, bribery) punishable by imprisonment under Title 18, United States Code, Section 152

Failed to keep or preserve adequate books or accounts or financial records

Obtained credit on the basis of a materially false statement concerning financial condition

Within one year prior to the filing of the petition transferred, removed, destroyed, or concealed, or permitted to be removed, destroyed, or concealed, any of this property with the intent to hinder, delay, or defraud his creditors

Within the past six years received a discharge in bankruptcy or had a composition, arrangement, or wage earner's plan confirmed under the Bankruptcy Act

Refused to obey any lawful order or answer any material questions in the course of the proceedings

Failed to explain satisfactorily any losses of assets or deficiency of assets to meet his liabilities

Failed to pay the required filing fees in full

59. In 1970, Section 2(a)12 of the Bankruptcy Act was amended to authorize the court to determine the dischargeability of debts and render judgments thereon. This amendment also provides that if a creditor believes an individual claim should be excluded from a discharge, the creditor must begin proceedings in the bankruptcy court within the time fixed by that court. If the creditor fails to do this, the grounds for exception are no longer available and after discharge the creditor "is perpetually enjoined from invoking them." [55] To obtain an exception from discharge due to misrepresentation of financial condition, the creditor must show that there was in fact a material fraudulent misrepresentation, moral turpitude by the debtor in making the representation with

[55] Vern Countryman, "New Dischargeability Law," *American Bankruptcy Law Journal*, Vol. 45 (Winter 1971), p. 26.

the intent that it be relied upon, and reliance in fact by the creditor.[56]

60. After confirmation of the plan and consummation of the proceedings, the court enters a final decree discharging the receiver or trustee, closing the estate, and making any other equitable provisions as may be necessary.[57]

Reasons for Dismissal of Proceedings

61. Certain conditions may arise enjoining the court to discontinue the arrangement proceedings. For a petition filed under Section 321, the court will enter an order directing that the prior bankruptcy proceedings be resumed. For a petition filed under Section 322, the court will either adjudicate the debtor a bankrupt and direct that bankruptcy proceedings be begun or merely dismiss the proceedings under Chapter XI. One of the following situations may cause the court to discontinue arrangement proceedings:

> The statement of executory contracts and the schedules and statement of affairs are not duly filed.
>
> An arrangement is not proposed in the manner and within the time fixed by the court.
>
> An arrangement is withdrawn or abandoned prior to its acceptance.
>
> An arrangement is not accepted by the creditors within the time fixed by the court.
>
> The required money is not deposited.
>
> The application for confirmation is not filed within the time fixed by the court.
>
> Confirmation of the arrangement is refused.[58]

62. Where the court has retained jurisdiction after confirmation and the debtor defaults in any of the terms or the arrangement terminates by reason of the happening of a condition specified in

---

[56] Stuart T. Waldrip, "Fraudulent Financial Statements and Section 17 of the Bankruptcy Act—The Creditor's Dilemma" (Notes), *Utah Law Review* (May 1967), p. 284.

[57] Bankruptcy Act, Sec. 372.

[58] *Ibid.*, Sec. 376.

the plan, the court must give notice of the hearing and dismiss the proceedings as provided for in Section 376.[59]

Provisions for Straight Bankruptcy

63. Upon entry of an order directing bankruptcy, Section 378 sets forth provisions for debts incurred in the superseded arrangement proceedings:

> For a petition filed under Section 321, bankruptcy proceedings shall be deemed reinstated.
>
> For a petition filed under Section 322, the proceedings shall be conducted as if a voluntary petition for adjudication in bankruptcy had been filed.
>
> Within 30 days of the order directing bankruptcy, the debtor-in-possession or receiver must file a separate schedule of all unpaid obligations incurred after the filing of the petition under Chapter XI and a statement of all executory contracts assumed or entered into.
>
> When the schedule of Chapter XI debts has been filed, the court must enter an order directing the filing of all claims against the debtor-in-possession or receiver within 60 days of such order and give notice of the order to the holders of such claims. Claims not filed within the prescribed period will not be allowed and the debtor-in-possession or receiver will be discharged from any liability.[60]

64. When a proceeding initiated by a petition filed under Section 322 is dismissed, the court shall enter a final decree discharging the receiver and closing the estate.[61]

65. The Bankruptcy Act also sets forth the provisions to be followed when the court enters an order directing bankruptcy proceedings after the arrangement has been confirmed:

> The trustee shall be vested with title to all the debtor's property as of the date of the entry of the order to proceed with bankruptcy.

[59] *Ibid.*, Sec. 377.
[60] Forman, p. 193.
[61] Bankruptcy Act, Sec. 380.

The unsecured debt incurred by the debtor between the confirmation of the arrangement and the order directing bankruptcy proceedings shall share on a parity with the prior unsecured debts of the same classes provable in the ensuing bankruptcy proceedings.

The provisions of Chapters I through VII of the Bankruptcy Act shall apply to the rights, duties, and liabilities of the creditors, for debts incurred between the confirmation of the arrangement and bankruptcy proceedings, and of all persons with respect to the property of the debtor. The date of bankruptcy shall be the date of the order directing that bankruptcy be proceeded with.[62]

Modifications of Plan After Confirmation

66. Under Section 386 the court has several options where an application is filed within six months after confirmation of the arrangement and attempts to show that fraud was practiced in the procuring of the arrangement and that the petitioners gained knowledge of such fraud subsequent to confirmation:

If the debtor has been guilty, the court may set aside the confirmation and direct that bankruptcy be proceeded with.

Confirmation may be set aside, the proceedings under the petition filed under Chapter XI reinstated, and the court may hear and determine applications for leave to propose alterations of the arrangement to correct the fraud.

The arrangement proceedings may be reinstated and the plan modified to correct the fraud without materially affecting the interests of other persons.

67. Where the court has retained jurisdiction and the confirmed arrangement provides for an extension of time for the payment of debts, a proposal to alter the plan, by changing the time of payment and/or reducing the amount of payment, may be filed by the debtor with the approval of the court after confirmation but before the deferred consideration has been fully paid. The proposal must state the proposed alterations, whether the deferred payments are evidenced by negotiable promissory notes and whether such notes have been delivered to the creditors, the reasons for proposing

[62] *Ibid.,* Sec. 381.

the modification, and a list of the parties who have extended credit to the debtor since confirmation. If the court permits the alterations to be filed, it shall call a meeting on at least 10 days' written notice and send a copy of the proposal to all parties of interest. At the meeting, if the plan as modified is accepted as required by Section 362, the court shall confirm the arrangement as altered.[63]

Provisions for the Results of Consummation

68. The Bankruptcy Act unequivocally states that any income or profit resulting from a modification or cancellation in whole or in part of an indebtedness under Chapter XI proceedings shall not be deemed taxable under any law of the United States or any state, unless it appears that one of the purposes of initiating the proceedings was the evasion of income tax.[64]

69. The basis of the debtor's property is to be decreased by an amount equal to the amount by which the debtor's indebtedness has been reduced or cancelled. However, the fair market value as of the date of entry of the order confirming the arrangement establishes the floor below which the basis of any particular property cannot fall.[65]

70. Special provision is also made in Section 397 for any taxes which are found to be due the United States or any state from a debtor within one year from the date of filing the petition and which have not been assessed before the date of confirmation, and all taxes which may become owing from a receiver, trustee, or debtor-in-possession. Such liabilities shall be assessed against, collected from, and paid by the debtor.

Advantages and Disadvantages

71. Chapter XI proceedings may be more appropriate under certain conditions than informal settlements made out of court:

> Rather than unanimous approval, majority approval in number and amount of claims of creditors whose claims have been filed and allowed is sufficient.

[63] *Ibid.*, Sec. 387, and Bankruptcy Rule 11–40.
[64] Bankruptcy Act, Sec. 395.
[65] *Ibid.*, Sec. 396.

The debtor's assets are in the custody of the court and safe from attack when the petition is filed.

The creditor has an opportunity to investigate the debtor and its business affairs.

Creditors are additionally protected by the requirements that to be confirmed by the court the arrangement must be for the best interests of creditors, feasible, and made in good faith.

72. The major disadvantages of this method of rehabilitation are that it is more time-consuming and more costly, resulting in smaller dividends to creditors.

5

Retention of the

Accountant and Fees

1. Because there are several ways of coping with financial difficulties and many different parties are involved, accountants have many avenues by which they may become involved in bankruptcy and insolvency. This chapter sets forth the ways in which the accountant may be retained and describes the procedures related to retention and to the determination of fees.

2. The retention of an accountant by the receiver, trustee, or debtor-in-possession must be by order of the court, which also issues notice on the amount of fees or the rate to be used. The accountant prepares an affidavit setting forth the scope of the services to be rendered and the estimated time required for such services. Based on this affidavit, counsel for receiver, trustee, or debtor-in-possession prepares an application for retention and submits it to the

court. If the court approves the retention, it will enter an order, confirm the scope of the services to be performed, and set the compensation for such services. An accountant may also be retained to render services for a debtor company that has not formally petitioned the court. In this situation the accountant will obtain a signed engagement letter similar in format to that of the usual engagement letter; however, provision for alternate sources of payment should be arranged if possible.

3. The accountant must keep adequate time and performance records while services are being rendered. After the services have been rendered the accountant files a petition for compensation in affidavit form with the court. The petition should contain enough information about the services rendered so the court may evaluate and compare them with the services authorized in the order of retention. After the hearings, if required, the judge or referee will fix the exact compensation which the accountant will receive.

RETENTION OF THE ACCOUNTANT

The Accountant's Role in the Proceedings

4. Usually the accountant becomes a party to the proceedings through retention by a creditors' committee, while serving a client who is headed for financial trouble, or through appointment by a trustee or assignee. In a voluntary arrangement under Chapter XI of the Bankruptcy Act, the debtor normally remains in possession and has the right to retain an accountant for necessary accounting functions. The same accountant may be retained by the creditors to conduct an audit as of the date of filing the petition. The creditors' committee may desire the services of an accountant other than the debtor's accountant, to inquire into the affairs of the debtor prior to insolvency and to aid the committee in developing a plan of arrangement. The trustee may also need the services of an accountant. (See Chapter 1, paragraphs 9–14.)

Retention Procedure—Formal

5. Bankruptcy Rule 215 holds that the retention of an accountant for the receiver or trustee must be by order of the court

and is granted upon the petition of the receiver or trustee, which must show among other things the necessity for such retention. This requirement also applies to an accountant employed by a debtor-in-possession. An accountant who is not an employee cannot be employed by a receiver, trustee, or debtor-in-possession except upon an order of the court expressly fixing the amount of the compensation or the rate by which it is to be measured. Thus the accountant should not consider the engagement confirmed until the court has signed an order authorizing the retention, and since compensation must come from the debtor's estate, authorization must be in advance by written order of the court fixing the rate or measure of compensation.

6. The receiver, trustee, or debtor-in-possession applies for the retention of an accountant by filing a petition with the bankruptcy judge of the District Court having jurisdiction. Included in the petition are the facts of the case, reasons why an accountant is necessary, the name and address of the proposed accountant, and a statement alleging that the particular accountant is qualified to perform such services.

Affidavit of Proposed Accountant

7. It is then necessary to obtain authorization by the court through an order for retention. This requires that the accountant make a preliminary survey of the debtor's books, records, and affairs and use the survey's findings to compose a letter under oath addressed to the receiver, trustee, or debtor-in-possession and containing the following information:

The accounting firm's name and address, and the name of the specific accountant (normally a partner) asking to be retained

Nature of any relationship or business association of the accountant with the debtor, the creditors, the attorneys, or any other party to the proceedings (normally in the form of a disclaimer of any type of business association)

The qualifications of the accountant, including any indication of past experience in bankruptcy and insolvency proceedings

A statement as to whether the accountant has already rendered services to the debtor, receiver, or trustee and whether he has a claim against the estate

A statement that a preliminary survey of the bankrupt's books and records has been completed and that the accountant is familiar with their general contents

A description of the extent and nature of the services expected to be rendered (the specific steps to be performed in the conduct of the audit should be detailed as much as possible)

An estimate of the time to be expended on the audit, broken down by class of employee and hourly billing rate

A request for retention for a maximum amount based on the estimate of hours and the stated billing rates

The accountant's notarized signature

8. It is important for the accountant to make a thorough preliminary survey of the work that is to be performed and to describe in the affidavit, in detail, the scope of the services to be rendered. An example of the type of information generally presented in the affidavit is shown in Figure 5–1.

Survey of Work To Be Performed

9. As mentioned in paragraph 7, the accountant must make a preliminary survey of the work that is to be performed in order to include in the affidavit the scope of the services to be rendered. If the accountant has performed audits for the debtor in the past, the condition of the records will be known and very little new information will be needed in order to prepare the affidavit.

10. When a new accountant is selected, as much information as possible about the company must be gained in a very short time period. Normally the accountant will receive a call from one of the attorneys representing the creditors' committee, requesting services for the engagement. The attorney will then describe some of the background information about the debtor. After providing the accountant with this information the attorney arranges, often the same day, to accompany the accountant to the office of the company to determine the nature of the debtor's operations. At the premises of the debtor the accountant will make an inspection of the facilities, very briefly examine the records, and obtain copies of the most recent financial statements which the company has issued.

UNITED STATES DISTRICT COURT
EASTERN DISTRICT OF NEW YORK

⁰ ⁰ ⁰ ⁰ ⁰ ⁰ ⁰ ⁰ ⁰ ⁰ ⁰ ⁰ ⁰ ⁰ ⁰
                                                    ⁰

In the Matter   ⁰

       of   ⁰   In Proceedings for an
                         ⁰   Arrangement

TOM CORPORATION,   ⁰
                         ⁰   No. 75–B–999

Debtor-in-Possession ⁰

⁰ ⁰ ⁰ ⁰ ⁰ ⁰ ⁰ ⁰ ⁰ ⁰ ⁰ ⁰ ⁰ ⁰ ⁰

AFFIDAVIT OF PROPOSED ACCOUNTANT

State of *New York*
County of *New York*: SS.:
City of *New York*

JOHN X. DOE, JR., being duly sworn, deposes and says:
1. He is a partner of the accounting firm of John X. Doe & Co., and he
is duly authorized to make this affidavit for and on its behalf.
2. The business addresses of said firm include its office at 90 Maple
Street, New York, New York 10005.
3. John X. Doe & Co. is a firm of certified public accountants and has
been in existence for over fifty years. The Firm operates through offices
located in 20 cities in the United States and in a number of offices located
overseas. He has been a Certified Public Accountant, licensed under the
laws of the State of New York, for over 15 years and his firm has been
retained as accountants in numerous matters to examine the books and
records of bankrupts and debtors-in-possession.
4. To the best of his knowledge, information and belief, neither he nor
the members of the firm of John X. Doe & Co. have any business
association with nor are related to any attorney, creditor, debtor-in-possession, or any party to the proceedings.
5. He has made an examination of the books and records of the
debtor-in-possession in order to determine the services which must be
rendered herein. Such examination indicates that it would be necessary to
perform the following services.

Figure 5–1.   Accountant's affidavit describing services to be performed in
proceedings for an arrangement.

a) Supervise and assist in the summarization of the books of account and posting to the general ledger in order to close the books for the period up to the date of the filing of the petition.

b) Prepare consolidated financial statements, including a consolidated balance sheet, consolidated statement of income and expense, consolidated statement of changes in financial position, and consolidated statement of affairs as of the date of the filing of the petition, May 31, 1975, encompassing the operation of the debtor-in-possession and its subsidiary, TIM CORPORATION.

c) Reconciliation of cash balances to amounts confirmed by depositories and analysis of outstanding checks.

d) Prepare schedules, review and analyze trade accounts receivable, including confirmation of certain accounts by direct correspondence. Confirmation of other receivables as may be considered necessary.

e) Review of adequacy of provision for bad debts.

f) Examination of the inventory of the debtor-in-possession's stock in trade, and review of the valuation and mathematical accuracy.

g) Review of prepared expenses, supplies, unexpired insurance, etc.

h) Review of transactions relating to investments and acquisitions, if any.

i) Review of additions and dispositions to the fixed assets and to the related allowances for depreciation.

j)   Confirmation of secured liabilities, if any, by direct correspondence with the creditors, and determination of the extent of collateral against each such liability.

k) Review of amounts of unsecured liabilities, including debts for merchandise, expenses, taxes, etc. Determination of adjustments that may be required to reflect such liabilities in the books of the Company. The scope of this work would recognize that creditors are to be notified to report directly to the Court the amount of such unsecured claims as of May 31, 1975. Assist counsel to the Creditors' Committee in resolving differences between amounts shown on the books and records of the debtor-in-possession as compared with claims filed by various creditors.

l) Examine all other material assets and liabilities reflected on the books and records of the debtor-in-possession to determine fair and reasonable balance sheet values.

m) Examine into the transactions of the corporation for the four months preceding the petition filing date to determine the existence of any possible preferences.

n) Review the claims filed by the various taxing authorities in order to determine the propriety and accuracy of said claims, including attendance at meetings with representatives of these agencies where necessary.

o) Attend meetings with the counsel to the Creditors' Committee, as well as attend examinations of the principal officers of the debtor-in-possession.

Figure 5–1.   Continued.

p) Examine into and review the transactions of the debtor-in-possession with its subsidiary, TIM CORPORATION, to determine the proper classification of all amounts; the validity of all intercompany charges; the existence of any preferential payments or other transactions which would be detrimental to creditors; and the proper financial statement presentation of the amount owing between companies.

q) Examine the books and records of TIM CORPORATION in order to prepare consolidated financial statements as of the petition filing date.

r) The affairs of the debtor-in-possession are in a considerably confused state and a substantial portion of the time required for analysis of the affairs of the debtor-in-possession will be expended in attempting to clarify the operations for the most recent fiscal period.

s) Furthermore, there are innumerable services which he and his firm will be required to render in relation to the aforesaid in order that a complete and proper understanding of the affairs of the debtor-in-possession may be presented.

6. The estimated charge for the accounting services proposed to be rendered is $18,800 plus actual out-of-pocket expenses for postage, telephone, etc. Such fee is based upon the regular standard hourly charges of the Firm for various categories of accountants and their assistants, as follows:

Assistant, typists, and clerks	80 hrs. @ $10.00	$ 800
Junior accountants	150	@ 24.00	3,600
Semi-senior accountants	150	@ 29.00	4,350
Senior accountants	70	@ 34.00	2,380
Supervisors and managers	90	@ 50.00	4,500
Partners	40	@ 80.00	3,200
Total			$18,830

7. The foregoing estimate has been prepared on the basis of our familiarity with accounting practices and procedures of the Company and presumes the reasonable continuity of the Company's activities in maintaining its own accounting records, under the direction of knowledgeable personnel.

JOHN X. DOE, JR.

Sworn to before me this

_____ day of June, 1975

Figure 5–1.   Continued.

The accountant should ascertain directly from the controller whether the records are current, whether major impediments exist, and whether the key accounting personnel plan to stay with the company. In certain cases, if the company's accountants are terminating their services, the accountant may decide not to take the engagement because the audit would become an impossible task without them and full compensation for all the efforts required would be doubtful.

11. The examination is very limited, with the accountant usually spending only part of a day at the debtor company. The accountant may be able to contact the debtor's independent accountant and obtain additional information. Based on this limited investigation, the accountant must prepare the affidavit.

Application for Retention

12. Counsel for the receiver, trustee, or debtor-in-possession uses the information in the accountant's affidavit on proposed services to prepare an application for retention of the accountant, to be submitted to the court for its approval. If the court approves the retention of the accountant, it will enter the order, confirm the scope of the services to be performed, and set the rate or maximum compensation to be allowed for such services. A sample of an application filed by counsel for retention of an accountant is shown in Figure 5–2. The format of a court order authorizing the retention of an accountant appears in Figure 5–3 (page 117).

Retention Order on a Retainer Basis

13. A retention order in addition to the one shown in Figure 5–2 is often required if the independent accountant assists the trustee, receiver, or debtor-in-possession in normal accounting duties including the preparation of monthly, and sometimes weekly, operating statements for the court. This type of order is essential if the time period between the date of bankruptcy and the acceptance of a plan of arrangement or reorganization is of considerable length. In many Chapter X and in some Chapter XI proceedings, the time span covers several years. A sample of the accountant's affidavit requesting retention as accountant for the debtor is shown in Figure 5–4 (page 118).

```
┌─────────────┐
│             │⎫
│  CAPTION    │⎬
│             │⎭
└─────────────┘
```

APPLICATION FOR RETENTION OF ACCOUNTANT

TO THE HON. ...., Referee in Bankruptcy:

The application of *William Roberts*, by *John Green*, his attorney, respectfully represents:

1. That he is the trustee herein, duly qualified and acting as such trustee.

2. The bankrupt was engaged in the business of [*state business*] with a place of business at (address).

3. The assets, after sale of the bankrupt's property and effects, amount to (amount) while the liabilities exceed (amount).

4. Applicant believes that it is necessary in the best interest of the estate to have a complete audit and examination of the books of account of the bankrupt for the following reasons:

(a) *Books of Account:* The bankrupt has turned over *ten* books of account. A preliminary survey by applicant discloses that these books of account are involved, and contain entries covering a period of several years. In addition, there are numerous cancelled vouchers which it will be necessary to check with the entries in the books.

(b) *Preliminary Survey:* A preliminary survey of the books of account discloses that said books were not kept in an orderly fashion, and it appears that certain entries are obviously incorrect and that entries have been made without proper explanatory detail. To determine accurately the condition of the bankrupt's affairs, a complete analysis of the books of account will be necessary.

(c) *Discrepancy Between Assets and Liabilities:* The bankrupt has failed to account for the discrepancy between his assets and his liabilities, nor do the books disclose the reason for the deficiency of assets.

(d) *Accounts Receivable:* Applicant is advised that there are numerous large outstanding accounts receivable, according to the records of the bankrupt, and that in order to determine the status of these accounts, an examination of the books of the bankrupt will be necessary.

Figure 5–2. Application for retention of accountant. (*Source:* Asa A. Herzog, Sheldon Lowe, and Joel B. Zweibel, *Herzog's Bankruptcy Forms and Practice* (New York: Clark Boardman Co., Ltd., 1971.)

(e) *[State any further reasons why applicant believes retention of accountants to be necessary.]*

5. That by reason of the premises aforesaid, applicant desires to retain the services of accountants to make the necessary examination and audit of the books of the bankrupt and applicant desires to retain the services of *Leon Robbin*, Certified Public Accountant, of (address). *[State reasons for selection.]* Said accountant has advised applicant that the cost of the proposed services will approximate (amount) which applicant verily believes to be a proper and reasonable charge.

WHEREFORE, applicant prays for an order authorizing the employment of *Leon Robbin* as accountant at a maximum compensation of ($500.00), the exact amount thereof to be fixed by this court upon the filing of a proper application for all of which no previous application has been made herein.

(Dated)

Signed _____

Attorney for Applicant

[Applicant signs where not represented by Attorney]

(Address)

Figure 5–2.   Continued.

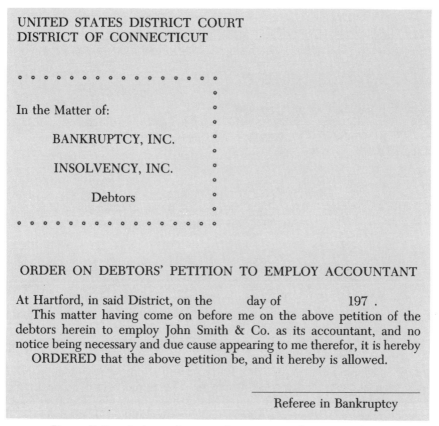

Figure 5–3. Order authorizing the retention of an accountant.

UNITED STATES DISTRICT COURT
EASTERN DISTRICT OF NEW YORK

* * * * * * * * * * * * * * *

In the Matter

of

TOM CORPORATION,

Debtor-in-Possession

* * * * * * * * * * * * * * *

In Proceedings for an
Arrangement

No. 75–B–999

AFFIDAVIT OF PROPOSED ACCOUNTANT
FOR RETENTION AS ACCOUNTANT
FOR THE DEBTOR-IN-POSSESSION

State of *New York* } SS.:
County of *New York* }

JOHN X. DOE, JR., being duly sworn, deposes and says
1. He is a partner of the accounting firm of John X. Doe & Co., and he is duly authorized to make this affidavit for and on its behalf.
2. The business addresses of said firm include its office at 90 Maple Street, New York, New York 10005.
3. John X. Doe & Co. is a firm of certified public accountants and has been in existence for over fifty years. The Firm operates through offices located in 20 cities in the United States and in a number of offices located overseas. He has been a Certified Public Accountant, licensed under the laws of the State of New York, for over 15 years and his firm has been retained as accountants in numerous matters to examine the books and records of bankrupts and debtors-in-possession.
4. To the best of his knowledge, information, and belief, neither he nor the members of the firm of John X. Doe & Co. have any business association with nor are related to any attorney, creditor, debtor-in-possession, or any party to the proceedings.

Figure 5–4. Accountant's affidavit requesting retention as accountant for the debtor.

5. He has made an examination of the books and records of the debtor-in-possession and has discussed the services required with officers of the debtor, counsel for the debtor, and counsel for the Creditors' Committee which consist of the following:

    a) The preparation of monthly statements to be submitted to the court.

    b) Review of the accounting records as deemed necessary.

6. He estimates that the cost of the foregoing services will be Two Hundred Fifty Dollars ($250.00) per month payable upon completion of each monthly review.

7. WHEREFORE your deponent asks for the making of an appropriate order of employment.

_____

JOHN X. DOE, JR.

Sworn to before me this

_____ day of June, 1975

_____

Figure 5–4.   Continued.

Deviations from Retention Order

14. The accountant should pay close attention to the scope of the accounting services to be rendered as they are described in the order for retention entered by the court. Deviation from the stated services will be closely scrutinized by the court and not included in the accountant's allowance for compensation. Likewise, if more time than the original estimate will be needed by the accountant, a supplemental court order must be obtained allowing additional compensation. A new order for retention must also be secured if the proceedings are transferred from one chapter to another.

15. Once the retention orders are entered by the court, the accountant may begin rendering services.

Retention Procedure—Informal

16. An accountant engaged to render services for a company in financial difficulty that has not formally petitioned the court should obtain a signed engagement letter before any work is

initiated. The format for the engagement letter is similar to that of the usual engagement letter; however, provision for alternate sources of payment should be arranged, in case the client becomes bankrupt in the formal sense. Through this procedure the accountant may avoid becoming a general creditor with a consequent reduction in claims. The alternate sources may consist of a guarantee of payment by one or more of the larger creditors or a personal guarantee by the principal officer or officers of the company. In certain cases it is possible for the accountant to receive an advance before beginning the engagement. One New York accounting firm actively involved in bankruptcy audits receives advance payment on about 10 per cent of its audits. Advances are more common where certain types of wrongdoing are suspected and the accountant is engaged to do a special investigation. It is also a good policy to have the client–debtor sign the engagement letter, if the officers will agree, even though the creditors may be the party requesting the audit. If the bankrupt firm has other affiliates that are solvent, it is desirable to have them sign the engagement letter, deposit funds for the payment of fees, or guarantee payment.

SCOPE OF WORK

Accountants as Quasi-Officers of the Court

17. Appointment by order for retention through the court makes the accountant a quasi-officer of the court, owing a primary duty to the court. Normally this duty involves reporting to and discussing problems with the trustee in the proceedings. Further, in all cases where persons seek compensation for services or reimbursement for expenses, they shall be held to fiduciary standards.[1] Such standards mean a special confidence has been imposed in the accountant who, in equity and good conscience, is bound to act in good faith and with due regard to the interest of the one imposing the confidence.[2]

[1] *Brown v. Gerdes*, 321 U. S. 178, 182, 1944.
[2] Chauncey Levy, "Creditors' Committees and Their Responsibilities," *Commercial Law Journal*, Vol. 74 (December 1969), p. 356n.

Purpose of the Audit

18. The trustee's accountant is primarily seeking to discover irregularities or transactions which are not in the normal course of business. After an audit of the books, records, and other sources, all the important facts are reported to the trustee for an evaluation of their legal implications (Chapter 8). The irregularities found are those which usually lead to the recovery of assets, barring of a discharge, or establishment of a case for criminal prosecution. The objective of the trustee and creditors in such an audit is to increase the size of the estate to maximize the distribution.[3]

Functions To Be Performed by the Accountant

19. The accountant assumes several roles in an insolvency proceeding and therefore has various functions to perform. These include the normal auditing functions of examining the accounts (Chapter 8) and preparing the financial statements (Chapter 9). An investigatory audit should also be conducted to discover any illegal or questionable transactions (Chapter 8, paragraphs 16–96). Finally, the accountant acts as a management and financial consultant in identifying the causes of difficulty and the measures necessary for effecting successful rehabilitation[4] (Chapter 6, paragraphs 20–27).

20. While included in the court-approved order for retention, the scope of the work to be done by the accountant is also outlined in detail by the attorney for the trustee[5] (Chapter 8, paragraphs 11–14). The accountant's services should normally be limited to an investigation and audit after the books are current. An all-inclusive list of the functions it is beneficial to have the accountant perform follows:

1. Establish the financial position of the debtor by performing an audit (Chapter 8).

---

[3] Asa S. Herzog, "CPA's Role in Bankruptcy Proceeding," *The Journal of Accountancy*, Vol. 117 (January 1964), p. 61.

[4] Edward A. Weinstein, "Accountant's Examinations and Reports in Bankruptcy Proceedings," *New York Certified Public Accountant*, Vol. 35 (January 1965), p. 31.

[5] "Certified Public Accountants Held to Fiduciary Standards," *Journal of the National Association of Referees in Bankruptcy*, Vol. 37 (January 1963), p. 8.

2. Investigate any assets or distribution made by the debtor to creditors or stockholders before the petition was filed which might be recoverable (Chapter 8).

3. Determine whether any wrongdoing occurred prior to the filing (Chapter 8, paragraphs 16–96).

4. Identify the causes of the business failure (Chapter 2).

5. Render an opinion as to the chance for continued operation of the business in the future (Chapter 9).

6. Maximize the provisions for creditors in the settlement while allowing for the relief necessary for the debtor to have a chance at successful rehabilitation.

7. Liquidate the court proceedings as quickly as possible.[6]

The performance of all of these tasks would result in high administrative expenses. The courts therefore try to restrict accounting services to a minimum and often, unfortunately, the fourth and fifth functions listed above are deleted from the court orders and the accountant's examination of the financial statements is restricted. A detailed discussion of functions performed by the accountant are described in the next chapter.

Duties of the Accountant When Retained by Creditors' Committee

21. The creditors' committee is most concerned with establishing the debtor's integrity, investigating its past transactions, and ascertaining whether a proposed plan of arrangement is in the best interests of creditors. The accountant will seek to determine whether there have been any preferential or fraudulent transfers and any losses which the debtor cannot explain. An attempt must be made to establish the value of the assets in liquidation so that the committee may decide whether that course of action would be more advantageous than an arrangement (Chapter 6, paragraph 21). And finally, an important function of the accountant for the creditors' committee is establishing the debtor's earning capacity to help determine the type of arrangement the committee should recommend for acceptance.[7]

---

[6] Weinstein, pp. 32–33.

[7] William J. Rudin, "Allowances in Chapter XI Proceedings," *Journal of the National Conference of Referees in Bankruptcy*, Vol. 40 (July 1966), p. 86.

22. The duties and functions of the accountant for the creditors' committee are described in detail in Chapter 7.

DETERMINATION OF ACCOUNTANT'S FEES

23. The accountant's fees are considered an administrative expense and receive first priority in payment. If the estate of the bankrupt is not large enough to pay the administrative claims in full, the accountant shares in the balance which is available with others having administrative claims.

24. Even though the services of the accountant when retained by the court are a part of the cost of administering the estate, this priority may be reduced if the debtor is removed from one type of bankruptcy and becomes subject to another. If a company which originally filed under Chapter XI is subsequently placed under the provisions of Chapter X, or declared a bankrupt, the cost of administrative expenses claimed under the provisions of Chapter XI is secondary to administrative expense claims incurred under subsequent filings. A separate claim must be filed for the services rendered in each phase of bankruptcy.[8] In order to protect the fees involved, it is important for the accountant to determine the condition of the debtor and the potential size of the debtor's estate.

SEC May Object to Fees

25. The SEC is considered a party in interest under Chapter X and under some Chapter XI proceedings. The accountant should be aware that the SEC may object to stated fees as being excessive in amount if it desires. In Chapter X or other proceedings where the SEC is involved, the judge is required to get an advisory report from the Washington office regarding fees. The rates acceptable to the SEC, as stated by one accountant, are "ten to fifteen years behind the times." Many of the accounting firms that deal with Chapter X and Chapter XI proceedings expect to get between 50 and 75 per cent of the "going rate." Most judges do at least accept the SEC recommendations although they are not bound by them,

[8] Edward A. Weinstein, "Examining a Company in Bankruptcy," *Quarterly* (Touche, Ross, Bailey and Smart), Vol. 9 (September 1963), p. 17.

and they will often impose an additional allowance over and above the recommended amount.

26. It is an advisable practice for the accounting firm to review with district representatives of the SEC the entire application for fees before the time records are sent to the Washington office so that the SEC is aware of the type of work performed, the time worked, and the quality of the work. The SEC often determines the average hourly rate for the entire engagement. As a result they may not only object to the hourly rates as established for partners, managers, seniors, and juniors, but may claim that partners and managers devoted too much time to the engagement. For example, the nature of the engagement may require that a considerable amount of time be spent on tax matters and settling litigation, and partners and managers may have to do most of the work. This should be pointed out to the SEC at the local level; a realistic awareness of some of the work involved and of the level of services required may prevent future reductions in the fees allowed. It is to the accountant's advantage to find out the SEC's views regarding the fees before the report is written. If the SEC evaluation is in error, the accountant then has an opportunity to try to answer its objections.

Compensation Must Be Approved by the Court

27. When retained by a receiver, trustee, or debtor-in-possession, the accountant's remuneration must come from either the bankrupt's estate or the debtor-in-possession. Payment from either source can only be made when the accountant is engaged upon an order of the court which expressly fixes the amount or rate of compensation.

28. To aid the court in setting the amount of compensation, the accountant is required to make a preliminary survey of the debtor's books and records to estimate the extent of the services it will be necessary to perform (see paragraphs 9–11). The amount then fixed by the court is the maximum compensation the accountant will be given for services in the proceedings. Thus, if the accountant believes the value of these services will exceed the maximum amount provided for, there should be an immediate attempt to obtain an additional order increasing the maximum.

Factors To Consider When Estimating Fees

29. The criteria most often used in setting reasonable fees are those given by the court in its decision concerning *Owl Drug Company*.[9] The factors to be weighed are:

The time spent in the proceedings

The complexity of the problems which arose

The relative size of the estate and the amount which is available for distribution

The quality of any opposition which is met

The results which are achieved, otherwise known as the *salvage theory* (rather than letting the time involved determine the remuneration, the fees are measured by the extent of success or accomplishments and benefits to the estate)[10]

The experience and standing of the accountant

The quality of skill necessary in the situation and the amount of care and professional skill used

The fee schedule in the area

The ethics of the profession

30. The court in the *Owl Drug* proceedings went on to note that any consideration of fee allowances must be according to the economy principle, which requires that all unnecessary expenses be curtailed to a minimum in insolvency proceedings. Thus the courts should attempt to set the fees at the least amount which is reasonable in order to maximize the distribution to creditors. Several accounting firms with considerable experience in bankruptcy proceedings estimate that the accountant normally receives about 75 per cent of the "going rate" for services rendered under Chapter XI proceedings and less than 50 per cent in straight bankruptcy cases. In addition, the accountant often finds it necessary to work a greater number of hours than is stipulated in the order of retention, for which no compensation is received.

31. The accountant should be aware when estimating fees that

[9] 16 F. Supp. 142, 1936.

[10] William J. Rudin, "Fees and Allowances to Attorneys in Bankruptcy and Chapter XI Proceedings," *Fordham Law Review*, Vol. 34 (March 1966), p. 399.

because of the nature of a bankruptcy engagement more seasoned personnel will be needed for this work than for a normal audit.

Compensation When Retained by Creditors' Committee

32. When engaged by a creditor or some party other than the receiver, trustee, or debtor-in-possession, the accountant must rely on that person rather than on the debtor's estate for compensation. However, under Section 339(2) of the Bankruptcy Act, as amended in 1967, the expenses of the creditors' committee for assistance rendered by agents, attorneys, or accountants, whether incurred before or after the filing of the petition, are allowed as an expense of administration to the extent deemed reasonable and necessary by the court, provided the arrangement is confirmed. Expenses incurred by the committee before its election pursuant to Section 338 shall not be disallowed because of a change in the committee's composition, provided a majority of the committee when it incurred the expense continue as members of the elected committee.

33. By the requirement that the expenses be such as the court deems reasonable and necessary, the court has retained discretion over the final allowance of expenses. Also, the provision for allowance of expenses incurred prior to official election of the committee recognizes the necessity and importance of a creditors' committee working prior to formal arrangement proceedings. The compensation for the accountant, as allowed by the court, must be included in the debtor's deposit before the plan of arrangement will be confirmed by the court.

34. Should the arrangement fail to be confirmed, the expenses of the creditors' committee would not enjoy first priority. Section 64(3) provides that the expenses of creditors incurred in obtaining a refusal, revocation, or setting aside of an arrangement or discharge, or obtaining evidence resulting in criminal conviction, shall be recoverable as third priority in later bankruptcy proceedings.[11] Thus, if the committee opposes the arrangement and confirmation is

[11] Lawrence King, "Creditor's Committees, Claims Arising During Pendency of Rehabilitation Proceeding and Filing Fees: 1967 Amendments to Bankruptcy Act," *Commercial Law Journal*, Vol. 73 (May 1968), p. 130.

refused, it is entitled to reimbursement for the expenses it incurred to obtain the refusal, including any fees paid for accounting services.[12]

35. Should an arrangement fail to be confirmed for reasons other than the efforts of the creditors' committee, there are no provisions for the committee to recover its costs and expenses. This offers a risk which accountants have been reluctant to accept. Therefore, the practice has developed whereby the debtor-in-possession is persuaded to engage the committee's accountant, or the debtor's accountant is forced upon the creditors' committee. In any subsequent liquidation proceedings the accountant would be remunerated as an expense of administration.

36. However, this arrangement is unacceptable to accountants because it violates the code of ethics of the AICPA which prohibits fee arrangements in which the fee is contingent upon the results of the service.[13] The accountant must see that an arrangement is approved in order to receive compensation for the services rendered. Furthermore, the accountant must avoid being forced into a position which causes a loss of independence, serving as watchdog for the creditors' committee and at the same time acting as a management and financial consultant for the debtor. It should be pointed out that this risk of non-payment for services has been reduced by the recently adopted Chapter XI Bankruptcy Rules. Rule 11–29(c) states that expenses of the committee including compensation for attorneys, accountants, and other agents may be allowed where there is no confirmation.

TIME RECORDS

37. It is important that the accountant keep adequate time and performance records while rendering services. When petitioning the court for a fee allowance, should the amount of the compensation be contested, such records would be vital. At the very least, the accountant should record the following information:

---

[12] Asa S. Herzog, "Bankruptcy Law—Modern Trends," *Journal of the National Association of Referees in Bankruptcy*, Vol. 37 (October 1963), p. 114.

[13] Rule 302, *Code of Professional Ethics* (New York: American Institute of Certified Public Accountants, 1973), p. 25.

The date and a description of the work which has been done

The time spent in the performance of the work

The name, classification, and per-diem billing rate of each staff member performing the work[14]

38. Many accounting firms use computerized forms for allocating time to their clients for services rendered. The court may not accept the computer runs unless there are authoritative records which support the work performed by the accountant. Computer cards are standardized and show only a minimum amount of information, usually including only the client's code number and time. In any accounting work performed for the court, it is advisable for the accounting firm to keep a hard set of records which clearly show in detail the nature of the work performed. In awarding fees the court also takes into consideration the quality of the services rendered by the accountant and the amount and types of reports issued. The accountant will often spend a great deal of time looking for preferential payments and other types of irregularities. If none is discovered, the court may not understand the reason for the fees charged by the accountant. Thus, the accountant may need these detailed records to support the request for payment.

PETITION FOR FEE ALLOWANCE

Court Discretion in Ruling on Fees

39. The requirement that the level of compensation be fixed in the court order of appointment has been held to be directory and not mandatory.[15] This means that when ruling on fees the court may exercise its discretion in light of all the circumstances surrounding the case.

40. The court also makes the final decision concerning compensation and the time when services were rendered. An accountant on loan to perform bookkeeping services for a debtor both

[14] Harold Gelb and Irving Goldberger, "Retention Order of the Accountant in Insolvencies and Bankruptcies and Petition for Compensation," *The New York Certified Public Accountant*, Vol. 23 (October 1953), p. 634.

[15] *Littleton v. Kincaid*, 179 F. 2d 848, 1950.

before and after bankruptcy can be allowed to recover for postbankruptcy costs under an order continuing the debtor-in-possession and allowing employment of outside help. On the other hand, an accountant completing a special examination of the debtor's financial position which was begun before bankruptcy was not entitled to first priority for the expenses of the work done after bankruptcy because an order of the court had not been obtained at the time of the commencement of the services.[16] Bankruptcy Rule 215 allows the trustee or receiver to engage an accountant as a salaried employee, if necessary to operate the business.

Procedure for Filing the Petition

41. When the accountant has completed the engagement, a petition for compensation should be filed in affidavit form with the court having jurisdiction over the proceedings. The petition should contain enough information about the services the accountant has rendered so that the court may evaluate and compare them with the services authorized in the order of retention. At a minimum, the application for compensation should include the following data:

The accountant's name, address, and firm affiliation

The source of the accountant's authorization to perform the services

Date the accountant began the engagement

List of the services the accountant rendered and the exhibits and schedules presented in the report

Total amount of compensation the accountant is requesting, accompanied by a schedule of the hours worked classified by the grade of accountant and the per-diem billing rate

The accomplishments believed to have resulted from the accountant's services, in light of the benefits which the estate has obtained from such services[17]

Sworn statement by the accountant concerning knowledge of the contents of the petition

Notarized signature of the accountant

42. An example of an affidavit applying for compensation is presented in Figure 5–5.

---

[16] *Century Chemical Corp.*, 192 F. Supp. 205, 1961.

[17] Gelb and Goldberger, p. 634.

UNITED STATES DISTRICT COURT
EASTERN DISTRICT OF NEW YORK

In the Matter

of   In Proceedings for an
                                        Arrangement
TOM CORPORATION,
                                    No. 75–B–999
Debtor-in-Possession

AFFIDAVIT FOR PETITION
FOR COMPENSATION OF ACCOUNTANTS

State of *New York* ⎱
County of *New York* ⎰ SS.:

JOHN X. DOE, JR., being duly sworn, deposes and says:

1. That he is a certified public accountant and a member of the accounting firm of John X. Doe & Co., with offices at 90 Maple Street, New York, New York 10005.

2. That his firm is well versed and experienced in the auditing of books and records of assignors, bankrupts and others involved in insolvency proceedings;

3. That neither he, nor any member of his firm, is related to or has had business association with any attorney, creditor, bankrupt, or debtor-in-possession or any other party to these proceedings;

4. That in accordance with an order signed by the Honorable Herbert Robertson dated June 15, 1975, the accounting firm of John X. Doe & Co. was retained to perform an audit and examine the books and records of the debtor-in-possession herein, and to render other miscellaneous services in connection with said audit and examination;

5. That pursuant to said retention, your petitioner rendered the following services:

1) Prepared an inventory of the books and records of the debtor-in-possession and its subsidiary, TIM CORPORATION.

Figure 5–5. Accountant's affidavit requesting compensation for services rendered.

2) Supervised and assisted in the summarization of the books of account and posting to the general ledgers of the debtor-in-possession and its subsidiary in order to close the books for the period up to the date of the filing of the petition.

3) Met with representatives of the debtor's former accountant, John Jones & Co., and obtained information as to the debtor's financial history, and photocopies of essential workpapers, tax returns, and documents contained in their files.

4) Examined the corporate minutes, resolutions, and stock records of the debtor and its subsidiary in order to determine their corporate history and ownership, and the existence and pertinent provisions of any significant contractual arrangements. In this connection, all significant contracts were examined and their pertinent provisions abstracted.

5) Assisted the debtor in planning and arranging for the taking of an inventory as at May 31, 1975.

6) Supervised and observed a portion of the inventory taken by the debtor as at May 31, 1975. In this connection, extensive tests of listed items were performed as to quantity, description, and physical existence.

7) Verified the mathematical accuracy of the May 31, 1975, inventory by checking all multiplication and addition on the final listings.

8) Determined that the inventory at May 31, 1975, was valued at the lower of cost or market values of each major category of items by extensive tests of the unit prices used therein against recent purchase and sales invoices, and internal cost records.

9) Examined into the relationships and transactions of the debtor with its subsidiary, TIM CORPORATION.

The intercompany account between TOM CORPORATION and TIM CORPORATION was examined and found to consist primarily of intercompany charges for expenses and purchases, payments made by the parent to creditors of its subsidiary, and cash advances for operations. It was also found that $96,000 of these advances were capitalized to pay for the debtor's investment in the subsidiary.

10) Examined into the transactions of the debtor and its subsidiary for the four months preceding the petition filing date to determine the existence of any possible preferences.

11) Prepared financial statements for the debtor and its subsidiary as of the petition filing date including:
   a) Statement of Financial Position at May 31, 1975
   b) Statement of Loss for the five months ended May 31, 1975.
   c) Schedules of operating expenses for the five months ended May 31, 1975.
   d) Statement of Affairs at May 31, 1975. Copies of these statements are annexed hereto.
   [See Chapter 9 for examples of the above statements.]

Figure 5–5.   Continued.

12) Reviewed the financial history of the debtor and its subsidiary to determine the existence and extent of any possible tax refund claims.

13) Reviewed the prior financial statements prepared by the debtor's former accountants.

14) Examined and reconciled the most recent statements for all bank accounts of the debtor and its subsidiary. In the process thereof, checks made payable to cash were reviewed to determine their purpose and authenticity.

15) Examined into the position of TED CORPORATION as relates to its financing transactions with the debtor and its subsidiary.

16) Prepared schedules of accounts receivable at May 31, 1975, showing names and amounts due from the various customers of the debtor and its subsidiary.

17) Reviewed the status of the accounts receivable of the debtor and its subsidiary and provided for possible bad debts thereon.

18) Analyzed the security deposits of the debtor and its subsidiary to determine any possible recoveries.

19) Reviewed the recent acquisitions of fixtures and equipment by the debtor and its subsidiary to determine their propriety and the existence of any liens or encumbrances.

20) Examined into the debtor's loans transactions with its officers and employees to determine the existence of any possible recoveries or preferential payments.

21) Prepared schedules of accounts payable at May 31, 1975, showing names and amounts due to the various trade creditors of the debtor and its subsidiary.

22) Prepared schedules of royalty and commission advances at May 31, 1975, showing names and amounts owing to the debtor and its subsidiary.

23) Reviewed the prepaid project development costs expended by the debtor and its subsidiary to determine any possible recoveries thereof.

24) Determined the amounts of unpaid wages of the debtor at May 31, 1975.

25) Reviewed the advances received by the debtor and its subsidiary from several of their distributors to determine the liability therefor.

26) Examined into amounts received by the debtor from various customers in advance of shipments, for which refunds are to be made.

27) Analyzed the debtor's insurance in force to determine any possible recoveries for unearned premiums and cash surrender values.

28) Prepared a schedule of royalties payable at May 31, 1975, showing names and amounts owing.

29) Determined the extent to which assets were security for loans received by the debtor, and the approximate amounts of any equity therein available to general creditors.

Figure 5–5. Continued.

30) Reviewed the liabilities of the debtor and its subsidiary for payroll taxes owing to the various tax authorities.

31) Examined into the status of the debtor's debenture bonds payable.

32) Examined the ledgers and journals and prepared analyses of all other significant balance sheet, income and expense accounts.

33) In addition to the foregoing, your deponent attended court and creditors' meetings and conferred with counsel to the creditors' committee and counsel to the debtor on numerous occasions in order to resolve the various problems which arose during the administration period.

6. In order for your petitioner to render the aforementioned services, it was necessary to expend approximately $550\frac{1}{2}$ working hours. Based upon the time expended, the reasonable value of the services rendered by petitioner is the sum of $17,637.00, computed on the expenditure of $38\frac{3}{4}$ hours of partners' time at an average of $81.50 an hour, $70\frac{3}{4}$ hours of supervisors' time at an average rate of $48.25 an hour, $71\frac{1}{4}$ hours of senior accountants' time at a rate of $34.00 an hour, 160 hours of semi-senior accountants' time at a rate of $29.00 an hour, 120 hours of time of junior accountants at a rate of $24.00 an hour, and 90 hours of assistant, typists, and clerks at a rate of $10.00 an hour, and out-of-pocket expenditures of $223.00.

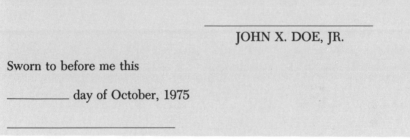

JOHN X. DOE, JR.

Sworn to before me this

_____ day of October, 1975

Figure 5–5.   Continued.

43. In straight bankruptcy proceedings, a notice of any such application and of a hearing concerning the petition must be sent to any party in interest, including the creditors. Section 58(a)(8) requires that creditors shall have at least 10 days' notice by mail of all applications by receivers, ancillary receivers, marshals, trustees, committees, and attorneys for compensation from the estate for services rendered, specifying the amount and by whom they were made. After the hearing, at which any objections may be given, the judge or referee will fix the exact compensation within the

maximum set in the order of retention. In an arrangement proceeding, notice to creditors of a petition for compensation is not required.

Payment for Services Rendered

44. The time the accountant will receive payment for the services rendered depends on the type of retention order. An accountant working under a retention order for special services normally receives payment at the time the case is completed. However, under some conditions, especially where the time period before a plan of arrangement or reorganization is accepted is of considerable length, the court may allow the accountant to receive payment, or at least partial payment, for services rendered. Under a retention order on a retainer basis the accountant receives payment for services rendered at various intervals, such as monthly or quarterly.

6

Accounting Services for

the Debtor-in-Possession

or Trustee

1. Bankruptcy proceedings are filled with various types of reports, emanating from the debtor, debtor-in-possession, or trustee, to the referee, the creditors, and finally the Administrative Office of the U. S. Courts in Washington. Since many of these reports deal with accounting information concerning the financial position of the debtor or estate, the projected profit or loss if the business continues, and other financial aspects of the bankrupt's operations, it is self-evident that the services of an accountant are essential in

many of today's business bankruptcies. This is especially true because of the complexities of modern business operations.

2. The unusual situations encountered in performing accounting services for a business involved in reorganization, arrangement, or straight bankruptcy liquidation often present several practical problems for the accountant. The unique aspects of this type of assignment require the accountant to be very resourceful in providing the additional information needed by the interested parties. This chapter describes the nature of services which may be rendered by the accountant for the debtor-in-possession and the trustee. Chapter 7 discusses the services of the accountant as they relate to the creditors' committee.

3. The accountant provides the attorney for the debtor with financial data to file the bankruptcy petition and with the background information needed to accurately present to the court the reason why the debtor is in difficulty. The accountant also performs the usual accounting services for the debtor, prepares operating statements for the courts, and assists the debtor in formulating a plan of arrangement.

4. The term "accountant" is used in this chapter to refer to both the independent accountant engaged by the debtor and the internal accountant of the debtor. Many accounting services in a bankruptcy proceeding may be performed by the debtor's internal accountant, and the debtor's accounting staff often assists the independent accountant. Auditing services and the preparation of certain schedules and reports for the court require the engagement of an independent accountant. Under these circumstances the accountant must refer to an independent accountant. There may be some advantages to having most of the services involved in the proceedings performed by an independent accountant; however, a discussion of this point is beyond the scope of this chapter.

RELATIONSHIP OF ATTORNEY AND ACCOUNTANT: THE PRE-FILING STAGE OF ARRANGEMENT PROCEEDINGS

5. The accountant will often be the first to become aware that a client is headed toward financial difficulties and will be unable to continue profitable operations and/or pay liabilities as they become

due. The debtor should be encouraged to employ an attorney to help effect a compromise or extension of the indebtedness. It would be to the debtor's advantage to have the accountant present at these first meetings.

6. There are two primary purposes for holding a conference between the debtor and the attorney before a petition is filed. First, the attorney will be supplied with the information needed to prepare the legal documents to accompany the petition. Second, it is necessary that the attorney obtain sufficient background and history concerning the debtor's business in order to present the facts to the court, meet with the creditors, knowledgeably discuss the situation with them, and explain why the debtor is in difficulty and why an arrangement should be consummated.[1]

7. The accountant plays a vital role in this conference. If the company's situation has not been closely followed, the accountant should determine the basic facts and gain a sound knowledge of the business, its history, and the causes of its present difficulties so that at this meeting the attorney can be given an overall view of the debtor's financial condition and the events which preceded it. In order to provide the attorney with this information it will be necessary for the accountant to analyze the activities of the debtor, to compare the financial statements for the last three or four years, and to determine what caused the cash shortage. A comparison of the income statements for the last four years may show that for the first three years the gross profit percentage was fairly constant; however, during the last year it dropped 10 per cent. What caused the change? This is the type of analysis that the accountant must make so that the major causes of the financial problem can be identified and possible corrective action can be discussed with the attorney. (See Chapter 2 for a discussion of the causes of business failure.) An independent accountant should discuss the company's financial condition with the members of the internal accounting staff. It is advisable to have the financial officer of the company present at this conference. In many initial conferences the debtor's internal accountants are intimately involved.

8. The attorney will request certain information from the accountant, including the most recent balance sheet, an income

[1] Asa S. Herzog, "CPA's Role in Bankruptcy Proceeding," *The Journal of Accountancy*, Vol. 117 (January 1964), p. 65.

statement, and a list of the debtor's creditors. Each individual asset will be examined and an attempt made to determine the property's value. The nature and extent of the liabilities will be discussed, and it should be indicated whether they are secured, unsecured, contingent, or unliquidated. In order to initiate the arrangement proceedings the attorney must have a complete and exact list of all creditors including their addresses, the amounts due, the dates incurred, the consideration for the debt, whether any security was given and, if so, its nature and value. The omission of any creditor from the list could result in serious consequences, including a charge of filing false financial statements.[2]

9. Under Chapter XI proceedings the debtor is permitted to reject any executory contracts which will be burdensome. Therefore the accountant should furnish the debtor's attorney with a list of all executory contracts including any contract which leaves something to be performed by either party, other than the obligation to pay money. Executory contracts may consist of long-term leases, commitments the company has made to produce goods for a specific customer at a set price over a long time period, construction contracts to expand the facilities, or agreements the company has signed for the purchase of a certain quantity of raw material. The accountant should also give an opinion as to which contracts will most likely be unprofitable and should be rejected.

10. It is also important to discuss at this conference what caused the debtor's current problems, whether the company will be able to overcome its difficulties, and if so, what measures will be necessary. The accountant should attempt to explain how the losses occurred and what can be done to avoid them in the future. To help with this determination, the accountant should project the operations for a thirty-day period over at least the next three to six months and indicate the areas where steps will be necessary in order to earn a profit (see paragraphs 22–24).

11. Discussion of the debtor's past history, including a thorough examination of its business conduct, is vital. The attorney will want to know whether any financial statements have been issued, the nature of such statements, whether they can be substantiated, and the possibility that they might be construed to be deceptive. Also investigated will be any preferential payments made to favored

[2] *Ibid.,* p. 66.

creditors or other transfers of property which are not in the regular course of business. Any unusually large purchases should be closely scrutinized, and the debtor should be able to account for all of the assets. Any other information concerning the debtor's activities which the attorney should be aware of to determine some of the problems which may arise in the course of the proceedings should also be supplied. It is necessary that the debtor's counsel have complete knowledge of the situation in order to decide what course of action it will be best to pursue. Obviously, the accountant plays a crucial role in obtaining this information.

12. One other area where the independent accountant's services are indispensable is in the determination of insolvency and the exact date at which it occurred. The lawyer is required to prove either equity or bankruptcy insolvency. But the independent accountant must determine the debtor's financial condition by an audit (Chapter 8), prepare worksheets, and compile supporting documents and records necessary to prove the client's condition.

13. If at this preliminary meeting it is decided to file a petition to initiate formal arrangement proceedings, all parties involved must act quickly because a tax lien may be impending or a judgment sale or foreclosure of a mortgage may be threatening. This emphasizes the necessity for the accountant to have complete knowledge in advance of the accounting functions that must be performed.[3]

ACCOUNTING SERVICES FOR THE DEBTOR

14. These services can be divided into four categories. First, the accountant provides the debtor's counsel with the information needed to prepare the schedules, statement of affairs, and other forms necessary to file a petition under Chapter XI. These requirements will be discussed more fully in the section entitled "Accounting Data Relative to the Petition" (paragraphs 25–39). Second, the accountant provides the usual accounting services for the client. The third function consists of periodic profit and loss statements for submission to the court. And fourth, the accountant

[3] Harris Levin, "Accounting Aspects of Arrangement Proceedings," *New York Certified Public Accountant*, Vol. 28 (June 1958), p. 430.

assists the client in formulating a plan of arrangement which will meet with the approval of creditors and at the same time allow the debtor to operate the business successfully.

Normal Accounting Services

15. It is still necessary for the accountant to render the usual services that would be given any other client, and normal accounting procedures will be followed. However, it is important to realize that the debtor-in-possession is a new legal entity which must be distinguished from the debtor. The accountant must close the debtor's books as of the date the petition is filed and open new books for the new entity. In the opening entries all of the debtor's assets but none of its liabilities should be transferred. This is because none of the debtor's liabilities which existed at the date of bankruptcy may be paid by the debtor-in-possession except upon specific order of the court.

Operating Statement of the Debtor

16. A complete periodic profit and loss statement setting forth the operations of the debtor's business must be filed with the court as required by local rules or by specific order of the court. It is important that this statement be carefully prepared because it is the court's only source of information concerning the financial operations of the debtor-in-possession.[4] It should be prepared on an accrual basis, and must be signed and verified under oath by an officer of the corporation. The attorney for the debtor must file two copies with the court and will usually also submit copies to the creditors' committee and their attorney.

17. The income statement filed with the court differs somewhat from the typical statement. The accountant generally prepares the report based on an estimated gross profit figure because it is highly unlikely that a physical inventory will be taken every month. The depreciation is put in a footnote rather than conventionally deducted as an expense because it only reduces profit and is immaterial to the court's present investigation. Also, nonrecurring expenses should be clearly labeled because the court is primarily interested in the next period's projected income. All liabilities

---

[4] Herzog, p. 67.

which become due after the petition is filed should be paid by the debtor in the regular course of the business, as should taxes which relate to the period after filing. However, taxes which accrued before the petition was filed should not be paid by the debtor as a normal business transaction.

18. The court does not require any particular form for the monthly operating statements. The revenue and expense are generally presented in the normal income statement format. Quite frequently, a cash receipts and disbursement statement is also filed with the income statement. Examples of an operating statement and a projected operating statement as filed with a court appear at the end of this chapter (pages 171–85).

19. The profit and loss statements are very important because they are the court's only source of information about the financial operations of a debtor who has remained in possession. It is required that the report be signed by an officer of the debtor and verified under oath. Two copies will usually be filed with the court by the attorney for the debtor-in-possession and one each with the chairman and attorney for the creditors' committee.

Assistance in Formulating Plan of Arrangement

20. The accountant will be asked to advise and give suggestions to the debtor and attorney in drawing up a plan of arrangement. The most important requirements of any plan are that it be in the best interests of creditors, meet with their approval, be feasible, and enable the debtor to resume operations successfully after confirmation. (See paragraphs 40–41.)

Liquidating Value of Assets

21. To be in the best interest of the creditors, the plan must give them an amount at least equal to the amount they would receive if the estate were to be liquidated. To determine the size of the liquidating dividends, the accountant must establish the distress-sale value of all assets which remain in the estate. Several methods are used by accountants to determine the immediate market price for the assets. The accountant may have another client in the same type of business who may be able to supply information about the values of some of the assets, especially

inventory. The accountant may be able to reasonably estimate the values of the assets through earlier experience with companies in the same industry. In order to determine the value of plant and equipment, the accountant may contact the manufacturer or a used-equipment dealer. It is often necessary for the court or the creditors' committee to employ an auctioneer or appraiser to evaluate the assets. The assets listed will include the property on hand and what may be recovered, such as assets distributed in preference of creditors or concealed by the debtor and any questionable transactions involving payments to creditors, returns of merchandise to vendors, sales of fixed assets, and repayment of loans to owners.

Projection of Future Operations

22. Feasibility refers to the ability of the debtor to carry out and perform the terms of the plan. To establish feasibility, the accountant must project the profitability potential of the business. Where the plan calls for installment payments, the accountant will be requested to prepare projected budgets, cash flow statements, and statements of financial position. The creditors must be assured with the projected income statement and cash flow statement that the debtor will be in a position to make the payments as they become due. The forecast of the results of operations and financial position should be prepared on the assumption that the proposed plan will be accepted and that the liability and asset accounts reflect the balance which would be shown after all adjustments are made relative to the debt forgiveness. See the projected operating statement on pages 177–85 for an example of the type of information presented in a forecast.

23. The forecast and the assumptions on which it is based originate with the debtor or trustee, who assumes the responsibility for them. However, the accountant would not want to be associated with the forecast in any way if the assumptions are believed to be incomplete or unreasonable.

24. The assumptions on which the forecast is based should be clearly stated in the report. An example of how the assumptions may be shown in the forecast is contained in the projected operating statement at the end of this chapter (pages 177–85). Any major changes in the operations of the business, such as the

elimination of a division or a given product line, should be clearly set forth. If the forecast depends on the success of new products or markets, this should be stated.

ACCOUNTING DATA RELATIVE TO THE PETITION

25. The accountant must supply the attorney with certain information necessary for an arrangement petition to be filed. This normally includes detailed schedules of the debtor's assets and liabilities, a statement of affairs regarding its past operations, and a statement of any executory contracts. Often the petition must be filed quickly to avoid pending legal proceedings, and the debtor's books are seldom up to date. Therefore the court may grant 15 additional days after the petition is filed for the inclusion of the aforementioned schedules and statements, provided a list of the names and addresses of all creditors and a brief statement of assets are with the petition.

Affidavit as to Projected Operations

26. Certain districts may require a sworn statement containing the data necessary to prove to the court that the debtor-in-possession will be able to operate the business at a profit. These projections, usually prepared in budget form and on a monthly basis, should be revised as new information becomes available and should indicate which areas, in the accountant's opinion, are unprofitable and which costs should be eliminated. The following data should be included in the affidavit:

> The total amount of the payroll each week and the salaries paid to the officers of the corporation
>
> All items which comprise overhead
>
> A list of the ten largest creditors
>
> A statement of any litigation or levies which are pending upon the debtor's property
>
> The reasons why it is in the best interests of the creditors that the debtor remain in possession of the property (it is most important to show that they will receive more under arrangement proceedings than they would if the estate were to be liquidated)

27. If there is reason to believe that the firm will not be able to at least break even, the independent accountant should notify the creditors and the trustee, citing the reasons for this suspicion. At the end of the period, a statement of operations should be prepared and compared with the projection so that those interested may come to their own decisions about the future of the business and subsequent budgets may be modified. These budgets as prepared by the accountant serve the dual function of controlling operations while the debtor remains in possession and guiding the preparation of the plan of arrangement. See paragraphs 22–24 for comments relating to the preparation of the forecasts.

Supporting Schedules

28. The schedules which must accompany the petition, as required by Section 7a(8) of the Bankruptcy Act, are sworn statements of the debtor's assets and liabilities as of the date the petition is filed under Chapter XI. These schedules consist primarily of the debtor's balance sheet broken down into detail, and the accountant will be required to supply the information generated in the preparation of the normal balance sheet and its supporting schedules. The required information is supplied on Schedules A–1 and A–3 which include a complete statement of liabilities, and Schedules B–1 through B–4 which are a complete statement of assets. Samples of these schedules appear as Official Form No. 6 in Appendix A (pages 347–51).

29. It is crucial that this information be accurate and complete because the omission or incorrect listing of a creditor might result in a failure to receive notice of the proceedings, and consequently the creditor's claim could be barred from a discharge when the plan is later confirmed. Also, omission of material facts may be construed as a false statement or concealment.[5]

Priority Claims

30. All claims holding priority under the Bankruptcy Act must be listed on Schedule A–1. The most frequent of such claims are wages, taxes, and any other debts expressly granted priority by law, including certain rent claims. For wages, the name and address of

[5] Levin, p. 432.

each claimant to whom the debtor owes salary or vacation pay when the petition is filed must be listed. Each taxing authority must be listed separately. For the Internal Revenue Service, the District Director of the office where the debtor files its returns should be listed, with a breakdown of all federal taxes which are due. All other taxing authorities must be listed, with the address of each agency and the amount owing.

Secured Creditors

31. Schedule A–2 is provided for listing the debtor's secured creditors, including all persons holding a deposit or property of the debtor. Required on the schedule is the name and address of each creditor, a description of the security which is being held, the present value of the security (usually the depreciated cost), and the amount owing to the creditor.

Unsecured Creditors

32. A list of all unsecured creditors is required on Schedule A–3 and must include their names, addresses, and the amount due each claimant. This information is generally taken from the books and records of the company. It is important to list all creditors and give the full name and correct address of each person because failure to notify any creditor may act to bar a discharge of the claim following confirmation of the arrangement. The exact amount due each creditor should be determined and the books posted so there is no doubt as to how much is owing. Unsecured creditors include not only general creditors, but also those who hold promissory notes, judgment creditors, and officers or directors of the debtor who have loaned money to the company. It is also important to list all claims which are disputed, contingent, or unliquidated, and indicate their status.[6]

33. Schedule A–3 also contains information regarding the debtor's liabilities on notes or bills discounted which are to be paid by the drawers, makers, acceptors, or endorsers. All creditors to whom the debtor is liable on accommodation paper are also listed on Schedule A–3. If the creditor is entitled to priority or is secured, the information should be included on Schedule A–1 or A–2. When

[6] *Ibid.,* p. 433.

Schedules A–1 through A–3 have been completed, all creditors who have or may have any interest in connection with the debtor's estate should have been listed.

Assets of the Debtor

34. Information concerning all property owned by the debtor is provided on Schedules B–1 to B–4. A statement of the real estate owned by the debtor with an estimated value of its interest is found on Schedule B–1.

35. Schedule B–2 concerns goods or personal property and where located, including cash, negotiable instruments and securities, stock in trade, all motor vehicles and machinery, fixtures, equipment, patents, copyrights, and trademarks. The most important section of this schedule is the information regarding the debtor's stock in trade, to be computed from the actual inventory with a disclosure of the method of valuation used. The method which is used to value the inventory should be consistent with prior periods and should be a method which is in accordance with generally accepted accounting principles. The figures required in this schedule are totals for each classification, not individual values for each item. Information about accounts receivable, insurance policies, all unliquidated claims (such as from fire, storm damage, and water damage), and deposits of money made by the debtor is also included in Schedule B–2.

36. Property in reversion, remainder, or expectancy, including property held in trust for the debtor or subject to any power or right to dispose of or to charge should be included as real property on Schedule B–1 or personal property on Schedule B–2. Schedule B–3 lists property not otherwise scheduled. Included in this schedule would be property transferred under assignment for benefit of creditors within four months prior to filing of the petition. Schedule B–4 applies only to an individual debtor filing a petition and concerns all property which is exempt from the proceedings, such as household furniture, clothing, etc.

37. A summary of debts and property taken from Schedules A and B is also included with the petition. A single oath for all of the schedules must be submitted specifying the number of sheets included in the schedules and acknowledging that the affiant has

read them. Separate forms of oath are provided for individuals, corporations, and partnerships. Form No. 7 which explains the information required on the schedules, summary, and oath is shown in Appendix A.

Statement of Affairs

38. The general purpose of the statement of affairs is to give both the creditors and the court an overall view of the principal items in connection with the debtor's operations when completed. It offers many avenues from which investigations into the debtor's conduct may be begun. The statement consists of twenty-one questions to be answered under oath concerning the following areas:

1. The nature, location and name of the business, including the employer's identification number, when the business was begun, where else and under what other names the debtor has conducted business.
2. Books and records, with the name and address of each person who kept and audited them during the preceding two years.
3. All financial statements which were issued within the previous two years.
4. The total dollar value of the last two inventories taken of the debtor's property, the valuation method used, the person who conducted the inventory, and the location of the records.
5. Income received from sources other than business operations.
6. Where and when income tax returns were filed for the last three years, tax refunds received or entitled to be received for the last two years.
7. All bank accounts and safe deposit boxes.
8. Property held in trust for another person.
9. Prior bankruptcy proceedings.
10. Prior receiverships, general assignments, and other modes of liquidation.
11. Property in the hands of a third person.
12. Party in suits pending at the time of the filing of the original petition; party in suits terminated within one year; any property attached, garnished, or seized within the last four months.

13. Any loans repaid during the year before the filing of the petition. Sufficient information must be given so as to determine whether any preferences have been made which might be recovered. Related to this will be a determination of the exact date when the debtor was insolvent.

14. Property transferred other than in the ordinary course of business during the preceding year. This is important because the transfer might have been fraudulent.

15. Assignment of accounts or other receivables.

16. Property returned or repossessed by a seller or secured party during the preceding year.

17. Business leases.

18. Losses from fire, theft, or gambling.

19. Personal withdrawals including loans made by officers, directors, or managing executives.

20. Payments or transfers to attorneys.

21. Names and addresses of all officers, directors, managing executives, and principal stockholders.

39. The statement of affairs which is required by Section 7a(9) of the Bankruptcy Act is to be submitted in triplicate at least five days prior to the first meeting of creditors.

FORMULATING AN AMENDED PLAN OF ARRANGEMENT

40. When a petition is filed under Chapter XI, an actual plan of arrangement may be included or it may just be stated that a plan will be devised. If a plan is filed with the petition, it is often done so only to halt other legal proceeding which may be pending and prove damaging if consummated. Thus the plan will most likely have to be amended and the changes are usually generated from meetings of the debtor with the attorney and the creditors' committee. Most problems arise in connection with a plan that grants an extension of time, and full agreement must be reached on the financial data the accountant provides to prove that such a plan is feasible. Figure 6–1 shows a typical plan of arrangement. Figure 6–2 illustrates a notice of a hearing on a modified arrangement and Figure 6–3 shows the proposed modified arrangement that would be sent to creditors with the notice.

UNITED STATES DISTRICT COURT
EASTERN DISTRICT OF NEW YORK

In the Matter

of

TIM CORPORATION,

Debtor-in-Possession

In Proceedings for an
Arrangement Under
Chapter XI

No. 75–B–999

PLAN OF ARRANGEMENT

The above-named debtor proposes the following arrangement with their unsecured creditors:

ARTICLE I
THE DIVISION OF CREDITORS INTO CLASSES

The unsecured debts of the debtor are divided into the following classes:

Class 1. All debts which have priority under Sections 64a (1) (2) (4) and (5) of the Bankruptcy Act.

Class 2. All other debts including claims arising from the rejection of executory contracts.

ARTICLE II
PROVISIONS MODIFYING OR ALTERING
THE RIGHTS OF UNSECURED CREDITORS

1. All debts included in Class 1 are to be paid in cash upon confirmation, or are to be paid in accordance with such agreement as may be made between the holder of such a debt and the debtor.

2. In settlement and satisfaction of all debts included in Class 2, the debtor agrees to deliver to the holders thereof, upon confirmation, five per cent of the indebtedness.

Figure 6–1. A plan of arrangement.

ARTICLE III
PROVISIONS FOR RETENTION OF
JURISDICTION BY THE COURT

1. The Court shall retain jurisdiction until all petitions, if any, to reject executory contracts, to nullify and set aside any liens, to recover property of the debtor, to turn over property to the debtor, or to accomplish any other purpose for which debtor relief is granted by the Bankruptcy Act, are finally adjudicated. The debtor shall have sixty days subsequent to the entry of the Order of Confirmation within which to file any such petition.

2. The Court shall retain jurisdiction for the purpose of allowing or disallowing all claims in accordance with the provisions of Section 369 of the Bankruptcy Act.

3. Except as set forth in paragraphs 1 and 2 above, after the date the Order of Confirmation becomes final, the Court shall retain no further jurisdiction in the matter.

Figure 6–1. Continued.

UNITED STATES DISTRICT COURT
FOR THE EASTERN DISTRICT OF MICHIGAN
SOUTHERN DIVISION

In the Matter of: No. 72–9999–P

TED, INC.,   In Proceedings for
A Michigan Corporation,   Arrangement Under
        Debtor   Chapter XI

NOTICE OF HEARING ON SECOND MODIFIED
ARRANGEMENT AND REOPENED MEETING OF CREDITORS

To the Creditors of the above named Debtor:

NOTICE IS HEREBY GIVEN that on August 16, 1972, the above named Debtor filed a Petition for Arrangement under Chapter XI of the Bankruptcy Act and on September 18, 1973, filed its Second Modified Arrangement. A Hearing on the Second Modified Arrangement and a Reopened Meeting of Creditors will be held in the Courtroom of the Bankruptcy Judge, 1057 Federal Building, Detroit, Michigan on October 25, 1973, at 2:00 P.M., at which time and place the creditors may attend, prove their claims, present written acceptances of the proposed Second Modified Arrangement, examine the Debtor and transact such other business as may properly come before said meeting. You will find a copy of the Second Modified Arrangement attached hereto. Acceptances of the Second Modified Arrangement must be in writing and must be filed with the Clerk of the Court before or at such meeting of the creditors or any adjournment thereof.

NOTICE: IF YOU HAVE PREVIOUSLY FILED A CLAIM, DO NOT FILE ANOTHER.

Dated this 1st day of October, 1973, at Detroit, Michigan.

JOHN DOE, Clerk
U. S. District Court

Figure 6–2.   Notice of a proposed modified arrangement.

In the Matter of:

TED, INC.,   No. 72–9999–P
A Michigan Corporation,
       Debtor

SECOND MODIFIED ARRANGEMENT
FILED SEPTEMBER 18, 1974

TED, Inc. ("Debtor") proposes the following Arrangement:

ARTICLE I
DEFINITIONS AND DIVISION OF UNSECURED DEBTS
INTO CLASSES

1.1 "Class One Debts" means all unsecured debts as allowed by the Court, which have priority under Section 64a(2), (4), and (5) of the Bankruptcy Act.

1.2 "Class Two Debts" means all other unsecured debts as allowed by the Court.

1.3 "Arrangement" means this Second Modified Arrangement.

ARTICLE II
PROVISION ALTERING AND MODIFYING THE
RIGHTS OF UNSECURED CREDITORS

2.1 Class One Debts. Class One Debts are to be paid in full upon confirmation, and allowance of claims.

2.2 Class Two Debts. Class Two Debts shall be settled and satisfied by the issuance to the Holders thereof ("Class Two Creditors") of one share of Debtor's Common Stock ("Stock") for each full $25.00 of Class Two Debts and by "Deferred Payments" to Class Two Creditors of 35% of Class Two Debts upon the terms and conditions set forth in Sections 2.3 through 2.8.

2.3 Distribution of Stock.

(a) The Stock shall be issued by Debtor to a Class Two Creditor upon the later of the following:

    (i) Ten days after date of entry of an Order Confirming this Arrangement.

    (ii) Ten days after the entry of an Order allowing the claim of a Class Two Creditor.

Figure 6–3. Text of a proposed modified arrangement.

(b) Pending the issuance of Stock to Class Two Creditors, and prior to date of hearing on Debtor's application for confirmation, Debtor shall deposit with the Disbursing Officer designated by the Court as nominee for Class Two Creditors, a certificate for 1,727,336 shares of Stock, registered in the name of the Disbursing Officer, which shall be used for transfer of Stock to be issued to Class Two Creditors. If said number of shares exceeds the amount of stock required, the excess shall be returned to Debtor and cancelled. If said number of shares is insufficient to satisfy the obligations of Debtor, Debtor shall issue such additional shares as may be required.

(c) No fractional shares shall be issued to any Class Two Creditor.

2.4 Deferred Payments. Deferred Payments shall be due and payable in the following installments:

Ten per cent	(10%) on or before December 28, 1973
Eight per cent	(8%) on or before December 31, 1974
Five per cent	(5%) on or before December 31, 1975
Three per cent	(3%) on or before December 31, 1976
Three per cent	(3%) on or before December 31, 1977
Six per cent	(6%) on or before December 31, 1978

2.5 Deferred Payments—Interest. The unpaid balance of the Deferred Payments due and payable after January 1, 1974 shall bear interest at the rate of six per cent (6%) per annum from January 1, 1974 to the date of payment. Interest on the entire unpaid balance shall be due and payable on December 31 of each year beginning December 31, 1974, unless any installment is prepaid, in which event accrued interest on the prepaid amount shall be payable at the time of such prepayment.

2.6 Deferred Payments—Collateral. As collateral for the obligation of Debtor to pay the Deferred Payments and the interest thereon, Debtor, when the Order confirming this Arrangement shall be final and all reviews and appeals, if any, from said Order of Confirmation have been dismissed and denied, or the time for taking an appeal or review from said Order of Confirmation has expired, will execute and deliver to a person designated in writing, by a majority of the Creditors' Committee as Trustee ("Trustee") an agreement or agreements ("Security Agreement") which will grant to Trustee a lien, encumbrance and security interest in the following property:

(a) First security interest in all of the issued and outstanding common stock of SEE, Inc.

(b) First mortgage on real estate owned by the Debtor at 10 East Park Road, Highland Park, Michigan.

(c) Security interest in Debtor's interest in store fixtures in operating stores on the date of confirmation, subject to then existing rights and interests of equipment lessors and any other secured party.

Figure 6–3. Continued.

(d) First security interest in all debts (and instruments evidencing said debts) owed to the Debtor as of December 31, 1973 by Hardware Supply and Credits, Inc. other than the following:

(i) Debts due and payable on or before December 31, 1973, and

(ii) Debts of Credits, Inc. to Debtor paid or offset after December 31, 1973 as a result of the transfer by Credits, Inc. to Debtor of the proceeds of loans to Credits, Inc. secured by its accounts receivable, as may be approved, from time to time, by Debtor's Board of Directors.

(e) The proceeds of the Collateral described in Section 2.6 (a) through (d).

(f) Any lien, encumbrance or security interest granted pursuant to this Section 2.6 shall terminate and become null and void if the Order confirming this Arrangement is finally reversed by review or appeal.

2.7 Deferred Payments—Terms of Security Agreement. The Security Agreement shall acknowledge Debtor's indebtedness to Trustee in behalf of all Class Two Creditors. The form of the Security Agreement shall (prior to confirmation) be approved by the Court and by the Creditors' Committee appointed in this cause pursuant to Section 338 of the Bankruptcy Act ("Creditors' Committee") and shall include the following provisions:

(a) At the option of the Trustee, acceleration of the maturity of installments of the Deferred Payments upon the occurrence of an Event of Default as defined in the Security Agreement (including default by Debtor for more than thirty (30) days in the payment of any installment of the Deferred Payments.)

(b) Authorization to Debtor to sell, mortgage or otherwise dispose of the Collateral, free from the lien of the Security Agreement, upon consent of a majority of the Creditors' Committee, which consent shall not be withheld in the event of a proposed sale at fair market value. The proceeds of any sale, mortgage or other disposition of the Collateral shall be applied on installments and accrued interest next due under Section 2.4.

(c) No Class Two Creditors shall institute any proceeding to enforce the Security Agreement unless Class Two Creditors holding a majority in principal amount of Class Two Debts or a majority of the Creditors' Committee shall make written request of Trustee to act and shall have offered Trustee reasonable indemnity against costs, expenses and liabilities to be incurred in connection therewith, and unless Trustee has failed to institute such action within thirty (30) days after such request.

(d) Trustee shall take or refrain from taking any action upon the written instructions of a majority of the Creditors' Committee, including the declaration of a default, and the subordination of the security interest to other security interests which may hereafter be created by Debtor, from time to time.

(e) Trustee shall, upon the written instructions of a majority of the

Figure 6–3. Continued.

Creditors' Committee, amend, modify or alter the Security Agreement in any respect and consent to the discharge or release or subordination of any security interest granted by the Security Agreement.

(f) Trustee shall, upon the written instructions of a majority of the Creditors' Committee, grant to Debtor extensions of time or other modifications of any nature whatsoever.

(g) Trustee may authorize Debtor to make payments of the installments directly to Class Two Creditors and may rely upon Debtor's certification that such payments have been made.

(h) The Security Agreement shall (i) require Debtor to reimburse Trustee and the Creditors' Committee for all costs and expenses, including reasonable attorneys' fees, incurred by them in performing their duties thereunder, and in enforcing or protecting the security interests, and (ii) secure such obligation of Debtor.

2.8 Deferred Payments—Partial Subordination. In the event of an entry by the Court of an Order directing that bankruptcy be proceeded with pursuant to Section 377 of the Bankruptcy Act, debts incurred by Debtor after the date of confirmation of this Arrangement shall have priority over the debts affected by this Arrangement to the extent that any installments of the Deferred Payments other than the 10% payment due on or before December 28, 1973 may not have then been paid, or may not thereafter be satisfied by liquidation of the collateral granted by Debtor, pursuant to Section 2.6. The collateral security provided for in Section 2.6 shall remain available at all times as security for the Deferred Payments pursuant to Section 2.4, notwithstanding the foregoing partial subordination.

2.9 Modification of Rights. The rights of the holders of Class Two Debts shall be modified and altered in accordance with the provisions of this Article II.

ARTICLE III

PROVISIONS FOR THE REJECTION OF EXECUTORY CONTRACTS

3.1 Certain Contracts.

(a) Debtor hereby rejects the executory contracts listed in Exhibit A to the extent that they have not as of the date of filing this Arrangement been terminated or rejected by the terms of the contract, or by action of the parties, or by Order of the Court.

3.2 Equipment Leases. Debtor hereby rejects the equipment leases and all extensions, modifications and supplements thereto, as described in Exhibit B attached hereto, and all covenants and agreements of Debtor contained in said leases, including the covenant of Debtor to return the goods to the lessor upon the expiration, termination or cancellation of the lease; provided however, that this section shall not be applicable to any of said leases which are determined by the Court to be security agreements as defined in the Uniform Commercial Code.

Figure 6–3. Continued.

3.3 Future Rejections. Debtor may reject such other executory contracts as Debtor may hereafter determine, which rejection shall be accomplished by filing a notice of rejection, together with an affidavit of mailing of such notice upon all parties affected by said rejection, with the Court on or before the entry by the Court of an Order of confirmation of Debtor's arrangement.

3.4 Cancellation of Rejections. Debtor may hereafter withdraw and cancel its rejection of any executory contract hereunder rejected by filing written notice of such cancellation, together with an affidavit of mailing thereof, upon all parties affected thereby, with the Court on or before the date of entry by the Court of an Order of Confirmation of Debtor's Arrangement.

Article IV
Special Provision Relating to Certain Equipment Leases

4.1 Purchase Agreements. During April and May of 1973, Debtor, with the approval of the Court, entered into purchase agreements with its major equipment lessors, Greyhound Leasing and Financial Corporation, Commercial Credit Industrial Corp., C C Leasing Corporation, General Electric Credit Corporation, Lease Financing Corporation, and Ford Motor Credit Company. Under said agreements, as modified, Debtor agreed to purchase and the equipment lessors agreed to sell the equipment described in various equipment leases for an aggregate consideration of $2,793,000.00. The rental payments made by the Receiver after dates specified in the agreements apply against the purchase price. Upon payment of the purchase price and performance by Debtor of its obligations under the purchase agreements, as modified, Debtor will become the owner of the leased equipment, and such payment and performance will be in full satisfaction of all claims of the equipment lessors. If the purchase price is paid in full on or before December 28, 1973 no interest shall accrue. If the purchase price is not paid in full on or before December 28, 1973, each equipment lessor has the option to declare its purchase agreement null and void. If said option is not exercised, and if the purchase price is paid after December 28, 1973, the purchase price shall bear interest at the rate of six per cent (6%) per annum commencing June 1, 1973.

4.2 Deposit of Purchase Price. The purchase agreements, as modified, require the deposit of the purchase price to be made as follows: one-half (½) of the present balance of the purchase price less an amount equal to the reductions attributable to rental payments made by the Receiver after the date hereof, shall be deposited by Debtor with the Disbursing Officer at the time Debtor makes its deposit under this Arrangement. The balance

Figure 6–3. Continued.

of the purchase price shall be deposited by Debtor with the Disbursing Officer prior to the date of hearing on Debtor's application for confirmation of this Arrangement.

4.3 Performance by Debtor. Debtor will perform its obligations under the purchase agreements as modified and will deposit the purchase price with the Disbursing Officer as set forth above.

4.4 Payment of Purchase Price. The purchase price shall be paid by the Disbursing Officer to said equipment lessors when the Order confirming this Arrangement shall become final and all reviews and appeals, if any, from said Order of Confirmation have been dismissed and denied, or the time for taking an appeal or review from such Order of Confirmation has expired.

Article V

Special Provisions Applicable to Holders
of Subordinated Debentures

5.1 Recital. The holders of the debentures (Subordinated Creditors) described in Exhibit C attached hereto are the holders of debts of Debtor which are subordinate in payment to the payment in full of certain other named creditors (Senior Creditors), as set forth in the instruments relating to said obligations and as described in Exhibit C. Said obligations are not subordinated to other creditors. Pursuant to the terms of the agreements relating to said obligations, Debtor will make all payments or distributions otherwise payable to a Subordinated Creditor by Article II of this Arrangement to Senior Creditors in proportion to their claims as Senior Creditors, unless otherwise mutually agreed by all of the Senior Creditors.

5.2 Stock Issuance. Debtor will, upon confirmation, issue to the Subordinated Creditors named in Exhibit C an aggregate of 263,305 shares of Debtor's common stock in the number of shares set forth next to his name on Exhibit C. Any right of a subordinated creditor or his successors and assigns to exercise any rights to convert into common stock or to purchase common stock of Debtor under warrants issued by Debtor are hereby terminated. To the extent that any such rights of conversion or stock warrants are executory contracts, they are hereby rejected by Debtor and the distribution provided in this Section 5.2 shall be in full settlement and satisfaction of any claim relating to such rejection.

5.3 Conditions Precedent. The obligation of Debtor to issue stock under Section 5.2 to any Subordinated Creditor is conditioned upon:

(a) Such subordinated Creditor furnishing to the Debtor within ten (10) days after entry by the Court of an Order determining Debtor's Arrangement to have been accepted, a written instrument executed by him and by the holders of all warrants which may have been

Figure 6–3. Continued.

issued to him together with his debentures, consenting to the termination of conversion or stock purchase rights (as the case may be) and waiving all claims against the Debtor arising from such termination and rejection.

(b) Such Subordinated Creditor furnishing to Debtor a written waiver and consent by each Senior Creditor who is senior to such Subordinated Creditor stating in substance that the Senior Creditor waives any right under the subordination provisions of the subordinated debenture to claim the stock to be issued to the Subordinated Creditor under this Section 5.2. Failure of any Subordinated Creditor to fulfill said conditions in whole or in part, shall reduce pro rata the stock to which such Subordinated Creditor would otherwise be entitled and shall not increase the number of shares to be issued to any other Subordinated Creditor.

ARTICLE VI
PROVISIONS FOR PAYMENT OF DEBTS INCURRED DURING
PENDENCY OF ARRANGEMENT AND PERFORMANCE OF
CONTRACTS ENTERED INTO BY RECEIVER

6.1 Assumption of Receiver's Contracts. Debtor assumes and agrees to perform all contracts entered into by the Receiver between the date of the filing of the petition herein and the date upon which Debtor's business is returned to Debtor, and Debtor agrees to indemnify and hold the Receiver harmless from any liability relating thereto.

6.2 Payment of Receiver's Debts. All debts incurred by Receiver after the filing of the petition herein and prior to the date upon which the Receiver returns Debtor's business to Debtor shall (to the extent not paid by the Receiver from funds retained by him) be paid by Debtor when said debts become due; and such debts until paid, shall have priority over debts affected by this Arrangement.

ARTICLE VII
PROVISIONS FOR RETENTION OF JURISDICTION BY THE COURT

After confirmation of Debtor's Arrangement and until entry of a final decree or judgment under Section 372 of the Bankruptcy Act, the Court shall retain jurisdiction for the following purposes:

7.1 Claims. To allow and disallow claims not finally allowed or disallowed prior to confirmation; and to disallow in whole or in part, any claim which, before confirmation, may have been provisionally allowed for voting purposes. The failure by Debtor to object to the voting of any claim shall not be deemed to be a waiver of Debtor's right to object to said claim, in whole or in part, thereafter.

Figure 6-3. Continued.

7.2 Pending Controversies. To hear and determine any controversy pending on the date of confirmation as a result of a petition filed before confirmation by a party to these proceedings or by any creditor or other person.

7.3 Valuation of Collateral. To value collateral held by secured creditors and to provide for payment thereof.

7.4 Injunctions. Upon the application of Debtor, and upon proper notice and showing of good cause, to issue such orders and injunctions as may be necessary or desirable to effectuate the rehabilitation purposes of Chapter XI of the Bankruptcy Act.

7.5 Classification of Creditors. As to claims timely filed, to hear and determine any controversy, relating to the classification of any creditor under Article I of this Arrangement, or to the classification of any creditor, in whole or in part, as a secured or unsecured creditor.

7.6 Allowance of Compensation. To enter orders allowing compensation to those persons entitled to receive compensation as expenses of administration under the provisions of the Bankruptcy Act.

7.7 Unliquidated Claims. To exercise jurisdiction relating to timely filed claims which are unliquidated or contingent or both, even though proceedings by the holder of any such claim may have been instituted in any state or federal court prior to the filing of the original Petition herein; and to allow or disallow any such claim on its merits, at any time after confirmation. Upon the allowance of unsecured claims against Debtor, they shall become Class Two Debts, and Debtor shall thereupon make payment and settlement thereof as provided in Article II.

7.8 Receiver's Obligations. To hear and determine all controversies relating to the obligations of the Receiver incurred in the conduct of Debtor's business prior to confirmation, and to the payment or performance thereof as provided in Article VI.

7.9 Distribution of Consideration. To hear and determine all controversies relating to the distribution of the stock to be issued by Debtor, pursuant to Article II hereof.

7.10 Jurisdiction over Defaults. If Debtor defaults in the payment of any installment under Section 2.4 for more than thirty (30) days without curing said default, or if any other Event of Default as defined in the Security Agreement shall occur, the Court may, upon petition by Trustee, enter an Order, pursuant to Section 377 of the Bankruptcy Act, adjudicating the Debtor a Bankrupt and directing that bankruptcy be proceeded with, or dismissing this proceeding, whichever in the opinion of the Court may be in the best interest of creditors.

7.11 Creditors' Committee. To hear and determine all controversies relating to the composition of the Creditors' Committee and to approve the filing of any vacancy in the Creditors' Committee caused by any reason

Figure 6–3. Continued.

whatsoever, if requested by any member of the Creditors' Committee. The Creditors' Committee shall remain in existence and continue to function until entry of final judgment or decree.

7.12 Controversies re Security Agreement. To hear and determine all controversies relating to the Security Agreement.

7.13 Election of Directors. To compel Debtor to elect directors as required by Section 8.1.

ARTICLE VIII
MISCELLANEOUS PROVISIONS

8.1 Corporate Action. Immediately after the entry of an Order of Confirmation, Debtor's Board of Directors will take such action as is necessary to have a Board of Directors consisting of five (5) persons and will cause three (3) persons designated by the Creditors' Committee to be elected as directors of the Debtor.

8.2 Costs and Expenses of Proceeding. All costs and expenses of this Arrangement proceeding as allowed by the Court, shall be paid in full, in cash upon confirmation.

8.3 Return of Business to Debtor. Immediately upon the entry of an Order of Confirmation of Debtor's Arrangement, Debtor's business shall be returned to it and shall thereafter be conducted by Debtor and not by the Receiver.

TED, INC., A Michigan Corporation
Debtor

By: JONES & JONES
Attorneys for Debtor

By   T. I. Jones
10 A Building Row
Detroit, Michigan 48221

DATED: 18th September, 1973

Figure 6–3.   Continued.

41. Any amended plan of arrangement must make provision for taxes which are due at the time the petition was filed. Certain principles govern such a situation. No compromise of taxes will be allowed, but installment payments may be allowed, if good cause is shown. The dollar-for-dollar principle and the time-limitation principle must also be followed. These mean that the taxing authorities must be paid in cash as a down payment a sum at least equal to the amount to be paid unsecured creditors upon confirmation of the plan, with the balance to be paid in monthly installments over a period of time no longer than that allowed for unsecured creditors.[7]

ADDITIONAL OR OTHER SERVICES

42. The independent accountant will normally expand an examination of a client with financial difficulties, ascertaining that all liabilities have been recorded, all requirements of loan agreements have been met, and any departures with their possible consequences have been disclosed. The accountant will also be concerned with determining that none of the assets has been stated at an amount exceeding its realizable value.[8]

43. In conducting an audit, the independent accountant will primarily examine the accounts and prepare the financial statements. This investigation will consist of examining any unusual transactions which occurred before proceedings were initiated, with utmost attention to any transactions which resulted in the dissipation of assets from factors other than losses in the ordinary course of the business. These normally include a transfer or concealment of assets; preferential payments to creditors; transactions with related parties not conducted at arm's length; major acquisitions, mergers, and investments which resulted in a loss; acquisitions of property at exorbitant prices; and any bulk sale of assets or of a part of the business. The independent accountant should describe these trans-

[7] *Ibid.,* p. 431.
[8] Paul Conner, "Financial Reporting for Companies in Financial Difficulty," *Oklahoma CPA,* Vol. 7 (October 1968), p. 22.

actions in as much detail as is possible and analyze their effect on the financial position of the firm.[9]

44. When retained for a proceeding under Chapter X, the independent accountant renders services for the trustee and has the same duties as for a debtor-in-possession, plus the responsibilities connected with an audit and investigation of the business. An investigation in a reorganization proceeding is much more extensive than that required in an arrangement. The independent accountant must conduct a thorough inquiry into the acts, conduct, property, financial condition, business transactions, history, and background of the debtor to determine whether the present management should be retained and whether a successful plan can be worked out. Everything that will help to establish the causes of the failure, including the conduct, attitudes, business judgment, and insight of the officers, directors, and managers, should be scrutinized.

45. In all liquidation proceedings, the independent accountant's primary duty is to indicate the areas where there may have been wrongdoing, misconduct, or misappropriation. It is then the attorney's job to determine whether there has been a violation of the law.

Accounting Services and the Granting of New Credit

46. The accountant may also assist the debtor in acquiring additional credit. Special schedules are prepared for the debtor in order to provide the credit grantors with the desired information.

47. Apart from the desire of the credit community to aid in the rehabilitation of a debtor, there are several business reasons for granting credit during a period of arrangement:

> Assets are unencumbered by old liabilities during this period and hence there is a substantial asset value as a basis for the granting of credit. This is true for all credit grantors, not only members of the creditors' committee and "pre-arrangement" creditors.
>
> Many creditors have obligations on bill-and-hold goods and on commitments. With proper credit lines, the liquidation of bill-and-hold goods and commitment position can be accomplished with minimum losses.

[9] Edward A. Weinstein, "Accountant's Examinations and Reports in Bankruptcy Proceedings," *New York Certified Public Accountant*, Vol. 35 (January 1965), pp. 31, 38–39.

Many creditors may be dealing with the debtor as an important customer and hence it is vital to keep this concern functioning as a user of their goods.

A proper credit line will provide for earlier distributions to the creditors without undue risk. Controls will prevent a distribution if it is felt that it would have a detrimental effect in any way on new creditors.

A debtor with credit lines should be able to operate the business in a more efficient fashion and thus maximize the payment to general creditors.

48. The debtor must not emerge from the arrangement as a credit risk. The company must be able to go to its creditors in the early stages of the arrangement period and receive the assistance it needs to re-establish itself in the business community and come out of the arrangement with the confidence of its creditors. During the arrangement period the accountant can be of valuable assistance by helping the creditors understand the problem areas and the financial statements so that the groundwork for future credit granting can be established.

ROLE OF THE SEC

49. The SEC has an interest in all Chapter X proceedings and an interest under other chapters if a public company is involved or if a considerable public interest is served by the company. Very frequently, the proceeding may be instigated as a result of an action brought by the SEC. The SEC has recently adopted a policy of examining with greater scrutiny financial reports which contain qualified statements as to viability or uncertainties involving the determination of financial position and the results of operations. A flood of letters to the SEC from dissatisfied shareholders, or volatility in the stock—primarily declines where shareholders may be hurt—may create immediate action from the SEC. Under these conditions, the SEC will hold an inquiry and often invite the accountant to explain the accounting treatment and position as to the statements. As a result of these hearings the stock may even drop further and the debtor may then become aware of the need to file a petition under Chapter X or Chapter XI.

50. Procedurally, once the company has filed the petition, the SEC's reorganization division will step in and assign an attorney and an analyst, who is often an accountant, to work on the case. If the company is a broker or dealer in securities, the SEC will assign someone from the broker–dealer section to the case. As a party to the proceedings the SEC must be served with copies of all motions and all papers filed with the court. From a practical standpoint, if the case is one of significance, the SEC will work very closely with the other parties to the proceedings. Representatives will attend meetings which are held among counsel, trustees, receivers, and accountants and they will participate in the discussion, at times almost to the point of making management decisions.

51. The SEC also determines whether the action taken by the debtor-in-possession or the trustee is within what it believes to be the interpretation of the law. It will see that proper notices are given for property sales, payments to creditors, or payments to shareholders. The SEC is also a source of background information for the accountant since it retains copies of all public documents filed. The accountants in an initial audit of a public company often spend the first week reviewing the documents that have been filed, collecting all published financial data, and obtaining copies of the statements filed with the SEC as a means of trying to determine what has happened. Also, the SEC may have subpoenaed records which the accountant needs to review. There is a need for close rapport and participation between the SEC and the accountants involved in the proceeding.

52. The SEC's chief role is to protect the public's interest. As a result the accounting firm may find that, even though the payment of its fees is a priority item, it often comes out second best. The SEC may not object to the principals' satisfying the demands of customers in order to avoid any criminal actions brought about by dissatisfied customers.

53. The SEC plays another role in keeping the proceedings moving. Very often, the attorneys for the debtor and creditors have a backlog of cases they are attempting to resolve. Consequently, after the initial impact a slowdown of activities will occur. The SEC acts as a very welcomed motivating influence to move things along.

54. The staff of the SEC has a high level of technical knowledge. They can very frequently offer the attorneys, and to some extent the accountants, guides as to how procedural problems may be resolved. They are a very fertile source of information.

PROFESSIONAL CONDUCT OF ACCOUNTANTS

55. As in any engagement, the accountant must be competent and ethical. The role of the accountant is crucial in the proceedings, especially for the referee who must preserve and restore the business, protect the rights of creditors, and decide between rehabilitation or liquidation. In making these decisions, the referee relies on the accountant for objective and unbiased opinions. It is important to remember that the accountant is a quasi-officer of the court and owes primary responsibility to it. All of the accountant's findings must be disclosed to the court.

Personal Liability—Preparation of Financial Statements

56. The accountant should strictly adhere to generally accepted auditing standards and procedures and statement presentation. Full disclosure is required, as well as clear and unambiguous language, in the report relating to any auditing procedures not undertaken by the debtor's independent accountant. These may include observation of physical inventory, confirmation of accounts receivable or cash in banks, verification of potential or present legal liabilities of the debtor, or verification of security arrangements. Generous use of footnotes and comments to the financial statements is advisable.

57. Where the practice has been to issue unaudited financial statements for the use of management only, particular care must be given by the debtor's independent accountant in the preparation of financial statements to be submitted to a creditors' committee or other interested third parties.

58. Since the report of the debtor's accountant is being examined by and relied upon by third parties, the accountant must be extremely careful about reliance upon management's oral representations as to various transactions, and must insist on written

documentation. This danger often lurks in non-cash transactions such as the following:

Accounts receivable–accounts payable set-offs where the same party is a customer and a creditor

Satisfaction of a trade liability by the transfer of fixed assets

Private arrangement involving the collection of a customer's account but an oral representation that the account is uncollectible

Professional Conduct of Debtor's Accountant—Toward Client

59. At the time the client recognizes that bankruptcy is imminent, there often exist unpaid bills for services rendered by the accountant. The decision as to whether to liquidate or reorganize will depend to a great extent on the information which the debtor's accountant prepares for review by the client and the attorney. The accountant must decide whether these additional, usually time-consuming services should be rendered when payment for them is very doubtful. Both ethical and practical considerations are involved. The resolution of the ethical aspects depends on the standards and the subjective motives of the individual practitioner. Some aspects of the practical side of this question which have bearing on the ethical issues should be considered.

60. The withdrawal of the accountant's services at this time will not prevent allegations from arising, however unjustified, regarding the failure of the accountant to exercise professional judgment prior to the withdrawal. It may be easier for the accountant to explain the basis of professional acts as an actively participating party in contact with the debtor's attorney, incoming creditors' accountant, or the creditors' committee, rather than as an outsider looking in while unjustified assumptions are being made. The creditors' committee is interested in finding as many recoveries as possible. One source is from the legal and professional staff of the debtor. If there is any indication, whether justified or unjustified, that the accountants of the debtor failed to exercise due care, this is often pursued by the legal staff of the committee.

61. Withdrawal at this time subjects the accountant's client to the findings of the accountant for the creditors' committee and to the assumptions drawn in the course of that review. The presence

of the debtor's accountant and interpersonal contact with the accountant representing the creditors' committee can explain or document various transactions which otherwise might be damaging to the client in negotiations with the creditors. If the debtor's accountant withdraws before the books and records are completed, treatment of individual items is left to the accountant for the creditors' committee. An example of this occurred where an accountant for a trustee in bankruptcy, working on the uncompleted books and records of a bankruptcy partnership, treated bank debit memos entered on the bank statements as an item of cost of goods sold. This resulted in a deficit gross profit on sales, which the trustee successfully used in court to deny the discharge in bankruptcy of the partnership and the individual partners on the basis of fraud. In reality, the debit memos represented insufficient-funds checks of customers; however, the damage had been done and no amount of oral testimony could correct the matter. Premature withdrawal of accounting services from an ailing business operation may result in a disservice not only to the client but to the accountant as well.

62. The debtor's accountant should appraise the client of what the creditors expect and what the debtor should or should not do during the interim period from the time of determination of imminent bankruptcy to the actual negotiations with creditors. The accountant will want to identify for the client the prebankruptcy acts that can result in criminal fraud charges, obviate the cooperation of creditors, or prevent a discharge in bankruptcy. The client should be aware of the fact that if the company's integrity is questioned very little cooperation can be expected from the creditors.

Professional Conduct of Debtor's Accountant— Toward Creditors' Accountant

63. One of the most frequent complaints of incoming independent accountants for creditors is the difficulties encountered in obtaining the necessary books of account of the debtor and various documentary evidence as the investigation proceeds. The duty of the incoming accountant is to the creditors and to the court. There is no room here for camaraderie between accountants but only for

the fulfillment of professional, legal, and ethical responsibilities. The debtor's accountant, therefore, should undertake to do the following in order to facilitate the work of the accountant for the creditors' committee:

> Assist in locating all books of accounts and records.
>
> Explain the debtor's accounting system.
>
> Aid in obtaining documents requested by the creditors' accountant.
>
> Permit the accountant for the creditors' committee to review the debtor's accountant's workpapers as they relate to specific questions raised. There would appear to be no obligation for the debtor's accountant to release possession of his workpapers for a general review by the creditors' accountant.
>
> Make available copies of all requested tax returns of the debtor and discuss potential trouble areas in the event of an audit by a taxing agency.

64. In one instance, an arrangement with creditors failed because of a New York City business tax audit assessment which reduced the available assets below the agreed settlement percentage. The reason for this unnecessary occurrence was the debtor's accountant's failure to forward copies of the debtor's tax returns as requested by the creditors' accountant. These returns revealed that the debtor had used an incorrect gross sales base in calculating the New York City gross business tax. If the creditors' accountant had been aware of this error, the potential audit assessment would have been considered in determining the percentage creditors would receive.

65. A question frequently asked the creditors' accountant by the creditors' committee is, "Did the debtor's accountant fully cooperate with you?" A negative answer will often result in the adoption of a poor attitude by the creditors' committee toward the debtor.

Direct Liability to Third Parties

66. The degeneration of the financial condition of a client's business operation creates natural alarm among creditors, credit agencies, bank loan officers and various other financial institutions dealing with the debtor. The debtor's accountant, who previously

had no direct contact with third parties, becomes very popular with them as they search for additional financial information relating to the debtor. The general integrity of the independent accountant will, no doubt, cause these very same third parties to rely upon any oral assertions made by the debtor's accountant. With complete awareness of professional status as it relates to conduct and to personal legal liability under these conditions, the accountant:

Should not engage in off-the-record conversation or written communication with third parties.

Should, officially and on the record, discuss the debtor's financial position when called upon by a proper third party, but only as to information reflected on the books and records of the client. It is advisable not to give personal opinions as to the future prospects of the client, whether they be good or poor, regardless of the sincerity of a personal opinion.

Should not submit a tentative financial statement to any third party unless all the required auditing standards and procedures and statement presentation standards have been followed.

Should seriously weigh the advisability of extending good offices in securing additional financing for the client where, in the accountant's judgment, repayment is highly doubtful.

Should avoid unofficial or informal contact with the various national and local credit reporting agencies but submit, as requested, financial statements fully documented and prepared in accordance with generally accepted accounting principles.

Other Professional Ethical Factors

67. Many ethical questions are raised when the accountant is involved in bankruptcy and insolvency proceedings. One question, which deserves careful consideration, arises when the accountant represents both the debtor and the creditors. This situation gives rise to some possible conflicts of interest, one of the largest involving the level of disclosure for which the accountant is responsible. The creditors will want to know as much as possible about the operations of the debtor. However, to reveal everything may prove misleading and unduly detrimental to the bankrupt. In this position the accountant must find the correct point between adequate disclosure so that creditors may protect their interests and avoid-

ance of excess disclosure which may injure the debtor. Because of the problem of independence created when the accountant represents both debtor and creditors, some firms actively involved in bankruptcy and insolvency engagements will not serve as accountants for both, while others believe they can effectively represent both debtor and creditors.

68. The accountant is often required to assist the creditors' committee in exercising control over the assets of the debtor. The accountant's independence would appear to be impaired by performance of functions for the debtor which are generally performed by management. The Ethics Division of the AICPA has ruled that the following functions cannot be performed if the accountant is to remain independent:

Cosign checks issued by the debtor corporation.

Cosign purchase orders in excess of established minimum amounts.

Exercise general supervision to insure compliance with the budgetary controls and pricing formulas established by management, with the consent of the creditors, as part of an overall program aimed at the liquidation of deferred indebtedness.

EXAMPLES OF OPERATING STATEMENTS

69. The preparation of financial statements to be filed with the court constitutes an important part of the accountant's function in bankruptcy proceedings. On the pages that follow, two examples of operating statements as filed are shown in their entirety. The first (pages 171–76) is an operating statement of a debtor as of a certain date. The second (pages 177–85) is a forecast or projection of operating results for a future period. Text discussion of these statements and the conditions surrounding their filing can be found in paragraphs 16–19 and 22–24 of the chapter.

UNITED STATES DISTRICT COURT
SOUTHERN DISTRICT OF NEW YORK

```
* * * * * * * * * * * * * * *
                              *
        In the Matter         *
                              *
            of                *          In Proceedings for
                              *          the Reorganization
    TRAC INDUSTRIES, INC.,     *          of a Corporation
                              *          _____
              Debtor          *            No. 73-B-999
                              *
* * * * * * * * * * * * * * *
```

OPERATING STATEMENT

August, 1975

**(With Summary of Receipts and Disbursements
and Federal Withholding Taxes)**

Exhibit I

JOHN JONES AND TIM DOE
AS TRUSTEES OF TRAC INDUSTRIES, INC. (DEBTOR)
UNDER CHAPTER X, IN PROCEEDINGS FOR REORGANIZATION

STATEMENT OF INCOME
For the Period August 1–August 31, 1975
(Unaudited)
(In Thousands)

	Totals	T. P. Lotter	Corporate Office
Net Sales	$381	$381	$ —
Cost of Goods Sold (Schedule 1)	191	191	—
Gross Profit	190	190	—
Direct Operating Expenses:			
Store Payroll	65	65	—
Rent and/or Building Depreciation	44	44	—
Advertising	2	2	—
Fixture Depreciation and Rentals	7	7	—
Other	48	48	—
Total Direct Operating Expenses	166	166	—
Other Expenses:			
Warehouse	8	8	—
Repair and Maintenance	2	2	—
General and Administrative Expenses (Schedule 2)	64	42	22
Credit Operations—Net	2	2	—
Total Other Expenses	76	54	22
Total Direct and Other Operating Expenses	242	220	22
Operating Income (Loss)	(52)	(30)	(22)
Other Income (Expense)—Note A	51	(2)	53
Income (Loss)—Note B	$ (1)	$ (32)	$ 31

Note A—Other Income (Expense) consists of the following:

	Totals	T. P. Lotter	Corporate Office
Allocation of corporate office expenses for the fiscal year ended 2/2/76	$ (2)	$ (2)	$ —
Interest income on certificates of deposit	53	—	53
Total	$ 51	$ (2)	$ 53

Note B—This statement does not reflect accrual of interest on any Trac Industries, Inc. indebtedness existing at May 27, 1973, nor of any legal or administrative costs of the trustees. Likewise, no provision has been made for interest charges by Trac Industries, Inc., to any of its subsidiary companies.

Schedule 1

JOHN JONES AND TIM DOE
AS TRUSTEES OF TRAC INDUSTRIES, INC. (DEBTOR)
UNDER CHAPTER X, IN PROCEEDINGS FOR REORGANIZATION

ANALYSIS OF COST OF GOODS SOLD

For the Period August 1–August 31, 1975
(Unaudited)
(In Thousands)

	Totals	T. P. Lotter	Corporate Office
Beginning Inventory	$1,643	$1,643	$ –
Material Purchases	183	183	–
Total Available for Sale	1,826	1,826	–
Ending Inventory	1,635	1,635	–
Cost of Goods Sold	$ 191	$ 191	$ –

Schedule 2

JOHN JONES AND TIM DOE
AS TRUSTEES OF TRAC INDUSTRIES, INC. (DEBTOR)
UNDER CHAPTER X, IN PROCEEDINGS FOR REORGANIZATION

GENERAL AND ADMINISTRATIVE EXPENSES

For the Period August 1–August 31, 1975
(Unaudited)
(In Thousands)

	Totals	T. P. Lotter	Corporate Office
Executive Salaries	$ 13	$ 9	$ 4
Other Payroll	28	21	7
Payroll Taxes and Fringes	3	3	–
Supplies	2	2	–
State and Local Taxes	8	–	8
Travel and Entertainment	4	4	–
Communications	3	2	1
Depreciation and Amortization	–	–	–
Equipment Rentals	2	2	–
Professional and Consulting Fees	1	1	–
Rent	2	–	2
Other	(2)	(2)	–
	$ 64	$ 42	$ 22

Exhibit II

JOHN JONES AND TIM DOE
AS TRUSTEES OF TRAC INDUSTRIES, INC. (DEBTOR)
UNDER CHAPTER X, IN PROCEEDINGS FOR REORGANIZATION

SUMMARY OF RECEIPTS AND DISBURSEMENTS

For the Period August 1–August 31, 1975

(Unaudited)

Cash Balance, August 1, 1975		$4,838,475
Receipts:		
Sales at Retail Stores	$455,905	
Interest	172	
Tax Refund	—	
Miscellaneous	7,468	
Allocated Corporate Overhead	10,787	
Total Receipts		474,332
Total Available		5,312,807
Disbursements:		
Net Payrolls	104,335	
Payroll Tax Withholding and Expense	25,489	
Sales and Real Property Taxes	16,217	
Merchandise Purchases and Freight	224,017	
Operating Expenses	50,265	
Real Property Rents	52,728	
Insurance	1,206	
Court Expenses	156	
Other Taxes	1,771	
Miscellaneous	—	
Administrative Allowances Disbursed per Court Order	131,653	
Total Disbursements		607,837
Cash Balance, August 31, 1975		$4,704,970*

*Includes short-term investment as follows:
Certificates of Deposit, due 9/4/75–10/23/75: $4,492,087

Exhibit III

JOHN JONES AND TIM DOE
AS TRUSTEES OF TRAC INDUSTRIES, INC. (DEBTOR)
UNDER CHAPTER X, IN PROCEEDINGS FOR REORGANIZATION

ANALYSIS OF FEDERAL WITHHOLDING TAXES

August, 1975

(Unaudited)

Period Ended	Gross Wages	Federal Taxes Withheld			Employer's Share of FICA	Total Taxes	
		FICA	Withholding Tax	Total		Amount	Date Paid
8/10/75	$ 23,422	$1,220	$ 3,304	$ 4,524	$1,220	$ 5,744	8/17/75
8/17/75	35,495	1,793	4,398	6,191	$1,793	7,984	8/21/75
8/24/75	39,490	2,162	5,400	7,562	2,162	9,724	9/ 7/75
8/31/75	34,619	1,784	4,336	6,120	1,784	7,904	9/11/75
Total	$133,026	$6,959	$17,438	$24,397	$6,959	$31,356	

STATE OF NEW YORK
COUNTY OF NEW YORK } ss.:

JOHN JONES, Trustee in reorganization herein, being duly sworn, deposes and says:

That he is the Trustee in reorganization of TRAC Industries, Inc. He has read the attached operating statement and summary of receipts and disbursements, which were prepared by the management of the debtor herein, and same are true and correct according to the best of his knowledge, information, and belief.

_____

JOHN JONES

Sworn to before me this
26th day of November, 1975

_____

Linda Smith
Notary Public, State of New York
No. 03–5464826
Qualified in Bronx County
Certificate filed in New York County
Commission Expires March 30, 1976

NO NAME INCORPORATED

PROJECTED OPERATING RESULTS

November 1, 1974, Through October 31, 1975

———

NO NAME INCORPORATED

COMMENTS ON MANAGEMENT ASSUMPTIONS
INCLUDED IN ACCOMPANYING PROJECTIONS

1. The Balance Sheet as of October 31, 1975, as shown in Exhibit I, has been adjusted to
   reflect the conditions set forth in the plan of arrangement. The adjustment is as
   follows:

Notes Payable—Unsecured	$ 89,592	
Accounts Payable	183,055	
Retained Earnings		$152,547
Goodwill		62,600
Leasehold Improvements		52,400
Additional Paid-In Capital		5,100

   All unsecured debt as of October 30, 1974, the date the petition was filed under
   Chapter XI, has been reduced by 60 percent for a total of $272,647. The deficit in
   Retained Earnings of $152,547 has been eliminated as a result of the anticipated debt
   forgiveness. The Goodwill account was completely written off and the Leasehold
   Improvements account was reduced by $52,400. The balance of the anticipated
   benefit from debt forgiveness of $5,100 has been credited to the Additional Paid-In
   Capital account.

2. Exhibit I reflects the Company's actual Balance Sheet after adjustments as of October 31, 1974, and the projected balance sheet as of October 31, 1975, after giving consideration to the projected operating results and changes in cash flow reflected in the remaining Exhibits.

3. Exhibits II and III reflect projected operating results for the year ending October 31, 1975, and are based on the following major assumptions:

   a. Sales are projected at $1,250,000 annual volume, and are based upon present backlog data as well as historical seasonal patterns.
   b. Cost of sales is projected as 73 per cent of sales.
   c. Purchase costs are assumed to be 46 per cent of sales, and purchase requirements are assumed to be three months prior to shipment.
   d. Payroll taxes are projected at 5.2 per cent of payroll costs.
   e. Building rent is anticipated to increase from $2,000 per month to approximately $3,000 per month in April, 1975, upon moving the Company's operations to new facilities. As of September 30, 1975, the lease agreement would have required payments of $5,000 per month. The lessor has agreed to reduce the payments to $2,000 per month until the expiration of the lease, March 30, 1975. At this time the debtor will be required to vacate the facilities.
   f. The officers of the Company have agreed to a 15 per cent reduction in salary. This reduction is reflected in the Exhibits.

4. Exhibit IV reflects the projected cash flow for the year ending October 31, 1975, and is based on the following major assumptions:

   a. Collections of Accounts Receivable are assumed to be as follows:

   10% of current month's sales
   80   of previous month's sales
   10   of second previous month's sales
   ___
   100%

   b. Additional long-term financing of $100,000 is anticipated. $38,000 will be used to acquire new equipment, which is essential if the company is to continue operating.
   c. All purchases are assumed to be paid for within 30 days of receipt of goods. Substantially all other creditors are paid within the same month of receipt of goods and services, except the ABC Advertising Company which has agreed to delay for one year the billings for advertising services rendered.

5. The forecast is based on the assumption that the plan of arrangement will be accepted.

Exhibit I

NO NAME INCORPORATED

BALANCE SHEETS

For the Year Ending October 31, 1975

(Based Upon Management Assumptions as Set Forth in Accompanying Comments)

Assets

	October 31 1975 (Projected)	October 31 1974 (Actual)
Current Assets:		
Cash (Exhibit IV)	$ 14,690	$ 33,545
Accounts Receivable	114,000	48,799
Inventory	258,049	254,875
Prepaid Expenses	3,388	3,388
Total Current Assets	390,127	340,607
Fixed Assets:		
Machinery and Equipment	119,874	81,874
Leasehold Improvements	28,974	28,974
Furniture and Fixtures	13,058	13,058
	161,906	123,906
Less: Accumulated Depreciation	65,118	47,118
	96,788	76,788
Other Assets:		
Deposits	2,636	2,636
Cash Surrender Value of Life Insurance	2,594	2,594
	5,230	5,230
Total Assets	$492,145	$422,625

Liabilities

	October 31 1975 (Projected)	October 31 1974 (Actual)
Current Liabilities:		
Current Notes Payable—Unsecured	$ 59,727	$ 59,727
Current Notes Payable—Secured	–0–	33,748
Accounts Payable	52,844	122,038
Accrued Expenses	88,496	10,740
Estimated Income Taxes Payable	16,033	–0–
Total Current Liabilities	217,100	226,253
Long-Term Debt	95,823	48,061
	95,823	48,061
Owners' Equity:		
Common Stock—$10 Par Value—8,000 Shares	80,000	80,000
Additional Paid-In Capital	68,311	68,311
Retained Earnings	30,911	–0–
	179,222	148,311
Total Liabilities and Owners' Equity	$492,145	$422,625

NO NAME INCORPORATED

PROJECTED STATEMENT OF OPERATIONS

For the Year Ending October 31, 1975
(Based Upon Management Assumptions As Set Forth in Accompanying Comments)

	Actual	Total	Period 1	Period 2	Period 3	Period 4
Net Sales, All Products	$ 0	$1,250,000	$ 85,000	$120,000	$ 90,000	$190,000
Cost of Sales:						
Beginning Inventory	0	254,875	254,875	304,719	280,703	258,754
Purchases	0	598,000	87,400	41,400	18,400	41,400
Direct Labor	0	141,920	11,700	9,360	12,350	9,880
Manufacturing Burden	0	175,754	12,794	12,824	13,001	14,281
	0	1,170,549	366,769	368,303	324,454	324,315
Less: Ending Inventory	0	258,049	304,719	280,703	258,754	185,615
Cost of Sales	0	912,500	62,050	87,600	65,700	138,700
Gross Profit	0	337,500	22,950	32,400	24,300	51,300
Selling, General and Adm.	0	282,333	23,885	22,595	23,764	22,664
Operating Income	0	55,167	(935)	9,805	536	28,636
Interest Expense	0	8,823	547	660	660	797
Other Income	0	600	50	50	50	50
Income Before Tax	0	46,944	$ (1,432)	$ 9,195	$ (74)	$ 27,889
Provision for Tax	0	16,033				
Net Income	0	30,911				
Retained Earnings (Beg.)	0	0				
Retained Earnings (End)	$ 0	$ 30,911				

Exhibit II

Period 5	Period 6	Period 7	Period 8	Period 9	Period 10	Period 11	Period 12
$ 90,000	$ 40,000	$ 90,000	$110,000	$115,000	$100,000	$105,000	$115,000
185,615	195,706	245,455	254,584	249,163	247,622	254,711	258,200
50,600	52,900	46,000	48,300	52,900	52,900	52,900	52,900
9,880	9,880	13,650	11,400	14,300	11,960	11,960	15,600
15,311	16,169	15,179	15,179	15,209	15,229	15,279	15,299
261,406	274,655	320,284	329,463	331,572	327,711	334,850	341,999
195,706	245,455	254,584	249,163	247,622	254,711	258,200	258,049
65,700	29,200	65,700	80,300	83,950	73,000	76,650	83,950
24,300	10,800	24,300	29,700	31,050	27,000	28,350	31,050
23,074	23,656	24,236	23,106	24,236	23,300	23,310	24,507
1,226	(12,856)	64	6,594	6,814	3,700	5,040	6,543
797	798	798	798	742	742	742	742
50	50	50	50	50	50	50	50
479	$ (13,604)	$ (684)	$ 5,846	$ 6,122	$ 3,008	$ 4,348	$ 5,851

NO NAME INCORPORATED

PROJECTED STATEMENT OF OPERATING EXPENSES

For the Year Ending October 31, 1975

(Based Upon Management Assumptions As Set Forth in Accompanying Comments)

	Actual	Total	Period 1	Period 2	Period 3	Period 4
Manufacturing Burden						
Salaries and Wages:						
Engineering	$ 0	$ 66,450	$ 4,600	$ 4,600	$ 4,600	$ 5,850
Indirect Labor	0	14,000	1,000	1,000	1,000	1,000
	0	80,450	5,600	5,600	5,600	6,850
Payroll Taxes	0	11,556	963	963	963	963
Building Rent	0	26,802	1,613	1,613	1,750	1,750
Heat, Light, and Power	0	10,140	660	670	680	690
Small Tools and Shop	0	1,500	100	100	110	110
Depreciation	0	14,000	1,050	1,050	1,050	1,050
Insurance	0	2,200	160	160	160	160
Property Taxes	0	2,000	400	400	400	400
Maintenance and Repairs	0	3,400	400	400	400	400
Engineering Supplies	0	2,400	200	200	200	200
Employee Benefits	0	7,200	490	510	530	550
Equipment Rental	0	5,550	445	445	445	445
Accrued Vacations	0	8,556	713	713	713	713
Total (Exhibit II)	$ 0	$175,754	$ 12,794	$ 12,824	$ 13,001	$ 14,281
Selling, General and Adm.						
Salaries and Wages:						
Officers	$ 0	$ 87,000	$ 7,250	$ 7,250	$ 7,250	$ 7,250
Office	0	57,015	5,325	4,260	5,325	4,260
	0	144,015	12,575	11,510	12,575	11,510
Payroll Taxes	0	7,492	654	599	654	599
Employee Benefits	0	3,640	270	280	290	300
Accrued Vacations	0	7,200	600	600	600	600
Building Rent	0	4,096	231	231	250	250
Utilities	0	2,220	150	160	170	170
Depreciation	0	4,000	200	200	200	200
Telephone and Telegraph	0	9,410	700	710	720	730
Professional Fees	0	8,000	667	667	667	667
Freight-Out	0	600	50	50	50	50
Office Supplies	0	3,900	325	325	325	325
Travel and Entertainment	0	7,560	630	630	630	630.
Insurance	0	2,800	233	233	233	233
Overtime Premium	0	600	200	0	0	0
Advertising	0	72,000	6,000	6,000	6,000	6,000
Equipment Rental	0	1,200	100	100	100	100
Miscellaneous	0	3,600	300	300	300	300
Total (Exhibit II)	$ 0	$282,333	$ 23,885	$ 22,595	$ 23,764	$ 22,664

Exhibit III

Period 5	Period 6	Period 7	Period 8	Period 9	Period 10	Period 11	Period 12
$ 5,850	$ 5,850	$ 5,850	$ 5,850	$ 5,850	$ 5,850	$ 5,850	$ 5,850
2,000	2,000	1,000	1,000	1,000	1,000	1,000	1,000
7,850	7,850	6,850	6,850	6,850	6,850	6,850	6,850
963	963	963	963	963	963	963	963
1,750	2,618	2,618	2,618	2,618	2,618	2,618	2,618
690	990	970	950	950	950	970	970
120	120	130	130	140	140	150	150
1,050	1,250	1,250	1,250	1,250	1,250	1,250	1,250
160	200	200	200	200	200	200	200
400	0	0	0	0	0	0	0
400	200	200	200	200	200	200	200
200	200	200	200	200	200	200	200
570	590	610	630	650	670	690	710
445	475	475	475	475	475	475	475
713	713	713	713	713	713	713	713
$ 15,311	$ 16,169	$ 15,179	$ 15,179	$ 15,209	$ 15,229	$ 15,279	$ 15,299
$ 7,250	$ 7,250	$ 7,250	$ 7,250	$ 7,250	$ 7,250	$ 7,250	$ 7,250
4,260	4,260	5,325	4,260	5,325	4,435	4,435	5,545
11,510	11,510	12,575	11,510	12,575	11,685	11,685	12,795
599	599	654	599	654	608	608	665
300	300	310	310	320	320	320	320
600	600	600	600	600	600	600	600
250	412	412	412	412	412	412	412
170	230	220	200	190	180	180	200
400	400	400	400	400	400	400	400
740	1,100	760	770	780	790	800	810
667	667	667	667	667	667	667	667
50	50	50	50	50	50	50	50
325	325	325	325	325	325	325	325
630	630	630	630	630	630	630	630
233	233	233	233	233	233	233	233
200	200	0	0	0	0	0	0
6,000	6,000	6,000	6,000	6,000	6,000	6,000	6,000
100	100	100	100	100	100	100	100
300	300	300	300	300	300	300	300
$ 23,074	$ 23,656	$ 24,236	$ 23,106	$ 24,236	$ 23,300	$ 23,310	$ 24,507

NO NAME INCORPORATED

PROJECTED STATEMENT OF CASH FLOW

For the Year Ending October 31, 1975

(Based Upon Management Assumptions As Set Forth in Accompanying Comments)

	Actual	Total	Period 1	Period 2	Period 3	Period 4
Beginning Balance (Exh. 1)	$ 0	$ 33,545	$ 33,545	$ 5,636	$ 938	$ 8,856
Add:						
Accounts Receivable	0	1,184,799	57,299	88,500	117,000	100,000
Other Income	0	600	100	100	0	0
Financing Proceeds	0	100,000	0	50,000	20,000	0
	0	1,285,399	57,399	138,600	137,000	100,000
Deduct:						
Accounts Payable	0	122,038	45,122	19,200	22,400	7,700
Purchases	0	545,100	0	87,400	41,400	18,400
Salaries and Wages	0	366,385	29,875	26,470	30,525	28,240
Payroll Taxes	0	19,048	1,617	1,562	1,617	1,562
Building Rent (Mfg.)	0	26,802	1,613	1,613	1,750	1,750
Heat, Light, and Power	0	10,140	660	670	680	690
Small Tools and Shop	0	1,500	100	100	110	110
Property Taxes	0	2,000	400	400	400	400
Maintenance and Repairs	0	3,400	400	400	400	400
Engineering Supplies	0	2,400	200	200	200	200
Employee Benefits (Mfg.)	0	7,200	490	510	530	550
Equipment Rental (Mfg.)	0	5,550	445	445	445	445
Employee Benefits (Non-Mfg.)	0	3,640	270	280	290	300
Building Rent (Non-Mfg.)	0	4,096	231	231	250	250
Utilities	0	2,220	150	160	170	170
Telephone and Telegraph	0	9,410	700	710	720	730
Freight-Out	0	600	50	50	50	50
Office Supplies	0	3,900	325	325	325	325
Travel and Entertainment	0	7,560	630	630	630	630
Overtime Premium	0	600	200	0	0	0
Advertising	0	10,000	0	0	1,000	1,000
Equipment Rental (Non-Mfg.)	0	1,200	100	100	100	100
Miscellaneous	0	3,600	300	300	300	300
	0	1,158,389	83,878	141,756	104,292	64,302
Insurance	0	5,000	0	0	0	0
Professional Fees	0	8,000	0	0	3,000	0
Capital Additions	0	38,000	0	0	0	5,000
Interest Expense	0	8,879	547	660	660	797
Notes Payable	0	52,238	883	882	882	22,271
Income Taxes	0	33,748	0	0	20,248	0
	0	1,304,254	85,308	143,298	129,082	92,370
Ending Balance (Exh. 1)	$ 0	$ 14,690	$ 5,636	$ 938	$ 8,856	$ 16,486

Exhibit IV

Period 5	Period 6	Period 7	Period 8	Period 9	Period 10	Period 11	Period 12
$ 16,486	$ 63,982	$ 37,461	$ 11,596	$ 1,611	$ 16,166	$ 22,533	$ 24,740
180,000	85,000	45,000	92,000	110,500	113,500	100,500	95,500
0	100	0	100	0	100	0	100
0	0	30,000	0	0	0	0	0
180,000	85,100	75,000	92,100	110,500	113,600	100,500	95,600
25,700	1,916	0	0	0	0	0	0
41,400	50,600	52,900	46,000	48,300	52,900	52,900	52,900
29,240	29,240	33,075	29,760	33,725	30,495	30,495	35,245
1,562	1,562	1,617	1,562	1,617	1,571	1,571	1,628
1,750	2,618	2,618	2,618	2,618	2,618	2,618	2,618
690	990	970	950	950	950	970	970
120	120	130	130	140	140	150	150
400	0	0	0	0	0	0	0
400	200	200	200	200	200	200	200
200	200	200	200	200	200	200	200
570	590	610	630	650	670	690	710
445	475	475	475	475	475	475	475
300	300	310	310	320	320	320	320
250	412	412	412	412	412	412	412
170	230	220	200	190	180	180	200
740	1,100	760	770	780	790	800	810
50	50	50	50	50	50	50	50
325	325	325	325	325	325	325	325
630	630	630	630	630	630	630	630
200	200	0	0	0	0	0	0
1,000	1,000	1,000	1,000	1,000	1,000	1,000	1,000
100	100	100	100	100	100	100	100
300	300	300	300	300	300	300	300
106,542	93,158	96,902	86,622	92,982	94,326	94,386	99,243
0	0	0	2,500	0	0	0	2,500
0	2,000	1,000	0	0	0	1,000	1,000
23,000	0	0	10,000	0	0	0	0
797	798	798	798	798	742	742	742
2,165	2,165	2,165	2,165	2,165	12,165	2,165	2,165
0	13,500	0	0	0	0	0	0
132,504	111,621	100,865	102,085	92,945	107,253	98,293	105,650
$ 63,982	$ 37,461	$ 11,596	$ 1,611	$ 16,165	$ 22,533	$ 24,740	$ 14,690

7

Accounting Services for

the Creditors' Committee

1. The creditors' committee is the representative and bargaining agent for the creditors. The committee often needs an accountant to assist them in protecting their interests. This chapter describes the aspects of the services rendered by the accountant as they relate to the creditors' committee. The auditing services performed for the committee will be only briefly mentioned since a later chapter will be devoted entirely to a discussion of the audit of the corporation involved in bankruptcy and insolvency proceedings. The accountant, in order to adequately represent the creditors, must be thoroughly familiar with the manner in which the creditors' committee works. The services rendered by the accountant include assisting the committee in exercising adequate control over the debtor's activities, completing an investigation and audit of the operations of the business, and assisting the committee in evaluating the proposed plan of settlement or arrangement. Unless specified differently, the term "accountant" as used in this chapter refers to an independent accountant engaged by the creditors' committee.

NATURE OF CREDITORS' COMMITTEE

2. The creditors' committee may be an unofficial or official committee. It is known as an unofficial committee if it is formed to effect a voluntary agreement, out of court, between the debtor and creditor. If the committee is established under the provisions of the Bankruptcy Act, it is known as an official committee. As was discussed in Chapter 3, there are no rigid rules governing the formation of the committee in bankruptcy or out-of-court matters. However, the Bankruptcy Act does include several restrictions designed to permit the selection of a fair and representative committee. If a committee was established before the petition in bankruptcy was filed, this committee is often elected as the committee authorized by the Bankruptcy Act. Although the functions performed by the committee may vary depending on the particular case, the circumstances surrounding the case, and the type of remedy sought, the objective is basically the same: to provide the supervision and control essential to protect the interests of the creditors.

3. The creditors' committee is the "watchdog" over the activities of the debtor. The committee examines all aspects of the firm's operations, including an evaluation of the assets and liabilities. During the period while a plan of settlement or arrangement is being formalized and the period immediately following the acceptance, the committee should closely and constantly supervise the debtor's business, in order to be sure that the assets do not continue to be diminished, wasted, or diverted.

4. The importance of the creditors' committee in Chapter XI proceedings cannot be overemphasized. The objective of the committee is similar to the SEC in Chapter X proceedings in that it counter-balances the strong position of control given to the debtor by the Act.[1] The debtor alone can seek relief under Chapter XI,[2] has the right to petition for continuance in possession,[3] may solicit for acceptance of a proposed plan either before or after filing,[4] and

[1] George Ashe, "Rehabilitation Under Chapter XI: Fact or Fiction," *Commercial Law Journal*, Vol. 72 (September 1967), p. 263.

[2] Bankruptcy Act, Secs. 321–322.

[3] *Ibid.*, Sec. 342.

[4] *Ibid.*, Sec. 336.

may offer amendments or modifications to the plan.[5] Complete domination by the debtor can only be overcome by active participation of the creditors' committee throughout all stages of the proceedings.

Bargaining Process

5. One of the basic functions performed by the creditors' committee is to negotiate a settlement and then make its recommendation to the other creditors. The accountant should be familiar with the bargaining process which goes on between the debtor and the creditors' committee in trying to reach a settlement. Bargaining can be both vigorous and delicate. The debtor bargains for a settlement that consists of a small percentage of the debt, one that demands only a small cash outlay now with payments to be made in the future. The debtor may want the debts outstanding to be subordinated or may ask that the agreement call for partial payment in preferred stock. The creditors want a settlement that represents a high percentage of the debt and consists of a larger cash down payment with the balance to be paid as soon as possible. If the creditors demand too high a percentage, the company may be forced to liquidate, either immediately or at some future date because it cannot make a large payment and still continue to operate. Creditors must not insist on more than the debtor has the ability to pay. However, the creditors cannot afford to accept a settlement that is very low because it establishes a bad example in the industry. In some trade areas all parties involved are almost of one large fraternity. Rutberg suggests that

> A meeting of creditors is like old home week. Everyone seems to know everyone else and there is much shaking of hands and slapping of backs and general good fellowship. It's something like the funeral of a lady who died at ninety-five after a full life and who left a great fortune to be divided up among the surviving relatives.[6]

The creditors do not want to establish a precedent with a settlement which is too low. As a result, the creditors' committee

---

[5] *Ibid.*, Sec. 363.
[6] Sidney Rutberg, *Ten Cents on the Dollar* (New York: Simon and Schuster, 1973), p. 45.

may demand that the debtor be liquidated although they will receive less than would have been received from a low out-of-court settlement.

6. Some basic guidelines may be applicable in certain situations in the bargaining process. First, if a cash payment is called for in the proposal in full or partial settlement, the down payment should at least be equal to the probable dividend to creditors if the business were liquidated. To offer this much is a strong selling point for the debtor. Also, creditors will probably not accept anything less. Second, when a settlement calls for future payments, the creditors' committee often insists that the payments be secured. The security may be in the form of notes of the debtor endorsed by its officers or other individuals acceptable to the committee. The creditors may also desire a mortgage on the debtor's real estate.[7] Third, when an out-of-court settlement includes installment payments over a period of time, Mulder suggests that creditors are likely to insist upon one or more of these safeguards:[8]

> The debtor must execute an assignment for the benefit of creditors. This will be held in escrow, by the creditors' committee, to become effective only if the debtor defaults in subsequent payment. In such an eventuality, the creditors can liquidate the debtor's assets through the assignment, or use the assignment as an act of bankruptcy.
>
> A corporate debtor must require all stockholders to endorse in blank all shares of stock to be held in escrow by the creditors' committee, to become effective only on default by the debtor.
>
> The directors and officers of a corporate debtor must tender resignations to the creditors' committee, to be held in escrow, to become effective only on default by the debtor.
>
> During any period when installment payments are pending, the creditors' committee will exercise control over the operation of the business. The committee, its counsel, its accountant, or a designated person will supervise or control purchases, credit sales, cash inflow and outflow, signing of checks, payrolls, etc.

[7] John E. Mulder, "Rehabilitation of the Financially Distressed Small Business—Revisited," *The Practical Lawyer*, Vol. 11 (November 1965), p. 44.

[8] *Ibid.*, pp. 43–44.

7. In addition, the debtor may be required to reduce expenses that the creditors consider excessive, such as travel and entertainment and officers' salaries.

Role of Creditors' Accountant in the Bargaining Process

8. A creditors' committee meeting will be called as soon as the accountant has completed the audit. If there is enough time, the audit report will be given in advance to all members of the committee. A copy may also be given to the debtor in advance; however, some committees request that the debtor not be given a copy of the report, other than the balance sheet, before the meeting. In an unofficial committee case, where time is crucial, especially in the textile industry, it is not unusual for the accountant to complete the audit only a day or two before the meeting. The first order of business is for the accountant to discuss the audit report orally with the committee. The highlights of the report should be pointed out, any irregularities discovered by the accountant should be described, and the reason for the debtor's financial difficulty should be discussed. The creditors will generally want to know the type of cooperation the accountant received from the debtor in the audit and whether they are dealing with an "honest" debtor.

9. The accountant will at this meeting go over the statement of financial position in general. Then each item will be analyzed and liquidating values will be assigned on the assumption that the business will be liquidated. (For an example of the type of statement of financial position that is issued, see Figures 9–1 and 9–2, on pages 260–65. Normally the accountant does not use liquidation values in preparing this statement; it is based on the going concern assumption. See Chapter 9, paragraphs 47–54.) Liquidating values are established on the basis of the information gained from the accountant's examination and inquiries, the knowledge of the creditors at the meeting, and any appraisals which have been made (see Chapter 6, paragraph 21). If the company is very large, the accountant may prepare for the committee a statement of affairs which would contain the liquidating values (Chapter 9, paragraphs 18–27). The accountant may be reluctant to

prepare a statement of affairs for this meeting without performing additional auditing procedures and inquiries, but there is usually not enough time or funds available for this additional work. If the accountant prepares the statement of financial position in accordance with the format in Figure 9–2, where the assets are reduced by the amount of the obligation for which they are pledged, it will facilitate the discussion.

10. The committee, with the assistance of the accountant, will determine the amount that will be available from the sale of the assets after all priorities are paid. The administrative fees are estimated and the balance represents the amount that would be available to unsecured creditors, a year or two hence.

11. At this point, the debtor and debtor's counsel are brought into the meeting. The debtor's counsel will present the defense of the debtor's operations, and may point out the cause of the financial difficulty and the steps management is prepared to take to prevent the problem from recurring. The counsel then indicates, if the debtor is ready, the terms of the debtor's offer to the creditors. With the assistance of the accountant and the creditors' counsel, the committee will question the debtor about the plan. After considerable discussion about the proposed plan, the committee will send the debtor out of the room and discuss the plan with the accountant and counsel. The committee may reject the plan as it is and submit to the debtor a plan that is acceptable to them, or they may simply suggest that the plan be modified, such as by increasing the cash payment by $.15 per dollar of debt. The negotiations will continue until they come to a consensus. Quite often in a Chapter XI case, where time is not as critical, the committee will want additional time to study the plan and compare, with the assistance of the accountant, the settlement amount in the plan with the amount that would be received upon liquidation.

12. The accountant, in addition to exercising control over the debtor's operations while a settlement is being arranged, will go over the plan with the committee and its counsel, make suggestions as to how it should be modified, and answer any questions the committee has about the plan.

Importance of Cash Flow in the Bargaining Process

13. The emphasis throughout the negotiations is on cash flow. The creditors' committee, as mentioned above, will first determine the amount the creditors would receive upon liquidation. This amount is compared with the suggested settlement amount as shown in the proposed plan. If the plan calls for a future payment, the committee must consider their prospects for receiving the payments. Before the committee can evaluate the plan, it must analyze the projected cash inflow. Normally the debtor, in presenting the plan, will supply statements of projected cash receipts and disbursements to support its claim that at some future date cash will be available to make these payments. The committee's accountant will examine these statements and assist the committee in evaluating the assumptions on which the statements were prepared. The accountant may, based upon the proposed changes suggested by management and the committee's evaluation of them and upon the audit and analysis of the debtor's past operations, prepare a cash flow statement which will be compared with the one prepared by the debtor (see paragraph 23).

IMPORTANCE OF SPEED

14. When the creditors' committee retains an accountant, it usually wants the audit and investigation and resulting statements and reports to be completed as soon as possible so that a plan may be agreed upon quickly. The committee asks for the accountant's report immediately because it is impossible for the committee to take any type of action until it has examined the report and discussed the operations of the bankrupt with the accountant. As soon as the accountant accepts the engagement, he must begin the audit. Accountants who are experienced representatives of creditors can complete the examination and issue the report in a relatively short time. A New York accounting firm recently issued a detailed report on the financial position of a debtor within ten days after the engagement was accepted, even though the company had a sales volume in excess of several million dollars. However, in some complex circumstances, it takes months just to establish the

financial position from the records and much longer to complete the audit.

15. It is advisable to seek a prompt settlement in order to halt the losses which the debtor may be incurring in the operation of its business and to block the possibility of misconduct by the debtor in the form of preferential payments, concealment of assets, or conversion of assets into property that is exempt from liquidation proceedings. Also, in an out-of-court settlement, if there is an extended delay, some of the creditors may file suit for their claims, eventually forcing the debtor to file a petition under Chapter XI.

CONTROLS

16. Supervision of the debtor and its activities is essential throughout the proceedings, beginning with negotiations concerning the settlement and ending only when the plan has been consummated. Control is normally aimed at conservation of the assets, and the creditors' committee holds an excellent position to perform such a function.

17. The importance of the supervisory function of the creditors' committee and of its representation of an unbiased viewpoint that protects the best interests of all the creditors was noted in the *Credit Service* case.[9] There the judge stated that a complete review of the debtor's conduct must be made to ensure that the proposed arrangement is fair, equitable, and feasible, and this "should be made by a disinterested and competent committee for the information of and action thereon by the creditors."[10]

18. The two most crucial time periods during which control must be exercised are the period after the filing of the petition but before agreement on a plan, and the period when installment payments are pending if called for by the plan. One of the key functions performed by the accountant, once the engagement for the creditors' committee has been accepted, is to preserve the assets through performance of an audit (Chapter 8). The first assignment of the accountant is to inventory the books and records (Chapter 8,

[9] 31 F. Supp. 979, 1940.
[10] *Ibid.*

paragraphs 39–42) and count the physical inventory. Recently an accounting firm received a telephoned request for services from the attorney for a creditors' committee. The call came in the morning; that same afternoon the accountants began and completed an inventory of the merchandise on the debtor's premises. The owner, unaware that the inventory had been taken, removed part of the inventory from the warehouse a few days later, hoping to conceal it from the assets of the estate. Obviously, the owner was unsuccessful in the attempt. The accountant, at times, must move very fast in order to exercise adequate control.

19. In addition to an audit, the accounting methods most frequently used to exercise control over the estate include some type of supervision or control over the receipts and disbursements and a statement of review of the debtor's operations.

Receipts and Disbursements Control

20. Direct control can be exercised over all disbursements by having the accountant countersign all checks. It is not unusual for the creditors' committee to make such a request and it was common practice, until very recently, for accountants to sign the checks as part of their services for the creditors' committee. This practice is undesirable because of the ethical and legal implications associated with the signature. The ethical aspects are discussed in Chapter 6 (paragraphs 67–68). If the accountant's signature is on all checks, the inference may be made that the accountant is assuming responsibility for the disbursements. One accounting firm countersigned payroll checks for the debtor, but failed to make sure that the taxes withheld from employees were remitted to the Internal Revenue Service. The funds were used for other purposes for which the accountant countersigned the checks. Officers, debtors-in-possession, and trustees may be held personally liable for failure to remit these taxes. Section 6672 of the Internal Revenue Code imposes a 100 per cent penalty upon a person required to collect and pay over taxes who willfully fails to do so. In this situation the Internal Revenue Service assumed that since the accountant was responsible for signing the checks, he was also responsible for remitting the taxes withheld. Since the debtor did not have any funds to cover the taxes, the accountant personally had to pay the

amount due. A New York accounting firm which formerly countersigned checks, when requested to do so by creditors' committees, now initials all checks before they are issued.

Receipts

21. Even when accountants do not countersign checks, they exercise a constant control function for the creditors because they are in contact with the debtor-in-possession on almost a daily basis. One of the first functions of the accountant is to establish some type of control over the receipts and disbursements. At one time the company may have had an adequate system, but during periods of financial difficulty divisions of responsibility and other internal controls are often not enforced. Key accounting and financial personnel of the company may resign. Responsibilities must be reestablished and proper control must be exercised over all receipts and disbursements. Adequate records of all sales must be maintained and the accountant must see that all cash received from sales and from collections of accounts receivable are deposited intact. Control must also be exercised over purchases, credit sales, returns, and payroll.

Disbursements

22. Before any disbursement is made, the accountant will review all invoices supporting the disbursement and in fact try to justify the expenditure. Certain types of expenditures such as travel and entertainment, professional fees, and other expenses of a personal nature should be carefully examined by the accountant. The accountant will see that only those liabilities are paid which were incurred after the filing of the petition or, in an out-of-court settlement, after the first creditors' meeting. It is also important to make sure that all liabilities incurred for new services are paid promptly.

Cash Flow Reports

23. By establishing a proper system of control, constantly monitoring the system to see that it is functioning properly, and frequently evaluating the cash flow, the accountant observes the day-to-day operations of the business during the time a settlement is

being arranged. Cash flow receives a great deal of attention, primarily because the creditors do not want to see the assets of the business continue to diminish. Normally, the accountant will develop, with the cooperation of the debtor-in-possession, a forecast of the anticipated receipts and disbursements on a periodic basis, usually weekly, for a period of four to six months. At the end of each period, the accountant will submit a report comparing the actual results with the projected estimates. Figure 7–1 is the letter of transmittal which would accompany the report. Figure 7–2 illustrates a statement of cash flow, and Figure 7–3 shows the actual and projected activity of a merchandise inventory account.

24. The accountant for the creditor's committee must take whatever steps seem necessary to insure that the assets do not continue to diminish because of mismanagement, or suspiciously disappear. The amount of control that must be exercised by the committee depends upon such factors as its faith in the debtor's honesty and integrity and whether the debtor has an accountant.

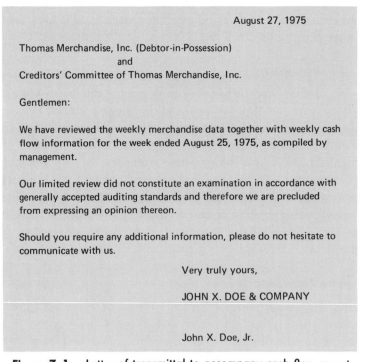

August 27, 1975

Thomas Merchandise, Inc. (Debtor-in-Possession)
            and
Creditors' Committee of Thomas Merchandise, Inc.

Gentlemen:

We have reviewed the weekly merchandise data together with weekly cash flow information for the week ended August 25, 1975, as compiled by management.

Our limited review did not constitute an examination in accordance with generally accepted auditing standards and therefore we are precluded from expressing an opinion thereon.

Should you require any additional information, please do not hesitate to communicate with us.

Very truly yours,

JOHN X. DOE & COMPANY

John X. Doe, Jr.

Figure 7–1.   Letter of transmittal to accompany cash flow report.

THOMAS MERCHANDISE, INC. (DEBTOR-IN-POSSESSION)

STATEMENT OF CASH FLOW

For the Week Ended August 25, 1975

(In Thousands)

	Actual (Unaudited)		Projected
Receipts:			
Transferred from Stores		$ 814	$ 850
Income—Leased Departments		67	54
Miscellaneous		304	120
Adam Drugs, Inc.		930	—
		2,115	1,024
Disbursements:			
Merchandise	$242		$990
Rents	22		—
Payroll	136		139
Other	263		155
		663	1,284
Excess of Receipts over Disbursements		1,452	(260)
Cash—Beginning		2,793	2,793
Cash—End		$4,245	$2,533

Note: This statement is subject to the accompanying letter of transmittal.

JOHN X. DOE & COMPANY

Figure 7–2. Cash flow statement.

THOMAS MERCHANDISE, INC. (DEBTOR-IN-POSSESSION)
MERCHANDISE DATA—APPAREL
Weekly—July–December, 1975

(In Thousands)

Week Ended	Sales Planned	Sales Actual	Orders Placed Retail	Orders Placed Cost	Orders Received Retail	Orders Received Cost	Open Orders— Cost	Cash in Banks	Payments on Purchases	Outstanding Debts to Vendors
1975										
July 28	$ 650	$764	$4,166.0	$2,249.8	$ 360	$ 194.6	$2,055.2	$2,102	—	$ 195
Aug. 4	800	869	2,666.0	1,439.5	1,276	689.1	2,805.6	1,936	$ 11	872
11	800	817	3,276.0	1,768.9	1,940	1,047.6	3,526.9	2,378	87	1,833
18	800	883	956.5	516.5	2,026	1,093.8	2,949.6	2,793	118	2,808
25	850	800*	(752.8)	(406.5)	1,907	1,030.0	1,513.1	4,245	242	3,596
Sept. 1	850		1,100.0	600.0						
8	900		1,100.0	600.0						
15	900		1,100.0	600.0						
22	950		1,100.0	600.0						
29	950		1,100.0	600.0						
Oct. 6	950		1,100.0	600.0						
13	950		1,100.0	600.0						
20	950		1,100.0	600.0						
27	850		1,200.0	650.0						
Nov. 3	1,000		1,200.0	650.0						
10	1,000		1,200.0	650.0						
17	1,000		—	—						
24	1,050		—	—						
Dec. 1	1,150		900.0	500.0						
8	1,250		900.0	500.0						
15	1,450		900.0	500.0						
22	2,350		900.0	500.0						
29	1,200		—	—						

*Estimated.

Figure 7-2.   Summary of merchandise inventory account.

Statement of Review or Preparation

25. Close supervision of the debtor's business operations is desirable to ensure that the assets do not continue to be diminished because of the mismanagement which originally caused the debtor's difficulties. Such control is also necessary to prevent the wasting or diversion of assets. To this end, the creditors' committee may require the debtor to furnish a monthly operating statement so that the committee may review the administration of the business, whether by the debtor or a receiver. In a Chapter XI proceeding, monthly operating statements must be filed with the court (Chapter 6, paragraphs 16–19). This will also put the committee in a better position to reveal to the court what is actually occurring, as well as enabling it to halt any undesirable events much more quickly.

26. Generally, if the debtor attempts to prepare these statements, the reports are inadequate and give a misleading impression of the company's profitability. It is therefore desirable that the committee engage an accounting firm to make an independent review of the debtor's records and prepare its own statements. In some proceedings the accountant for the creditors may also be retained by the debtor to perform the necessary accounting services and prepare the required statements for the committee and the court. At other times the debtor may have its own independent accountant who will prepare the required operating statements. The accountant for the creditors' committee will review the statements and advise the committee of the status of the company's operations. The operating statements are described and illustrated in Chapter 6 (paragraphs 16–19, and pages 171–85).

INVESTIGATION

27. An important function performed by the accountant for the creditors' committee is a thorough examination of the debtor's past business transactions. The primary purpose of such an investigation is to ensure that all assets have been accounted for and any misconduct adequately explained (Chapter 8).

Discovery of Assets

28. It is crucial that the creditors have a knowledge of all the debtor's assets and their value. This includes all that property which may be recovered because it was involved in a preferential transfer, assets which were concealed, and the like. The total assets available to creditors in liquidation must be determined, to ascertain the dividend the creditors would receive in straight bankruptcy and to indicate whether a proposed plan is in their best interests. (See Chapter 8, paragraphs 55–69.)

Discovery of Malfeasance

29. During the audit and investigation of the debtor, the accountant will be on the alert for any transactions which are believed to be questionable, including dishonesty, issuance of false financial statements, concealments, preferential payments, fraudulent transfers, etc. (Chapter 8). Any misconduct even merely suspected by the accountant should be reported to the creditors' committee because it will be taken into consideration by them when deciding whether the debtor should be rehabilitated. Such behavior may also influence the court in deciding to appoint a receiver and not allow the debtor to remain in possession or in requiring that the debtor furnish indemnity to protect the assets of the estate.[11] The discovery of certain types of transactions may cause the debtor to be barred from a discharge of his debts or may constitute an act of bankruptcy to be used in an involuntary petition as provided in the Bankruptcy Act.

AUDIT OF DEBTOR'S BOOKS AND RECORDS

30. The basic duty of the accountant engaged by the creditors' committee is to perform a thorough audit of the debtor's books and records (Chapter 8). This work serves as a foundation from which the accountant will issue statements and reports and conduct any necessary investigations into the debtor's conduct. The creditors must have the results of any such examination to judge whether a

[11] Asa S. Herzog, "CPA's Role in Bankruptcy Proceeding," *The Journal of Accountancy,* Vol. 117 (January 1964), p. 68.

proposed plan is feasible and in their best interests and to decide whether they should accept it.

Special Areas of Interest

31. In formulating an acceptable plan of arrangement the accountant must focus on the following areas, in addition to performing the usual examination of the debtor's books:

> Since an attempt is being made to rehabilitate the business, the creditors will be interested in not only prior years' operations, but also the future potential of the business. The accountant should attempt to provide information regarding the projected volume of the business and estimated gross and net profits. To determine the future success of the business, comparisons should be made of these figures with those typical of the industry.
>
> The causes of the debtor's past losses should be ascertained and measures necessary to eliminate them in the future determined so that the debtor will be able to earn a profit.
>
> The liquidating value of the debtor's assets should be fixed so that while attempting to agree on a plan creditors will know the smallest dividend acceptable to them and have a basis for judging a proposed plan.
>
> To determine the size of the initial payment which it would be possible to make to creditors, it will be necessary to ascertain the status and extent of any liens existing on the debtor's property and secured claims and the amounts owed on priority claims.
>
> The market value of the debtor's assets should be established as this value may be used in any proposed plan. Assets may be reduced to their market values at the time part of the indebtedness is forgiven (Chapter 9, paragraph 81).
>
> An opinion should be given as to the best settlement creditors may expect while also allowing the debtor to be successfully rehabilitated. The accountant should determine whether a better offer could be negotiated for the creditors.
>
> As previously discussed, any unusual transactions should be investigated.

32. In straight bankruptcy proceedings, rather than emphasizing the future potential of the business as in an arrangement,

creditors are concerned with the liquidation value of the debtor's assets and with discovery of any unusual transactions, including the transfer or concealment of assets. Examples of the types of unusual transactions the accountant would seek to discover through the audit are listed below:

Preferential payments made within four months of bankruptcy

Sales of inventory to vendors or other creditors

Fixed assets sold to creditors or others for less than their full value, sold to creditors as an account offset, or resold to the manufacturer as an account offset

The misappropriation of receipts, especially advances from factors

Liens given creditors prior to bankruptcy to enable them to obtain a greater percentage distribution than other creditors

Any assets withdrawn by stockholders in the form of dividends, loans, transfer of assets, etc.

Potential assets, such as pending lawsuits, which might enlarge the size of the estate

All other transactions which may have arisen outside of the ordinary course of the business[12]

PLAN OF ARRANGEMENT

33. As was noted in the previous chapter, the accountant for the debtor provides advice and assistance in the formulation of a plan of arrangement or settlement. An important function of an accountant employed by the creditors is to help them evaluate the proposed plan of action. The accountant is able to provide valuable assistance to the committee because of the familiarity with the financial background, the nature of the operations, and the management of the company gained from the audit. In committee meetings a great deal of time is spent in discussions between the committee members and the accountant concerning the best settlement they can expect and how it compares with the amount they would receive if the business were liquidated. The accountant also gives an opinion as to the debtor's future prospects for profit,

[12] Edward A. Weinstein, "Examining a Company in Bankruptcy," *Quarterly* (Touche, Ross, Bailey and Smart), Vol. 9 (September 1963), p. 18.

assuming the business were not liquidated. (See Chapter 6, paragraphs 20–24 and 40–41.)

RESPONSIBILITIES OF CREDITORS' ACCOUNTANT

34. An accountant retained by the creditors has a primary duty to them and performs all work in their interest. One of the accountant's first concerns will be to inquire into the transactions which have occurred, which will require an audit of the debtor's books and records. One of the purposes of this investigation will be to determine whether there have been any preferential or fraudulent transfers, unexplained losses, or other unusual and suspicious transactions. The creditors' accountant should, however, first ask the debtor about any questionable items rather than indiscriminately making accusations. In the same manner, the accountant will seek to establish the debtor's integrity and the soundness of the debtor's records and statements.

35. Another important function of an accountant employed by the creditors is to help them reach a conclusion about the proposed plan of arrangement. This involves advising them as to the best settlement they can expect and comparing this with the distribution to be received if the business were liquidated. To accomplish this, the forced sale value of the assets must be ascertained and the accountant must give an opinion as to the debtor's future earning power. Here the accountant should also contact the debtor to gain awareness of any situations that should be given consideration.

36. Finally, both the creditors and the accountant are concerned with closely supervising the debtor in order to be sure that the assets do not continue to be diminished, wasted, or diverted, either before a plan is effected or after a settlement is reached. This includes studying the financial statements issued by the bankrupt and being aware of all its actions.

37. The creditors' accountant thus owes them the duty of making sure they know all the facts, investigating anything about which there may be a question, and helping them choose the most advantageous course of action. At the same time there is a responsibility to the debtor to conduct all inquiries in a fair manner and to make sure the information given to the creditors is correct.

8

Audit Procedures and

Special Areas of Inquiry

1. Reporting on insolvent companies requires the application of audit procedures which vary somewhat from those utilized under normal conditions. Much more emphasis is placed on the balance sheet. The audit of a company in financial difficulty is very similar in many respects to the audit of a company that is in the process of being acquired by another. Emphasis is placed on selected accounts and others are completely ignored. In a normal audit the accountant searches for unrecorded liabilities and uses great care to see that the assets are not overstated; however, in a bankruptcy audit the accountant must ascertain that there are no unrecorded or concealed assets.

2. The accountant must be on the alert for indications that occurrences out of the ordinary have taken place. Any transactions which could possibly result in the dissipation of the debtor's assets in a manner other than by loss in the ordinary course of business should be examined closely. These include irregular transfers, transactions with related parties, concealment of assets, false entries and statements, financing irregularities, or preferential payments. In the course of the investigation the accountant may discover a more serious type of irregularity that constitutes fraud. A comparison of the statements filed by the debtor with the company's records may reveal deliberate discrepancies, or missing books or records, erasures and alterations, or the age of the records may indicate that fraud exists.

3. The generally accepted standards and procedures which apply to the normal audit are also relevant to bankruptcy and insolvency proceedings. The financial statements should be presented in accordance with generally accepted principles of accounting.

4. Most of the emphasis in this chapter is on audit procedures which differ from those utilized under normal conditions. The term "accountant" as used in this chapter refers to an independent accountant for either the debtor or the creditors' committee.

NATURE OF AUDIT

5. The steps performed in an audit of a company in financial difficulty are considerably different from the normal audit designed to render an opinion. The purpose of the audit in most bankruptcy

and insolvency cases is to assist interested parties in determining what should be done with the "financially troubled debtor."

Objectives

6. The objective of an audit of the assets is to determine the existence and extent of understated or undisclosed assets. The accountant searches for hidden bank accounts, assets in the name of the owner that were purchased with the bankrupt's funds, preferential payments, valuable assets written off or sold without adequate consideration, and any other unrecorded or concealed assets. Emphasis in the liability accounts is placed on the discovery of transactions which resulted in the reduction or modification of liabilities. The debtor may have granted invalid liens to secured creditors or overstated obligations to related companies. The accountant will search for executory contracts which may have been incorrectly recorded as actual liabilities. The claims filed by creditors will be examined to see that they are not overstated. The equity accounts must be examined to determine whether there are any improprieties which would result in an increase in equity. The debtor may have purchased treasury stock illegally, received inadequate consideration for stock issues, or written off uncollected stock subscriptions.

7. In examining the income, the accountant looks for unrecorded sales, interest income, or other types of income where a failure to record may have resulted in an understatement of assets of considerable value. In the examination of the expense accounts, the accountant ascertains whether there were any payments for overstated or non-existent expenses such as wage payments to fictitious employees or payments for purchases which were never delivered.

Balance Sheet Emphasis

8. In a straight bankruptcy audit, all attention is focused on the balance sheet; the profit and loss statement is of very little importance. Even in a Chapter X or Chapter XI proceeding, less emphasis is placed on the income statement. The creditors want to know the amount they would receive if the debtor were liquidated so that they can compare it with the amount promised under a plan of arrangement.

9. Not enough attention is given to the income statement, and especially to projected statements, in most Chapter XI proceedings. An analysis of the income statements for the past few years is helpful in predicting future profits, and the success of the business in the long run will depend on its ability to make a profit. Over several years, the income statements provide information about the types of expenses that should be eliminated. They pinpoint the time period when the profits began to decline and often give some indication as to the causes of the company's failure. In most proceedings, both the creditors and the stockholders would be better off if the company can be successfully rehabilitated.

10. The long-run profitability of the company often does not emerge clearly because long-range operating plans are not prepared or no analysis is made of the past operating results. One of the major reasons for this can be found in the background and attitude of the representatives of the creditors. Many banks, financial institutions, and other large credit grantors have a separate department which handles all accounts of debtors in financial difficulty. These specialists do not have the interest in the future of the company that the credit manager or a salesman for the firm would have. Their primary interest is in obtaining the maximum amount from a particular account. It is immaterial that they may be able to keep a debtor in business, even when this means that an account which may have represented a large amount of sales for ten or fifteen years will continue. Their performance is measured by the size of the cash settlement.

Modifications of Audit

11. Examinations of companies involved in bankruptcy and insolvency can be extended endlessly. Throughout the examination, a judgment has to be rendered by the accountant as to the extent of detailed work which must be performed. The accountant does not have a blank order to go in all directions and probe as deeply as seems necessary. If the accountant goes beyond the scope of the examination as set forth in the retention order, payment for the extra work may not be authorized. (See Chapter 5, paragraph 14.)

12. If at any time major revisions in the scope of the examination are required, it is a good policy for the accountant to

discuss the changes with the creditors' committee and their attorneys, the trustee, the receiver, or other parties to the proceedings. The accountant should point out the initial findings and give an opinion on the direction that the investigation or review should take. With a consensus from the interested parties the accountant will continue the audit. The accountant should be very careful when selecting one or two areas to concentrate on and consequently making a judgment on the other areas that it is not feasible to cover. A year or two later the accountant may be open to criticism for not including certain areas that perhaps should have been examined. It takes a certain amount of experience and know-how to be able appropriately to tailor the scope of an audit to particular situations. Restriction of time, fees, and various other influences often limit the scope of the engagement.

13. The priority of work assignments can also be affected by outside influences. The debtor may be faced with imminent foreclosure, and the conditions under which certain debts arose may have to be determined immediately. Very often while the accountant is carrying out the work assignment in an orderly manner, the trustee may say, "Forget about everything else. Put four people on this problem and find out what happened." Or the trustee's attorney may demand that another problem area be examined. The interruptions may cause the progression of the scope of the audit to become disorderly and as a consequence the same phase of the examination may be reperformed a second or third time. The accountant may become resentful of this type of pressure, but these are the realities of bankruptcy and insolvency engagements. They are *not* all conducted in an orderly manner, nor are they the traditional type of examination. Pressure upon the attorney for the debtor-in-possession, or the trustee, or even the attorney for the creditors' committee is transferred upon the accountant. The orderliness and scope of an examination sometimes become completely uncontrollable, especially in the initial stages.

14. Since the audit of a company involved in bankruptcy and insolvency proceedings is not the traditional type of audit, the accountant's effectiveness will be measured in terms of creativity, imagination, and resourcefulness in finding out what really happened.

Audit Program Guide

15. An audit program guide for bankruptcy and insolvency proceedings appears on pages 243–55, at the end of this chapter. It is presented to assist the accountant in developing a program related to the needs of a particular engagement.

INTRODUCTION TO THE SPECIAL AREAS OF INQUIRY

16. The opportunity for manipulation of the books and transactions by the debtor means that the accountant must be on the alert for indications that occurrences out of the ordinary have taken place. Several types of transactions commonly found in insolvency cases demand extra attention on the part of the accountant.

Irregularities

17. An irregularity is any transaction which is not in the ordinary course of business, and especially includes any transaction which results in the apparent dissipation of the debtor's assets in a manner other than by loss in the ordinary course of business. The period of time during which irregularities may have occurred is not limited to the four months prior to the filing of the petition or the period of insolvency. Instead, the time period covered during the audit may extend to a year or more, depending on the circumstances.[1]

18. Irregularities are of utmost importance in the accountant's audit. The fundamental concern is with discovering transactions on the part of the debtor company which may act to bar it from a discharge of its debts, result in the recovery of assets, or provide information for a case for criminal prosecution. Recovered assets would enlarge the bankrupt's estate and make available a greater amount for distribution to creditors.

19. There are several common types of transactions which the accountant should carefully scrutinize as being suspect of irregulari-

---

[1] Edward A. Weinstein, "Accountants' Examinations and Reports in Bankruptcy Proceedings," *New York Certified Public Accountant*, Vol. 35 (January 1965), p. 38.

ties. These will be briefly described here and the important items more fully covered in the remainder of this chapter.

20. *Fraudulent transfers.* These primarily include transfers made or incurred by the debtor company, without fair consideration and within one year prior to bankruptcy, which render it insolvent or leave it with an unreasonably small amount of capital. The transfers are made when the debtor believes it will incur debts beyond its ability to pay as they mature, or with an intent to hinder, delay, or defraud the creditors. Thus, for sales of assets made within one year prior to the filing of a petition, the accountant must determine whether full value was received and the effect or intent of such transfer. See paragraphs 43–54.

21. *Transactions with related parties such as officers, employees, and relatives.* It is especially important to ascertain that such transactions were made at arm's length, that fair consideration was received for any transfer of assets, and that there are no paddings, incorrect cash expenses, misappropriated receipts, or improper purchases. The withdrawal of assets by stockholders as dividends, loans, transfers of assets, etc., should all be very carefully examined for any manipulation or bad intent. See paragraphs 48–54.

22. *Concealment of assets.* This category usually includes an attempt to misappropriate property and hide the shortage. This is often difficult to prove since investigation must rely on records previously kept by the bankrupt. If it seems possible to show a concealment, turnover proceedings can be attempted, to try to regain possession of the property. See paragraphs 55–69.

23. *False entries and statements.* Common examples of this irregularity are mutilation or alteration of the books, concealment or destruction of records, forgery of any document, and issuance of false statements. See paragraphs 70–74.

24. *Financing irregularities.* These include any schemes whereby the debtor attempts to obtain goods or money using methods outside the ordinary course of business. The most frequently manipulated accounts are receivables and inventory. See paragraphs 75–85.

25. *Preferential payments.* These are defined as an irregularity by the Bankruptcy Act. Included are any transfers of property made by the debtor while insolvent, within four months prior to the filing of a petition, and in payment of an antecedent debt, when the

effect of such payment was to cause one creditor to receive a greater percentage of debt than some other creditor of the same class. In order for the trustee to recover preferential payments, the Bankruptcy Act further requires that the creditor receiving the payment have reasonable cause to believe that the debtor was insolvent at the time of the transfer. Transactions which should be carefully examined by the accountant include sales of inventory or other assets back to vendors as an account offset which would favor certain suppliers, liens given to creditors in contemplation of bankruptcy, and repayment of loans to certain creditors in anticipation of bankruptcy. See paragraphs 86–93.

26. *Other types of transactions.* The types of transactions listed below should also be carefully examined by the accountant:

Any major acquisition, merger, or investment which results in a loss.

Bulk sales of assets or portions of the debtor's business.

Indications that the bankrupt deliberately allowed liabilities to increase, causing hardship to the more recent creditors. An analysis of the accounts payable may indicate that for several months prior to the filing of the petition, no payments were made on accounts even though new orders were being placed and some cash was received from sales.

Attempts on the part of creditors to inflate their claims (paragraphs 94–96).

Any potential assets which may increase the size of the estate if settled favorably for the bankrupt, such as pending lawsuits or insurance claims.

All other transactions which may have arisen outside the normal course of business.

27. The above list does not purport to include every type of irregularity possible in an insolvency case, but mentions only those most frequently encountered. Regardless of the reasons for any suspicions, the accountant's report should include any and all recoverable assets such as assets involved in preferential payments, assets concealed by the debtor, certain assets which have been sold and are suspected of being involved in a fraudulent transfer, and any other assets relating to questionable transactions. It is also

crucial that the trustee's attorney be aware of such irregularities, in order to initiate proceedings to recover such property for the estate.

Fraud

28. A specific and somewhat more serious irregularity sometimes found in bankruptcy cases is fraud, or intentional deception in relinquishing some property or lawful right. This usually relates to the debtor's books and records (paragraphs 70–74), and may include a false oath in the administration period, or the filing of false schedules and the giving of false testimony under oath.[2]

29. The accountant normally attempts to discover fraud by comparing the schedules which the debtor has filed and the company's statement of affairs with the amounts for assets and liabilities as found in the books. Indications that fraud may exist include missing books or records; erasures and alterations; and evidence that the books were written at one point in time—a uniform color of ink, one handwriting, or an apparent age of the books that does not support the stated age of the books.[3]

30. In addition to its own penalties under commercial law, fraud acts to bar a debtor from a discharge of liabilities. Section 14c(3) of the Bankruptcy Act provides that a discharge shall be denied when it has been proven that the bankrupt obtained money or property on credit or as an extension or renewal of credit by making or publishing or causing to be made or published in any manner whatsoever a materially false statement, in writing, representing its financial condition. Thus any attempt intentionally to deceive creditors and thereby gain money or property will mean the debtor remains liable for the debts so incurred.

Proof of Fraud

31. To prove misrepresentation and thereby block a discharge of debt, the creditor must show the existence of three basic elements:

[2] Robert Bronsteen, "The Accountant's Investigation of Bankruptcy Irregularities," *New York Certified Public Accountant*, Vol. 37 (December 1967), p. 941.

[3] Asa S. Herzog, "CPA's Role in Bankruptcy Proceeding," *The Journal of Accountancy*, Vol. 117 (January 1964), p. 62.

A fraudulent misrepresentation which is material (any substantial variation from the truth is considered material)

Moral depravity by the debtor in making the representation with the intent that it be relied upon

Reliance in fact by the creditor

Methods of Discovering Irregularities and Fraud

32. The accountant's major source for the discovery of unusual transactions is the debtor's books and records. Where it is believed that documents may be missing, the accountant may request the trustee to arrange to have all mail addressed to the debtor delivered to the trustee instead. In this manner, all checks which are received can be recorded and deposited, improprieties might be revealed by correspondence, and any gaps in the current records may be filled in.[4] An analysis of purchase returns may also reveal fraud.

33. The following is a list of schedules which, when prepared, may aid the accountant in the discovery of irregularities. Each worksheet includes those accounts most subject to manipulation:

A schedule of all payments made by the debtor preceding the filing of the petition, to determine whether any preferential payments were made to creditors. Such a schedule should include all major payments made during the period from insolvency or during the four months preceding the filing of the petition.

A worksheet of changes in major creditors' accounts, to indicate whether any payments were made to certain creditors for current or prior purchases and whether certain suppliers were being favored through substantial returns or other offsets.

A report of all repayments of debt, to ascertain whether some creditors were paid in anticipation of the filing of a petition in bankruptcy. Especially included should be repayments to officers, directors, stockholders, and other related parties.

A schedule of the sale of fixed assets, to reveal any sales to creditors for less than full value, to creditors as an account offset, or back to the manufacturer for cash or as an account offset.

A study of the trend of liabilities, purchases, and sales, to indicate the pattern by which debts grew, whether purchases were not being

---

[4] Bronsteen, p. 935.

paid for even though sales were large, and whether this was occurring to the detriment of the bankrupt's more recent creditors. This report would be of value in establishing the intent of the bankrupt, always a difficult procedure.

A reconciliation of the creditors' account balances per the debtor's books with the creditors' claims, including, if possible, explanation of any differences between the creditors' claims and the debtor's books.[5]

34. Even if the accountant harbors no suspicions about the debtor's actions, all transactions should be described in as much detail as possible and their effect upon the financial position of the business should be analyzed. Two different approaches have most commonly been used in reporting the bankrupt's history. One approach is a chronological index which is simply a schedule including a monthly chronology of all major inflows and outflows of cash and all major unusual transactions. Another approach consists of a narrative description which outlines the sequence of events. Either approach, used as a normal audit procedure, would give indications of those areas where the accountant should conduct further inquiry.

AVAILABILITY OF BOOKS AND RECORDS

Locating and Obtaining Possession of the Records

35. After receiving the retention order, one of the first steps performed by the accountant is to make a survey of the debtor's books and records and their condition. At the same time, examples of documents used by the business may be obtained. These are helpful in outlining the nature of the operations of the business, in determining how its systems operate and its procedures flow, and in identifying the responsible parties. For some types of audits—for example, where a broker or dealer in securities is involved—examination of documents is absolutely essential. Ideally, management should prepare for the accountant the list of books and records and certify that the list is complete. If the records are turned over to the

---

[5] Weinstein, pp. 36–38.

accountant, the list should be signed indicating receipt of the records.

36. In a straight bankruptcy proceeding or a situation where fraud is suspected, the accountant will assist the trustee in securing all the bankrupt's books and records and transferring them to the accountant's office. Speed is of the utmost importance in the removal process, for several reasons. Such records often disappear with no explanation as to their whereabouts. They may be disposed of innocently by persons who have no idea of their value. The receiver or trustee normally wants to vacate the premises as quickly as possible, to minimize rental expense. Thus, quick removal means greater insurance that the records will be adequately safeguarded. It is highly desirable for the accountant to supervise this activity, since the accountant is best able to determine which books are most useful and therefore should be preserved.

37. In a proceeding where the debtor remains in possession, the debtor will retain the records but the auditor will ascertain that all records are accounted for. The books cannot be removed if the entity continues in existence. Even under these conditions it is good practice to have management prepare a list of the books and records. The list should be signed by management and placed in the auditor's file for future reference.

38. It is important to realize that, as an appointee of the court, the accountant is correspondingly entitled to see all of the debtor's books and records (paragraphs 39–41).

Scheduling the Books; Procedure
Followed for Missing Records

39. The accountant is responsible for preparing a list of all the books and records turned over by the debtor, and for ascertaining whether any records are missing. Any such findings must be reported to the trustee's attorney. It is then the duty of the attorney to establish the existence and location of the missing books and initiate proceedings to recover them if such action is deemed necessary.

40. Again, speed is crucial. The shorter the time period between possession of the books by the trustee and proceedings to

obtain missing records, the higher the probability that the books will be successfully recovered.

41. The trustee's attorney may employ turnover proceedings to obtain the debtor's books and records. This action is generally invoked for recovery of property which belongs to the bankrupt estate. The accountant's role in this process would be to reconstruct the debtor's bookkeeping system in order to show what books were kept in the system and what books are therefore missing.

42. Once the books and records have been successfully located and obtained, they should be very carefully stored and made available only to those persons who are authorized to have access to them.

FRAUDULENT TRANSFERS

Transfer of Assets Without Fair Consideration

43. Fraudulent transfers are defined in Section 67d(2) of the Bankruptcy Act and include transfers which are presumed fraudulent regardless of whether the actual intent was to defraud creditors. A transfer is deemed to be fraudulent when made within one year prior to the filing of the petition to initiate insolvency proceedings and made or incurred:

Without fair consideration by a debtor who is or will be thereby rendered insolvent

Without fair consideration by a debtor who is engaged in or is about to engage in such business or transaction, for which the property remaining in the debtor's hands is an unreasonably small amount of capital

Without fair consideration by a debtor who intends to incur or believes that it will incur debts beyond its ability to pay as they mature

With actual intent, as distinguished from intent presumed in law, to hinder, delay, or defraud either existing or future creditors

44. Insolvency as employed in the determination of fraudulent transfers is defined in Section 67d(1)(d) to occur when the present fair salable value of the debtor's property is less than the amount

required to pay its debts. Furthermore, Section 70e(1) stipulates that any transfer or obligation incurred by the debtor which is fraudulent or voidable by any creditor under any federal or state law is also null and void as against the trustee.

45. It is important to ascertain when a fraudulent transfer has in fact occurred, because Section 14c(4) of the Bankruptcy Act provides that fraudulent transfers made by the debtor within one year prior to bankruptcy are grounds for denying the bankrupt a discharge of its debts. However, in this action it is necessary to prove that the debtor intended to hinder, delay, or defraud the creditors.

Sales of Assets Below Market Values

46. Upon realization that a business is in financial difficulty, those who are involved may attempt to minimize their personal losses by removing the company's assets. Or the business may be a sham operation, meaning that the company was created solely for the purpose of obtaining personal gain at the expense of creditors. The methods used to accomplish such objectives normally involve the transfer of assets without fair consideration or for no consideration at all. The proceeds which are withheld from the business are kept by the owners and thereby concealed from the trustee in bankruptcy.

47. The accountant should examine all sales of the debtor's assets for a period of at least one year before bankruptcy in order to determine whether any sales were made without adequate consideration. Any price discounts which are recorded should be investigated, for these may have been paid in cash to the owners. The accountant should also be on the alert for any price variations and compare sales of merchandise made to various customers.[6]

Transfer of Assets to Officers, Employees, Relatives, and Others

48. Any payments made to those with a close relationship to the business, such as the owners, their relatives, employees, or other businesses controlled by these parties, should be closely investigated

[6] Bronsteen, pp. 935–36.

by the accountant. The usual question is whether fair consideration was received for the assets transferred. Assets may also be given to companies controlled by the bankrupt's owners in payment of various goods and services at highly inflated prices.[7]

Padding

49. Padding, a form of payment of cash without fair consideration, attempts to obtain funds from the business by adding fictitious claims to expense accounts and then retaining the extra payment. The most common example is payroll padding: checks are prepared for employees who have been terminated or for fictitious employees who have been added to the payroll. It is very difficult to detect payroll padding which occurred in prior periods. The payroll records can be compared with the salaries reported to the Internal Revenue Service, but the tax records may agree with the payroll records because they also have been padded. One of the first steps usually taken by accountants is to compare the payroll for the period audited with prior periods. If there are any differences, the auditor will then attempt to determine what caused them. The payroll records are also examined for unusual names, addresses, and amounts. Confirmation can be sent to past employees for verification that wages were actually received by the employee and that the employee really exists. The auditor should examine the files to see whether any W–2 mailings were returned. (See the audit program guide on pages 243–55 at the end of this chapter for procedures related to the current period's payroll.) The supplies expense might be padded through the presentation of invoices for supplies that were never received. Or a repairs expense account could be enlarged by a claim for services never performed. The rent expense which is paid to a related party may be inflated by a substantial amount.

Cash Expenses

50. Manipulation of cash expenses may be accomplished in the same ways as in the padding schemes described above. Other abstractions may be accomplished through improper petty cash

[7] *Ibid.*, p. 939.

withdrawals by using fictitious vouchers or increasing the amount on valid claims. Checks may be drawn to cash without the proper documentation. Individuals may have the corporation pay for large personal expenses, such as travel and entertainment. The methods of obtaining funds from a business through improper cash expenses are unlimited.

Non-Deposit or Diverting of Receipts

51. Individuals may abstract the cash from a sale or collection on an account and attempt to cover up the shortage in various ways. The sale may be recorded at less than is collected or deleted entirely.

Improper Purchases

52. Invoices for amounts greater than the actual purchase price may be submitted for payment of assets purchased. Employees may submit for payment by the firm bills pertaining to merchandise bought for their own personal use. Purchase discounts may be unrecorded and the resulting overpayment retained by an owner. Again, the methods of manipulating purchases are numerous and similar to those found in a business not experiencing financial difficulties.

Improper Loans

53. Individuals may borrow funds in the company's name without recording the note on the books, and abstract the cash. During one audit, an independent accountant discovered sealed envelopes containing information about the notes the president had signed without authorization.

Improper Sales of Merchandise

54. A less obvious method of transferring or diverting assets out of the bankrupt corporation is by selling merchandise at ridiculously low prices to a newly formed corporation or to a relative or friend. To uncover this possibility, the accountant usually examines the sales invoices for the months immediately preceding the bankruptcy, compares the prices charged thereon

with prices charged at least six months prior to bankruptcy, and attempts to establish whether any substantial reduction occurred in the selling price of the bankrupt's merchandise.

CONCEALMENT OF ASSETS

55. In an attempt to minimize their own personal losses, those involved with a bankrupt corporation may conceal the debtor's assets. Regardless of the type of assets involved, the basis for determining whether the assets on hand at the time of bankruptcy were depleted by possible concealment is usually the financial statements as found in the debtor's files. The accountant should closely examine these statements and supplement them with statements from the files of the accountant who was retained by the debtor company before it entered bankruptcy.[8]

Merchandise

56. Merchandise concealments or shortages must often be proven theoretically or technically, that is, through a reconstruction of the accounts rather than a physical count. The beginning inventory is ascertained from a financial statement or physical inventory and the purchases to the date of bankruptcy are added to it. From this total, the cost of sales is subtracted, which should yield the value of the merchandise in inventory as of the date of bankruptcy. After a physical inventory is taken, if a lower figure results, the difference represents the amount of inventory which has been lost or concealed.

57. As an illustration of transfers of inventory by the bankrupt in a fraudulent matter, it was reported to a trustee that trucks had been seen loading up at the doors of the bankrupt's stores within a few days preceding the bankruptcy. The trustee obtained a copy of the auction inventory sheets for the accountant, in the hope that the missing inventory could be established. Unfortunately, the bankrupt had been operating five-and-dime stores which stocked and sold hundreds, if not thousands, of different items. The accountant could not make an actual unit count. Although the number of units

[8] Sydney Krause, "Accountant's Role in a Liquidation Proceeding," *New York Certified Public Accountant*, Vol. 28 (July 1958), p. 508.

purchased within the short period of time the debtor was in business could be established, it was impossible to determine how many units were sold since the sales records consisted of only the register tapes. However, the accountant did pursue the following approach:

> Since the debtor was in business only a few months, the total amount of purchases made by the debtor for its stores was established from the paid and unpaid bills.

> Since the debtor commenced its operations without any inventory, the only inventory available for sale was that which the purchase records clearly indicated had been procured.

> The auctioneer indicated (on an overall basis) that the merchandise brought at auction approximately 50 per cent of the cost. Accordingly, the accountant doubled the auction proceeds, that is, the gross auction proceeds, to arrive at the approximate cost of the inventory on hand at the bankruptcy date.

> Therefore, the difference between the total purchases made and the inventory on hand for the auction at cost was the merchandise that had been used or consumed in the sales.

> The records then indicated what the sales were—that is, what the debtor reported as its sales—and by deducting the normal mark-up for this type of store from the sales, the cost of sales was determined. As might be expected, the inventory that evidently was consumed for the sales was far in excess of the indicated cost value of the sales. As a matter of fact, even if it were assumed that all sales were made at cost and that there was no mark-up on the sales, the merchandise consumed still far exceeded the sales, a clear indication that inventory was missing.

Unrecorded Sales

58. Other assets may be concealed through unrecorded sales. Merchandise may be removed from the business with no consideration given or accounting entry made. The delivery of merchandise purchases may be diverted to the owners of the firm. Cash may be concealed by not recording the sale of scrap or waste or by recording a sale of good merchandise as a sale of scrap or waste with a lower value.[9]

[9] Bronsteen, pp. 936–37.

59. Several methods may be employed to discover the diversion of assets by unrecorded sales. The gross profit earned in previous periods should be compared with that currently being received, and large drops in the amount should be investigated for possible uncompensated removal of merchandise. A schedule for the immediate period, including sales, purchases, and direct labor and production costs, should be prepared to uncover any unusual occurrences. Concealments might be discovered through a theoretical unit merchandise audit, where a list is made by unit and dollar amount of the opening inventory, purchases, sales, and ending inventory. Individual, specific units of the merchandise might be traced through serial, style, or identification numbers. Purchase bills should be checked against receiving records. A schedule of all sales of scrap and waste materials should be prepared. And an analysis should be made of all the processing and contracting bills to establish that all raw material purchased and not now in inventory has been incorporated into the finished product and that all units which were processed were later accounted for either in sales or in the closing inventory.[10]

60. Merchandise may be held as collateral by creditors and not disclosed. Or, merchandise may never have been delivered by the supplier, although notes were issued in payment and the purchases are reflected on the books. Collateral may have been given for notes received by the debtor. The loans may have been entered on the books but the merchandise transferred or the collateral never recorded.

Cash Surrender Value of Officers' Life Insurance Policies

61. Although the purchase of life insurance policies on the lives of corporate officers is not a deductible tax expense for the corporation, it is often deemed advisable to obtain life insurance on the officers of the corporation in order to provide the cash funds necessary to repurchase their capital stock from the widow or estate. Consequently, a large number of bankrupt corporations own such life insurance policies. The asset is the cash value of the policy. Since the corporation normally is in dire need of cash funds prior to the filing of the petition, loans have usually been taken by

[10] *Ibid.*, pp. 937–38.

the corporation from the insurance company against the policies either for payment of the premiums due or for other working capital needs. The accountant can uncover the existence of these policies by finding proper entries on the corporate books of account, by the discovery of the policies themselves, by premium notices found among the paid or unpaid bills, or by entries made on the books such as payments to life insurance companies for premiums.

62. The cash value can be determined by an examination of the policy itself or by direct communication with the insurance broker or the life insurance company in question. At the same time, the accountant must ascertain the loan, if any, outstanding against the policy either from entries on the books or from information received from the insurance company. Also, the accountant must determine that all dividends receivable on the policies have been credited to the bankrupt corporation. Once this information is compiled, the equity in the policy is readily ascertainable. A judgment can then easily be made as to whether an offer made by a former officer of the bankrupt to repurchase the policy is equitable. It is interesting to note that most corporate officers are well aware that these policies are a good buy for themselves and their families and they quite often will make an offer to repurchase the policies for the equity therein, whereas they may not as anxiously provide other information having a bearing on the administration of the bankrupt corporation.[11]

Deposits and Security

63. Deposits and security are usually assets of the corporation arising from down payments made on the purchase of machinery or items of merchandise, or security left with landlords for the performance of the terms of a lease. Where a complete set of books is available, these items are self-evident and present no problems to the auditor. However, many examinations have not uncovered such assets until more detailed searches were made of the records.

64. Among the records the accountant seeks are leases and receipts for deposits left with utilities. Naturally, the leases clearly indicate the security left with the landlord and the utility receipts

---

[11] Elliot G. Meisel, "Services Rendered by the Accountant to the Trustee" (accounting firm of Roberts & Leinwander Co.), p. 7 (mimeographed).

likewise provide the information on utility deposits. Down payments on the purchase of machinery or equipment are a little more difficult to uncover and the accountant often relies on information provided by creditors. A search of correspondence is often helpful in uncovering deposits of this nature. There can also be a corresponding liability for deposits or security, if the bankrupt was a landlord or manufacturer of equipment for which such deposits are usually required.

Investments and Real Estate

65. Investments in stocks or bonds can be uncovered from brokers' statements or payments to brokerage houses among the cash disbursements. Investments in real estate usually appear in the form of unusual cash disbursements, that is, disbursements that normally would not be made for the business under review. Again, examination of the correspondence files will often lead to the discovery of such investments, and a reading of the minute books of the corporation can be a lead to such assets. Included in this category is the ownership of subsidiary companies whose stock may have value (where the subsidiaries are solvent corporations). An abundance of transactions with another corporation, clearly not in the nature of normal purchases by the bankrupt corporation, usually indicates an affiliation with that corporation through holdings of common stock, or a relationship of parent and subsidiary companies. A bankrupt corporation is often found to be the parent company of a real estate corporation that owns the premises from which the bankrupt corporation had conducted its business. The real estate frequently turns out to be quite valuable, notwithstanding the fact that usually the mortgages are substantial in amount.[12] Ownership of real estate by a bankrupt corporation is apparent where tax payments are made to the local real-estate taxing authorities or where payments of similar amounts are made to banks on a monthly or quarterly basis, indicating mortgage payments.

Machinery and Equipment

66. The accountant's inventory or an auctioneer's report will show the machinery and equipment located at the premises of the

---

[12] *Ibid.*, p. 9.

bankrupt, but the accountant is more interested in reporting on the machinery and equipment *not* at the premises. The most common assets of this type are the automobiles used personally by the corporate officers. Though registered in the officers' own names, the cars are often purchased by the corporation, with all operating expenses completely paid by the corporation. Insurance brokers' bills will usually point out the existence of these assets as well as chattel mortgage payments made on a monthly basis. Often a letter will arrive, or will be discovered in the company's files, from an irate bailee wanting to know when someone is going to remove machinery from a warehouse or premises or who is going to pay for its storage cost. A review of the contracts file may uncover some assets that do not appear on the books of the corporation. Machinery or equipment usually does appear (at least in summary form) and the corporate tax returns ordinarily will have detailed schedules of the items included in this category.

67. Assets may also be concealed by the withdrawal of unusual receipts such as recovery of bad debts or insurance recoveries.

68. These investigations and determinations become the basis for a turnover proceeding, which is used to compel the debtor to surrender the property or its value which is unaccounted for and therefore presumably concealed by the bankrupt. Thus the challenge to the accountant is to prove that certain assets exist, even though their physical existence is not immediately evident.

69. The concealment of assets, when intended to hinder, delay, or defraud creditors, is grounds for barring a debtor from the discharge of debts under Section 14c(4) of the Bankruptcy Act.

FALSE ENTRIES AND STATEMENTS

Mutilation and Alteration of Records

70. Any suspicion that the books have been tampered with should be quickly and carefully acted upon by the accountant and the trustee's attorney. There may be attempts on the part of the firm's owners or employees to conceal assets, make preferential payments, hide a fraudulent transfer, or effect some other irregularity. Indications of such activities include suspicious erasures, names

or amounts which have been crossed out, and pages which have been rewritten. Documents which should receive the closest attention are checks, payroll records, deposit slips, and petty cash slips. The most reliable method of examining and investigating any unusual condition is to contact an independent third party to verify the debtor's records. An example of this procedure would be a comparison between the duplicate deposit tickets retained by the bank and the debtor's cash receipts journal. Other examples are given below:

> Examination of purchase bills and receiving records, to bring to light fictitious purchase bills used to siphon off business funds.
>
> Examination of sales invoices and shipping documents, to reveal fictitious invoices used to obtain loans.
>
> Review of loans received, to determine whether they were bona fide loans or disguised sales.
>
> Analysis of receivable and payable subsidiary accounts, to see whether non-existent or unusual accounts appear.
>
> Audit of petty cash slips, to check for alterations.

Concealment and Destruction of Records

71. As previously discussed, locating and obtaining possession of the bankrupt's books and records is one of the accountant's first and most important tasks. Should the investigation reveal that the debtor is withholding records, the attorney may initiate turnover proceedings to obtain possession of them. Intentional destruction of records, if proven, may give the attorney grounds for further legal actions. Section 14c(2) of the Bankruptcy Act explicitly states that a discharge of debts will be denied when it is proven that the bankrupt destroyed, mutilated, falsified, concealed, or failed to keep or preserve books of account or records, from which the financial condition and transactions of the business might be ascertained.

Forgery

72. Officers of the bankrupt may falsify a third party's signature, for numerous reasons. The debtor may attempt to receive credit illegally by forging notes, mortgages, warehouse receipts, trust receipts, shipping documents, and other evidences

often used as security. Forgery might also be used to endorse a check and divert the monies to personal use. The proceeds from the sale of marketable securities might be misappropriated through forgery.[13] Forgery is a form of deception and as such carries its own punishment under the federal laws.

Issuance of False Statements

73. The following list explains how several accounts may be altered for financial statement purposes.

Cash:
    Kiting of receipts
    Withdrawals not recorded
    Deposits of worthless checks from insolvent affiliates

Accounts Receivable:
    Worthless accounts not written off
    Insufficient reserve for bad debts
    Large returns and allowances in subsequent period
    Fictitious sales
    Invoices billed in advance of shipping dates
    Fictitious accounts created to cover withdrawals to officers, etc.
    Non-disclosure of hypothecation to banks or factors

Notes Receivable:
    Worthless
    Insufficient reserve for bad debts
    Forging or fictitious notes created to cover withdrawals
    Contingent liability for discounted notes not shown

Merchandise Inventory:
    Non-disclosure of pledged inventory or liens against
    Inflated values and quantities
    Items billed in advance of shipping dates included in inventory
    Old obsolete inventory not disclosed

---

[13] Bronsteen, p. 941.

Cash Value—Officers' Life Insurance:

Liability for loans not shown

Corporation not beneficiary

Fixed and Other Assets:

Mortgages not disclosed

Inflated values by reappraisals and not shown

Inadequate reserve for depreciations

Leased equipment recorded as fixed assets

Personal assets (such as autos) not registered in corporate name but recorded as assets

Capitalized expenses that have no value

Inter-Company Receivables:

From affiliates to cover withdrawals of officers

From affiliates that are insolvent

Investments:

Worthless, but shown at original cost

Pledged and not recorded

Not registered in corporate name

To cover withdrawals to insolvent affiliates

Liabilities:

Not recorded

Withdrawals of subordinated debts not shown

Capital:

Notes and loans payable recorded as capital

False subordinations

74. The accountant discovers the issuance of false financial statements by comparing the statements the debtor has issued with the books and records. The comparison can be presented in schedule form, which explains the difference between the statements and the records. Figures 8–1 and 8–3 present the statement of financial position and statement of income and profit or loss, respectively, as originally issued by the debtor. Figures 8–2 and 8–4 show the statements prepared by the accountant, comparing the debtor's statements with the records.

A RETAIL CORPORATION

STATEMENT OF FINANCIAL POSITION

At December 31, 1975

Assets

Current Assets:		
Cash in Banks		$ 20,730
Accounts Receivable	$26,530	
Less: Allowance for Doubtful Accounts	3,500	23,030
Merchandise Inventory		131,810
Prepaid Expenses		4,470
Total Current Assets		$180,040
Investments:		
Common Stock—Jones & Co.		4,760
Preferred Stock—Smith, Inc.		5,000
Total Investments		9,760
Fixed Assets		49,530
Less: Accumulated Depreciation		22,720
Net Fixed Assets		26,810
Other Assets:		
Deposits as Security		8,500
Goodwill		8,000
Total Other Assets		16,500
Total Assets		$233,110

Liabilities and Capital

Current Liabilities:		
Loan Payable—Bank		$ 20,000
Accounts Payable		80,560
Taxes and Accrued Expenses		7,960
Total Liabilities		$108,520
Capital:		
Capital Stock Issued		75,000
Additional Paid-In Capital		35,000
Accumulated Earnings, January 1, 1975	$ 5,170	
Profit for Period [Figure 8-3]	9,420	14,590
Total Capital		124,590
Total Liabilities and Capital		$233,110

Figure 8–1.   Statement of financial position, as prepared by debtor.

A RETAIL CORPORATION

COMPARISON OF ISSUED STATEMENT OF FINANCIAL POSITION WITH BOOKS OF ACCOUNT

At December 31, 1975

	Per Books	Per Financial Statement	Apparent Errors Assets Overstated	Apparent Errors Liabilities Understated
Assets				
Current Assets:				
Cash in Banks	$ 2,730	$ 20,730	$18,000	
Accounts Receivable—Net	21,030	23,030	2,000	
Merchandise Inventory	121,810	131,810	10,000	
Prepaid Expenses	4,470	4,470		
Total Current Assets	150,040	180,040	30,000	
Investments:				
Common Stock—Jones & Co.	4,760	4,760		
Preferred Stock—Smith, Inc.	—0—	5,000	5,000	
Total Investments	4,760	9,760	5,000	
Fixed Assets—Net	26,810	26,810		
Other Assets	16,500	16,500		
Total Assets	$198,110	$233,110	$35,000	
Liabilities and Capital				
Current Liabilities:				
Loan Payable—Bank	$ 20,000	$ 20,000		
Notes Payable—John Doe	6,000	—0—		$ 6,000
Accounts Payable	103,560	80,560		23,000
Taxes and Accrued Expenses	7,960	7,960		
Total Current Liabilities	137,520	108,520		29,000
Due After One Year:				
Notes Payable—John Doe	9,000	—0—		9,000
Total Liabilities	146,520	108,520		$38,000
Capital:				
Capital Stock Issued	75,000	75,000		
Additional Paid-In Capital	—0—	35,000		
Accumulated Earnings (Deficit)	(23,410)	14,590		
Total Capital	51,590	124,590		
Total Liabilities and Capital	$198,110	$233,110		
Reconciliation of Capital				
Accumulated Deficit Per Books		$ 23,410		
Accumulated Earnings Per Statement		14,590	$38,000	
Paid-In Capital Per Statement			35,000	
Total To Be Accounted For				$73,000
Assets Apparently Overstated			35,000	
Liabilities Apparently Understated			38,000	
Total Accounted For				$73,000

Figure 8–2. Accountant's comparative statement of financial position, as prepared from debtor's books.

A RETAIL CORPORATION

STATEMENT OF INCOME AND PROFIT OR LOSS

For the Period From January 1 to December 31, 1975

Net Sales		$592,010
Cost of Goods Sold:		
Merchandise Inventory, January 1, 1975	$ 98,490	
Net Purchases	364,230	
Freight-In and Other Costs	10,510	
Available for Sale	473,230	
Less: Merchandise Inventory, December 31, 1975	131,810	
Cost of Goods Sold		341,420
Gross Profit		250,590
Expenses:		
Sales Salaries	101,790	
Administrative Salaries	20,180	
Rent	53,890	
Advertising	19,850	
Taxes	8,790	
Utilities	10,040	
Depreciation	5,820	
Other Expenses	20,810	
Total Expenses		241,170
Net Profit for Period [Figure 8-1]		$ 9,420

Figure 8–3. Statement of income and profit or loss, as prepared by debtor.

A RETAIL CORPORATION

COMPARISON OF ISSUED STATEMENT OF INCOME AND PROFIT
OR LOSS WITH BOOKS OF ACCOUNT

For the Period From January 1 to December 31, 1975

	Per Books		Per Financial Statement	
Net Sales		$562,010		$592,010
Cost of Goods Sold:				
Merchandise Inventory, 1/1/75	$ 98,490		$ 98,490	
Net Purchases	340,230		364,230	
Freight-In and Other Costs	10,510		10,510	
Available for Sale	449,230		473,230	
Less: Merchandise Inventory, 12/31/75	121,810		131,810	
Cost of Goods Sold		327,420		341,420
Gross Profit		234,590		250,590
Expenses:				
Sales Salaries	111,790		101,790	
Administrative Salaries	20,180		20,180	
Rent	53,890		53,890	
Advertising	24,850		19,850	
Taxes	8,790		8,790	
Utilities	10,040		10,040	
Depreciation	5,820		5,820	
Other Expenses	27,810		20,810	
Total Expenses		263,170		241,170
Net Profit or (Loss)		$ (28,580)		$ 9,420

SUMMARY

	Sales	Gross Profit	Expenses	Net Profit
Per Financial Statement	$592,010	$250,590	$241,170	$ 9,420
Per Books	562,010	234,590	263,170	(28,580)
Apparent Misstatement	$ 30,000	$ 16,000	$ 22,000	$ 38,000

Figure 8–4. Accountant's comparative statement of income and profit or loss, as prepared from debtor's books.

FINANCING IRREGULARITIES

75. Many schemes have been devised whereby the debtor attempts to receive goods or money using very confusing methods so that payment is delayed or the amount received is more than is actually due. The most common accounts manipulated to accomplish these goals are accounts receivable and inventory.

Receivables

76. Many different types of abuses may be found in the financing of accounts receivable. Customers may be sent bills before the goods are shipped or the sale is consummated. Documents such as sales invoices or customers' signatures on financing agreements may be forged. Employees may fail to record merchandise which has been returned, thus showing an inflated accounts receivable total. Invoices may be padded so that if the receivables were factored, the debtor would receive funds in excess of the actual costs.[14]

77. In analyzing the receivables of a paint company an auditor noticed that excessive amounts of returns were being made by customers, depreciating the value of the accounts receivable. Salesmen were inflating the receivables by making sales which would later be returned. This practice was encouraged because the plant producer paid commissions on acceptance of the order, rather than after payment. Further analysis indicated that the salesmen were promising customers exclusive rights to the paint in their geographic area and then selling the same type of paint to a local competitor of the first customer. They camouflaged this action by placing a different trade name label on the cans of paint.

78. The business should have full ownership of its receivables and there should be no liens outstanding against them or any contingent liabilities for receivables which have been discounted. The total which is shown for accounts receivable should be the realizable cash value. Items which should not be included in accounts receivable but would be presented separately are:

[14] *Ibid.*

Shipments made on consignment

Accounts for which there is indication that collection will not be possible because the customer was a bad credit risk

Permanent investments of capital in or loans to affiliated or subsidiary businesses

Receivables which resulted from transactions with officers, employees, or subsidiary companies

Loans or advances to employees or officers

Claims which will never be enforced, such as those resulting from transactions conducted under false pretenses

Installment receivables

Receivables arising from transactions other than the sale of merchandise—the sale of plant assets, insurance claims, etc.

Credit balances in accounts receivable

79. To discover any of these irregularities, the most reliable procedure would be for the accountant to confirm the transactions with the third party involved. If there is a suspicion that merchandise was returned but not recorded, the customer should be contacted. Confirmation of a certain number of receivables is a normal audit procedure. If the receivables have been factored, they should be directly confirmed with the customer and all shipping documents, receipts, and the method and means of payment should be carefully examined to insure the transactions are valid. If the accountant suspects that a shipment shown as a sale was actually made on consignment, the receiver of the goods should be contacted to see whether title did actually pass. Doubtful credit risks should be investigated and any transactions made with employees or officers should be carefully scrutinized. Many of the procedures followed in determining whether irregularities exist in accounts receivable are extensions of those found in a normal audit.

Inventory

80. Inventories, the methods of financing purchases, and the use of inventories to obtain further credit are also subject to manipulation by the debtor. Signatures may be forged on receiving reports attesting that material was received and payment is therefore due the vendor. Subsequent payment may then be

abstracted by the officers or employees. Other documents may be falsified to record a higher inventory value, cover up a shortage, etc. As with receivables, these transactions may be best verified through confirmation with outside parties.

81. A company with warehouses on its premises had a substantial amount of inventory subject to warehouse liens which were held by Lexington Warehouse Company. The accountant's investigation disclosed that items were not properly recorded in the warehouse receipts issued by Lexington Warehouse. As a result, in the recorded contents of certain lots there were variances from the description in the warehouse receipts, and inventory was over-stated. Lot number 5589, for example, was on warehouse receipt number 36673 as 17,425 pounds headless shrimp at $.80 per pound for a value of $13,796. This lot actually contained fish which was valued at $.38 per pound for a total value of $6,621, for a difference of $7,175. It was determined that when the inventory of shrimp came into the facilities of the company, it would be proper inventory. A warehouse receipt would be prepared which went to a New York bank for financing. The shrimp were then taken out the front door and a lesser quality of shrimp—and in some cases even catfish—was substituted. The higher-quality shrimp were then taken to the back door and processed again.

82. The discrepancies were discovered by taking a detailed inventory. Also, the auditor discovered two black books which the company used to keep up with the changes it had made in the inventory which was placed in the warehouse.

83. Inventories may be financed through a technique known as kiting. This scheme uses the float period, or the time it takes for a check to clear the bank on which it is drawn. It is an attempt to prevent an overdraft from being detected by the bank and in effect uses the bank's credit without authorization or payment of interest. Kiting may also be tied in directly with the inventory. In the example described above, the local warehouse was slow in notifying the Lexington Warehouse Company (Lexington, Ky.) that the items had been sold. The company used the proceeds, which should have been directly applied to the payment of the loan since the inventory had been sold, until the bank in New York received notice of the sale of the inventory. The company continued to list the item in inventory even though the sale was recorded.

84. Inventories may also be used as collateral to obtain credit. They may become the security for new credit or be pledged to secure outstanding obligations. If the debtor has inflated the inventory figure, the collateral is actually insufficient for the amount borrowed and the creditors have been deceived.

85. In a typical audit not involving insolvency the accountant attempts to establish the correct quantity of items in inventory and the proper valuation of the goods. These are very important aspects of an audit involving a bankrupt where it is necessary to ascertain whether the collateral which has been pledged is adequate and the amounts paid were for items which actually represented purchases. The correct quantity as shown in the inventory figure is determined through observation of a physical inventory and statistical sampling of the correspondence between the inventory records and actual goods. Valuation is tested by examining sales invoices, obtaining prices paid by other vendees, and questioning the seller as to how much was actually received. All these procedures must be conducted with a higher degree of suspicion on the part of the accountant than would normally be the case, due to the nature of the proceeding.

PREFERENTIAL PAYMENTS

86. A preferential payment as defined in Section 60a(1) of the Bankruptcy Act is a transfer of any of the property of a debtor to or for the benefit of a creditor, for or on account of an antecedent debt made or suffered by the debtor while insolvent and within four months before the filing of a petition initiating bankruptcy proceedings, when the effect of such transfer is to enable the creditor to receive a greater percentage of debt than some other creditor of the same class. Preferences include the payment of money, a transfer of property, assignment of accounts receivable, or a mortgage on real or personal property.

87. A preferential payment is not a fraud but rather a legitimate and proper payment of a valid antecedent debt. It is created by law and its goal is to effect equality of distribution among all the creditors. The four-month period prior to bankruptcy has been arbitrarily selected by Congress as the time period during

which the debtor's assets belong to his creditors ratably. During this period, a creditor who accepts a payment is said to have been preferred and may be required to return the amount received and later participate in the enlarged estate to the extent of a pro rata share.

Recovery of Preferential Payments

88. The trustee will attempt to recover preferential payments. For the payment to be voidable the Bankruptcy Act further requires that the creditor who receives it had to have reasonable cause to believe that the debtor was insolvent at the time when the transfer was made.[15] The accountant may be of value in proving the creditor had cause to believe that the debtor was insolvent through a discovery of any changes in the pattern of transactions occurring between the bankrupt and the creditor, such as a shortening of credit terms.[16]

89. If the creditor accepts the payment in good faith with no knowledge of the financial affairs of the bankrupt, the trustee will be unable to recover the payment. Also, if the preference is to be voidable, payment must have been made within four months of bankruptcy. Furthermore, insolvency at the time of payment is necessary and only someone with the training of an accountant is in a position to prove insolvency.[17]

90. It is important that the accountant note an exception provided for in Section 60c of the Bankruptcy Act. Here it is stipulated that if a creditor has been preferred, and afterward in good faith gives the debtor further credit without security of any kind for property which becomes part of the debtor's estate, the amount of the new credit remaining unpaid at the time of the adjudication in bankruptcy may be set off against the amount which would otherwise be recoverable from the debtor. Therefore, to establish the final amount of preferential payments to one creditor, it is necessary to set off all new credits against the prior preferential payments.[18]

---

[15] Bankruptcy Act, Sec. 60b.
[16] Bronsteen, p. 942.
[17] Krause, p. 505.
[18] Herzog, p. 62.

Search for Preferential Payments

91. Any payments which have been made within the four months preceding bankruptcy and which are not in the ordinary course of business should be very carefully scrutinized. Suspicious transactions would include anticipations of debt obligations, repayment of officers' loans, repayment of loans which have been personally guaranteed by officers, repayment of loans made to personal friends and relatives, collateral given to lenders, and sales of merchandise made on a contra-account basis.[19]

92. Sales which are unrecorded and result in the transfer and concealment of merchandise may result in benefit to preferred creditors in several ways. Collateral may be given to creditors but not recorded on the debtor's books. Merchandise may be concealed from the trustee by suppliers who send bills for undelivered merchandise under a "bill and hold" arrangement. Or merchandise may be returned to creditors for a direct or indirect consideration. All these schemes are intended to prefer a certain creditor over another.

93. In seeking to find voidable preferences, the accountant has two crucial tasks: to determine the earliest date on which insolvency can be established within the four-month period, and to report to the trustee's attorney all payments, transfers, or encumbrances which have been made by the debtor after that date. It is then the attorney's responsibility to determine which payments are voidable. However, the accountant's role should not be minimized for it is the accountant who initially determines those payments which are suspect.

INFLATED CLAIMS

94. Just as it is important to minimize the priority and administration creditors in order to provide the maximum dividend to unsecured creditors, it is likewise important to limit the filing of the unsecured creditors to their proper amounts. Excessive amounts allowed for unsecured creditors will naturally diminish the dividend payable to those in that group.

[19] Bronsteen, p. 942.

95. After establishing the book balances for the unsecured creditors, the accountant compares the schedule with the claims filed, to determine their accuracy. Discrepancies are analyzed and, if they are not reconcilable, this information is communicated to the trustee or counsel and also to the creditors' committee.

96. Where a Chapter XI or X has preceded the adjudication, the accountant determines (by dates of delivery as compared to the filing dates of the arrangement proceedings) whether a claim is properly classified as administrative or non-administrative. All the above verification naturally requires examination of the original documents, including receiving reports, purchase orders, and the actual supplier's invoices. Where the supplier has not given credit for payments made or credits allowed, the accountant locates the checks proving payment or the paperwork substantiating the allowance. In an interesting recent Chapter XI proceeding, the debtor (prior to the Chapter XI proceeding) had settled a claim with a supplier for $9,800, payable by adding $.10 to each item of goods purchased in the future until the $9,800 had been paid. This settlement was for an original invoice of approximately $60,000; however, the accounts payable records showed no liability at all to the creditor. Although the settlement preceded the filing of the arrangement petition and although there had been partial performance on the settlement, the creditor nonetheless presented a confirmation to the accountant showing the $60,000 balance as still due. Fortunately, the accountant noticed the $.10 additional payments on the invoices of the supplier (which aroused the accountant's suspicions) and the true facts were then uncovered. Consequently, instead of allowing a claim for $60,000, the statement reflected the true liability of $9,800 less partial payment thereon.

APPLICABILITY OF GENERALLY ACCEPTED AUDITING STANDARDS

97. When the accountant states that an examination was conducted in accordance with generally accepted auditing standards, this normally means that the examination performed was adequate to support an opinion on the financial statements and that it was performed with professional competence by properly trained

persons. Such standards are really measures of an acceptable level of quality and are judged by the "prudent-man standard," or what other competent auditors would conclude to be necessary if given the same set of facts.

98. Two broad classifications of auditing standards are universally referred to. One is termed personal or general standards and concerns the auditor's training and experience and the quality of the work done. The second is the field work and reporting standards and refers to the evidence to be obtained and the means of reporting the results of the audit.

99. These standards are obviously quite general in their applicability. This is necessary because no one set of auditing procedures can be applied in all situations. Therefore, the accountant must select and apply the appropriate auditing procedures as required in the particular circumstances.

100. Because of their generality, the auditing standards as set forth in Statement on Auditing Standards No. 1 certainly apply to the audit of a client involved in insolvency. The auditor must obviously have adequate technical training, maintain an independent mental attitude, and exercise due professional care. The work must be planned and supervised, internal control must be studied and evaluated, and sufficient competent evidential matter must be obtained. Finally, the statements must be presented in accordance with generally accepted accounting principles, consistently applied. There must be adequate disclosures, and either an expression of an opinion or reasons why one cannot be given should be included in the report.

Auditing Procedures

101. The nature of the insolvency proceedings determines the specific procedures which will be followed. A bankruptcy situation allows for greater manipulation of the books and transactions, so in many areas the accountant will need to scrutinize the records and supporting documents more closely than might otherwise be necessary. Special attention must be given to uncovering any irregularities such as fraudulent transfers, preferential payments, false entries, concealment of assets, and the like. These investigations may necessitate greater reliance on sources outside the

debtor's records than is normal, including confirmation with third parties. It may be necessary to reconstruct some accounts because of a lack of adequate data or the dubious nature of the bankrupt's information.

102. Other considerations also arise because of the nature of the situation. For example, the question may be posed as to whether the auditor can represent the debtor and still be independent when supplying information for the creditors. Or, if the accountant helps devise a plan for rehabilitation and recommends its acceptance, can the same accountant later be independent when auditing the debtor's progress? Is it ever possible to rely on the system of internal control in insolvency proceedings, or should the examination be conducted as if there were no adequate safeguards? These and other specific questions arise when applying auditing standards to a bankruptcy case.

103. The various audit steps which will be necessary must be individually determined for each case. Whether such procedures are adequate can only be measured by a consideration of what a reasonable person with the same training would do in a similar situation. But it still remains true that those standards which generally apply to all audit cases are also relevant to insolvency and bankruptcy proceedings.

104. The first generally accepted auditing standard of reporting requires that the auditor state whether the financial statements are presented in accordance with generally accepted principles of accounting. This means that any financial statements prepared by an accountant must not deviate from the standard presentation and treatment of accounts and transactions as commonly used by the profession.

105. There is no definitive list of accounting principles which has been written down and may be referred to by auditors. Rather, the accountant must have a sound and thorough knowledge of accounting theory. It is also necessary to be aware of the pronouncements of the AICPA, FASB, other areas of accounting literature, and current industry practice. Using these sources, the accountant must then apply personal judgment to determine whether a particular principle is generally accepted and appropriate in the circumstances.

106. The most common sources of accounting principles are

the Accounting Research Bulletins and Opinions previously issued by the rule-making bodies of the AICPA, and Standards issued by the Financial Accounting Standards Board. The principles set forth in these publications are deemed to have substantial authoritative support and therefore are considered to be generally accepted accounting principles. Any departures in the financial statements from these pronouncements must be disclosed in a footnote to the statement or in a separate paragraph of the auditor's report. Such deviations are to be acceptable to the auditor only if they have substantial authoritative support and are acceptable practices. This decision is made by the accountant after examining all the relevant and authoritative sources of literature, and evaluating what is commonly done in such situations.

107. The next chapter presents a discussion of the application of the reporting standards to reports issued in bankruptcy and insolvency proceedings, and includes an analysis of the going-concern concept as it relates to entities facing financial difficulties.

108. The art of accounting is comprised of the talent, training, experience, and knowledge which result in the accountant's judgment as to which auditing standards are appropriate and which accounting principles are applicable to a particular circumstance. Overriding these specific decisions are the general standards which apply to all cases, including bankruptcy and insolvency proceedings.

AUDIT PROGRAM GUIDE
BANKRUPTCY AND INSOLVENCY

The following audit guide has been prepared for the purpose of assisting accountants who are conducting audits of companies involved in bankruptcy and insolvency proceedings. By definition, it is designed to *guide* the auditor in preparing a customized program for each individual engagement; it is not intended that it be used as a final program. Modification should and must be made depending upon the nature and characteristics of each situation.

Judgment on the part of the auditor is of paramount importance, as it will determine the total time consumed on the engagement and the relative value of such input to the creditors and debtor. The auditor must see that the efforts expended are efficient and in the proper area.

The procedures and responsibilities of the auditor may also vary depending on whether retention was by a creditors' committee for an out-of-court settlement or assignment under state court, or by the courts in a Chapter X, Chapter XI, or straight bankruptcy proceeding.

General Procedures

1. Prepare memorandum outlining:
   a. How the account was acquired (if by referral, give source and date of referral)
   b. Principal creditors and members of creditors' committee
   c. Attorneys for creditors' committee and debtor
   d. Background information about the company, including type of business, locations of offices, and any other general information about the firm
   e. Estimated assets and liabilities of the company
   f. Any affiliates or subsidiaries
2. Prepare engagement letter or request for retention order. In a committee case, the accounting firm should make sure the attorney for the creditors and the chairman of the creditors' committee arrange for covering of all fees, especially if debtor talks cease and court action occurs. In an assignment case (state court), Chapter XI, or straight bankruptcy, an order is generally required. However, if the work is accepted because of the

"credit body," the cooperation of the creditors' committee must be obtained to protect the accounting firm in payment of fees. If there are affiliates or subsidiaries which are not involved in the "official" action, acquire an advance payment if at all possible.

3. Prepare petition for fee allowance in tentative form as soon as major part of work is complete, then update the petition before filing with court.

4. Obtain copies of:
   a. Recent reports issued to credit agencies
   b. Financial statements for last three to five years issued to stockholders, creditors, banks, and others
   c. Bank statements for last year
   d. Federal, state, and local income and franchise tax returns and revenue agents' reports for last three years
   e. Copies of inventories for last tax return, for last interim statement, and for last issued statement

5. Prepare comparative statement of income or loss for last three to five years. Prepare comparative gross profit ratios for same period.

6. Determine whether it will be necessary to have fixed assets and inventories appraised for liquidation value by appraiser or auctioneer.

7. Prepare or, if possible, have management prepare list for the following books and records, and state their location (on premises, in warehouse, attorneys' office, or accountants' office):
   a. General ledger
   b. Journals
   c. Subsidiary ledgers
   d. Supporting records, such as minutes of directors' meetings, perpetual inventory cards, production records, cost sheets, and stock records
   Management should sign the list stating that the list includes all of the books and records of the company.

8. Obtain name, address, and telephone number of:
   a. Controller
   b. Key bookkeeping personnel
   c. Principals

9. Prepare trial balance.

10. Review audit program guide considering the information determined from above and modify accordingly.

11. Maintain a "time and expense" log showing name of each person, hours expended, nature of function performed, and other expenses incurred.

Specific Procedures

Cash in Bank

1. Prepare bank reconciliations of all bank accounts for last statement to verify balances and uncover unusual disbursements.
2. Request "cut off" bank statement and reconcile.
3. Examine and review a selected number of months' bank statements for erasures, alterations, unusual disbursements, and other improprieties.
4. Examine canceled checks for several months, especially last four, for endorsement and cancellation dates. Be alert for endorsements indicating:
   a. Payments to owners and/or officers
   b. Loan and exchange transactions
   c. Checks made payable to cash
   d. Cashing by "check cashers" (numbered endorsements) or other suspicious endorsements which may indicate fraudulent payments
5. Test-check duplicate deposit slips to entries in cash receipts journal and to remittance advices.
6. Verify all general journal entries affecting cash, including an examination of all debit and credit memos.
7. Prepare reversal entry for outstanding checks which are unissued and on hand or for which there are no funds in the bank account.
8. Confirm balances with bank.
9. Review interbank transfers for names of banks not reflected on books.
10. Scan cash receipts records and returns and allowance registers for possible unwarranted credits.
11. Examine receipts for disclosure of unusual sources of income which may lead to otherwise unknown assets.

Cash on Hand

1. Determine existing funds and take possession and control.
2. Count and reconcile funds simultaneously.

3. Test vouchers for supporting documents, signatures, and approvals.
4. Note all vouchers relating to loans or any other unusual vouchers.
5. Return funds to custodians.
6. If funds include loans and vouchers not recorded, adjust account to actual cash balance.

Accounts and Notes Receivable

1. Obtain or prepare aged schedule showing:
   a. Name and address
   b. Balance due
   c. Accounts which are assigned
   d. Aging based on invoice date as follows:
      (1) Current month
      (2) First preceding month
      (3) Second preceding month
      (4) Third preceding month
      (5) Fourth preceding month and prior
2. Review aged schedule and determine required allowance for uncollectible accounts.
3. Tie-in supporting records with statement amount of receivables.
4. Calculate allowance for trade and cash discounts.
5. Determine existence and approximate amount of possible advertising or other types of allowances.
6. Determine possibility and approximate amount of recorded and unrecorded sales on consignment.
7. Review sales contracts for unrecorded contractual rights of a recoverable nature.
8. Determine method of recording sample lines in possession of sales representatives or agents.
9. Review propriety of recent write-offs, large returns, and compromises of receivables.
10. Request confirmation of receivable balances with customer or collection agent.
11. List subsequent collections of receivables on separate schedule indicating full details. (This may be required in final accounting for court.)

12. Determine that collection agents have turned over all accounts collected.

13. Compare list of receivables with accounts payable to determine whether the business is also obligated to any of its debtors. In preparing reports for the creditors' committee, it may be desirable to offset a customer's balance in accounts payable against the receivable. In all reports, the amounts and accounts should be disclosed.

Inventories

1. Obtain copies of all previous physical inventories or statement from management as to their disposition.

2. Establish basis of valuation of prior inventories.

3. Observe physical inventory. If business has been closed and no employees are available, arrange to have inventory examined, listed, and valued by a public auction company. Expense should be arranged through attorney and/or referee in bankruptcy.

4. Make test counts of inventory items, tracing them to completed inventory records.

5. Confirm inventory at contractors, if material. Prepare separate schedule of this inventory and list related "liens" by contractors.

6. Inventory at contractors should be evaluated to determine advisability of paying off contractor and obtaining merchandise.

7. Review cut-offs on all merchandise—incoming, outgoing, and in process.

8. Review internal procedures for recording flow of raw materials.

9. Review costing of product lines and verify existence of pricing by book and/or formula.

10. Obtain copies of insurance report forms reflecting inventory values, and compare to recorded values.

11. Test-check pricing of:
    a. Raw materials
    b. Work in process
    c. Finished goods
    d. Packing supplies
    e. Factory supplies
    f. Obsolete inventory

12. Ascertain the amount of incremental cost required to complete the work in process, to determine whether completion is advisable.

13. Perform unit reconciliation from previous to current physical inventory date.

14. Determine whether there are merchandise liens outstanding and disclose them in detail.

15. Make separate list of "bill and hold" merchandise in hands of creditors, and evaluate.

16. Obtain inventory representation letter from management.

Prepaid Insurance

1. Prepare detailed analysis of insurance accounts showing the prepaid amounts, the cash and loan values of life insurance, and the recoverable deposit premiums.

2. Obtain schedule of insurance in force from brokers and compare with records.

3. Review calculation of premium earned based on payroll figures. If the advance exceeds the amount determined from payroll, set it up as a prepaid expense. If the premium is greater than the deposit, show the difference as an accrued liability.

4. Determine the short rate cancellation values of insurance in force.

5. Determine whether life insurance policies on the lives of corporate officers exist by examining entries on corporate books, by searching for the policies themselves, by analyzing the paid and unpaid bills, or by looking for entries on the books which represent payments to life insurance companies for premiums.

6. Confirm cash and loan values of life insurance with insurer.

7. Determine that all dividends received on the policies have been credited to the corporation.

Loans and Exchanges

1. Analyze charges and credits to account in detail.

2. List all disbursements possibly recoverable as follows:
   a. Date
   b. Payee
   c. Amount
   d. Endorsement
   e. Date paid
   f. Where paid
   g. Address of payee

3. Note all charges and credits which did not arise from cash transactions and obtain explanations.

4. Confirm large balances.

Plant and Equipment

1. Analyze property accounts and evaluate the provision for depreciation.

2. Ascertain that additions to plant asset accounts have been properly entered in the records.

3. Ascertain that retirements of plant assets have been properly recorded.

4. Verify that there are no unrecorded retirements.

5. Establish the existence of plant assets by inspecting major items.

6. Inspect contracts, deeds, title guarantee policies, and other related documents to determine ownership.

7. Determine existence of property items and extent to which they are security for existing debts.

8. Determine potential loss on abandonment of leasehold improvements.

9. Determine status of real estate tax arrearages.

10. Obtain estimates of realizable value of fixed assets from approved appraisers or equipment manufacturers.

Other Assets

1. Analyze all accounts such as:
   a. Security deposits
   b. Deposits on fixed asset acquisitions
   c. Prepaid interest
   d. Royalty and commission advances
   e. Prepaid professional fees
   f. Tax refunds
   Show, as a minimum, date, folio, and amount.

2. Prepare schedule of investments and obtain market values.

3. Confirm material items.

Accounts Payable

1. Prepare schedule including names and addresses of creditors, amount owed, and distribution by size of debt.

2. Group liabilities due to factors. If a supplier factors its accounts, the obligation is to the factor. Obligations to suppliers using the same factor should be shown under the factor's name.

3. Examine all material payments and other debits within the prior four months to determine possible preferential treatment to specific creditors. List details with respect to large returns of merchandise and payments before maturity.

4. Compare creditors' statements mailed the first of the month to the debtor, with ledger accounts.

5. Compare balance shown on the books with claim filed by the creditor and reconcile significant differences.

6. Confirm selected balances and especially indebtedness to large creditors.

7. Scrutinize accounts payable for names of related companies or relatives and investigate nature and circumstances of any such accounts.

Notes Payable

1. Prepare schedule showing:
   a. Creditor's name and address
   b. Original principal amount and unpaid balance
   c. Arrearages in principal and interest payments
   d. Date of inspection
   e. Interest rate
   f. Due date
   g. Description of security given and date lien was granted
   h. Guarantors and extent of their obligation
   i. Restrictive clauses and breaches thereof

2. Determine possibility of preferential treatment either in liquidation of debt or granting of security.

3. Obtain copies of notes and supporting documents.

4. Examine selected paid and canceled notes.

5. Confirm selected obligations.

Taxes Payable

1. Determine the amount of tax liability indicated in the records.

2. Examine the most recently filed returns.

3. Carefully examine the records to determine the amount unpaid. In order to determine the liability it is often necessary to complete the unfiled tax returns. The list below indicates the number of returns that must be filed:
   a. Federal, state, and local corporate tax returns
   b. Federal, state, and local payroll tax returns
   c. State and local sales tax returns
   d. State and local property tax returns
   e. Commercial rent, gross receipts, or occupancy tax returns (usually of a local nature)
   f. Truck mileage tax returns
   g. Capital stock franchise tax returns or stock transfer tax returns

4. Compute accrued payroll taxes to date of bankruptcy or date of report if out-of-court settlement is being considered.

5. Analyze expense accounts and establish relationship to payroll.

6. Reconcile tax claims filed by various government authorities to amounts determined from examination of returns and records. Notify counsel of any difference so that claims or records can be adjusted.

7. Verify that all tax claims are properly classified as administrative or non-administrative claims.

Wages Payable and Other Accrued Expenses

1. Prepare or have management prepare schedule including name, address, social security number, gross wages due, period covered, and taxes to be withheld for each employee.

2. Verify amounts due against payroll records to establish that the particular employee in question actually worked for the period claimed.

3. Where union contracts exist, scrutinize the contracts to determine how much severance or vacation pay employees are entitled to receive.

4. Segregate the wages and accrued vacation and severance pay into priority and non-priority classifications.

5. Accrue other wage-related obligations such as union fund contributions and retirement fund contributions.

6. Schedule all other unpaid and unrecorded expenses.

7. Determine existence and terms of any employee benefit plans.

Mortgages and Other Secured Debts

1. Prepare schedule showing:
   a. Creditor's name and address
   b. Original principal amount and unpaid balance
   c. Arrearages in number of payments and total amount and interest payments
   d. Date of inception
   e. Interest rate
   f. Copy of amortization schedule, including any balloon payment
   g. Description of security given and date lien was granted
   h. Guarantors and extent of their obligation
   i. Restrictive clauses and indication of breaches
   j. Extent of real estate tax arrearages
   k. Assessed value of real estate given as security

2. Determine possibility of preferential payment in liquidation of debt and in granting of security.

3. Where accounts receivable are financed or factored, obtain a copy of agreement and list special terms. List monthly debits and credits for a minimum of twelve months showing:
   a. Cash advances
   b. Factor charges
   c. Interest charges
   d. Chargebacks

4. Determine for factored or financed accounts receivable:
   a. That no improprieties exist
   b. Whether the lendor has unreasonably improved its position by taking collateral for less than fair value
   c. That the lendor has at all times maintained dominion and control over its collateral with particular emphasis on promptness of remittances to the debtor
   d. That chargebacks on factored accounts have not been duplicated

5. Obtain executed copy of:
   a. Mortgage
   b. Financing agreement
   c. Factoring contract
   d. Appraisal of collateral

6. Obtain copies of U.C.C. filings from Secretary of State.

7. Confirm selected accounts.

Contributed Capital

1. Obtain stock certificate book and prepare schedule indicating:
   a. Certificate number
   b. Shareholder
   c. Number of shares
   d. Date issued
   e. Date canceled
   f. Restrictions noted in stubs (or obtain information from transfer agent)
2. List significant characteristics of each class of stock.
3. Determine consideration received for stock, noting:
   a. Whether cash, services, or tangible assets
   b. Per-share amount
   c. Total amount
   d. Amount paid in excess of par
4. Obtain details surrounding all stock redemptions and reacquisitions, with particular emphasis on legally defined capital of company at such times.
5. Determine valuation basis of treasury stock.
6. Determine status of stock subscriptions receivable.
7. Examine and abstract all available minutes and resolutions related to contributed capital.
8. Analyze stock option and warrant activity and determine status of those not exercised.

Retained Earnings

1. Analyze for previous four to five years, with full explanations for all debits and credits.
2. Establish propriety of all charges not arising from operations.
3. Segregate any amounts which would properly be classified as donated or arising from revaluation of assets.

Sales

1. Test the cut-off of sales transactions.
2. Check recent common carriers' receipts to determine unrecorded amounts.
3. Test-check last six months or more for sales at less than customary or list prices. Also check for prices which, although customary, are generally below those of competitors.

4. Prepare schedule showing, by month, comparative sales, sales returns, sales allowances, and net sales for last three years and indicate customers constituting in excess of 10 per cent of total volume.

5. Prepare brief summary of sales procedures.

6. Determine potential cost of fulfillment of product guarantees.

7. Review sales, sales orders, and cancellations subsequent to date of filing petition.

8. Determine unfilled orders and management's plans for completing orders.

9. The above procedures are normally not performed in as much detail for assignment and straight bankruptcy cases as they are for an out-of-court settlement, a reorganization, or an arrangement.

Purchases

1. Test the cut-off of cost of sales.

2. Test cost of goods sold entries against shipping records.

3. Prepare schedule showing, by month, comparative purchases for the last three years.

4. Prepare brief description of purchasing procedure.

5. Test-check purchases during previous six to twelve months for adequacy of receiving documentation.

6. Examine purchase returns and allowances for unusually large recent items. Also examine for returns and allowances to relatives or related companies.

7. Review purchase commitments for potential losses or excessive commitments.

Payroll

1. Test selected payroll entries against time cards or piecework reports, union contracts, rate authorization, and deductions authorized.

2. Determine that payroll has been distributed to proper account classifications.

3. Scrutinize selected weeks of payroll for payments to relatives or principals, for unusual payments of back wages, and for inordinately high rates of pay.

4. Compare recent payroll periods with those of the previous year. Justify any differences.

5. Observe a payroll distribution. Compare payroll checks which are to be distributed with the payroll register and prove register totals.

6. Determine date of last union audit and potential additional liability over and above reported contributions.

Other Costs, Expenses, and Income

1. Investigate month-to-month and year-to-year changes in amounts of various costs and expenses.

2. Analyze rent expense and abstract pertinent lease terms.

3. Inquire as to possibility of sublease of all or part of leased premises.

4. Analyze professional fees and determine services rendered.

5. Analyze officers' salaries and expense accounts.

6. Scan other revenue accounts for unusual items and make appropriate examination where required.

7. Search for unrecorded liabilities that may involve losses or expenses.

8. Analyze all other significant expense accounts.

Contracts and Agreements

1. Examine and obtain copies of:
   a. Shareholders' buy/sell agreements
   b. Retirement agreements
   c. Employment contracts
   d. Insurance agreements

2. Examine and abstract all other significant information in contracts and agreements.

9

Financial Reporting

1. The accountant will prepare not only current financial statements but supplementary statements which are helpful in evaluating the future prospects of the business. Three important questions must be answered in order to determine the direction in which the company's future will lie:

What is the current financial position of the business?

If the current position looks financially feasible, what about the future?

If, after projecting the company's operations, the future looks fairly promising, what financial methods can be employed to pump new, healthy financial "blood" into the business?

The report issued by the accountant states the results of operations, and hopefully provides needed information about the possibility of the company's future existence.

2. Among the documents the accountant will submit, at the time the petition is filed or shortly thereafter, are the Statement of Affairs (sworn answers to twenty-one questions about the debtor's past operations; see Chapter 6), recent financial statements, schedules with detailed information about the assets and liabilities of the debtor, and a statement of the amount due each creditor. Also, the accountant may prepare a statement of affairs showing realizable values, and other special-purpose statements to assist the debtor in securing additional funds. These various statements are discussed in detail in paragraphs 4–32.

3. The accountant's report, since it contains an opinion on the statements submitted, is of great importance in bankruptcy proceedings. Because of the nature of the proceedings, there are limitations on the scope of the accountant's examination, and any uncertainty concerning the ability of the company to continue operations may require the accountant to disclaim an opinion on the statements. The nature of the report is described in paragraphs 33–69. The last part of the chapter (paragraphs 70–81) deals with the effect of settlements on future statements.

FORM AND SUBSTANCE OF FINANCIAL STATEMENTS

4. Many of the statements and schedules the accountant is required to prepare in bankruptcy or insolvency proceedings are the same as those used by companies not experiencing financial difficulty. But in insolvency proceedings these reports are used in specific ways to provide the information needed to effect a fair and equitable settlement to all those involved.

Financial Data Required at the Date of Filing of Petition in Chapter XI

5. When a petition is filed to initiate proceedings under Chapter XI, certain documents must be filed at that time or shortly thereafter. Among the most important are the following.

Statement of Affairs. This consists of answers to twenty-one questions concerning the debtor's past operations, and should not be confused with the report titled "Statement of Affairs," to be discussed later, which shows the realizable value of the assets and the liabilities in the order in which they will be paid.

Recent financial statements including:
1. Statements of Financial Position and income statements issued during the two years prior to filing
2. Current Statement of Financial Position
3. Statement of Operations covering the period from the date of the last balance sheet to the date of the petition
4. Statement of Capital Deficiency as of date of petition

Schedules with detailed information about the assets and liabilities of the debtor as of the date of the petition.

Schedule showing the summary of operations and the percentage relationship of each item to sales for each of the previous three to five years.

Correct statement of the amount due each creditor, including secured, unsecured, contingent, and unliquidated claims.

A statement of all executory contracts.

6. The accountant obviously plays a very valuable role in obtaining the information required in these statements, and any attempt to file a petition without the aid of an accountant would reduce the reliability of the data accompanying the petition. Chapter 6 contains a more detailed description of the schedules and other information filed with the petition.

Balance Sheets (Statements of "Condition")

7. In addition to balance sheets relating to prior years, the debtor is required to furnish a current balance sheet. This statement, while having importance on its own, also forms the basis for several other statements which must be filed. While balance sheets are normally prepared in the conventional manner, alternative forms are sometimes used because of the doubts surrounding the balances as they are found in the accounts. Three columns might be presented, showing balances as per books, certain proposed corrections, and balances after certain proposed correc-

tions, so that all those using the statement will be aware that the figures are tentative. Figure 9–1 (pages 260–61) shows this type of balance sheet.

8. Figure 9–2 (pages 262–65) shows the conventional balance sheet for the ABC Company as of December 31, 1974, along with the notes to the statement. This balance sheet and other statements of the ABC Company will serve as the focal point of discussion throughout this chapter. Four months after the date of the balance sheet presented in Figure 9–2, the ABC Company appealed to its creditors for their assistance. Figure 9–3 (pages 266–67) shows the balance sheet as of April 28, 1975, which is prepared in the normal manner except that all secured liabilities are subtracted from the assets to which they relate. In this balance sheet, the balance of accounts receivable is reduced to zero since they are pledged to the First National Bank in the amount of $600,000 and the net realizable value is only $584,800. Priority claims are subtracted from the total unpledged assets before arriving at the total book value of assets available to unsecured creditors. Also listed are factors which may create an increased capital deficit, such as additional losses that may be sustained on realization of assets, and administrative expenses or additional contingent or undisclosed liabilities.

9. This type of balance sheet is very useful in meetings with creditors' committees, in Chapter XI arrangement proceedings, or in out-of-court settlements. The final total represents the assets that are available for unsecured creditors. All assets are normally presented at book value less any necessary adjustments which should be made as a result of the audit. These are not liquidation values. It is assumed that the business will be rehabilitated and continue operations. The balance sheet differs from the Statement of Affairs in that the balance sheet is not prepared on the assumption that the business will be liquidated. The Statement of Affairs is described in detail in a subsequent section (paragraphs 18–27).

JIM STORES, INC. (A BANKRUPT)
AND SUBSIDIARY COMPANIES
CONSOLIDATED BALANCE SHEET

October 14, 1975

	Balances, as Per Books	Certain Proposed Corrections— Increase/ (Decrease)	Balances, After Certain Proposed Corrections
Assets			
Cash	$ (66,857)	$ 116,257	$ 59,953
		(42,899)	
		53,452	
Accounts Receivable—Trade	2,968,661	10	2,900,516
		(61,746)	
		(6,409)	
Less: Allowance for Doubtful Accounts	829,765	5,584	1,300,000
		(475,829)	
		10	
	2,138,896		1,600,516
Notes and Other Accounts Receivable—Non-Trade	591,536	6,000	597,536
Merchandise Inventories	1,005,344	105,987	1,043,072
		(68,259)	
Prepaid Expenses	27,261	(12,538)	14,723
Investments and Advances	1,323,262	(10,235)	1,579,651
		11,127	
		292,997	
		(37,500)	
Deposits and Other Assets	134,878	(25,863)	109,015
Property and Equipment:			
Land	673,750	—	673,750
Furniture, Fixtures, and Leasehold Improvements	667,760	(238,220)	429,540
Less: Accumulated Depreciation and Amortization	491,630	197,909	293,721
	176,130		135,819
Construction in Progress	615,000	(615,000)	—
Total Assets	$6,619,200	$ (805,165)	$5,814,035

Figure 9–1.   Balance Sheet presentation showing proposed corrections

	Balances, as Per Books	Certain Proposed Corrections— Increase/ (Decrease)	Balances, After Certain Proposed Corrections
Liabilities and Stockholders' Equity			
Collateralized Obligations:			
Notes Payable—GCA Company	$ 122,500	$ (4,756)	$ 117,744
Advances from Jones Company	1,226,771	(42,899)	1,183,872
Mortgage Payable	73,750	—	73,750
Lorraine Co. Chapter XI Notes	53,954	—	53,954
	1,476,975		1,429,320
Uncollateralized Obligations:			
Construction Loan	615,000	(615,000)	—
5% Debenture Bonds, Due 2/1/77	800,000	—	800,000
Notes Payable—Banks	162,000	—	162,000
Note Payable—Other	493,830	1,000	464,830
		(30,000)	
Checks Written in Excess of Bank Balances	—	116,257	116,257
Accounts Payable and Accrued Liabilities	1,261,734	53,741	1,312,043
		(25,120)	
		4,617	
		2,071	
		15,000	
Affiliated Companies	—	293,882	293,882
	3,332,564		3,149,012
Deferred Income Taxes	360,000	—	360,000
Deferred Income	1,425	—	1,425
Ledger Imbalance	94,347	(58,310)	5,060
		(44,503)	
		13,527	
Stockholders' Equity:			
Common Stock (par value 50¢ per share; authorized 500,000 shares, plus 36,000 shares reserved for issuance pursuant to acquisition of subsidiary NPR Co., less 23,856 shares held in treasury)	240,283	750	231,033
		(10,000)	
Paid-In Surplus	1,008,337	10,377	1,024,714
		6,000	
Retained Earnings (Deficit)	105,269	(13,527)	(386,529)
		87,021	
		(2,286)	
		(563,007)	
	1,353,889		869,218
Total Liabilities and Stockholders' Equity	$6,619,200	$ (805,165)	$5,814,035

to bankrupt's books and final balances after corrections.

ABC COMPANY, INC.

BALANCE SHEET

December 31, 1974

Assets

Current Assets:			
Cash			$ 35,295
Accounts Receivable		$553,200	
Less: Allowance for Discounts	$ 40,200		
Allowance for Uncollectibles	92,300	132,500	420,700
Inventories			650,000
Tax Refund Receivable			294,673
Total Current Assets			1,400,668
Fixed and Other Assets:			
Property, Plant, and Equipment (Note 4):			
Land		22,000	
Building	$1,150,000		
Less: Accumulated Depreciation	510,000	640,000	
Fixtures and Equipment	93,000		
Less: Accumulated Depreciation	22,000	71,000	733,000
Investment in XYZ Company		20,000	
Goodwill (Notes 1 and 5)		10,250	763,250
Total Assets			$2,163,918

Figure 9–2. Example of standard Balance Sheet with explanatory Notes,

Liabilities and Stockholders' Equity		
Current Liabilities:		
Accounts Payable		$ 511,618
Salaries Payable		100,500
Commissions Payable		10,000
Taxes Payable		100,000
Notes Payable (Note 3)		570,000
Payable to Contractors		125,000
Reserve for Liquidation Losses (Note 2)		200,000
Total Current Liabilities		1,617,118
Long-Term Liabilities:		
Mortgages Payable (Note 4)		487,500
Other Liabilities:		
Notes Payable—Officer		36,000
Total Liabilities		2,140,618
Stockholders' Equity:		
Common Stock ($10 par, 20,000 shares authorized, 18,000 shares outstanding: see Note 5)	$180,000	
Deficit	(156,700)	23,300
Total Liabilities and Stockholders' Equity		$2,163,918

showing financial condition of ABC Company as of December 31, 1974.

ABC COMPANY, INC.

NOTES TO BALANCE SHEET

Note 1. Basis of Presentation and Summary of Significant Accounting Policies

Basis of Presentation:

ABC Company, Inc., had sustained losses from its operations during the four years ended December 31, 1974, and based on subsequent unaudited financial information, losses have continued since December 31, 1974. The accompanying financial statements have been prepared on a going-concern basis. Continuation of the Company's operations, realization of its assets, and liquidation of its liabilities are dependent upon the ability of the Company to achieve a profitable level of operations and to obtain additional financing.

Summary of Significant Accounting Policies:

Inventories—The total merchandise inventory at December 31, 1974, is stated at the lower of cost or market, determined by the FIFO method.

Property, Plant, and Equipment—Property, plant, and equipment are carried at cost. Additions and improvements are capitalized; maintenance and repairs are charged to operations as incurred. Depreciation is calculated using the straight-line method over the estimated useful lives of the assets.

Goodwill—The goodwill was transferred to the Company in 1968 (see Note 5) and is being amortized at the rate of $1,000 per year.

Note 2. Operations To Be Discontinued and Estimated Liquidation Losses

On October 29, 1974, the Board of Directors resolved to discontinue the operations of one division. A summary of the assets of this division is as follows:

Accounts Receivable—Net	$100,000
Inventories	225,000
Property, Plant, and Equipment	130,000
	$455,000

The liquidation of this division will probably result in liquidation losses. The Company had provided a reserve for estimated losses of $200,000; however, no determination can be made at this time as to the total amount of such losses.

Figure 9–2.　Continued.

Note 3. Notes Payable

The Company entered into a financing agreement in 1972 with the First National Bank of Boston wherein it applied for a revolving credit of $600,000. As security for the payment of the Company's debt to the bank, it granted and assigned to the bank a continuing security interest in all accounts receivable owned or created by the Company. The continuation of this agreement is conditioned upon (1) a cash projection (unaudited) for the six months ending June 30, 1975, furnished to the bank by the Company, (2) the ability of the Company to improve cash flow (including the program set forth in Note 2), and (3) the assumption that there will be no material adverse changes in the Company's financial plans and projection on an overall basis.

Note 4. Mortgage Payable

Property, plant, and equipment are pledged as collateral for mortgages payable of $487,500. The mortgages payable mature in varying amounts to January 31, 1989, bearing interest from 5 per cent to 9 per cent per annum.

Note 5. Stockholders' Equity

ABC Company, Inc., was incorporated under the laws of the State of New York on September 17, 1968. Prior to that date, on April 6, 1968, AB Company, Inc., a wholly owned subsidiary of AF Industries, Inc., transferred certain assets to the new company, ABC Company, Inc., as follows:

Merchandise Inventory	$296,000
Fixed Assets (Net of Accumulated Depreciation)	22,306
Goodwill	17,000
Cash Surrender Value of Life Insurance (Net of Loans Thereon of $42,670)	5,775
Prepaid Expenses	12,600
Other Assets	4,500
	$358,181
Represented by: Capital Stock (8,000 Shares)	$ 80,000
Loans Payable	278,181
	$358,181

On August 5, 1969, ABC Company issued 10,000 shares of stock at par value of $10 to the public. As of December 31, 1974, AF Industries owned 30 per cent of the outstanding stock and the President, Irving J. Stein, owned 10 per cent.

Figure 9–2.   Continued.

ABC COMPANY, INC.

STATEMENT OF FINANCIAL CONDITION

April 28, 1975

Assets

Current Assets:			
Cash			$ 7,327
Accounts Receivable—Assigned		$710,100	
Less: Allowance for Discounts	$ 50,100		
Allowance for Uncollectibles	75,200	125,300	
		584,800	
Less: Due to First National Bank of Boston			
(see contra)		$600,000	
Inventories		$795,000	
Less: Due to Contractors		75,000	720,000
Tax Refund Receivable			7,673
Total Unpledged Current Assets			735,000
Fixed and Other Assets:			
Property, Plant, and Equipment:			
Land		22,000	
Building	$1,150,000		
Less: Accumulated Depreciation	550,000	600,000	
Fixtures and Equipment	93,000		
Less: Accumulated Depreciation	25,000	68,000	
		690,000	
Less: Mortgage Payable		487,500	202,500
Investment in XYZ Company		20,000	
Goodwill		10,000	232,500
Total Unpledged Assets			967,500
Less: Priority Claims			247,500
Total Assets Available to General Creditors			$720,000

Figure 9–3.   Balance Sheet, or Statement of Financial Condition,
to its creditors

Liabilities, Less Capital Deficiency			
Priority Claims:			
Taxes Payable			$100,000
Salaries Payable			127,500
Commissions Payable			20,000
Total Priority Claims			$247,500
Fully Collateralized Claims:			
Mortgages Payable			$487,500
Contractors Payable (see contra)			75,000
Total Fully Collateralized Claims			$562,500
Partially Collateralized Claims:			
First National Bank of Boston:			
Notes Payable		$500,000	
Accounts Payable (see below)		100,000	
		600,000	
Less: Accounts Receivable—Assigned (see contra)		584,800	$ 15,200
General Claims:			
Due to ABC Company, Inc.—Employees' Profit Sharing			
Trust		25,000	
Accounts Payable	$682,000		
Less: Accounts Payable—First National Bank of			
Boston (see above)	100,000	582,000	607,000
Notes Payable—Officer			36,000
Total General Claims			658,200
Reserve for Liquidation Losses			200,000
Capital Deficiency			(138,200)
Subject to:			
1. Additional losses that may be sustained on realization			
of assets and administrative expenses			
2. Contingent and undisclosed liabilities			
Total Liabilities (General Claims) Less			
Capital Deficiency			$720,000

of the ABC Company as of April 28, 1975, after it had appealed
for assistance.

Notes to Statements

10. The notes to the balance sheet should also receive greater attention than is conventional. They should explain the content of each account, include some of the major audit steps that were performed, and discuss any information that was not available during the examination and any deficiencies in the books and records. For example, a physical inventory might not have been taken at the date the petition is filed and the accountant may wish to disclose the method used to satisfy the requirement that the inventory be correctly stated. The notes in support of accounts receivable and inventories, which are only two of the many that were needed to explain the accounts in the balance sheet of Jim Stores, Inc. (Figure 9–1), are shown in Figure 9–4 to illustrate how detailed the notes to the financial statements must typically be.

11. The balance sheet becomes the basis for the schedules of assets and liabilities which the bankrupt must file. These schedules consist of sworn statements of the debtor's assets and liabilities as of the date of filing the petition and include the same basic information found in the debtor's balance sheet. (For detailed discussion, see Chapter 6, paragraphs 25–39.)

12. Section 7a(8) of the Bankruptcy Act requires that the debtor file its detailed schedules within five days of adjudication as an involuntary bankrupt or within five days of filing a voluntary petition. However, the debtor may be allowed to petition the court with only a balance sheet and file the detailed schedules within a short time period thereafter. In this case, the balance sheet gains added importance.

13. Quite clearly, in addition to its conventional significance as a statement of position at one point in time, the balance sheet prepared as of the date of bankruptcy derives greater importance because of the schedules that are prepared from it.

Income Statements

14. The debtor is required to file a statement in duplicate on the fifteenth day of each month setting forth the results from operations of the previous month. Because of the complexities involved in preparing such a statement, an accountant's services

JIM STORES, INC.

NOTES TO CONSOLIDATED BALANCE SHEET (PARTIAL)

Accounts Receivable, Trade—$2,900,516

The amount of accounts receivable shown in the accompanying balance sheet as of October 14, 1975, represents the aggregate amount appearing in the general ledgers of the companies, less a correction for certain accounts receivable which had been sold. Prior to October 14, the companies had closed a number of stores and had sold the accounts receivable originating at these stores. However, such accounts had inadvertently not been eliminated from the books of the companies and we have made a correction for such sold accounts.

In addition, the accounts receivable are subject to the following comments:

1. The accounts receivable have been pledged as collateral under a financing agreement with Jones & Company, Inc. Prior to our engagement, Jones & Company had requested each of the stores to prepare trial balances of its accounts receivable on or about October 14, 1975 (detailed accounts receivable information is available only at the stores). We have obtained such trial balances from Jones and have compared the totals thereon to the companies' general ledger control accounts as of October 14, taking into consideration intervening sales and collections in cases where the trial balances were prepared as of a date other than October 14. In making this comparison, we find that the trial balances do not agree with the general ledger control accounts by an aggregate of $3,460.80 (trial balance totals in excess of ledger balances). These differences range from one corporation in which trial balances exceed the ledger balance by $6,402.32 to another where the aggregate of individual store balances is $16,693.02 less than the corporate ledger balance. We have not corrected for these differences because we did not investigate them to the extent necessary to determine their origin and their effect on other accounts. To the extent that we did investigate, we noted that the following factors contributed to the differences:

   a. As described in the Cash section of this report, there was considerable confusion and erroneous handling of cash collections on or about October 14, 1975.

   b. Customers occasionally make deposits for layaway purchases and these deposits are entered in the accounts receivable control accounts without further segregation or detailed accounting. The trial balances prepared on or about October 14 did not include the amounts of open customer deposits. Such deposits, which are not otherwise segregated in the companies' records, represent unsecured obligations of the companies to the customers and should be recognized as such.

2. Jones & Company maintains a record of the amount of accounts receivable representing its collateral. We requested that Jones report to us the balance as shown on its records, for comparison with the companies' ledgers. The amount reported by Jones to us differs from the amount recorded on the companies' books. We understand that Jones has attempted to identify this difference.

3. In 1974 the companies sold certain accounts receivable which had previously been written off as uncollectible. Approximately $2,400,000 of such receivables were sold for a consideration of $300,000. Subsequent to that time the companies have collected at least $140,000 on accounts receivable which had been written off, but these collections have not been segregated into sold accounts and unsold accounts. The collections have been taken into income on the companies' books.

The purchase price for the accounts sold had been received in the form of a five-year $300,000 note; to the extent that collections may have been made by the companies on sold accounts, the companies should apply such collections against the face amount of the note.

Figure 9–4. Selected Notes to the Balance Sheet for Jim Stores, Inc., shown in Figure 9–1.

4. As a part of our work with the companies' accounts receivable, we selected a number of accounts for direct verification by correspondence with the customers. In the course of this work, we made the following observations which we feel are significant:

a. In the trial balances selected by us for circularization, almost 5 per cent of the accounts listed did not have any mailing address for the customer.

b. We made a circularization from among those customers for whom mailing addresses were listed on the trial balance and found that a number of these were returned undelivered because of incomplete or wrong addresses. Where the companies' officials were able to furnish better addresses, the circulars were remailed to the new addresses, and in some cases these too were returned undelivered. Of the customers selected, we were unable to contact about 5 per cent due to lack of accurate mailing addresses.

Inventories—$1,043,072

Physical inventories were taken by the companies on or about November 30, 1975. We visited six stores during the inventory counts to observe the procedures in operation, and visited six other stores after the inventory counts to check the accuracy of the results. We are satisfied that a reasonably accurate inventory was taken on or about November 30, 1975.

Such physical inventories, after compilation, were worked back to October 14, 1974, at retail prices by taking into consideration intervening sales and transfers. The information for such sales and transfers was obtained from machine tabulations prepared by a machine accounting service agency affiliated with Smith & Company in Atlanta, Georgia. We found that these tabulations do not tie in to sales and transfer data developed by alternate sources. While we have made corrections for certain types of differences, we have not satisfied ourselves that the data used, after correction, are reliable. Furthermore, while we have been informed that purchases during this period were nominal and would not materially affect the reconstruction of October 14 inventory amounts, we have not been able to gather any acceptable data with respect to such purchases.

The inventory amount appearing in the accompanying balance sheet represents the inventory, reconstructed as described above, as of October 14, 1975, at retail prices, less a reduction from retail, based on an average normal profit percentage for the companies. This method of valuing inventories is commonly used by retail organizations and is designed to state inventories at the lower of cost or market. However, the method presupposes that the retail prices used as the base for the computations will represent realistic prices at which it can normally be expected that the merchandise will be sold, that adequate mark-downs in retail prices will have been made whenever necessary to move merchandise, that excessive quantities of aged merchandise are not accumulating, and that the inventory will be liquidated in an orderly manner in the ordinary course of business. We were informed, however, that the companies had for some time experienced considerable difficulty in replenishing their inventories with new merchandise. This necessarily resulted in a general deterioration of the quality and age of merchandise remaining unsold. Furthermore, mark-downs appear to have been less extensive than would have been expected under the circumstances. Under the present financial difficulties of the companies, it would appear that inventories will not be liquidated in an orderly manner in the ordinary course of business. We understand that a considerable amount of inventory was liquidated during the past Christmas season but we have not reviewed the extent of such liquidation or the disposition to be made of unliquidated merchandise.

Figure 9–4.   Continued.

usually prove to be necessary. For example, the statement must be prepared on an accrual basis (Chapter 6, paragraphs 16–19).

15. A detailed income statement or Statement of Operations is presented for the last complete year of operation and for the subsequent period to the date of filing the petition in bankruptcy. In addition to the amount, the percentage of each item listed on the statement is given in relation to net sales. Figure 9–5 is an example of this type of statement for the ABC Company. Comparative incomes are often prepared in less detail, but percentages for the last three to five years are included, as shown in Figure 9–6.

Cash Receipts and Disbursements Statements

16. In some instances the court may require that a Cash Receipts and Disbursements Statement be filed each week, although an order may be secured deleting this requirement. The preparation of cash receipts and disbursements statements becomes extremely important where the debtor's plan calls for installment payments and it is necessary for the accountant to show that such payments will be made. See Chapter 7, paragraphs 13 and 23.

Statement of Capital Deficiency

17. A Statement of Capital Deficiency is often prepared, setting forth in summary form the changes in the capital accounts for the last few years. This statement indicates the time period when the losses began to occur, any withdrawals by the owners, and all other major transactions dealing with the capital accounts. The Statement of Capital Deficiency for the ABC Company as of April 28, 1975, is presented in Figure 9–7 (page 274).

Statement of Affairs

18. A Statement of Affairs is quite commonly prepared when a business is experiencing financial difficulty and considering initiation of some type of remedy. This statement should not be confused with the statement of affairs which must be filed under the Bankruptcy Act when a debtor files a petition, and consists merely of answers to questions regarding the debtor's past operations (Chapter 6, paragraphs 38–39). The statement of affairs is often

ABC COMPANY, INC.

STATEMENT OF OPERATIONS

Prior Year and Current Year to Date of Filing

	January 1 to April 28, 1975		For the Year Ended December 31, 1974	
Sales	$1,050,000		$3,750,000	
Less: Returns	100,000	(9.5% of gross sales)	250,000	(6.7% of gross sales)
	950,000		3,500,000	
Less: Discounts and Allowances	75,000	(7.9% of sales, less returns)	160,000	(4.6% of sales, less returns)
Net Sales	$ 875,000	100.0%	$3,340,000	100.0%
Cost of Goods Sold:				
Inventories—Beginning	650,000		840,000	
Raw Materials	505,000		1,827,000	
Labor and Factory Overhead	427,500		600,000	
	1,582,500		3,267,000	
Inventories—End	795,000		650,000	
Cost of Goods Sold		787,500	90.0	2,617,000	78.4
Gross Profit		87,500	10.0	723,000	21.6
Operating Expenses [Figure 9-6]:				
Production and Designing	52,000		310,000	
Selling and Shipping	95,000		450,000	
General and Administrative	102,000		300,000	
		249,000	28.5	1,060,000	(31.7)
Operating Loss		(161,500)	(18.5)	(337,000)	(10.1)
Estimated Liquidation Losses		—		(200,000)	(6.0)
Federal Income Tax Credit		—		(287,000)	(8.6)
Net Loss		$ (161,500)	(18.5)	$ (250,000)	(7.5)

Figure 9–5. Statement of Operations of ABC Company for completed calendar year and for subsequent period to date of filing of petition in bankruptcy.

ABC COMPANY, INC.

SUMMARY OF STATEMENT OF OPERATIONS

Prior Three Years and Current Year to Date of Filing

	January 1 to April 28, 1975		For the Years Ended					
			December 31, 1974		December 31, 1973		December 31, 1972	
Net Sales	$ 875,000	100.0%	$3,340,000	100.0%	$4,400,000	100.0%	$4,700,000	100.0%
Cost of Sales	787,500	90.0	2,617,000	78.4	3,100,000	70.5	3,200,000	68.1
Gross Profit	87,500	10.0	723,000	21.6	1,300,000	29.5	1,500,000	31.9
Operating Expenses	249,000	28.5	1,260,000*	37.7	1,500,000	34.1	1,570,475	33.4
Loss from Operations	(161,500)	(18.5)	(537,000)	(16.1)	(200,000)	(4.6)	(70,475)	(1.5)
Income Tax Credits	—		(287,000)	(8.6)	(100,000)	(2.3)	(40,475)	(.9)
Net Loss	$ (161,500)	(18.5)	$ (250,000)	(7.5)	$ (100,000)	(2.3)	$ (30,000)	(.6)

*Includes liquidation losses estimated at $200,000.

Figure 9–6. Summary of Statement of Operations of ABC Company for three completed calendar years and for subsequent period to date of filing of petition in bankruptcy.

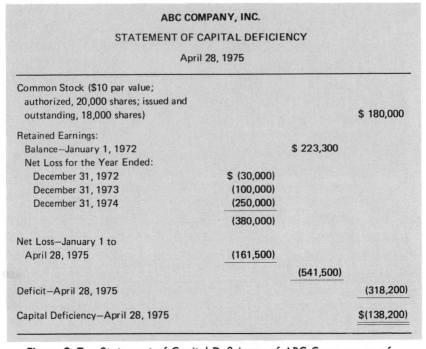

Figure 9–7. Statement of Capital Deficiency of ABC Company as of April 28, 1975, the date of filing of petition in bankruptcy.

prepared under the direction of the bankruptcy judge or at the request of the creditors' committee in out-of-court proceedings and it provides information which assists the creditors in deciding on the course of action they should take in their dealings with the insolvent debtor. The Statement of Affairs, developed from the balance sheet in Figure 9–3, for the ABC Company as of April 28, 1975, is shown in Figure 9–8 (pages 276–77).

19. The report prepared by the accountant is a statement of the debtor's financial condition as of a certain date, and presents an analysis of its financial position and the status of the creditors with respect to the debtor's assets. It has been termed "a statement of position from a 'quitting concern' point of view."

20. The Statement of Affairs is based on assumptions which differ quite clearly from those on which the balance sheet is based. Some of the major differences follow:

It is hypothetical or pro forma; that is, it is an estimate of the probable outcome if the debtor's business were liquidated.

Liquidation is assumed to occur and therefore it is necessary to establish a time period over which the assets will be sold so that their value may be estimated. The shorter the time period, the smaller the proceeds from sales which will be realized.

Correspondingly, the assumption of a going concern is abandoned and the emphasis is shifted from measuring periodic profit to establishing the debts and resources available to meet those obligations.

The form used for the statement of affairs is that which will reveal the legal status of the several groups of creditors.

21. The normal procedure followed in constructing the Statement of Affairs consists of setting up the section headings; reporting each liability in the appropriate section, and, if the liability is secured, reporting the related asset in the appropriate section; listing all the remaining assets which should be the unpledged assets; and summarizing the asset and liability data. Clearly, before the Statement of Affairs can be prepared a balance sheet must be drawn up and additional data secured. In addition to the balance sheet, the following information is needed:

Reliable estimates of the amount which can be expected to be realized from the sale of each asset

All pledges of assets which have been made on specific obligations

Any obligations which are expected to arise while liquidation is proceeding, but which are not currently found in the balance sheet[1]

22. Several values may be shown on the Statement of Affairs for each asset, but the most important is the realizable value or the cash value of each asset in liquidation through forced sale. The columns normally found for assets on the Statement of Affairs are:

Book Value—the balance of each asset as it is found in the debtor's books and would appear on a balance sheet at that date

[1] Harry Simons and Wilbert E. Karrenbrock, *Advanced Accounting—Comprehensive Volume* (Cincinnati: Southwestern Publishing Co., 1968), p. 643.

ABC COMPANY, INC.

STATEMENT OF AFFAIRS

April 28, 1975

Book Value	Assets	Appraised	Estimated Amount Available	Loss or (Gain) on Realization
	Assets Pledged With Fully Secured Creditors:			
$ 795,000	Inventories	$ 400,000		$395,000
22,000	Land	35,000		(13,000)
600,000	Building	650,000		(50,000)
68,000	Fixtures and Equipment	20,000		48,000
	Total	1,105,000		
	Less: Fully Secured Claims (see contra)	562,500	$542,500	
	Assets Pledged With Partly Secured Creditors:			
584,800	Accounts Receivable	450,000		134,800
	Total	$ 450,000		
	Free Assets:			
7,327	Cash	$ 7,327	7,327	
7,673	Tax Refund Receivable	7,673	7,673	
20,000	Investment in XYZ Company	20,000	20,000	
10,000	Goodwill	–0–		10,000
	Trademarks	5,000	5,000	(5,000)
	Estimated Amount Available		582,500	
	Liabilities With Priority (see contra)		257,500	
	Estimated Amount Available for Unsecured Creditors (Approximately 33¢ per Dollar)		325,000	
	Estimated Deficiency on Unsecured Liabilities		468,000	
	Reserve for Liquidation Losses Established December 31, 1974 (see contra)			(200,000)
$2,114,800	Totals		$793,000	$319,800

Figure 9–8. Statement of Affairs of ABC Company as of

Book Value	Liabilities and Stockholders' Equity		Amount Unsecured
	Liabilities With Priority:		
$ –0–	Estimated Liquidation Costs	$ 10,000	
100,000	Taxes Payable	100,000	
127,500	Salaries Payable	127,500	
20,000	Commissions Payable	20,000	
	Total Liabilities With Priority (deducted contra)	$257,500	
	Fully Secured Liabilities:		
75,000	Payable to Contractors	$ 75,000	
487,500	Mortgages Payable	487,500	
	Total Fully Secured Liabilities (deducted contra)	$562,500	
	Partly Secured Liabilities:		
	First National Bank of Boston:		
500,000	Notes Payable	$500,000	
100,000	Accounts Payable	100,000	
	Total Partly Secured Liabilities	600,000	
	Less: Accounts Receivable Assigned (see contra)	450,000	$150,000
	Unsecured Liabilities:		
	Due to ABC Company, Inc., Employees' Profit		
25,000	Sharing Trust		25,000
	Accounts Payable	682,000	
582,000	Less: Payable to First National Bank of Boston	100,000	582,000
36,000	Notes Payable to Officer		36,000
200,000	Reserve for Liquidation Losses (deducted contra)	$200,000	
	Stockholders' Equity:		
180,000	Common Stock		
(318,200)	Deficit		
$2,114,800	Totals		$793,000

April 28, 1975, the date of filing of petition in bankruptcy.

Appraised Value—the amount of cash expected to be realized upon sale of the asset

Estimated Amount Available—the proceeds which will be available for unsecured creditors as a result of the sale of the asset; obtained by subtracting the fully and partially secured claims and liabilities with priority from the total appraised value of assets

Estimated Loss or Gain on Realization of the Asset

23. The basis of the classification scheme used for assets in the Statement of Affairs is the availability of assets to unsecured creditors, and this form is related to the liability classifications. It is important that all those assets which will probably be accruing to the debtor also be included. The groups and the order in which they are usually found are as follows:

Assets pledged with fully secured creditors, including all those assets with a realizable value expected to be at least equal to the claims against them

Assets pledged with partly secured creditors, including assets with a realizable value expected to be less than the claims against them

Free assets, which are those available to meet the claims of general creditors

24. Liabilities and owners' equity are shown in the Statement of Affairs in the order in which the claims against the assets will be liquidated. The accountant should be careful to include all those liabilities expected to be incurred. Two columns are normally found for the liability section, one giving the book value or balance sheet amount of the claim and a second indicating the amount of the liability which is unsecured. They are classified in terms of their legal priority and secured status, with the following groups most commonly used:

Liabilities with priority—creditors who, under the priority granted by the Bankruptcy Act, must be paid before anything is given to unsecured creditors

Fully secured liabilities—creditors with claims against which assets have been pledged with a realizable value equal to or greater than the debt

Partly secured liabilities—debts for which the assets pledged have a realizable value less than the claim which they are intended to secure

Unsecured liabilities—liabilities with no legal priority and not secured by pledged assets; these claims must be satisfied by the free assets

Capital accounts

25. The foregoing information readily gives an estimate of the amount which the unsecured creditors may expect to receive. The percentage of each claim which will be paid is equal to the total realizable value of the free assets divided by the total amount of unsecured claims.

26. Along with the Statement of Affairs, a deficiency statement is often prepared to show the source of the deficiency to unsecured creditors. Normally included is the estimated gain or loss on the realization of each asset and any additional costs associated with liabilities which have not been recorded, thus giving the total estimated loss from liquidation. The amount of this loss to be suffered by the owners and the deficiency to creditors are then shown. This statement is valuable in that it reveals how the capital contributed to the business was used and why it is not possible to pay all the creditors. Figure 9–9 presents the Statement of Deficiency to Unsecured Creditors for the ABC Company.

27. The preparation of a Statement of Affairs is virtually mandatory when a company is experiencing difficulty and attempting to decide which course of action it would be best to follow. Its main advantage to the creditors is that it assists them in ascertaining what actions should be taken by setting forth the probable results from alternative policies.

Special-Purpose Statements

28. If the accountant is conducting an investigation aimed at uncovering irregularities, the preparation of special schedules is crucial. It may be necessary to prepare a statement of all the payments made preceding the filing of the petition, to reveal any preferential payments; or a schedule of all sales of assets may have to be devised to uncover fraudulent transfers.

29. The accountant will normally be asked to prepare, for a given time period following the filing of the petition, statements

ABC COMPANY, INC.

STATEMENT OF ESTIMATED DEFICIENCY
TO UNSECURED CREDITORS

April 28, 1975

Estimated Losses on Realization:		
On Inventories	$395,000	
On Fixtures and Equipment	48,000	
On Accounts Receivable	134,800	
On Goodwill	10,000	$587,800
Estimated Gains on Realization:		
On Land	13,000	
On Buildings	50,000	
On Trademarks	5,000	68,000
Net Loss on Realization		519,800
Unrecorded Expenses		—0—
Liquidation Expenses:		
Legal Fees and Liquidation Costs	7,000	
Accountants' Liquidation Fees	3,000	10,000
Total Estimated Losses and Costs of Liquidation		529,800
Less: Stockholders' Equity:		
Common Stock	180,000	
Less: Deficit	(318,200)	(138,200)
Estimated Deficiency to Unsecured Creditors Before Adjustment		668,000
Less: Reserve for Liquidation Losses		200,000
Estimated Deficiency to Unsecured Creditors		$468,000

Figure 9–9. Statement of Estimated Deficiency to Unsecured Creditors filed by the ABC Company as of April 28, 1975, the date of filing of petition in bankruptcy.

projecting the profit expectations of future operations. These statements provide a tool for working out a plan of arrangement and should include budgets, cash flow statements, and profit projections.[2]

[2] Edward A. Weinstein, "Accountants' Examinations and Reports in Bankruptcy Proceedings," *New York Certified Public Accountant*, Vol. 35 (January 1965), p. 35.

30. It may also be necessary to show why it would be in the best interests of the creditors for the debtor to remain in operation of the business. This involves proving that creditors would profit more from a plan of arrangement than from liquidation, and is usually accomplished with a schedule estimating the size of the dividend creditors would receive if the business were liquidated. To obtain such a figure, the forced-sale value of the assets must be determined and all those assets which may be recovered for the bankrupt's estate must be included.

31. If a plan of arrangement providing for installment payments over a period of time is proposed, the accountant will be required to prepare a projected budget, a cash flow statement, and a balance sheet, to show that the debtor will be able to make the payments and that the plan is feasible.

32. Thus, the two main categories where special statements are found are in the search for irregular transactions and in drawing up a plan to effect rehabilitation. However, each insolvency proceeding is unique and the individual situation will govern what additional reports the accountant must prepare so that the proceeding will be fair and equitable to all involved.

REPORTING ON AN INSOLVENT CONDITION

33. The report containing the accountant's opinion on the statements prepared and submitted has supreme importance in the bankruptcy proceedings. It is the chief source of information for all those who are interested in the debtor's affairs, and the degree of reliance placed on the statements is dependent upon the accountant's opinion concerning them.

Accountants' Reports

34. It is first necessary to point out that the reports issued by accountants concerning companies in liquidation, reorganization, or arrangement proceedings are very similar. The primary differences which arise relate mostly to the material which is covered rather than to the basic format. It is crucial for the accountant to realize, however, that straight bankruptcy proceedings involve audits of

companies being liquidated, while arrangements or reorganizations are audits of going concerns.

35. The reports issued in insolvency proceedings do differ significantly in certain respects from those issued as a result of a traditional audit. When reporting on a going concern, the emphasis is on allocating costs into expired and unexpired portions to determine the results of operations. However, when reporting on a firm involved in insolvency proceedings, the concern shifts to the realizable value of the assets and the legally enforceable obligations which have been incurred by the debtor. Thus the emphasis shifts from the income statement to the balance sheet. It may become desirable to disclose the fair market value of certain assets, when possible, and a comprehensive review of the assets is required to assure that none is stated at a value significantly in excess of its realizable value. The examination would also be expanded to insure that all liabilities are recorded, the requirements of all loan agreements have been met, and any deviations with their probable consequences have been disclosed. Included in the footnotes or elsewhere might also be management's appraisal of the situation.

Limitations on Scope

36. The accountant's examination usually includes all the standard auditing procedures followed in a normal audit and conforms to generally accepted auditing standards. However, certain limitations do arise in the scope of the accountant's examination. The accountant's report is usually needed as soon as possible, to effect a plan, and the time necessary to perform the audit procedures is therefore not available. Or the court may attempt to keep administrative expenses to a minimum and accordingly may restrict professional services to those deemed absolutely essential. The most common limitations in scope include an inability to confirm accounts receivable, to request vendors' statements, and to confirm deposits, prepaid expenses, and the like.

37. The scope of the examination may be limited further by certain obstacles and unusual situations which emerge during insolvency proceedings. Examples of problems which may be encountered include poor, incomplete, or missing books and records; lack of written explanation for occurrences such as major

investments, loan repayments to insiders, and other transactions with parent companies or stockholders; absence of employees familiar with the books and records; major transactions which have not been recorded; and executives who refuse to cooperate or are not familiar with major financial transactions.[3]

38. When such situations arise, unusual audit procedures must frequently be employed. Alternative techniques, which are described in detail in Chapter 8, paragraphs 5–96, include the following:

> Interviews with those people who might have a knowledge of the unusual transactions being investigated
>
> Inspection of all available correspondence files
>
> Examination of the prior accountant's working papers
>
> Inspection of all documents held by the company's former attorneys
>
> Confirmation of transactions, either orally or in writing, with second parties
>
> Scheduling of all unusual transactions chronologically
>
> Extensive tracing and retracing[4]

39. The obstacles and limitations in the scope of the examination and the subsequent employment of alternative procedures inevitably affects the type of report the accountant will be able to issue. Whether a qualified opinion or an actual disclaimer of opinion should be given depends on the severity of the limitations. Other conditions which are prevalent in insolvency proceedings must also be considered. These are discussed more fully in paragraphs 47–60.

40. Certain statements are normally found in an accountant's report concerning a company experiencing financial difficulty. Comparative balance sheets and income statements for a period of years may reveal the source of the debtor's problems. A statement of affairs, or a balance sheet with assets classified as free or pledged and liabilities shown as priority, secured, and unsecured may assist in deciding the best remedy to adopt. It may also be advantageous

---

[3] *Ibid.*, p. 33.
[4] Edward A. Weinstein, "Examining a Company in Bankruptcy," *Quarterly* (Touche, Ross, Bailey and Smart), Vol. 9 (September 1963), p. 15.

to include a statement showing the debtor's capitalization with a schedule of all withdrawals of capital.[5]

Unique Disclosures in Report

41. The accountant's report covering these statements (and any additional ones prepared) contains some disclosures that are unique to insolvency proceedings. Frequently the following items are found:

> A brief history of the debtor, including a discussion of the reasons for bankruptcy and any changes in management which have been made.
>
> If the accountant has disclaimed an opinion, the reasons for so doing.
>
> A discussion of any areas of the examination which were not completed and an indication as to why they were left undone. This includes disclosure of any books or records of the debtor which are withheld by an officer of the company.
>
> Documentation of sources used to obtain information for the report other than the debtor's books and records.
>
> Any corrections made to the book balances and the reasons for such changes.
>
> A detailed description of all unusual transactions including a schedule of all possible preferential payments and a list of all discrepancies found between the debtor's books and records and the financial statements issued to the trade, bank, and credit agencies.
>
> An assessment of the probability of successfully continuing the business under a plan of arrangement or reorganization.

42. The four standards of reporting established by the AICPA Committee on Auditing Procedures are to be followed by the auditor in presenting the report. The reporting standards are as follows:

> The report shall state whether the financial statements are presented in accordance with generally accepted accounting principles.

[5] Chauncey Levy, "Creditors' Committees and Their Responsibilities," *Commercial Law Journal*, Vol. 74 (December 1969), p. 358.

The report shall state whether such principles have been consistently observed in the current period in relation to the preceding period.

Informative disclosures in the financial statements are to be regarded as reasonably adequate unless otherwise stated in the report.

The report shall either contain an expression of opinion regarding the financial statements taken as a whole, or an assertion to the effect that an opinion cannot be expressed. When an overall opinion cannot be expressed, the reasons therefor should be stated. In all cases where an auditor's name is associated with financial statements, the report should contain a clear-cut indication of the character of the auditor's examination, if any, and the degree of responsibility being taken.[6]

Full Disclosure

43. When writing the report, the accountant must decide the necessary and appropriate degree of disclosure about the debtor and its situation. In all cases, the third standard of reporting, adequacy of informative disclosure, must be followed. In order for the financial standards to be fairly presented in accordance with generally accepted accounting principles, adequate disclosure is required of all material matters.[7] Strengthening this requirement even further is the AICPA Code of Professional Ethics, Rule 2.02, which sets forth that members will be held guilty of an act discreditable to the profession if they fail to disclose a material fact known to them, the disclosure of which is necessary to make the financial statements not misleading.

44. The amount of disclosure required is more difficult for the accountant to determine in a situation involving insolvency than in a normal audit. Thus, it might not be wise to indiscriminately reveal that a company is experiencing financial trouble. Knowledge of this fact might unjustifiably discourage customers from placing new orders, make credit more difficult for the debtor to obtain, or provide important information to competitors. However, some disclosure is necessary for the benefit of interested parties who lack

[6] *Codification of Auditing Standards and Procedures: Statement on Auditing Standards No. 1* (New York: American Institute of Certified Public Accountants, 1973), Secs. 410, 420, 430, and 450.

[7] *Ibid.*, Sec. 430.02.

the training to be able to discern the possibility of financial difficulty from the statements or when this information is not readily apparent from a mere reading of the financial statements. The accountant is again limited because the need to remain independent places a restraint on any interpretation of the data or forecast of future events. Some suggestions which have been made for more adequate disclosure involve a clear statement in the footnotes that the company is headed toward financial trouble, and disclosure of any recent appraisals or other special studies.[8] However, if the enterprise is facing financial difficulty which may affect the continuance of general business operations, adequate disclosure of this fact is required in the opinion (paragraphs 47–60).

Accountant's Responsibility for Disclosure

45. The accountant's responsibility for disclosure in a bankruptcy proceeding is greater than in a normal audit because the accountant is an appointee of the court. In *Food Town, Inc.* it was ruled that when accountants are appointed by an order in such a proceeding, they become quasi-officers of the court and owe their primary duty to the court.[9] Analogously, in *Brown v. Gerdes* the court further decided that, in all cases, persons who seek compensation for services or reimbursement for expenses are held to fiduciary standards.[10] These standards imply that a special confidence has been imposed in another who, in equity and good conscience, is bound to act in good faith and with due regard to the person granting the confidence. These relationships and requirements mean that accountants must include in their report all those facts which come to their attention during the examination, even if detrimental to the bankrupt or its management. Clearly then, when preparing a report, the accountant must realize that the special proceedings impose additional requirements and responsibilities, beyond the normal considerations, as to the facts that must be disclosed.

46. The type of opinion which the accountant issues on the

---

[8] Paul Conner, "Financial Reporting for Companies in Financial Difficulty," *Oklahoma CPA*, Vol. 7 (October 1968), pp. 22 and 25.

[9] "Accountant's Role in a Bankruptcy Case," Statement in Quotes, *The Journal of Accountancy*, Vol. 115 (June 1963), p. 62n.

[10] 321 U.S. 178, 182, 1944.

financial statements submitted with the report has a strong effect on the degree of confidence which other interested parties place in the statements. This is important because the accountant's report is often the only source of information available to those who are trying to decide the relationship they wish to have with the debtor in the future.

Going Concern Concept

47. According to the first standard of reporting, "The report shall state whether the financial statements are presented in accordance with generally accepted accounting principles." [11]

48. The accounting principle which presents the greatest obstacle for the accountant who is examining a company facing financial difficulty is the going concern concept. The concept is basic to accounting theory and was one of the first concepts to gain general acceptance. Hatfield called it in 1909 a "general principle which with various applications, is now universally accepted." [12]

Going Concern Concept Defined

49. The going concern concept means a continuance of general enterprise situations. The assumption is made that assets are expected to have continuing usefulness for the general purposes for which they were acquired and that liabilities are expected to be paid at maturity. Statement No. 4 of the Accounting Principles Board (APB) recognizes the going concern concept as one of the basic features of financial accounting, determined by the characteristics of the environment in which financial accounting operates. It is described as follows: "Going concern—continuation of entity operations is usually assumed in financial accounting in the absence of evidence to the contrary." [13]

50. The APB recognizes the following elements of modern economic organization as helping to provide an underlying continu-

---

[11] *Codification of Auditing Standards and Procedures, op. cit.*, Sec. 410.01.

[12] Henry Hatfield, *Modern Accounting* (New York: D. Appleton-Century Co., Inc., 1909), p. 80.

[13] AICPA, *Accounting Principles* (Chicago: Commerce Clearing House, Inc., 1972), Sec. 1002, 17(2).

ity and stability to some aspects of economic activity and hence to
the task of measuring that activity:

(1) Several forms of enterprise, especially the corporate form, continue to
exist as legal entities for extended periods of time.

(2) The framework of law, custom, and traditional patterns of action
provides a significant degree of stability to many aspects of the economic
environment. In a society in which property rights are protected, contracts
fulfilled, debts paid, and credit banking and transfer operations efficiently
performed, the degree of uncertainty is reduced and the predictability of the
outcome of many types of economic activities is correspondingly increased.[14]

51. The going concern concept was recognized by Moonitz in
Accounting Research Study No. 1, and by Grady in ARS No. 7. The
American Accounting Association recognized "enterprise continu-
ity" as an underlying concept in its 1957 publication:

The "going concern" concept assumes the continuance of the general
enterprise situation. In the absence of evidence to the contrary, the entity is
viewed as remaining in operation indefinitely. Although it is recognized that
business activities and economic conditions are changing constantly, the
concept assumes that controlling environmental circumstances will persist
sufficiently far into the future to permit existing plans and programs to be
carried to completion. Thus the assets of the enterprise are expected to have
continuing usefulness for the general purpose for which they were acquired,
and its liabilities are expected to be paid at maturity.

To the extent that termination of important activities can be predicted with
assurance, a partial or complete abandonment of the assumption of
continuity is in order. Otherwise, the assumption provides a reasonable basis
for presenting enterprise status and performance.[15]

Absence of Evidence to the Contrary

52. The assumption is made that the entity's operations will
continue "in the absence of evidence to the contrary." The
problem for the accountant is to determine what constitutes
evidence to the contrary. A business which has had profits for
several years and is expanding its operations is clearly a going

14 *Ibid.*, Sec. 1023.16.
15 AAA Committee on Accounting Concepts and Standards, *Accounting and Reporting
Standards for Corporate Financial Statements and Preceding Statements and Supplements*
(Columbus, Ohio: American Accounting Association, 1957), p. 2.

concern. An entity that is in the process of liquidating its assets in straight bankruptcy is clearly not a going concern. However, what assumption should the accountant make for a business that has had losses for the past three years, or for an entity that is in a Chapter X reorganization or a Chapter XI arrangement?

53. In the issuance of the report the accountant must be satisfied that evidence contrary to the going concern assumption does not exist. Carmichael classified the elements of contrary evidence in the following manner:

a. Financing problems—difficulty in meeting obligations.
   (1) Liquidity deficiency—the company's current liabilities exceed its current assets, which results in difficulty in meeting current obligations.
   (2) Equity deficiency—the company's solvency is questionable because of a retained earnings deficit or, in more extreme cases, an excess of total liabilities over total assets.
   (3) Debt default—the company has been unable to meet debt payment schedules or has violated one or more other covenants of its loan agreements.
   (4) Funds shortage—the company has either limited or no ability to obtain additional funds from various capital sources.

b. Operating problems—apparent lack of operating success.
   (1) Continued operating losses—no net profit has been earned for more than one past period.
   (2) Prospective revenues doubtful—revenue is insufficient for day-to-day operating needs, or there have been cut-backs in operations, such as personnel reductions.
   (3) Ability to operate is jeopardized—legal proceedings related to operations may severely curtail operations, or suppliers of operating materials may refuse to transact with the company.
   (4) Poor control over operations—the company management has been unable to control operations, as evidenced by repetitive, uncorrected problems.[16]

54. If any of the above problems or any of the difficulties described in Chapter 2 exists in the entity, the accountant should clearly evaluate their consequences before issuing the report. The independent accountant may determine that it is best to qualify the

[16] D. R. Carmichael, *The Auditor's Reporting Obligation: Auditing Research Monograph No. 1* (New York: American Institute of Certified Public Accountants, 1972), p. 94. Copyright © 1972 by the American Institute of Certified Public Accountants, Inc.

report, disclaim an opinion, or issue an adverse report. The following discussion on the type of opinion is not restricted to reports issued under Chapter X or XI, but applies to entities having any type of financial difficulty.

Qualified Opinion

55. A company experiencing financial difficulties is normally trying to correct the situation. If the accountant is of the opinion that evidence points to future operating success and if favorable financial arrangements are possible, a qualified or even an unqualified opinion may be issued. Many factors must be considered by the accountant before an opinion is expressed: the nature of the company's operations, the type of financial problem, the confidence that can be placed in the key personnel, and the manner in which the company has solved its problems in the past. In order to illustrate the nature of a qualified opinion it is assumed that there is a good possibility the ABC Company will have future operating success if the financial support it now receives continues and if the unprofitable division can be liquidated as planned. The qualified opinion based on the above assumptions for the ABC Company as of December 31, 1974, is presented in Figure 9–10. The notes referred to in this qualified opinion are those illustrated in Figure 9–2.

Disclaimer of Opinion

56. If additional financial arrangements are uncertain and if the ability of the company to reverse the trend of unprofitable operations is in doubt, the auditor may disclaim an opinion in lieu of issuing an unqualified or qualified report. The fact that a company has a deficit in retained earnings does not necessarily mean that an unqualified report cannot be issued. The ability of the company to survive is the important factor which must be evaluated. Generally, for a company experiencing financial and operating difficulties, the first deviation from an unqualified report comes in the form of a qualified report. If corrective action is not taken, then the auditor, after studying and evaluating the operating and financial problems, may decide that an opinion cannot be expressed. The ABC Company has experienced three successive years of operating losses

To the Board of Directors and Stockholders
ABC Company, Inc.
New York, New York

We have examined the balance sheet of ABC Company, Inc., as of December 31, 1974, and the related statements of income, retained earnings, and change in financial position for the year then ended. Our examination was made in accordance with generally accepted auditing standards, and accordingly included such tests of the accounting records and such other auditing procedures as we considered necessary in the circumstances.

As set forth in Note 2, the Company has provided a reserve for estimated liquidation losses of $200,000 applicable to the operation of a division which it has recently decided to close. We are unable to determine the adequacy of such reserve. As set forth in Note 3, a lending arrangement is conditioned upon future events which are not susceptible of determination.

In our opinion, subject to the effect, if any, on the financial statements of the ultimate resolution of the matters discussed in the preceding paragraph, the financial statements referred to above present fairly the financial position and the results of its operations and the change in financial position for the year then ended, in conformity with generally accepted accounting principles applied on a basis consistent with that of the preceding year.

New York, New York
February 15, 1975

Figure 9–10. Qualified opinion on the financial statements of the ABC Company as of December 31, 1974. The text of the Notes referred to may be found in Figure 9–2.

as stated in Figure 9–7. If there is very little possibility of reversing this loss trend and a good chance the financing agreement explained in Note 3 of Figure 9–2 will be cancelled, the auditor for the ABC Company will find it necessary to issue a disclaimer of an opinion similar to the one illustrated in Figure 9–11.

57. Quite often the accountant will disclaim an opinion on the statements issued in an insolvency proceeding. Usually this is because of the uncertainties surrounding the entity's continuance or because the auditor is unable to obtain sufficient competent evidential matter during the course of the examination. Also, audit

ABC Company, Inc.
New York, New York

We have examined the consolidated balance sheet of ABC Company,
Inc., as of December 31, 1974, and the related consolidated statements
of net loss and deficit, and changes in financial position for the year
then ended. Our examination was made in accordance with generally
accepted auditing standards, and accordingly included such tests of the
accounting records and such other auditing procedures as we considered
necessary in the circumstances.

The accompanying financial statements have been prepared in conformity with generally accepted accounting principles consistently
applied on the basis of the continuation of the Company as a going
concern. However, the Company has operated at a loss during the past
three years and its current liabilities exceed its current assets. The continuation of the business as a going concern is dependent upon the
continued forbearance of certain creditors, the Company's ability to
obtain additional working capital, and future profitable operations.
Further, we are unable to evaluate the effect on the financial statements
of the future outcome of the matters mentioned and described in Notes
2 and 3.

Because of the possible material effect on the financial statements
of these uncertainties, we do not express an opinion on the financial
statements referred to above.

New York, New York
March 30, 1975

Figure 9–11. Disclaimer of opinion on the statements of the ABC
Company, issued three months after the qualified opinion. For the text of the
Notes referred to, see Figure 9–2.

obstacles may have been encountered, resulting in incomplete field
work, or the scope of the examination may have been limited in the
retention order. These situations clearly require that the accountant deny an opinion so that third parties will not rely on the
financial statements when such reliance is not warranted.

58. It is important that the accountant state all the reasons for
disclaiming an opinion. These include disclosure of all areas of the
examination which were not completed, any obstacles encountered,
other limitations placed on the scope of the examination, and any
sources of information other than the debtor's books and records.[17]

[17] Weinstein, "Accountants' Examinations and Reports in Bankruptcy Proceedings," p. 33.

ABC Company, Inc.
New York, New York

We have examined the books and records of ABC Company, Inc., for
the purpose of ascertaining its financial condition as of April 28, 1975,
as set forth in the accompanying report.

Our review did not include the application of audit procedures sufficiently
comprehensive to constitute an examination in accordance with generally accepted auditing standards. In accordance with prevailing standards of professional practice, the foregoing statements are deemed to be
unaudited. We therefore do not express an opinion on the financial
statements in the accompanying report.

The realization of asset values and the ability to continue as a going concern are dependent upon successful arrangement with creditors, attaining
sufficiently profitable operations, and/or adequate additional financing.

New York, New York
May 14, 1975

Figure 9–12. Sample of a disclaimer of opinion issued to creditors'
committees and in Chapter XI arrangements.

59. An example of the type of disclaimer often issued to
creditors' committees and in Chapter XI arrangements is shown in
Figure 9–12. This is the type of disclaimer that would be issued
with the statements as of April 28, 1975 (see Figures 9–3 and 9–5),
which the auditor prepared for the creditors' committee of the ABC
Company.

Adverse Opinion

60. The evidence to the contrary may be so convincing that
the statements prepared on a going concern basis are not fairly
presented. This type of situation may also arise when, even if the
entity does continue, its assets are in such a condition that it is
impossible for them to be worth their book values. If the statements
are not corrected, the accountant would be required to issue an
adverse opinion.

Statement on Auditing Procedure No. 38—"Associated With"

61. Accountants may encounter situations where they are
associated with statements of a firm involved in insolvency pro-

ceedings but no audit of the company is conducted. In this case, Statement on Auditing Procedure (S.A.P.) No. 38, "Unaudited Financial Statements," issued in 1967, is meant to apply.

Unaudited Financial Statements

62. It is first necessary to ascertain when financial statements are unaudited. The second paragraph of S.A.P. No. 38 states that this situation arises if the accountant (a) has not applied any auditing procedures to them or (b) has not applied auditing procedures which are sufficient to permit the expression of an opinion concerning them, as described in Statement on Auditing Procedure No. 33.[18] The third paragraph of S.A.P. No. 38 states that accountants are considered to be associated with unaudited financial statements, first, when they consent to the use of their firm name in a report, document, or written communication setting forth or containing the statements, or second, when they submit to the client or others, with or without a covering letter, unaudited financial statements which they have prepared or assisted in preparing, even if the firm name is not appended to the financial statements or the letter is written on "plain paper" rather than on the firm's own stationery.

63. Prior to the issuance of S.A.P. No. 38, the accountant could allow financial statements to be presented on plain paper without disclaiming an opinion. However, it is now required that whenever the accountant is associated with unaudited statements there must be a disclaimer of an opinion, making it clear that the accountant has not audited the statements and does not express an opinion on them. Furthermore, each page of the financial statements must be marked as unaudited. These steps are required so that anyone who becomes aware of the accountant's association with these statements will not place unwarranted reliance on them.

64. S.A.P. No. 38 goes on to say that the accountant has no responsibility to apply any auditing procedures to unaudited financial statements and is not expected to have an opinion as to whether the statements were prepared in conformity with generally accepted accounting principles. But if the accountant concludes on the basis of known facts that the statements are not in conformity

[18] See *Codification of Auditing Standards and Procedures, op. cit.,* Secs. 511–16.

with generally accepted accounting principles, the following steps should be taken:

> Insist upon appropriate revision; failing that,
>
> Set forth in the disclaimer any reservations and the effect of the deviation on the statements; failing that,
>
> Refuse to be associated with the statements and withdraw from the engagement.

65. Furthermore, the accountant should refuse to be associated with any unaudited financial statements which are believed to be false or intended to mislead.

66. The recent case involving *1136 Tenants' Corporation v. Max Rothenberg & Co.*[19] clearly points out how important it is for the accountant to be very careful in the issuance of unaudited statements. The accountant should have a written agreement with the client as to the nature and scope of the engagement. In addition, the manner in which the statements are to be used should be understood between the accountant and the client and this understanding should be confirmed in writing and signed by both parties.

67. When unaudited statements for a prior year are presented with audited statements for the current year for comparative purposes, S.A.P. No. 38 requires appropriate disclosure so that no opinion is expressed on the prior-year unaudited statements.

68. An accountant for the creditors' committee will receive compensation allowed by the court for services which give the committee the necessary information so that it may reach an informed conclusion on the plan of arrangement. This normally requires only an investigatory audit, which does not constitute an examination sufficiently extensive to justify the accountant's association with the statements. However, if any type of report is issued by the accountant, it must be accompanied by a disclaimer of opinion, making it clear that the accountant has not audited the statements and does not express an opinion on them. See Figure 9–12.

---

[19] 36 A.2d 804, 219 N.Y.S. 2d 1007 (1st Dept. 1971); *aff'd* Court of Appeals, March 15, 1972.

69. Pursuant to S.A.P. No. 38, the accounting firm involved in insolvency proceedings must be extremely careful to avoid having its name linked with a company it has not audited. Unless a complete investigation of the debtor's affairs and transactions has been conducted, the accountant does not have an adequate foundation from which to issue an opinion as to whether the financial statements correctly present the debtor's financial position and results from operations. For example, merely looking for preferential payments does not constitute a thorough examination. False association with a company experiencing financial difficulties can be especially dangerous because of the increased number of people interested in the bankrupt's affairs.

EFFECT OF SETTLEMENTS ON FUTURE STATEMENTS

70. When a company is liquidated and all its assets are sold, the business is dissolved and the books are permanently closed. In a reorganization proceeding, the debtor emerges as a new entity with a new set of accounts, the balance of which is determined by the settlement. However, when a plan of arrangement is enacted, the debtor retains its present form and books, but the terms of the plan call for certain adjustments. The following sections discuss the most common entries made and the situations in which they are required.

Additional Paid-In Capital

71. Under the Bankruptcy Act and the Internal Revenue Code, the forgiveness of indebtedness is explicitly held not to be income. Instead, the reduction is construed to be a form of contributed capital.

72. However, although the Bankruptcy Act and the Internal Revenue Code do not consider the forgiveness of indebtedness as income, the question remains as to how the amount should be presented in external financial statements. The difference between the amount of the liability and the amount which must be paid under the plan of arrangement or settlement is either a gift or an item of revenue in a very broad sense. The Accounting Principles Board defines revenue as:

. . . a gross increase in assets or a gross decrease in liabilities recognized and measured in conformity with generally accepted accounting principles that results from those types of profit-directed activities of an enterprise that can change owners' equity (see section 1025.21). Revenue under present generally accepted accounting principles is derived from three general activities: (a) selling products, (b) rendering services and permitting others to use enterprise resources, which result in interest, rent, royalties, fees, and the like, and (c) disposing of resources other than products—for example, plant and equipment or investments in other entities. Revenue does not include receipt of assets purchased, proceeds of borrowing, investments by owners, or adjustments of revenue of prior periods.[20]

73. In 1948 the American Accounting Association suggested that revenue represents an inflow of assets or net assets into the firm as a result of sales of goods or services. Revenue also included gains from the sale or exchange of assets other than stock in trade and gains from advantageous settlement of liabilities.[21]

74. A gift is a voluntary transfer of property without any consideration being given for the transfer. If a gift is made to a bankrupt, its debts are cancelled without any consideration on the part of the bankrupt. Gifts to the enterprise may be classified as capital or revenue. If the contributions are in the form of "conscience payment," they are normally considered revenue. Otherwise, gifts are normally considered a contribution to capital. The criteria to be used in determining how to classify the gift are the intent of the donor and the events surrounding the gift. The philosophy underlying the enactment of Chapters X and XI was to allow the debtor to have a new start. The debtor comes out of the proceedings without any commitments of any type directly related to the amount of debt forgiven. The cancellation may be viewed as a type of gift, in part directly from the majority creditors who agree to the plan and in part from Congress which has imposed the plan on the minority dissenting creditors.

75. However, it should be pointed out that one of the main reasons why the majority creditors accept a plan is that they believe they will receive a greater return under the plan than under complete liquidation. Thus, the handling of the cancellation as a gift raises some questions which need additional analysis. The

---

[20] AICPA, *Accounting Principles*, Sec. 1026.12.
[21] AAA Committee on Accounting Concepts and Standards, p. 15.

general practice is to consider the cancellation as an addition to paid-in capital.

76. Under this practice, the accounting entries made when the amount of the liability is reduced and the debt is paid off are as follows: the liability is debited for the full amount of the original indebtedness, cash is reduced by the amount actually paid out, and paid-in capital is increased by the difference. If any of the assets are subsequently written down, the contributed capital account must also be reduced by this amount.

Chapter XI and Quasi-Reorganization

77. There is some question as to whether an adjustment under Chapter XI constitutes a quasi-reorganization. To some it does not appear reasonable to adjust the assets downward only to the extent of the debt forgiveness. Since the company is in fact trying to make a "new start," it has been argued that all of the assets should be reduced to market values and that the deficit in retained earnings should be completely eliminated under the provisions of a quasi-reorganization. It has also been contended that the theory of quasi-reorganization should allow the assets to be revalued upward if they are stated below market values. The AICPA has not looked favorably upon such a procedure. The SEC has also opposed the procedure until in a very recent quasi-reorganization it not only allowed but insisted that market values be used, even though they were greater than cost, for a given asset.

78. The practice has been not to consider the adjustments under a Chapter XI arrangement as a quasi-reorganization. However, the entire area of quasi-reorganization needs to be restudied. If it is determined that there is justification for this type of reorganization, then some type of criteria must be established as to when the quasi-reorganization should or should not be used.

Retained Earnings

79. As previously stated, when a debtor receives a forgiveness of indebtedness, no profit or income is held to have been realized. The reduction of debt may not be used to produce or increase a positive balance in the retained earnings account. However, the amount realized from debt forgiveness may be used to eliminate a debit balance in the retained earnings account provided there is a

reorganization or a quasi-reorganization. The following rule was adopted by the AICPA in 1934:

> Capital surplus, however created, should not be used to relieve the income account of the current or future years of charges which would otherwise fall to be made thereagainst. This rule might be subject to the exception that where, upon reorganization, a reorganized company would be relieved of charges which would require to be made against income if the existing corporation were continued, it might be regarded as permissible to accomplish the same result without reorganization provided the facts were as fully revealed to and the action as formally approved by the shareholders as in reorganization.[22]

Liabilities—Classification: Long-Term Versus Current

80. Liabilities remaining on the books of the debtor, regardless of whether they have been scaled down, retain the classification, according to the length of repayment, that they originally held before the proceedings. Some plans, however, may call for repayment of debt in installments over a period of time much longer than provided for in the original agreement. This may cause an obligation to be reclassified from short- to long-term debt. On the other hand, a promise to pay now a smaller sum than was originally pledged to be paid later would call for reclassification as a current obligation. Thus, the terms found in the plan of arrangement govern the adjustments which will be made in the classification of liabilities.

Assets—Write-Down to Realizable Values

81. Reduction in the book values of assets and when this is required are discussed more fully in Chapter 10, "Tax Aspects." Briefly, once again, when a debtor company secures a reduction of its liabilities in a proceeding under the Bankruptcy Act, it is not held to have realized any income from the difference between the original debt and the actual payment. It is required, however, that the debtor's property be reduced in value by an amount equal to the amount of indebtedness which has been cancelled.[23] The one proviso is that the basis of any one specific asset cannot be reduced

[22] AICPA, *Accounting Principles*, Sec. 5511.01. Also see Sec. 5581.
[23] Bankruptcy Act, Secs. 270 and 396.

below its fair market value on the date on which the order confirming the plan is entered. Thus, in an arrangement where debt is reduced, the assets will usually emerge at a value equal to the proceeds which could be received if the property were sold on the date of confirmation.

10

Tax Aspects

1. The income tax effect of certain transactions during the administration period and of tax assessments related to prebankruptcy periods can impose undue hardship on the bankrupt, who is already in a tenuous financial position. It is not uncommon for a bankrupt to realize substantial taxable income during the administration period, from the sale of all or part of the assets or from taxable recoveries. Net operating loss carryovers and other offsetting tax deductions are often unable to minimize the income tax

effect. Therefore, in addition to insuring that all statutory tax reporting and filing requirements are satisfied at the due dates, the accountant must be aware of those tax aspects which will permit the preservation and enlargement of the bankrupt's estate.

NOTIFICATION OF PROCEEDINGS AND FILING OF RETURNS

Notice to Governmental Agencies

2. Pursuant to Section 6036 of the Internal Revenue Code, every receiver, trustee in bankruptcy, assignee for the benefit of creditors, or other fiduciary, and every executor must give notice of qualification to the Secretary of the Treasury or a delegated representative, in the manner and within the time limit required by regulations of the Secretary or delegate.

3. Section 301.6036–1 of the Treasury Regulations requires that the individual in control of the assets of a debtor in any bankruptcy proceeding shall, within ten days of the date of an appointment or authorization to act, give notice in writing to the District Director of Internal Revenue for the district where the debtor is or was required to file returns. The notice shall not be required if, prior to or within ten days of the date of the fiduciary's appointment or authorization to act, any notice regarding the proceeding has been given under any provision of the Bankruptcy Act to the Secretary or other proper officer of the Treasury Department.

Form of Notice

4. Where written notice is required, it may be made on Treasury Form 56 (Notice to Commissioner), and should include:

> The name and address of the person making such notice and the date of appointment or of taking possession of the assets
>
> The name, address, and employer identification number of the debtor or other person whose assets are controlled

In the case of a court proceeding:
1. The name and location of the court in which the proceedings are pending
2. The date on which the proceedings were instituted
3. The number under which the proceedings are docketed
4. The date, time, and place of any hearing, meeting of creditors, or other scheduled action with respect to the proceedings

5. Similar notices may be required by other governmental taxing authorities and should be filed in accordance with their prescribed procedures.

6. The Clerk of the Bankruptcy Court is required to mail a certified copy of all orders of adjudication in bankruptcy to the Commissioner and notice of the first meeting of creditors to the Treasury Department and the District Director.[1] If a copy of the petition in bankruptcy is submitted to the Treasury within the ten-day period, this will constitute adequate notification under a provision of the Bankruptcy Act as provided for in the Treasury Regulations (Section 301.6036–1).

7. The Internal Revenue Code (Section 6903) requires that a fiduciary give to the Treasury Department a notice of relationship (statement that any person is acting for another in a fiduciary capacity).   This notice also may be made on Treasury Form 56.

Failure To Give Notice

8. If notice is not given pursuant to Section 6036 where notification is required, the period of limitations on the assessment of taxes is suspended from the date the proceeding is instituted to the date notice is received by the District Director, and for an additional thirty days thereafter. However, the suspension in no case shall exceed two years.[2]

Responsibility for Filing Income Tax Returns—Corporations

9. The trustee or receiver having possession of or title to all or substantially all the property or business of a corporation shall file

---

[1] Bankruptcy Act, Sec. 58(e).
[2] I.R.C., Sec. 6872, and Treas. Reg., Sec. 301.6872–1.

the income tax return for the corporation in the same manner and form as the corporation would be required to file the return.[3]

10. Both liquidating and operating trustees must file returns and pay taxes on certain items of income and gain received during the liquidation or operation of the bankrupt's estate. A receiver in charge of only part of the property does not have to file a federal income tax return.[4]

11. When a corporation is discharged from its debts after it has filed a petition and then resumes business operations, the discharge acts to separate the estate of the bankrupt corporation from the corporation itself in all proceedings except those under Chapter XI. A trustee is held responsible for the income from the property administered during the bankruptcy proceeding; a discharged corporation which has resumed operations must file a corporate tax return.

Responsibility for Payment of Tax

12. When a payment of tax is due, the person who is required to file the return is also responsible for the payment of the tax.[5] Thus, the trustee in bankruptcy, who is responsible for filing the corporate income tax return, must pay any tax which may be due. Failure to do so may result in personal liability on the part of the trustee.

13. When the bankrupt estate is created, no tax is levied on the transfer of the debtor's assets to the new entity, and there is no change in the tax basis of the assets transferred. Any gain which is realized on the disposition of the bankrupt's property results in an imposition of tax directly against the estate and indirectly against the creditors by the reduction of their bankruptcy dividend. Thus, the effect of bankruptcy is to shift the tax burden from the debtor to the creditors.[6]

[3] I.R.C., Sec. 6012b(3), and Treas. Reg., Sec. 1.6012–3(b)(4).
[4] *Ibid.*
[5] I.R.C., Sec. 6151(a).
[6] Sydney Krause and Arnold Kapiloff, "The Bankrupt Estate, Taxable Income, and the Trustee in Bankruptcy," *Fordham Law Review*, Vol. 34 (March 1966), p. 417.

When To File a Corporate Tax Return

14. A corporate income tax return should be filed annually, regardless of whether the corporation has any income, as long as the corporation exists for tax purposes. A corporation in existence during any portion of the year must file a return. A corporation is not in existence after it ceases business and dissolves, retaining no assets, even though under state law it may thereafter be treated as continuing as a corporation for certain limited purposes connected with winding up its affairs, such as for purposes of suing and being sued.[7] If the corporation has valuable claims for which it will bring suit during this period, it has retained assets and therefore continues in existence. A corporation does not go out of existence if it is turned over to receivers or trustees who continue operations.

15. A trustee who continues to liquidate the assets of the bankrupt estate after the corporation has obtained a discharge under Section 14 of the Bankruptcy Act should, it appears, file a fiduciary income tax return (Form 1041), reporting income realized during the trusteeship. The trustee also has the right to claim income tax refunds.[8]

Responsibility for Filing Income Tax Returns— Individual and Partnership

16. With the intervention of bankruptcy proceedings into the affairs of an individual (or partnership), a separate taxable entity consisting of the bankrupt estate is created. Thus the bankrupt, as an individual, and the trustee in bankruptcy for that individual are required to file separate returns since they are separate taxable entities.[9]

17. The creation of the new taxable entity is not held to be a taxable transaction, and therefore the trustee acquires the debtor's basis for the assets received. The provisions of Subchapter J of the Internal Revenue Code are held to apply to bankrupt estates, because legal title to the bankrupt's property vests by operation of

[7] Treas. Reg., Sec. 1.6012–5.
[8] Bankruptcy Act, Sec. 70.
[9] P. B. Chabrow, "Estates in Bankruptcy: Return Requirements, Rules Concerning Income and Deductions," *Journal of Taxation*, Vol. 31 (December 1969), p. 363.

the law in the trustee.[10] After transferring the property to the trustee, the individual may acquire new employment or assets. The creation of a new entity and other provisions applicable to individuals do not apply to a corporation which has been liquidated because if the debtor subsequently wishes to resume business operations, a new corporation will be formed.[11]

18. The trustee in bankruptcy for an individual (or partnership) has no authority to file an income tax return for the individual. Instead, the bankrupt individual or partnership continues to file an individual or partnership tax return, reporting income and expenses for the entire taxable period on Form 1040 or Form 1065, whichever is applicable.

19. The trustee in bankruptcy of an individual does file a return of income of the bankrupt estate and pay the taxes. Using Form 1041, the trustee reports the income and expenses during the administration of the estate.

TREATMENT OF INCOME DURING BANKRUPTCY PERIOD

Income Required To Be Reported

20. Generally it is not thought that income would be a consideration during bankruptcy proceedings since an insufficiency of profits has contributed to the insolvency. However, during the administration of the estate transactions may occur which generate taxable income. Any income derived from the sale or operation of the debtor's assets must be reported as it is earned.

21. There may be many sources of income to a bankrupt estate. Proceeds will be received from the sale or liquidation of assets. Rental income may be realized from any real estate owned, royalties from patents, dividends from securities, and interest on savings and other deposits of the debtor (or the trustee, who may deposit the bankrupt estate's funds). The cancellation of the indebtedness of the bankrupt by the creditors may also be construed as a form of income.[12]

---

[10] Bankruptcy Act, Sec. 70(a).

[11] Jerome R. Hellerstein and Victor Brudney, "Tax Problems in Bankruptcy or Insolvency Reorganization," *Lasser's Encyclopedia of Tax Procedures*, 2d Ed. (Englewood Cliffs, N. J.: Prentice-Hall, Inc., 1960), p. 405.

[12] *Ibid.*, p. 401.

Deductions Allowed

22. In the determination of taxable net income, the trustee is allowed certain deductions. Most common are:

The costs of administration in general.

The costs of administration directly associated with the production of income by the estate, provided that they are construed as ordinary and necessary business expenses.

Payments made to priority and general unsecured creditors if such distributions are allocable to a debt associated with an item which would have been deductible by the bankrupt. However, it is necessary to realize that debtors using an accrual basis may have already deducted the expense, while payment is just being made by the trustee.

Payments for priority tax claims incurred before the date of adjudication and which therefore would have been deductible by the debtor if paid prior to bankruptcy.

Income tax carryforward and carryback losses.[13]

23. Thus, in calculating the taxable income from the operation of the bankrupt's estate for which the trustee is responsible, special consideration must be given to prior transactions and their possible effects on the proceeds currently being received.

Gain or Loss on Disposition of Assets

24. The trustee may realize a gain or loss through sale of the assets of the debtor's estate. The basis used by the trustee in determining the gain or loss is the same as the debtor's basis. The trustee is required to assume the debtor's basis because the transfer of assets from the bankrupt to the trustee is a non-taxable transaction. As to which of the debtor's bases is to be used, Treasury Regulation 1.1016–7(b)(1) states that the basis shall be determined as of the date of entry of the order confirming the plan, composition, or arrangement under which the indebtedness shall have been cancelled or reduced.

25. In addition to acquiring the debtor's basis, when determining whether a sale has resulted in a short- or long-term capital gain,

---

[13] Chabrow, pp. 365–66.

the trustee's holding period of the bankrupt's assets is equal to the holding period of the debtor plus that of the trustee.[14]

26. Thus, using the debtor's basis and holding period, the trustee is held to have realized taxable income when the sale price of the asset exceeds the basis. Correspondingly, there is a deductible capital loss when the proceeds from sale are less than the basis.

Cancellation or Adjustments of Indebtedness— Out of Court

27. In some cases, when a debtor is permitted to settle a liability for less than the face amount of the debt, the difference may be construed as income to the debtor. Thus, when a debt owed by a solvent taxpayer is discharged, cancelled, or forgiven without a bankruptcy proceeding, taxable income is held to arise. However, when an insolvent taxpayer transfers property to a creditor in settlement of a debt and remains insolvent after the transfer, no income is held to be realized for tax purposes from the amount of debt which has been forgiven.

Cancellation or Adjustments of Indebtedness— Bankruptcy Proceedings

28. When insolvency proceedings are conducted under the Bankruptcy Act, the reduction, forgiveness, or cancellation of debt is explicitly held not to be taxable income as set forth in Sections 268 and 269, concerned with Chapter X reorganizations, and Section 395, dealing with Chapter XI arrangements. Section 268 states that

> . . . no income or profit, taxable under any law of the United States or of any state now in force or which may hereafter be enacted, shall, in respect to the adjustment of the indebtedness of a debtor in a proceeding under this chapter, be deemed to have accrued to or to have been realized by a debtor, by a trustee provided for in a plan under this chapter, or by a corporation organized or made use of for effectuating a plan under this chapter by reason of a modification in or cancellation in whole or in part of any such indebtedness in a proceeding under this chapter.

---

[14] I.R.C., Sec. 1223(2).

However, if it appears that the plan had as one of its principal purposes the evasion of any income tax, the exemption will be disallowed or confirmation of the plan denied. The regulations under Internal Revenue Code Section 61 set out rules implementing these provisions.[15]

29. Internal Revenue Code Section 108 is also concerned with income from the discharge of indebtedness:

> (a) *Special rule of exclusion.*—No amount shall be included in gross income by reason of the discharge in whole or in part, within the taxable year, of any indebtedness for which the taxpayer is liable, or subject to which the taxpayer holds property, if
>   (1) the indebtedness was incurred or assumed
>   (a) by a corporation, or
>   (b) by an individual in connection with property used in his trade or business, and
>   (2) such taxpayer makes and files a consent to the regulations prescribed under Section 1017 (relating to the adjustment of basis) then in effect at such time and in such manner as the Secretary prescribes.

Reduction of Basis

30. Section 1017 of the Internal Revenue Code, entitled "Discharge of Indebtedness," states that where any amount is excluded from gross income under Section 108(a) on account of the discharge of indebtedness, the whole amount or a part of the amount so excluded shall be applied in reduction of the basis of any property held by the taxpayer. This reduction affects the basis used for depreciation purposes and for the determination of gain or loss on disposition of the property.

31. However, specific rules with respect to cancellation of indebtedness and reduction of basis apply to Chapter X or XI situations.[16] Sections 270 and 396 of the Bankruptcy Act state that in determining the basis of property for any purposes of any law of the United States or of a state imposing a tax upon income, the basis of the debtor's property shall be decreased by an amount equal to the amount by which the indebtedness of the debtor has been cancelled or reduced. The basis of any particular property is not to

---

[15] Treas. Reg., Sec. 1.61–12(b)(1).
[16] Treas. Reg., Sec. 1.1016–7.

be decreased, however, to an amount less than the fair market value of such property as of the date of entry of the order confirming the plan.

32. Because the reduction of indebtedness is held not to be income, but a reduction in basis of assets, dividends paid from the earnings created by the forgiveness of debt are not taxable. The write-down may be held to be a form of gift, in part by voluntary action of the consenting creditors in reducing the outstanding debts of a corporation and in part by an act of Congress which imposes its will on the dissenting creditors. Pursuant to this interpretation, the amount of reduction of the indebtedness is construed to be a form of contributed capital.[17]

33. An important distinction must be made between proceedings held informally and proceedings which are conducted under the auspices of a court. Current large operating losses often lead to potential claims for income tax refunds. However, in informal settlements such losses may be reduced or diminished because of the ordinary income created by the cancellation of indebtedness by creditors. But the losses will be reduced only to the extent that the debtor is made solvent.[18]

AVAILABILITY OF LOSS CARRYOVERS AND CARRYBACKS

34. In general, the sections of the Internal Revenue Code which are concerned with net operating losses are held to apply to bankruptcy proceedings. This includes Section 172(b)(1) which provides that losses from business operations may be carried back to the three years preceding the year of loss and, if any losses remain, they may be carried forward for the five subsequent years to offset future profits.

Loss Carrybacks

35. Loss carrybacks result in claims for tax refunds attributable to profits on which taxes were paid in years before the time of

---

[17] Philip J. Erbacher, "Is the National Bankruptcy Act Paramount over the Internal Revenue Code in Federal Tax Matters?," *TAXES—The Tax Magazine*, Vol. 48 (March 1970), p. 161. See also *Meyer v. Commissioner*, 383 F.2d 883 (1967).

[18] Rev. Rul. 58–600, 1958–2 C.B. 29.

bankruptcy proceedings. If the debtor suffered operating losses in years preceding the year in which the petition was filed and has the right to claim a refund on taxes paid in earlier years, this right has been construed as property under Section 70 of the Bankruptcy Act and thus passes to the trustee. The trustee may therefore file a claim for the refund of these taxes.

36. If the debtor has incurred losses in the same year in which bankruptcy proceedings are initiated, the right to claim a refund at the end of the taxable year is also held to be property of the bankrupt which passes to the trustee. However, the claim may not be made until the end of the taxable year so that the amount of the loss may be exactly determined.[19] To illustrate, assume that a corporation on a calendar-year basis sustained losses of $350,000 from January 1 to June 30, 1973, the date the petition was filed. These losses may be used by the trustee to claim a refund of tax paid on income earned for 1970, 1971, and 1972. However, the trustee must wait until the bankrupt's taxable year ends (December 31, 1973) before filing a claim for refund. Any income earned during the balance of the year would be used to offset the $350,000 loss. Thus, the trustee gets the benefit of any refund resulting from the use of a pre-petition net operating loss of the debtor as well as any loss incurred during the operation of the estate prior to discharge in bankruptcy.

37. Where a corporation is being reorganized and there are large losses which may be carried back to prior periods (in the absence of possible claims for refund of taxes on filing of assignee's or trustee's tax return), it is not necessary to prepare final tax returns. Instead, a letter may be sent to the various governmental agencies stating the fact of the large loss, accompanied by a final statement of financial position and income.[20]

Loss Carryforwards

38. Loss carryforwards are concerned with the prospective use of operating losses. The question is whether the trustee may use any part of an unused loss to offset any income generated during the

---

[19] *Segal v. Rochelle*, 86 Sup. Ct. 511 (1966).

[20] Irwin Lutsky, "Tax Services in Insolvency Proceedings," *New York Certified Public Accountant*, Vol. 38 (June 1968), p. 435.

administration or liquidation of the estate. The basic premise of the tax law is that only the taxpayer who suffers the loss may enjoy the benefits of it. A limited exception is made under Internal Revenue Code Section 381 with respect to corporations undergoing certain tax-free reorganizations.

39. For individuals, the trustee in bankruptcy cannot use the operating loss carryforward even though profits may be earned directly as a result of the operations of the business, or as a gain on liquidating the assets, or as interest on time deposits of the bankrupt. The individual taxpayer who incurred the losses is the only one who can receive benefits from them. Even a corporation which does not undergo any corporate change but has a significant change in its stockholdings may be treated as not the same taxpayer who suffered the loss. Thus, to determine the availability of net operating losses, changes in ownership and the business activities of the corporation must be examined.[21]

40. The trustee of the estate of a corporate bankrupt is required to file a corporate tax return, and the benefit of any operating losses is carried forward by the trustee when filing for post-bankruptcy periods. However, when the corporation obtains a discharge and then resumes business activity, it would appear that any unused net operating loss would not pass to the trustee to offset income obtained during the administration of the estate because the discharged corporation continues to file its corporate tax return while the trustee files a fiduciary tax return.[22] It is doubtful, however, whether the unused losses will be available to the discharged corporation if, as likely, there has been a substantial change in stock ownership.[23]

41. Even if proceedings are not held under the Bankruptcy Act, the benefit of a loss carryforward may still be lost. Unless a remedy is sought in an official court settlement, any reduction of indebtedness results in a taxable gain to the extent that the company is made solvent. In the absence of an election to reduce the basis of the debtor's property under Section 108 of the Internal Revenue Code, the taxable gain would dissipate the tax loss

[21] Krause, pp. 414–15.

[22] See *New Colonial Ice Co. v. Helvering*, 292 U. S. 435 (1934).

[23] See *Huyler's v. Commissioner*, 327 F.2d 767 (1964); *Willingham v. U. S.*, 289 F.2d 283 (1961); *cert. den.* 368 U. S. 828 (1961).

carryover.[24] However, no taxable income results from a cancellation of debt under Chapter X or Chapter XI.

ADJUSTMENTS TO ASSET, LIABILITY, AND CAPITAL ACCOUNTS

Situations Necessitating Adjustments

42. In Section 270 (reorganizations) and Section 396 (arrangements), the Bankruptcy Act requires that the basis of the debtor's property be decreased by an amount equal to the amount by which the indebtedness of the debtor has been cancelled or reduced in a proceeding under the relevant chapter. However, the basis of any particular property is not to be decreased to an amount less than the fair market value of that property as of the date of entry of the order confirming the plan. Thus, the reduction of a liability means the debtor's assets must correspondingly be reduced, unless the property has a basis already equal to or below the fair market value. Those bankrupts who will be insolvent after any adjustment of their liabilities are not required to reduce the basis of their property. Reorganization aimed at remedying financial difficulties also does not call for an adjustment in the basis of the assets because the reorganized company assumes the basis of the old company.

43. When property which passed to the trustee in bankruptcy reverts to the debtor after discharge under an arrangement or reorganization, the debtor usually acquires the original basis along with any adjustments it was necessary to make.[25]

44. Section 1017 of the Internal Revenue Code also sets forth the procedure to be followed where debt is reduced. Under Section 108(a), where any amount is excluded from gross income on account of the discharge of indebtedness, the whole amount or the part of it so excluded is to be applied in reduction of the basis of properties held by the taxpayer (whether before or after the time of discharge) during any portion of the taxable year in which such discharge occurred. As can readily be seen, the provisions of the Bankruptcy Act and the Internal Revenue Code concerning the procedure to be followed when debt is reduced are similar.

[24] Rev. Rul. 58–600, 1958–2 C.B. 29.
[25] Chabrow, p. 365.

45. The theoretical considerations of how to treat the economic gain realized from the reduction of indebtedness revolve around whether such gain becomes part of the permanent capital of the corporation or is a part of the earnings and profits of the corporation.

46. If the amount cancelled is considered a part of the earnings and profits, the dividends received by stockholders from the earnings and profits will be taxable. If it is considered a part of contributed capital, any dividend received by stockholders that was paid from the capital resulting from the cancellation would be a return of capital and not subject to tax.

47. The tax effect depends upon how the Internal Revenue Service interprets the cancellation. Earnings and profits as a source of dividends is a statutory term. The statute does not define it, but contains a number of specific rules which provide some guidance. Earnings and profits as determined by accounting principles may not necessarily be considered a part of earnings and profits for tax purposes. However, in all conditions, it appears that the item in question must have the characteristic of income to be included in earnings and profits. The Eighth Circuit Court of Appeals recently held that an adjustment of the debts of a corporation in a bankruptcy arrangement did not result in the creation of earnings and profits for the corporation, regardless of the collateral effect of the debt cancellation on the basis of the assets.[26] Thus, any dividends paid from capital resulting from an adjustment of debt are not considered as taxable income under this decision. See Chapter 9, paragraphs 71–81 for the accounting treatment of the gain due to debt forgiveness.

48. The entries required to be made in the debtor's books upon consummation of the plan follow from the theory just discussed. At the time the debtor's liabilities are reduced, the payable is debited for the full amount, cash is credited for the amount paid, and the capital account is increased by the difference. When it is necessary to reduce the asset basis on the debtor's books pursuant to Sections 270 or 396 of the Bankruptcy Act, the capital account is debited and assets are credited for the amount by which the indebtedness has been forgiven. These transactions in the

[26] *Meyer v. Commissioner, supra;* see Erbacher, pp. 158–62, for a detailed description of the evidence supporting this interpretation.

capital account do not always cancel out, for example, when the basis cannot be reduced because it is already below fair market value.

Tax Benefit Rule

49. Sections 270 and 396 of the Bankruptcy Act require that the basis of the taxpayer's property be reduced by the amount by which the debt has been cancelled, provided that the reduction does not result in a tax benefit on any income tax return. The cancellation of indebtedness cannot result in a double favorable tax treatment for the debtor. Thus, this may result in recapture of previously allowed investment credits.[27]

Interest

50. An additional provision to the requirement of an adjustment in the asset basis is that it be reduced by the amount by which the debt is cancelled, not including accrued interest unpaid.

51. As a general rule, interest is not paid during the bankruptcy period. The accrual-basis taxpayer may deduct the interest expense, even though the ability to pay is uncertain, providing the liability to pay is fixed and determinable. The full amount of the interest is deductible during the year of accrual regardless of the fact that the taxpayer is undergoing reorganization under the Bankruptcy Act and there is doubt as to whether all or part of the interest will actually be paid.

TAX ASSESSMENTS, INTEREST, AND PENALTIES

Tax Assessments

52. Normally, when a tax liability arises an additional tax may not be assessed unless the correct procedure is followed. Thus, Section 6213(a) of the Internal Revenue Code prohibits an assessment of any income tax deficiency until a notice of the deficiency is mailed to the taxpayer. However, the filing of a taxpayer's petition in bankruptcy means that Section 6871 then governs and the

[27] Treas. Reg., Sec. 1.47–2(c).

Commissioner is thereby given authority to immediately assess any tax deficiency not previously assessed.

53. The petition must be approved by the court in a Chapter X reorganization before the proceedings start. In a Chapter XI arrangement, approval of the court is not necessary. When the petition is filed in straight bankruptcy, there is an automatic adjudication.

54. This assessment under Section 6871 is normally made even if a deficiency notice has been sent or a case is before the Tax Court.[28] The taxpayer loses the right to receive a ninety-day letter, provided one had not been sent at the time of the immediate assessment. This immediate assessment is not a notice of deficiency as provided in Section 6861(b). Instead of such notice, a letter will be sent to the taxpayer, receiver, trustee, debtor-in-possession, or other fiduciary, giving detailed notification of the tax deficiency computation. The taxpayer may furnish evidence showing wherein the deficiency is incorrect and upon request may be granted an informal conference by the District Director with respect to the deficiency, provided a Tax Court petition had not been filed prior to the bankruptcy petition. Under certain conditions during the course of the bankruptcy proceedings, the bankrupt may compromise the tax claims by filing application for offer and compromise before the Appellate Division of the Internal Revenue Service. Also, in Chapters X and XI, a debtor may be released from a tax liability by the payment of a reduced claim under a plan accepted by the Secretary of the Treasury. The Treasury has ninety days to accept or reject the plan after it is received from the court. If the plan is not accepted or rejected within ninety days, consent shall be conclusively presumed.[29]

55. Except for the conditions described above, the bankruptcy courts have jurisdiction under the Bankruptcy Act to determine the amount and validity of taxes claimed. The trustee can object to the Internal Revenue Service claims and will not be required to pay the tax and then sue for refund.

56. If there are no pending tax deficiencies to be assessed, the Internal Revenue Service will normally conduct an audit to

---

[28] T. H. Kingsmill, Jr. "When and How Is a Bankrupt Discharged from Federal Tax Debt?," *Journal of Taxation*, Vol. 31 (September 1969), p. 181.

[29] Bankruptcy Act, Sec. 199.

determine the amount of the bankrupt tax liability. This presents several problems for the independent accountant. The books and records often are not current and complete. The bankrupt's staff may not be qualified to explain and support the nature of underlying transactions. Thus, the tax authorities often look to the independent accountant for assistance. However, the accountant is faced with the compensation and time restraints contained in the retention orders granted to him by the court.

57. The independent accountant should file with the Internal Revenue Service a declaration of qualifications to practice before the Internal Revenue Service (Form 3–204) and have the fiduciary execute and file a general power of attorney (Form 2848) in each Internal Revenue Service office where the fiduciary is to be represented by the attorney or accountant.

Interest on Unpaid Taxes

58. Any federal tax which is not paid when due causes the taxpayer to be charged 9 per cent interest from the due date to the payment date. This interest accrual ends at the date of bankruptcy, and interest which arose before bankruptcy is held to be a valid claim against the estate.

59. Should a tax arise during the period of bankruptcy, interest would be charged until the end of the bankruptcy proceedings. This interest claim has been held to be non-allowable; that is, it is usually dischargeable as is the interest on other discharged debts.[30]

60. However, if after the proceedings the estate is solvent or tax liabilities arise from the administration of the estate, the Treasury then has a valid claim for interest on unpaid taxes in the postbankruptcy period.[31]

Tax Penalties

61. Any tax penalty which relates to operations before bankruptcy is held to be non-allowable, with the exception of the amount of monetary loss arising from the act, transaction, or

---

[30] Richard Kaye, "Federal Taxes, Bankruptcy and Assignments for the Benefit of Creditors—A Comparison," *Commercial Law Journal*, Vol. 73 (March 1968), p. 79.

[31] Kingsmill, p. 182.

proceeding out of which the penalty arose.[32] Thus, only the amount actually lost by the government because of the bankrupt's actions will constitute a valid claim in insolvency proceedings. However, penalties levied against an estate due to current taxes incurred by the trustee during the administration of the estate are allowable claims. Since they are attributable to conduct or misconduct of the trustee, penalties are never deductible in determining taxable income.

PRIORITIES OF FEDERAL, STATE, AND LOCAL TAX CLAIMS

General Tax Liabilities

62. Section 64(a) of the Bankruptcy Act enumerates the debts of the bankrupt which are to be afforded priority in advance of the payment of dividends to creditors, and are to be paid in full out of bankrupt estates. Fourth in the order of payment are taxes legally due and owing by the bankrupt to the United States or any state or subdivision thereof which are not released by a discharge in bankruptcy. Taxes which are not included in this priority category shall not have priority over general unsecured claims, and no order shall be made for the payment of a tax assessed against any property of the bankrupt in excess of the value of the interest of the bankrupt estate therein as determined by the court.

63. It is quite evident that no preference is given to the federal government over the states in the payment of taxes. Furthermore, those claimants who hold perfected specific liens on the debtor's property are to be satisfied from the liened property or its proceeds before any unsecured tax claims may be collected, provided that the trustee acquires the debtor's property subject to such liens.[33]

64. The date on which the tax liability arises is crucial in determining the priority to be granted that claim. In general, taxes which became due before bankruptcy are accorded fourth priority. However, taxes which became due more than three years prior to bankruptcy are denied this priority and treated instead as general

---

[32] Bankruptcy Act, Sec. 57j.
[33] Hellerstein, p. 402.

claims.[34] And taxes which accrue during the bankruptcy period are a cost of administration and are therefore granted first priority to be paid before any other unsecured claim.

65. The Bankruptcy Act also gives the court the power to determine the validity and amount of taxes whenever such decision is necessary. Pursuant to Section 2a(2A), the bankruptcy courts are invested with jurisdiction to hear and determine any question arising as to the amount or legality of any unpaid federal or state tax.

Tax Liens

66. Under Section 6321 of the Internal Revenue Code, the federal government acquires a lien for taxes on all property of any taxpayer liable for such taxes when it makes a demand for payment and the taxpayer neglects or refuses to pay. The tax is said to have been assessed as of the date when the liability is recorded on the assessment list in the District Director's office.[35]

Recording of Liens

67. Whether a tax lien has been recorded, and the rights which are given to the trustee, are crucial considerations. Section 6323 of the Internal Revenue Code states that such a lien is not valid against a mortgagee, pledgee, purchaser, or judgment creditor until notice of the lien is recorded. Therefore, unless the trustee in bankruptcy is construed to occupy one of the aforementioned categories, with respect to a tax lien which is acquired by the government before the bankruptcy is initiated, the liability will be paid as a secured claim before priority claims and general unsecured creditors even if the lien has not been recorded.[36] Section 70c of the Bankruptcy Act as amended in 1966, often called the "strong-arm clause," has been construed to give the trustee in bankruptcy all the powers of a judgment creditor.[37] Therefore, even if a tax was assessed and consequently secured, if a notice of the lien was not filed, the claim will lose its priority and be treated as a general unsecured liability.

[34] Bankruptcy Act, Sec. 17.

[35] Kaye, p. 79.

[36] Joseph P. Logan III, "Federal Tax Liens in Bankruptcy," *Washington and Lee Law Review*, Vol. 23 (Fall 1966), p. 372.

[37] *Ibid.*

Priority of Federal Liens

68. A federal tax lien in bankruptcy which has been recorded is superior to state and local tax claims. But in regard to personal property, unless the lien has been accompanied by possession, it is subordinated to administration costs and wage claims. Section 67c of the Bankruptcy Act provides that the payment of statutory liens, including tax liens, may be postponed until the payment of administrative expenses and wages, if:

The bankrupt estate is insolvent,

The lien is on personal property,

The lien is not accompanied by possession, or

The lien has not been enforced by sale prior to the filing of the petition in bankruptcy.

DISCHARGEABILITY OF TAX LIABILITIES

69. In general, the tax liabilities which may be discharged in bankruptcy proceedings are those which became legally due and owing more than three years before bankruptcy. Such debts, also called stale tax claims, are denied the fourth priority usually given taxes and the fifth priority given federal claims other than taxes. Instead, they are allowable as claims having equal priority with the general creditors.[38] Taxes become legally due and owing as of the date when the Internal Revenue Code requires the return to be filed.

Taxes Not Dischargeable

70. Section 17(a) of the Bankruptcy Act delineates the debts which are not to be affected by a discharge. It states that the bankrupt shall not be released from taxes which became legally due and owing to the United States or any state or subdivision thereof within three years preceding bankruptcy, provided that a discharge will not release a bankrupt from any taxes:

[38] W. T. Plumb, Jr. "Federal Tax Liens and Priorities in Bankruptcy—Recent Developments," *Journal of the National Conference of Referees in Bankruptcy*, Vol. 43 (April 1969), p. 43.

Which were not assessed in any case in which the bankrupt failed to make a return required by law

Which were assessed within one year preceding bankruptcy in any case in which the bankrupt failed to make a return required by law

Which were not reported on a return made by the bankrupt and which were not assessed prior to bankruptcy by reason of a prohibition on assessment pending the exhaustion of administrative or judicial remedies available to the bankrupt

With respect to which the bankrupt made a false or fraudulent return, or willfully attempted in any manner to evade or defeat the tax

Which the bankrupt has collected or withheld from another as required by the laws of the United States or any state or political subdivision thereof, but has not paid over

71. Any discharge which is granted shall not act to bar any remedies available under applicable law to the United States or any State or subdivision thereof, against the exemption of the bankrupt allowed by law. Also, a discharge in bankruptcy shall not release or affect any tax lien.

Dischargeability and Tax Liens

72. As noted above, a discharge in bankruptcy does not release or affect a tax lien. The federal government has taken the position that it may pursue the bankrupt on taxes which have been discharged by levying on his after-acquired property, provided the lien has been perfected. The courts have ruled that a deficiency cannot be asserted against any assets acquired by the bankrupt after bankruptcy.[39]

73. Also non-dischargeable is a liability arising from the failure to remit taxes which are required by law to be withheld or collected from others. Included in this category are withholding taxes, the employees' share of social security payments, and a state sales tax.[40]

---

[39] Leslie W. Abramson, *Basic Bankruptcy: Alternatives, Proceedings and Discharges* (Ann Arbor, Mich.: The Institute of Continuing Legal Education, 1971), p. 172. See *Braund*, 423 F.2d 719 (1970); *Carlson*, 423 F.2d 714 (1970); *United States v. Sanabria*, 424 F.2d 1121 (1970).

[40] Gary L. Blum, "Ramifications of Bankruptcy in Federal Tax Matters," *New York University Institute of Federal Taxation*, Vol. 29 (1971), p. 939.

Tax Claims and Dischargeability

74. The non-dischargeability aspect of some tax claims has further ramifications. The Bankruptcy Act requires that all tax claims be filed within six months after the date of the first meeting of creditors. But if such liabilities are not dischargeable in bankruptcy, the failure to file such claims within the required time period will not bar them because the government will be able to pursue them outside the insolvency proceedings.[41]

75. The non-dischargeability and priority of distribution aspects of tax claims have an important relationship to one another. Taxes which are not discharged pursuant to Section 17(a) of the Bankruptcy Act are granted priority under Section 64a(4) of the same statute. Conversely, when tax claims are dischargeable, those debts become general claims which are entitled to dividend distribution with the other general creditors after the claims with priority have been paid.

TAX CONSIDERATIONS IN REORGANIZATIONS

76. The usual outcome of a Chapter X or Chapter XI proceeding is the takeover of the corporation by its creditors, by creditors and stockholders, or by new interests. Many reorganizations in the past have involved only the debtor's creditors; however, with today's business conditions, it is often feasible for the debtor's corporation to be bailed out by new interests. No doubt, this change is a result of the interest many of today's corporations have in acquisitions.

77. Certain characteristics emerge from reorganizations which have been construed as non-taxable. They must fit into one of the definitions of a reorganization as found in the Internal Revenue Code; there must be a continuity of business enterprise and interest; and there must be a business purpose for the transaction.

Section 371

78. By its terms, Section 371 of the Internal Revenue Code applies only to a proceeding under Chapter X or to a corresponding

[41] Hellerstein, p. 923.

receivership or foreclosure proceeding under state law. It does not apply to Chapter XI proceedings. It deals with situations where property is transferred by a corporation under the jurisdiction of a bankruptcy court to another corporation which has been organized to consummate the plan. Section 371 states that no gain or loss shall be recognized if property of a corporation is transferred, in pursuance of an order of the court having jurisdiction of the corporation in a proceeding under Chapter X of the Bankruptcy Act, to another corporation which is organized or made use of to effectuate a plan of reorganization approved by the court in the proceeding, in exchange solely for stock or securities in the other corporation.

Transfer of Property

79. For a debtor who is insolvent, the transfer of property is non-taxable and the reorganized corporation acquires the debtor's basis for the assets it receives. Furthermore, any stockholders or security holders of the original corporation who give securities of the insolvent for securities of the reorganized corporation are not held to have realized any gain or loss on the transaction.[42] Sections 371(a)(2) and 371(b)(2) of the Internal Revenue Code provide for recognition of gain by the corporation or by the stockholders or security holders to the extent of boot received and retained in addition to stock and securities of the transferee.

Acquisitive Reorganization

80. There is some question about the application of Section 371 to an acquisitive reorganization by unrelated companies.[43] No authorities have directly applied this section to this type of reorganization; however, the Regulations take a very liberal view and only look to the end result of a series of steps to see whether Section 371 is applicable. A liberal interpretation would not preclude this application.[44]

[42] I.R.C., Sec. 371(b).
[43] David R. Tillinghast and Stephen P. Gardner, "Acquisitive Reorganizations and Chapters X and XI of the Bankruptcy Act," *New York University Tax Law Review*, Vol. 26 (May 1971), p. 690.
[44] Theodore Berger, "Acquisitions of Financially Troubled Businesses," *TAXES—The Tax Magazine*, Vol. 50 (December 1972), p. 811.

81. The reasons why Chapter XI arrangements were omitted from Section 371 are unknown; however, the accountant must assume that the omission was intentional and that Chapter XI proceedings are governed by Section 368 of the Internal Revenue Code. Certain parts of Section 368 may also apply to Chapter X reorganizations.[45]

Continuity of Interest

82. The reorganization must pass the continuity of interest test, which means that the owners of the debtor corporation must establish that they have retained a continuing equity interest in the acquiring corporation. Notes and bonds of the acquiring company do not constitute a continuing proprietary interest but preferred and common stock do.[46] For an insolvent company, the concept has developed that the creditor's interest is transferred into a proprietary interest prior to the acquisition.[47] Section 1.371–1(a)(4) of the Treasury Regulations states:

> Thus, the nonrecognition accorded by section 371(a)(1) applies only to a genuine reorganization as distinguished from a liquidation and sale of property to either new or old interests supplying new capital and discharging the obligations of the old corporation. For the purpose of determining whether the requisite continuity of interest exists, the interest of creditors who have, by appropriate legal steps, obtained effective command of the property of an insolvent corporation is considered as the equivalent of a proprietary interest. But the mere possibility of a proprietary interest is not its equivalent. . . .

83. In order for the continuity test to be met, according to the position of the Internal Revenue Service, the shareholders of the acquired company as a class must receive and intend to retain stock in the acquiring company which is at least 50 per cent of the value of their prior stock interests.[48]

---

[45] See Tillinghast and Gardner, pp. 663–723.
[46] *LeTulle v. Scofield*, 308 U. S. 415 (1940).
[47] *Helvering v. Alabama Asphaltic Limestone Co.*, 315 U. S. 179 (1942).
[48] Rev. Proc. 66–34, 1966–2 C.B. 1232.

Continuity of Business Enterprise

84. The requirements for the continuity of business enterprise are set forth in the Regulations under both Section 368 and Section 371.[49] The courts make a distinction between a lull in business caused by financial distress and a complete liquidation. The entire former business of the surviving corporation may be discontinued if the business of the acquired corporation is retained.[50]

WITHHOLDING

85. There is a tendency for the debtor or debtor-in-possession to pay the creditors who pressure the most for payment, and the funds from taxes (federal, state, and local) withheld from employees are often used to satisfy these creditors. The debtor, debtor-in-possession, trustee, and accountants (Chapter 7, paragraph 20) should realize that Section 6672 of the Internal Revenue Code and some state laws hold a person required to collect and remit these taxes, who willfully fails to do so, personally liable. Taxes withheld from wages during the bankruptcy period are granted first priority. The Section is unclear as to the priority (first, second, or fourth) of taxes withheld on pre-bankruptcy wages paid during bankruptcy.[51]

CONCLUSION

86. A corporation in financial difficulty has many pressing problems to examine. Because of these problems, attention is unlikely to be directed toward the tax consequences of one course of action compared to another. However, the consequences of this oversight can be very costly if an operating loss carryover is lost or additional taxes are levied on income earned during the proceedings which could have been avoided. The role of the accountant is to bring these facts to the attention of the trustee, debtor, or debtor-in-possession, and creditors.

[49] Treas. Reg., Secs. 1.368–1(b) and 1.371–1(a)(4).
[50] Rev. Rul. 63–29, 1963–1 C.B. 77.
[51] See *Fogarty*, 164 F.2d 26 (1947); *Connecticut Motor Lines, Inc.*, 336 F.2d 96 (1964); and *Freedomland, Inc.*, 480 F.2d 184 (1973).

11

The Proposed Bankruptcy Act

1. The Bankruptcy Act of 1973 was introduced in the U. S. House of Representatives as H. R. 10792 on October 9, 1973, and referred to a subcommittee of the House Committee on the Judiciary. The proposed Act was also introduced in the Senate. Congress started considering the Act during February of 1975. The Act is designed to replace the Bankruptcy Act of 1898 and the well known 1938 Chandler Amendment. The proposed Act is the result of more than two years of study by the Commission on the Bankruptcy Laws of the United States, which was created by a joint Congressional resolution. The Commission was composed of two members each from the U. S. Senate and U. S. House of Representatives, a California attorney known for his expertise in securities law, a representative of Dun & Bradstreet, a professor, and two federal district judges.

2. The Commission took a theoretical approach to the solution of bankruptcy problems and ignored, in the opinion of some, the practical difficulties encountered in business bankruptcies. One writer has stated that the problems of the proposed Act are

". . . the result of a theoretical and academic approach to the problems of consumer bankruptcy and a misapplied transference of these problems and solutions to a business bankruptcy system. . . ."[1] There was not a full-time practicing bankruptcy attorney or bankruptcy judge (referee) appointed to the Commission.

3. Another writer has stated: "The Commission concludes that bankruptcy should be easier and go much further in giving debtors a 'fresh start' irrespective of moral or ethical considerations."[2] There is also considerable support for the provisions of the new Act. A research director for the Commission feels that "the Commission took the philosophical and practical stand that bankruptcy and related relief should support, not upset the nation's credit system. . . ."[3]

4. The proposed Act is divided into ten chapters; only the last chapter applies to the period of transition from the present Act to the proposed one. Chapter I contains definitions of several terms used in the proposed Act and a description of the general provisions of the Act. Chapter II describes the organizational structure, jurisdiction, and procedure of the Bankruptcy Court created by the Act. Chapter III describes the functions, duties, powers, and methods of operation for the Bankruptcy Administration. The provisions which apply to more than one chapter are described in Chapter IV. Chapter V covers liquidations, voluntary and involuntary. Chapter VI applies to plans for debtors with regular income. It includes and expands the provisions of the present Chapter XIII. Reorganization is the title given to Chapter VII. Most of the cases which would be classified as Chapter X, XI, or XII proceedings under the current Act would be Chapter VII proceedings under the proposed Act. Chapter VIII covers adjustment of debt of public agencies, instrumentalities, and political subdivisions. Railroads are governed by Chapter IX.

[1] Robin E. Phelan, "The Proposed Bankruptcy Administration (The 'FBA')—Bureaucratic Alphabet Soup Gets A Bigger Bowl," *The American Bankruptcy Law Journal*, Vol. 48 (Fall 1974), p. 343.

[2] Linn K. Twinem, "Bankruptcy Report: Some Limitations on Creditors' Rights," *The Business Lawyer*, Vol. 29 (January 1974), p. 368.

[3] Robert M. Viles, "Non-Revolutionary Bankruptcy Act Proposed by the National Bankruptcy Commission," *The Business Lawyer*, Vol. 29 (July 1974), p. 1117.

5. The objectives of this chapter are to describe some of the major provisions of Chapters II, III, IV, V, and VII of the proposed Act, after briefly discussing why the Commission was created.

WHY THE COMMISSION ON THE BANKRUPTCY LAWS OF THE UNITED STATES WAS CREATED

6. The number of bankruptcies has increased over 1,000 times since World War II. A large part of this increase is due to consumer bankruptcies, which account for roughly 90 per cent of all petitions filed. The duties and responsibilities of the Commission were not restricted to the study of consumer bankruptcies, but most of those who testified in support of the establishment of the Commission emphasized consumer problems. The reason for this is fairly obvious. Although there have certainly been changes in commercial credit and financial practices of business, these have in no way compared with the revolution in the consumer credit field. In general, Congress has been more willing to make changes in Chapters X and XI than it has in the areas that relate to consumers.

7. Another reason for the establishment of the Commission was the lack of uniform practices of courts and officers. There are major differences in policies among the federal bankruptcy courts. For example, in the fiscal year ended June 30, 1972, almost 20 per cent of the petitions filed under Chapter XIII were filed in the State of Alabama while in the Southern District of New York only one petition was filed. These differences caused unequal treatment of both debtors and creditors.

8. The large administrative cost (around $17 million for fiscal 1972) and the inefficiencies due to a lack of information about the operations of the various districts, a lack of simplified procedures for handling routine cases, and the requirements of redundant paperwork are other reasons given for the need for a new bankruptcy law.

9. A controversial study conducted by The Brookings Institution pointed out most of the weaknesses discussed above and was, no doubt, partly responsible for the establishment of the Commission.

ORGANIZATION AND STRUCTURE

10. The proposed Act would eliminate the referees in bankruptcy which exist under the present law and create a Bankruptcy Court and a Bankruptcy Administration. These agencies would be similar to the Tax Court and the Internal Revenue Service in that an administrator and a staff would handle all non-contested matters and as soon as an act of the Bankruptcy Administration is challenged, the matter would go to a bankruptcy judge.

Bankruptcy Court

11. The Commission recommends that the Bankruptcy Courts be separate from the United States District Courts and that they have jurisdiction over all controversies arising out of a case which commenced under the Act.[4] Under the present law it is often difficult to determine whether a proceeding in a bankruptcy court is acceptable or whether it is necessary to sue in an appropriate non-bankruptcy court; however, under the proposed Act this controversy is eliminated. The proposed Act will also eliminate the problem of the debtor in attempting to determine which of the several rehabilitation chapters is most appropriate to its needs. The Bankruptcy Court will have the authority to determine what property is exempt.[5] The Court does not have the authority to try criminal cases; however, it can enforce obedience to its order by fine and/or imprisonment and can punish persons for contempt.[6]

12. The President of the United States shall appoint the judges by and with the advice and consent of the Senate for a term of fifteen years.[7] An appeal from a bankruptcy court shall be taken to a district court and further appeals would proceed in the normal way to a court of appeals and the Supreme Court.[8]

[4] Bankruptcy Act of 1973, Sec. 2–201(a). All Section references in footnotes to the end of this chapter, unless otherwise noted, are to Sections of the Bankruptcy Act of 1973, as proposed in the House of Representatives (see paragraph 1 of the chapter).
[5] Sec. 2–201(a)(2).
[6] Sec. 2–201(d).
[7] Sec. 2–102.
[8] Sec. 2–210.

Bankruptcy Administration

13. The proposed Act calls for the creation of a Bankruptcy Administration with the power to handle almost all matters except those which involve some form of litigation. The agency is to be established in the executive branch of the government and the principal officer will be an administrator appointed by the President with the advice and consent of the Senate for a term of seven years. The administrator is authorized to appoint a deputy, regional administrators, and other officers as is found necessary to conduct the business of the Bankruptcy Administration.[9] In addition to the officers and employees, who are under Civil Service, the administrator may employ attorneys, accountants, appraisers, auctioneers, management consultants, business advisors, and other individuals and organizations on a part-time, temporary, or intermittent basis.[10]

14. Section 3-202 states that the administrator has the power necessary to discharge the duties and functions assigned under this Act. The powers given to the administrator are found throughout the balance of the Act, and are described in greater detail in the discussion of the various chapters of the Act. Some of these powers are listed here to give the reader an idea of the broad nature of the judicial and administrative scope of this office:

Determine schedule of fees and charges[11]

Adopt, amend, or repeal rules and regulations not in conflict with the Act[12]

Promulgate rules describing the duties of trustees and receivers under the Act[13]

Approve the trustees' requests for employment of attorneys, accountants, appraisers, auctioneers, and other personnel [14]

Appoint creditors' committee[15]

Under certain conditions serve as trustee[16]

[9] Secs. 3-101 and 3-102.
[10] Sec. 3-102(d).
[11] Sec. 3-302(b).
[12] Sec. 3-202(b)(1).
[13] Sec. 4-306.
[14] Sec. 4-309(9).
[15] Secs. 5-102(a) and 7-101(a).
[16] Sec. 5-101.

Authorize a trustee, receiver, or debtor to issue certificates of indebtedness which have priority over other unsecured debt[17]

15. The Bankruptcy Administration is to be financed from funds appropriated by Congress and from fees and charges received by the administrator under the Act. The fee and charges established by the administrator should be reasonable and equitable and the income from fees and charges should equal as nearly as practicable the costs of the Administration.[18] An annual audit will be performed by a certified public accountant and the accounts and operations will also be audited by the General Accounting Office.[19] The administrator will submit annually to Congress and to the Office of Management and Budget a business-type budget program.[20]

CHAPTER VII: REORGANIZATION

16. The proposed new Chapter VII, which will consolidate the present Chapter X and Chapter XI proceedings, is designed to more effectively free a financially troubled business from burdensome prebankruptcy commitments and to facilitate the operations of the business free from court and administrative regulation when only ordinary business transactions are involved. The Act attempts to provide an environment where debtor and creditor can bargain for the adjustment of their respective interests free from outside influence other than that necessary to protect the rights of dissenting creditors and shareholders. The purpose then is to provide an efficient, timely, and fair adjustment of the rights of all parties and to provide a forum for timely and fair judicial determination of controversies that arise from the proceedings.[21] There is considerable diversity of opinion as to whether the Act accomplishes these objectives.

[17] Sec. 7–106.
[18] Secs. 3–301 and 3–302(c).
[19] Sec. 3–401.
[20] Sec. 3–402.
[21] J. Ronald Trost, "Corporate Reorganizations Under Chapter VII of the 'Bankruptcy Act of 1973': Another View," *American Bankruptcy Law Journal*, Vol. 48 (Spring 1974), p. 119.

Functions of Administrator and Bankruptcy Judge

17. The administrator will be primarily responsible for presiding over the day-to-day proceedings during the reorganization of the business. All matters which are contested will be decided by the judge. The judge will also have the responsibility for any action to recover money or property of the estate. Under this chapter, the administrator does not have any responsibility for managing the business. One important change made by the proposed Act, in the opinion of some writers, is that it separates the judicial function of resolving issues from the day-to-day operations of the business.

Filing of Petition

18. Involuntary and voluntary petitions may be filed under the provisions of Chapter VII. Sections 4–205(b) and 4–205(c) provide that one or more creditors whose claims total at least $10,000 may file a petition. Relief may be requested when the debtor is unable to pay current liabilities as they become due or generally fails to pay debts as they become due, or if any agent takes possession of substantially all of the debtor's property in a rehabilitation or liquidation proceeding not under the proposed Act. Thus, the "acts of bankruptcy" which are required under the current law would be abolished. Also, it takes only one creditor to force a debtor into bankruptcy; under the current law it takes three.

19. Critics of the proposed law suggest that by allowing one creditor to file an involuntary petition and by eliminating the acts of bankruptcy, a large number of going concerns will be forced into liquidation.

Creditors' Committee

20. Section 7–101(a) of the proposed Act provides that the administrator will appoint a creditors' committee as soon as practical after a petition is filed. The committee will ordinarily consist of seven members selected from the creditors holding the largest amount of unsecured claims who are representative of the different types of creditors holding claims. The committee size may be increased or decreased in order to obtain a representative committee. The administrator has the power to appoint other

committees of unsecured creditors or equity security holders if a need for such a committee exists. The court, on the petition of any interested party, may change the membership on the grounds that the committee is not representative.[22] The major change between the proposed Act and the present law is that currently the creditors select the committee and it does not necessarily have to come from the creditors with the largest claim.

21. The committee at a scheduled meeting with a majority of the members present may appoint, subject to the approval of the administrator, an attorney, an accountant, or other agencies to represent and perform services for the committee.[23]

22. The functions of the creditors' committee are as follows:

Consult with the administrator as to the administration of the estate, the issuance of certificates of indebtedness, the sale or lease of property, and the appointment of a trustee

Consult with the trustee or debtor concerning the operation of the business

Examine into the conduct of the debtor's affairs and the causes of the insolvency, the inability to pay debts as they mature, or the cessation of payment of debts

File a proposed plan or a modification of a proposed plan

Consider any plan and negotiate with the debtor or others concerning the terms of any plan

Advise those represented of its recommendations as to any plan and the progress of the case

Collect and file with the court acceptances of any plan

Perform such other services as may be in the interest of creditors[24]

Operation of Business

23. The administrator has the right to authorize a trustee, a receiver, or the debtor to operate the business—whichever is in the best interest of the estate.[25] If the debtor is a corporation with liabilities of at least $1,000,000 and there are at least 300 creditors, the court will order the administrator to appoint a trustee unless it

---

[22] Secs. 7–101(b) and 7–101(c).
[23] Sec. 7–101(d)(1).
[24] Sec. 7–101(d)(3).
[25] Sec. 7–104.

finds that the protection afforded by a trustee is unnecessary or the expense would be greater than the benefit. Regardless of the size of debt and the number of creditors, the court may order the administrator to appoint a trustee on the application of any interested party or the administrator.[26]

Plan of Reorganization

24. On the plan of reorganization, the proposed Act takes part of the provisions of Chapter XI and part of Chapter X and adopts some new characteristics. Provisions for developing a plan for Chapter VII apply to all types of business reorganizations. Some of the key provisions dealing with the proof of claims, the development of the plan, and the acceptance and confirmation of the plan are described in this section.

Proofs of Claims and Interests

25. The proposed Act eliminates the need for creditors to file proofs of claims. Section 7–301 provides that claims, and interests which are not disputed, contingent, or unliquidated, are established by the list filed by the trustee or debtor as required by Section 7–103. This provision does not differ from the proposed Chapter X rules.

Development of Plan

26. On or before the date set by the administrator, the trustee or the debtor is required to file a plan or a report why the plan cannot be formulated with the administrator.[27] The debtor, a creditor, or an equity security holder may also file a plan at any time prior to the date set by the administrator.[28] The plan of arrangement filed under Chapter XI is the debtor's plan and the creditors are not allowed to file.

Acceptance and Confirmation

27. Before a plan will be confirmed by the court, it must be accepted by a majority in amount of each class of creditors

[26] Sec. 7–102(a).
[27] Sec. 7–304(a).
[28] Sec. 7–304(b).

materially and adversely affected who have accepted or rejected the plan.[29] The two-thirds majority required by Chapter X is reduced to a majority and the requirement under Chapter XI that a majority in number of creditors must vote for the plan is eliminated.

28. Another major difference in the conditions which must be met before confirmation under the proposed Act and confirmation under Chapter X and Chapter XI is the "fairness standard." Chapter X now requires the court to make a determination, even if accepted by the creditors, that the plan is "fair and equitable." [30] Under Chapter XI the plan has to be in the best interest of the creditors, which means that the amount they receive under the plan is at least as much as they would have received if the debtor's estate were liquidated.[31] The stockholders under a Chapter XI proceeding are allowed to retain an interest even though creditors are not paid in full. Under a Chapter X proceeding the "absolute priority" doctrine applies and if the corporation is insolvent, the shareholders cannot participate. The same principle applies to creditors. Senior creditors must receive payment in full before the junior creditors can participate in the reorganization process.

29. The "absolute priority" rule has been relaxed in the proposed Act. The requirements are that there be a reasonable basis for the valuation on which the plan is based and that the plan must be fair and equitable, offering a reasonable probability that the consideration distributed to creditors and stockholders will fully compensate for their interests.[32] The priority rule is further relaxed in that if the business valuation does not provide any benefits for some junior interests, they may participate in either of two ways. First, Section 7–303(4) provides that stockholders may participate if they make a contribution which is important to the operations of the corporation on a basis which reasonably approximates the value of their interests and the additional estimated value of such a contribution. This appears to be a procedure for allocating the excess of the going-concern value over the liquidating value among the interested parties.

---

[29] Sec. 7–310(d)(1).
[30] Bankruptcy Act, Sec. 221(2).
[31] *Ibid.*, Sec. 336(2).
[32] Sec. 7–210(d)(2)(B).

30. A second provision of the proposed Act which would allow junior interests to participate involves another look at the valuation of the corporation. Section 7–303(3) provides that if junior interests are precluded from participation, provision for delayed participation is allowed, within a specified time period not later than five years from the confirmation date, provided the financial condition of the entity warrants such participation.

31. The proposed Act would allow confirmation of a plan that is acceptable to all creditors materially and adversely affected with the fairness standard described above, provided the plan does affect holders of publicly held securities.[33]

32. The plan, of course, must provide for payment of priority claims specified in Section 4–405(a)(1)–(5).

33. The proposed Act provides for making modifications and objecting to the proposed plan. However, if an objection could have been made during the process of acquiring approval of the creditors and/or stockholders, it cannot be made at the hearing on confirmation of the plan.[34]

Discharge

34. The provisions of the confirmed plan are binding on all parties involved in the proceedings regardless of whether they have accepted it.[35] The confirmation of a plan terminates all interest of equity security holders as provided in the plan or in the order confirming the plan and it extinguishes all claims against the debtor except those exempted from discharge under Section 4–506.[36]

Role of the SEC

35. The SEC has a very important part in bankruptcy proceedings under the present Chapter X and a.;o under Chapter XI if the company is publicly owned. The SEC must receive an advisory report under the present law; under the proposed Act this report must be filed with the administrator according to the requirements of Section 7–306. However, the SEC is to receive

[33] Ibid.
[34] Sec. 7–310(b).
[35] Sec. 7–311(b).
[36] Sec. 7–311(c).

notice of any corporation which files a petition if there are 300 or more security holders.

CHAPTER V: LIQUIDATION

36. The objective in drafting the provisions for the distribution of the assets of the bankrupt was to simplify and eliminate certain special interests.

Filing of Petition

37. The petition may be voluntary or one or more creditors having claims totaling at least $2,500 in excess of any security may file an involuntary petition requesting relief. The basis for relief under Chapter V is the same as was described for Chapter VII (see paragraph 18). The administration of the estate under this chapter will be suspended, if the debtor or creditor files a petition under Chapter VII, until the court decides under which chapter to provide relief.

Election of Trustee and Creditors' Committee

38. A private trustee may be elected to liquidate the estate if elected by a majority in amount voting and if the number voting hold at least 35 per cent of the amount of unsecured claims of creditors qualified to vote.[37] Until a private trustee is elected the administrator may appoint a trustee to operate the business.[38]

39. The administrator may appoint a creditors' committee on his own initiative or as a result of an application of any interested party. The committee is to consist of a suitable number from the largest non-priority unsecured claims which is representative of all types of claims. The purpose of the creditors' committee is to consult with and make recommendations to the administrator and trustee and to submit to the court any questions which affect the administration of the estate.[39]

---

[37] Sec. 5–101(a).
[38] Secs. 5–101(c) and 4–302(a).
[39] Secs. 5–102(a) and 5–102(c).

Distribution of Assets

40. The trustee is free to sell property of the estate in a way that is determined appropriate, without hearing or order of the court; however, the administrator must give notice of the public sale, including the time and place, to the creditors' committee and other creditors who request such notice. Notice is not required where it is impracticable or if the sale is in the ordinary course of a business authorized to be operated.[40]

41. The Commission (see paragraph 1) has recommended that the claims which should have priority be reduced to basically those for administrative expenses, wages, and taxes. The administrative expenses are allowed to the extent they are reasonable and necessary and are for a reason stated in Section 4–403(a). The wages allowed are increased from $600 (under the present law) to $1,200 and they can include up to $300 in fringe benefits. (Under the present law fringe benefits are denied priority as wages.) The wages must have been earned within three months prior to the date of the petition or the cessation of the debtor's business, whichever is earlier.[41]

42. The proposed Act also reduces the time period when taxes are a priority, from three years to one year prior to bankruptcy. Those taxes accruing in this one-year period represent the only priority given to the government.[42]

43. Section 4–406(a) provides that certain claims should be subordinated to other debts. Among them are debts owed to officers or directors, or to an affiliate of a debtor or any member of the debtor's immediate family.

CONCLUSION

44. The features of the proposed Bankruptcy Act of 1973 described above are those which relate to a corporation seeking relief under either Chapter V or VII. Emphasis has been placed on those provisions which differ from the present law and those which

[40] Secs. 5–203(a) and 4–307(c)(3).
[41] Sec. 4–405(a).
[42] *Ibid.*

would appear to have the greatest impact on the debtor and the creditors.

45. If the proposed Act is enacted in its present form, which is highly unlikely, it could have a profound effect on the credit community. Any professional person who is in any way associated with bankruptcy and insolvency proceedings will, no doubt, carefully follow the action which Congress takes on the Commission's report.

APPENDIXES

A

Official Bankruptcy Forms

Form No. 1. Petition for Voluntary Bankruptcy

United States District Court for the _____ District of _____

In re

_____ _____,
Bankrupt [*include here all names* } Bankruptcy No._____
used by bankrupt within last
6 years]

VOLUNTARY PETITION

1. Petitioner's post-office address is_____

_____.

2. Petitioner has resided [*or* has had his domicile *or* has had his principal place of business] within this district for the preceding 6 months [*or* for a longer portion of the preceding 6 months than in any other district].

3. Petitioner is qualified to file this petition and is entitled to the benefits of the Bankruptcy Act as a voluntary bankrupt.

Wherefore petitioner prays for relief as a voluntary bankrupt under the Act.

Signed: _____,
Attorney for Petitioner.
Address: _____,

_____
[*Petitioner signs if not represented by attorney.*]

_____,
Petitioner.

STATE OF _____
County of _____, *ss:*

I, _____, the petitioner named in the foregoing petition, do hereby swear that the statements contained therein are true according to the best of my knowledge, information, and belief.

_____,
Petitioner.

Subscribed and sworn to before me on _____.

_____,

_____
[*Official character*]

[*Unless further time is granted by the court pursuant to Rule 108, this petition must be accompanied by a schedule of the petitioner's debts and property, his claim for such exemptions as he may be entitled to, and a statement of his affairs. These additional statements shall be submitted on official forms, shall include the information about the petitioner's property and debts required by the Bankruptcy Rules and by the forms, and shall be verified under oath.*]

Form No. 2.   Application To Pay Filing Fees in Installments

[Caption, other than designation, as in Form No. 1]

APPLICATION TO PAY FILING FEES IN INSTALLMENTS

1. Applicant is filing herewith a voluntary petition in bankruptcy.
2. He is unable to pay the filing fees except in installments.
3. He proposes to pay such fees to the clerk of the district court upon the following terms:

----

4. He has paid no money and transferred no property to his attorney for services in connection with this case or any pending case under the Act, and he will make no payment or transfer to his attorney for such services until the filing fees are paid in full.

Wherefore applicant prays that he be permitted to pay the filing fees in installments.

Dated: _____.

Signed: _____,
Applicant.

Address: _____,
_____.

Form No. 3.   Order for Payment of Filing Fees in Installments

[Caption, other than designation, as in Form No. 1]

ORDER FOR PAYMENT OF FILING FEES IN INSTALLMENTS

The application of the bankrupt for permission to pay the filing fees in this case in installments having been heard;

It is ordered that the bankrupt pay the filing fees still owing, namely, $_____, as follows: _____

It is further ordered that all payments be made at the office of the clerk of the United States District Court located at _____; and that until the filing fees are paid in full, the bankrupt shall pay no money and shall transfer no property to his attorney, and his attorney shall accept no money or property from the bankrupt for services in connection with this case.

Dated: _____.

_____.
Bankruptcy Judge.

Form No. 4. Verification on Behalf of a Corporation

STATE OF _____
County of _____, *ss:*

I, _____, the President [*or other officer or* an authorized agent] of the corporation named as petitioner in the foregoing petition, do hereby swear that the statements contained therein are true according to the best of my knowledge, information, and belief, and that the filing of this petition on behalf of the corporation has been authorized.

_____.

Subscribed and sworn to before me on _____.

_____,
[*Official character*]

Form No. 5. Verification on Behalf of a Partnership

STATE OF _____
County of _____, *ss:*

I, _____, a member [*or* an authorized agent] of the partnership named as petitioner in the foregoing petition, do hereby swear that the statements contained therein are true according to the best of my knowledge, information, and belief, and that the filing of this petition on behalf of the partnership has been authorized.

_____.

Subscribed and sworn to before me on _____.

_____,
[*Official character*]

Form No. 6. Schedules

[*Caption, other than designation, as in Form No. 1*]

SCHEDULE A.—STATEMENT OF ALL DEBTS OF BANKRUPT

Schedules A–1, A–2, and A–3 must include all the claims against the bankrupt or his property as of the date of the filing of the petition by or against him.

SCHEDULE A-1.—CREDITORS HAVING PRIORITY

Nature of claim	Name of creditor and residence of place of business (if unknown, so state)	Specify when claim was incurred and the consideration therefor; when claim is contingent, unliquidated, disputed, or subject to setoff, evidenced by a judgment, negotiable instrument, or other writing, or incurred as partner or joint contractor, so indicate; specify name of any partner or joint contractor on any debt	Amount of claim
(a) Wages and commissions owing to workmen, servants, clerks, or traveling or city salesmen on salary or commission basis, whole or part time, whether or not selling exclusively for the bankrupt, not exceeding $600 to each, earned within 3 months before filing of petition_____			$_____
(b) Taxes owing (itemize by type of tax and taxing authority):			
(1) To the United States_____			
(2) To any State_____			
(3) To any other taxing authority_____			
(c) (1) Debts owing to any person, including United States, entitled to priority by laws of United States (itemize by type)_____			
(2) Rent owing to a landlord entitled to priority by laws of any State accrued within 3 months before filing of petition, for actual use and occupancy_____			
Total_____			

SCHEDULE A-2.—CREDITORS HOLDING SECURITY

Name of creditor and residence or place of business (if unknown, so state)	Description of security and date when obtained by creditor	Specify when claim was incurred and the consideration therefor; when claim is contingent, unliquidated, disputed, subject to setoff, evidenced by a judgment, negotiable instrument, or other writing, or incurred as partner or joint contractor, so indicate; specify name of any partner or joint contractor on any debt	Market value	Amount of claim without deduction of value of security
			$_____	$_____
Total_____				

SCHEDULE A-3.—CREDITORS HAVING UNSECURED CLAIMS WITHOUT PRIORITY

Name of creditor (including last known holder of any negotiable instrument) and residence or place of business (if unknown, so state)	Specify when claim was incurred and the consideration therefor; when claim is contingent, unliquidated, disputed, subject to setoff, evidenced by a judgment, negotiable instrument, or other writing, or incurred as partner or joint contractor, so indicate; specify name of any partner or joint contractor on any debt	Amount of claim
		$_____
Total_____		

SCHEDULE B.—STATEMENT OF ALL PROPERTY OF BANKRUPT

Schedules B–1, B–2, B–3, and B–4 must include all property of the bankrupt as of the date of the filing of the petition by or against him.

SCHEDULE B-1—REAL PROPERTY

Description and location of all real property in which bankrupt has an interest (including equitable and future interests, interests in estates by the entirety, community property, life estates, leaseholds, and rights and powers exercisable for his own benefit)	Nature of interest (specify all deeds and written instruments relating thereto)	Market value of bankrupt's interest without deduction for secured claims listed in schedule A–2 or exemptions claimed in schedule B–4
		$
Total		

SCHEDULE B-2 —PERSONAL PROPERTY

Type of property	Description and location	Market value of bankrupt's interest without deduction for secured claims listed in schedule A–2 or exemptions claimed in schedule B–4
a. Cash on hand		$
b. Deposits of money with banking institutions, savings and loan associations, credit unions, public utility companies, landlords, and others		
c. Household goods, supplies, and furnishings		
d. Books, pictures, and other art objects; stamp, coin, and other collections		
e. Wearing apparel, jewelry, firearms, sports equipment, and other personal possessions		
f. Automobiles, trucks, trailers, and other vehicles		
g. Boats, motors, and their accessories		
h. Livestock, poultry, and other animals		
i. Farming supplies and implements		
j. Office equipment, furnishings, and supplies		
k. Machinery, fixtures, equipment, and supplies (other than those listed in items j and l) used in business		
l. Inventory		
m. Tangible personal property of any other description		
n. Patents, copyrights, franchises, and other general intangibles (specify all documents and writings relating thereto)		
o. Government and corporate bonds and other negotiable and nonnegotiable instruments		
p. Other liquidated debts owing bankrupt or debtor		
q. Contingent and unliquidated claims of every nature, including counterclaims of the bankrupt or debtor (give estimated value of each)		
r. Interests in insurance policies (itemize surrender or refund values of each)		
s. Annuities		
t. Stocks and interests in incorporated and unincorporated companies (itemize separately)		
u. Interests in partnerships		
v. Equitable and future interests, life estates, and rights or powers exercisable for the benefit of the bankrupt or debtor (specify all written instruments relating thereto)		
Total		

SCHEDULE B-3.—PROPERTY NOT OTHERWISE SCHEDULED

Type of property	Description and location	Market value of bankrupt's interest without deduction for secured claims listed in schedule A-2 or exemptions claimed in schedule B-4
a. Property transferred under assignment for benefit of creditors, within 4 months prior to filing of petition (specify date of assignment, name and address of assignee, amount realized therefrom by the assignee, and disposition of proceeds so far as known to bankrupt)		$
b. Property of any kind not otherwise scheduled		
Total		

SCHEDULE B-4.—PROPERTY CLAIMED AS EXEMPT

Type of property	Location, description, and so far as relevant to the claim of exemption, present use of property	Reference to statute creating the exemption	Value claimed exempt
			$
Total			

SUMMARY OF DEBTS AND PROPERTY
[From the statements of the bankrupt in schedules A and B]

Schedule	Debts and property	Total
DEBTS		
A-1/a	Wages having priority	
A-1/b(1)	Taxes owing United States	
A-1/b(2)	Taxes owing States	
A-1/b(3)	Taxes owing other taxing authorities	
A-1/c(1)	Debts having priority by laws of the United States	
A-1/c(2)	Rent having priority under State law	
A-2	Secured claims	
A-3	Unsecured claims without priority	
Schedule A total		
PROPERTY		
B-1	Real property (total value)	
B-2/a	Cash on hand	
B-2/b	Deposits	
B-2/c	Household goods	
B-2/d	Books, pictures, and collections	
B-2/e	Wearing apparel and personal possessions	
B-2/f	Automobiles and other vehicles	
B-2/g	Boats, motors, and accessories	
B-2/h	Livestock and other animals	
B-2/i	Farming supplies and implements	
B-2/j	Office equipment and supplies	
B-2/k	Machinery, equipment, and supplies used in business	
B-2/l	Inventory	
B-2/m	Other tangible personal property	
B-2/n	Patents and other general intangibles	
B-2/o	Bonds and other instruments	
B-2/p	Other liquidated debts	
B-2/q	Contingent and unliquidated claims	
B-2/r	Interests in insurance policies	
B-2/s	Annuities	
B-2/t	Interests in corporations and unincorporated companies	
B-2/u	Interests in partnerships	
B-2/v	Equitable and future interests, rights, and powers in personality	
B-3/a	Property assigned for benefit of creditors	
B-3/b	Property not otherwise scheduled	$
B-4	Property claimed as exempt	$
Schedule B total		

350

OATH OF INDIVIDUAL TO SCHEDULES A AND B

STATE OF_____

County of_____, ss:

I, _____, do hereby swear that I have read the foregoing schedules, consisting of ____ sheets, and that they are a statement of all my debts and all my property in accordance with the Bankruptcy Act, to the best of my knowledge, information, and belief.

Signed: _____.

Subscribed and sworn to before me on _____.

_____,

_____.

[*Official character*]

OATH ON BEHALF OF CORPORATION TO SCHEDULES A AND B

STATE OF_____

County of_____, ss:

I, _____, the president [*or other officer or* an authorized agent] of the corporation named as bankrupt in this proceeding, do hereby swear that I have read the foregoing schedules, consisting of ____ sheets, and that they are a statement of all the debts and all the property of the corporation in accordance with the Bankruptcy Act, to the best of my knowledge, information, and belief.

Signed: _____.

Subscribed and sworn to before me on _____.

_____,

_____.

[*Official character*]

OATH ON BEHALF OF PARTNERSHIPS TO SCHEDULES A AND B

STATE OF_____

County of_____, ss:

I, _____, a member [*or* an authorized agent] of the partnership named as bankrupt in this proceeding, do hereby swear that I have read the foregoing schedules, consisting of ____ sheets, and that they are a statement of all the debts and all the property of the partnership in accordance with the Bankruptcy Act, to the best of my knowledge, information, and belief.

Signed: _____.

Subscribed and sworn to before me on _____.

_____,

_____.

[*Official character*]

Form No. 7.   Statement of Affairs for Bankrupt Not Engaged in Business

[Caption, other than designation, as in Form No. 1]

STATEMENT OF AFFAIRS FOR BANKRUPT NOT ENGAGED IN BUSINESS

[Each question should be answered or the failure to answer explained. If the answer is "none," this should be stated. If additional space is needed for the answer to any question, a separate sheet, properly identified and made a part hereof, should be used and attached.

The term, "original petition," as used in the following questions, shall mean the petition filed under Bankruptcy Rule 103, 104, or 105.]

1. Name and residence

a. What is your full name and social security number?

b. Have you used, or been known by, any other names within the 6 years immediately preceding the filing of the original petition herein? (If so, give particulars.)

c. Where do you now reside?

d. Where else have you resided during the 6 years immediately preceding the filing of the original petition herein?

2. Occupation and income

a. What is your occupation?

b. Where are you now employed? (Give the name and address of your employer, or the address at which you carry on your trade or profession, and the length of time you have been so employed.)

c. Have you been in a partnership with anyone, or engaged in any business during the 6 years immediately preceding the filing of the original petition herein? (If so, give particulars, including names, dates, and places.)

d. What amount of income have you received from your trade or profession during each of the 2 calendar years immediately preceding the filing of the original petition herein?

e. What amount of income have you received from other sources during each of these 2 years? (Give particulars, including each source, and the amount received therefrom.)

3. Tax returns and refunds

a. Where did you file your last federal and state income tax returns for the 2 years immediately preceding the filing of the original petition herein?

b. What tax refunds (income and other) have you received during the year immediately preceding the filing of the original petition herein?

c. To what tax refunds (income or other), if any, are you, or may you be, entitled? (Give particulars, including information as to any refund payable jointly to you and your spouse or any other person.)

4. Bank accounts and safe deposit boxes

a. What bank accounts have you maintained, alone or together with any other person, and in your own or any other name within the 2 years immediately preceding the filing of the original petition herein? (Give the name and address of each bank, the name in which the deposit maintained, and the name and address of every other person authorized to make withdrawals from such account.)

b. What safe deposit box or boxes or other depository or depositories have you kept or used for your securities, cash, or other valuables within the 2 years immediately preceding the filing of the original petition herein? (Give the name and address of the bank or other depository, the name in which each box or other depository was kept, the name and address of every other person who had the right of access thereto, a brief description of the contents thereof, and, if the box has been surrendered, state when surrendered, or, if transferred, when transferred, and the name and address of the transferee.)

5. Books and records

a. Have you kept books of account or records relating to your affairs within the 2 years immediately preceding the filing of the original petition herein?

b. In whose possession are these books or records? (Give names and addresses.)

c. If any of these books or records are not available, explain.

d. Have any books of account or records relating to your affairs been destroyed, lost, or otherwise disposed of within the 2 years immediately preceding the filing of the original petition herein? (If so, give particulars, including date of destruction, loss, or disposition, and reason therefor.)

6. Property held for another person

What property do you hold for any other person? (Give name and address of each person, and describe the property, or value thereof, and all writings relating thereto.)

7. Prior bankruptcy

What proceedings under the Bankruptcy Act have previously been brought by or against you? (State the location of the bankruptcy court, the nature and number of each proceeding, the date when it was filed, and whether a discharge was granted or refused, the proceeding was dismissed, or a composition, arrangement, or plan was confirmed.)

8. Receiverships, general assignments, and other modes of liquidation

a. Was any of your property, at the time of the filing of the original petition herein, in the hands of a receiver, trustee, or other liquidating agent? (If so, give a brief description of the property, the name and address of the receiver, trustee, or other agent, and, if the agent was appointed in a court proceeding, the name and location of the court and the nature of the proceeding.)

b. Have you made any assignment of your property for the benefit of your creditors, or any general settlement with your creditors, within one year immediately preceding the filing of the original petition herein? (If so, give dates, the name and address of the assignee, and a brief statement of the terms of assignment or settlement.)

9. *Property in hands of third person*

Is any other person holding anything of value in which you have an interest? (Give name and address, location and description of the property, and circumstances of the holding.)

10. *Suits, executions, and attachments*

a. Were you a party to any suit pending at the time of the filing of the original petition herein? (If so, give the name and location of the court and the title and nature of the proceeding.)

b. Were you a party to any suit terminated within the year immediately preceding the filing of the original petition herein? (If so, give the name and location of the court, the title and nature of the proceeding, and the result.)

c. Has any of your property been attached, garnished, or seized under any legal or equitable process within the 4 months immediately preceding the filing of the original petition herein? (If so, describe the property seized or person garnished, and at whose suit.)

11. *Loans repaid*

What repayments on loans in whole or in part have you made during the year immediately preceding the filing of the original petition herein? (Give the name and address of the lender, the amount of the loan and when received, the amounts and dates of payments and, if the lender is a relative, the relationship.)

12. *Transfers of property*

a. Have you made any gifts, other than ordinary and usual presents to family members and charitable donations, during the year immediately preceding the filing of the original petition herein? (If so, give names and addresses of donees and dates, description, and value of gifts.)

b. Have you made any other transfer, absolute or for the purpose of security, or any other disposition, of real or tangible personal property during the year immediately and preceding the filing of the original petition herein? (Give a description of the property, the date of the transfer or disposition, to whom transferred or how disposed of, and, if the transferee is a relative, the relationship, the consideration, if any, received therefor, and the disposition of such consideration.)

13. *Repossessions and returns*

Has any property been returned to, or repossessed by, the seller or by a secured party during the year immediately preceding the filing of the original petition herein? (If so, give particulars including the name and address of the party getting the property and its description and value.)

14. *Losses*

a. Have you suffered any losses from fire, theft, or gambling during the year immediately preceding the filing of the original petition herein? (If so, give particulars, including dates, names, and places, and the amounts of money or value and general description of property lost.)

b. Was the loss covered in whole or in part by insurance? (If so, give particulars.)

15. *Payments or transfers to attorneys*

a. Have you consulted an attorney during the year immediately preceding or since the filing of the original petition herein? (Give date, name, and address.)

b. Have you during the year immediately preceding or since the filing of the original petition herein paid any money or transferred any property to the attorney or to any other person on his behalf? (If so, give particulars, including amount paid or value of property transferred and date of payment or transfer.)

c. Have you, either during the year immediately preceding or since the filing of the original petition herein, agreed to pay any money or transfer any property to an attorney at law, or to any other person on his behalf? (If so, give particulars, including amount and terms of obligation.)

STATE OF_____
County of_____, ss:

I, _____, do hereby swear that I have read the answers contained in the foregoing statement of affairs and that they are true and complete to the best of my knowledge, information, and belief.

------------------,
Bankrupt.

Subscribed and sworn to before me on _____.

------------------,

------------------.
[*Official character*]

Form No. 8. Statement of Affairs for Bankrupt Engaged in Business

[*Caption, other than designation, as in Form No. 1*]

STATEMENT OF AFFAIRS FOR BANKRUPT ENGAGED IN BUSINESS

[Each question should be answered or the failure to answer explained. If the answer is "none," this should be stated. If additional space is needed for the answer to any question, a separate sheet properly identified and made a part hereof, should be used and attached.

If the bankrupt is a partnership or a corporation, the questions shall be deemed to be addressed to, and shall be answered on behalf of, the partnership or corporation; and the statement shall be verified by a member of the partnership or by a duly authorized officer of the corporation.

The term, "original petition," as used in the following questions, shall mean the petition filed under Bankruptcy Rule 103, 104, or 105.]

1. Nature, location, and name of business

a. Under what name and where do you carry on your business?

b. In what business are you engaged? (If business operations have been terminated, give the date of such termination.)

c. When did you commence such business?

d. Where else, and under what other names, have you carried on business within the 6 years immediately preceding the filing of the original petition herein? (Give street addresses, the names of any partners, joint adventurers, or other associates, the nature of the business, and the periods for which it was carried on.)

e. What is your employer identification number? Your social security number?

2. Books and records

a. By whom, or under whose supervision, have your books of account and records been kept during the 2 years immediately preceding the filing of the original petition herein? (Give names, addresses, and periods of time.)

b. By whom have your books of account and records been audited during the 2 years immediately preceding the filing of the original petition herein? (Give names, addresses, and dates of audits.)

c. In whose possession are your books of account and records? (Give names and addresses.)

d. If any of these books or records are not available, explain.

e. Have any books of account or records relating to your affairs been destroyed, lost, or otherwise disposed of within the 2 years immediately preceding the filing of the original petition herein? (If so, give particulars, including date of destruction, loss, or disposition, and reason therefor.)

3. Financial statements

Have you issued any written financial statements within the 2 years immediately preceding the filing of the original petition herein? (Give dates, and the names and addresses of the persons to whom issued, including mercantile and trade agencies.)

4. Inventories

a. When was the last inventory of your property taken?

b. By whom, or under whose supervision, was this inventory taken?

c. What was the amount, in dollars, of the inventory? (State whether the inventory was taken at cost, market, or otherwise.)

d. When was the next prior inventory of your property taken?

e. By whom, or under whose supervision, was this inventory taken?

f. What was the amount, in dollars, of the inventory? (State whether the inventory was taken at cost, market, or otherwise.)

g. In whose possession are the records of the 2 inventories above referred to ? (Give names and addresses.)

5. Income other than from operation of business

What amount of income, other than from operation of your business, have you received during each of the 2 years immediately preceding the filing of the original petition herein ? (Give particulars, including each source, and the amount received therefrom.)

6. Tax returns and refunds

a. In whose possession are copies of your federal and state income tax returns for the 3 years immediately preceding the filing of the original petition herein?

b. What tax refunds (income or other) have you received during the 2 years immediately preceding the filing of the original petition herein?

c. To what tax refunds (income or other), if any, are you, or may you be, entitled? (Give particulars, including information as to any refund payable jointly to you and your spouse or any other person.)

7. Bank accounts and safe deposit boxes

a. What bank accounts have you maintained, alone or together with any other person, and in your own or any other name, within the 2 years immediately preceding the filing of the original petition herein ? (Give the name and address of each bank, the name in which the deposit was maintained, and the name and address of every person authorized to make withdrawals from such account.)

b. What safe deposit box or boxes or other depository or depositories have you kept or used for your securities, cash, or other valuables within the 2 years immediately preceding the filing of the original petition herein? (Give the name and address of the bank or other depository, the name in which each box or other depository was kept, the name and address of every person who had the right of access thereto, a description of the contents thereof, and, if the box has been surrendered, state when surrendered or, if transferred, when transferred and the name and address of the transferee.)

8. Property held for another person

What property do you hold for any other person? (Give name and address of each person, and describe the property, the amount or value thereof and all writings relating thereto.)

9. Prior bankruptcy proceedings

What proceedings under the Bankruptcy Act have previously been brought by or against you? (State the location of the bankruptcy court, the nature and number of proceeding, and whether a discharge was granted or refused, the proceeding was dismissed, or a composition, arrangement, or plan was confirmed.)

10. Receiverships, general assignments, and other modes of liquidation

a. Was any of your property, at the time of the filing of the original petition herein, in the hands of a receiver, trustee, or other liqui-

dating agent? (If so, give a brief description of the property and
the name and address of the receiver, trustee, or other agent, and, if
the agent was appointed in a court proceeding, the name and location
of the court and the nature of the proceeding.)

b. Have you made any assignment of your property for the benefit of your creditors, or any general settlement with your creditors,
within the 2 years immediately preceding the filing of the original
petition herein? (If so, give dates, the name and address of the assignee, and a brief statement of the terms of assignment or settlement.)

11. *Property in hands of third person*

Is any other person holding anything of value in which you have
an interest? (Give name and address, location and description of the
property, and circumstances of the holding.)

12. *Suits, executions, and attachments*

a. Were you a party to any suit pending at the time of the filing of
the original petition herein? (If so, give the name and location of the
court and the title and nature of the proceeding.)

b. Were you a party to any suit terminated within the year immediately preceding the filing of the original petition herein? (If so,
give the name and location of the court, the title and nature of the
proceeding, and the result.)

c. Has any of your property been attached, garnished, or seized
under any legal or equitable process within the 4 months immediately
preceding the filing of the original petition herein? (If so, describe
the property seized or person garnished, and at whose suit.)

13. *Payments on loans and installment purchases*

What repayments on loans in whole or in part, and what payments
on installment purchases of goods and services, have you made during
the year immediately preceding the filing of the original petition
herein? (Give the names and addresses of the persons receiving payment, the amounts of the loans and of the purchase price of the goods
and services, the dates of the original transactions, the amounts and
dates of payments, and, if any of the payees are your relatives, the
relationship; if the bankrupt is a partnership and any of the payees is
or was a partner or a relative of a partner, state the relationship; if
the bankrupt is a corporation and any of the payees is or was an officer,
director, or stockholder, or a relative of an officer, director, or stockholder, state the relationship.)

14. *Transfers of property*

a. Have you made any gifts, other than ordinary and usual presents
to family members and charitable donations, during the year immediately preceding the filing of the original petition herein? (If so, give
names and addresses of donees and dates, description, and value of
gifts.)

b. Have you made any other transfer, absolute or for the purpose of
security, or any other disposition which was not in the ordinary course
of business during the year immediately preceding the filing of the

original petition herein? (Give a description of the property, the date of the transfer or disposition, to whom transferred or how disposed of, and state whether the transferee is a relative, partner, shareholder, officer, or director, the consideration, if any, received for the property, and the disposition of such consideration.)

15. Accounts and other receivables

Have you assigned, either absolutely or as security, any of your accounts or other receivables during the year immediately preceding the filing of the original petition herein? (If so, give names and addresses of assignees.)

16. Repossessions and returns

Has any property been returned to, or repossessed by, the seller or by a secured party during the year immediately preceding the filing of the original petition herein? (If so, give particulars, including the name and address of the party getting the property and its description and value.)

17. Business leases

If you are a tenant of business property, what are the name and address of your landlord, the amount of your rental, the date to which rent had been paid at the time of the filing of the original petition herein, and the amount of security held by the landlord?

18. Losses

a. Have you suffered any losses from fire, theft, or gambling during the year immediately preceding the filing of the original petition herein? (If so, give particulars, including dates, names, and places, and the amounts of money or value and general description of property lost.)

b. Was the loss covered in whole or part by insurance? (If so, give particulars.)

19. Withdrawals

a. If you are an individual proprietor of your business, what personal withdrawals of any kind have you made from the business during the year immediately preceding the filing of the original petition herein?

b. If the bankrupt is a partnership or corporation, what withdrawals, in any form (including compensation or loans), have been made by any member of the partnership, or by any officer, director, managing executive, or shareholder of the corporation, during the year immediately preceding the filing of the original petition herein? (Give the name and designation or relationship to the bankrupt of each person, the dates and amounts of withdrawals, and the nature or purpose thereof.)

20. Payments or transfers to attorneys

a. Have you consulted an attorney during the year immediately preceding or since the filing of the original petition herein? (Give date, name, and address.)

b. Have you during the year immediately preceding or since the filing of the original petition herein paid any money or transferred any property to the attorney, or to any other person on his behalf? (If so, give particulars, including amount paid or value of property transferred and date of payment or transfer.)

c. Have you, either during the year immediately preceding or since the filing of the original petition herein, agreed to pay any money or transfer any property to an attorney at law, or to any other person on his behalf? (If so, give particulars, including amount and terms of obligation.)

(If the bankrupt is a partnership or corporation, the following additional question should be answered.)

21. Members of partnership; officers, directors, managers, and principal stockholders of corporation

a. What is the name and address of each member of the partnership, or the name, title, and address of each officer, director, and managing executive, and of each stockholder holding 25 per cent or more of the issued and outstanding stock, of the corporation?

b. During the year immediately preceding the filing of the original petition herein, has any member withdrawn from the partnership, or any officer, director, or managing executive of the corporation terminated his relationship, or any stockholder holding 25 per cent or more of the issued stock disposed of more than 50 per cent of his holdings? (If so, give name and address and reason for withdrawal, termination, or disposition, if known.)

c. Has any person acquired or disposed of 25 per cent or more of the stock of the corporation during the year immediately preceding the filing of the petition? (If so, give name and address and particulars.)

STATE OF _____
County of _____, *ss*:

I, _____, do hereby swear that I have read the answers contained in the foregoing statement of affairs and that they are true and complete to the best of my knowledge, information, and belief.

--------------------,
                                                            Bankrupt.

Subscribed and sworn to before me on _____.

--------------------,
_____.
                                    [*Official character*]

[*Person verifying for partnership or corporation should indicate position or relationship to bankrupt.*]

Form No. 9. Creditors' Petition for Bankruptcy

[*Caption, other than designation, as in Form No. 1*]

CREDITORS' PETITION

1. Petitioners, _____,
of *_____, and _____,
of *_____, and _____,
of *_____, are creditors of _____
_____, of *_____, having
provable claims against him, not contingent as to liability, amounting
in the aggregate, in excess of the value of securities held by them, to
$500 or over. The nature and amount of petitioners' claims are as fol-
lows: _____
_____.

2. The alleged bankrupt has had his principal place of business [*or*
has resided*] within this district for the 6 months preceding the filing
of this petition [*or* for a longer portion of the 6 months preceding the
filing of this petition than in any other district].

3. The alleged bankrupt owes debts to the amount of $1,000 or over
and is a person who may be adjudged an involuntary bankrupt under
the Bankruptcy Act.

4. Within the 4 months preceding the filing of this petition, the
alleged bankrupt committed an act of bankruptcy in that he did on
_____.

Wherefore petitioners pray that _____ be adjudged
a bankrupt under the Act.

Signed: _____,
Attorney for Petitioners.
Address: _____,
_____.

[*Petitioners sign if not
represented by attorney.*]

STATE OF _____
County of _____, *ss:*

I, _____, one of the petitioners named in the
foregoing petition, do hereby swear that the statements contained
therein are true according to the best of my knowledge, information,
and belief.

_____,
Petitioner.

Subscribed and sworn to before me on _____.

_____,
_____.

[*Official character*]

*State post-office address.

Form No. 10.   Summons to Bankrupt

[Caption, other than designation, as in Form No. 1]

SUMMONS

To the above-named bankrupt:

A petition in bankruptcy having been filed on_____, in this court of bankruptcy, praying that you be adjudged a bankrupt under the Bankruptcy Act,

You are hereby summoned and required to file with this court and to serve upon the petitioners' attorney, whose address is_____ _____, a motion or an answer [1] to the petition which is herewith served upon you, on or before _____. If you fail to do so, you will be adjudged a bankrupt by default,

                                                 _____,
                                                 Clerk of District Court.

[Seal of the United States District Court]
Date of issuance : _____.

[1] If you make a motion, as you may in accordance with Bankruptcy Rule 112, that rule governs the time within which your answer must be served.

Form No. 11.   Adjudication of Bankruptcy

[Caption, other than designation, as in Form No. 1]

ADJUDICATION

On consideration of the petition filed on _____, it is adjudged that _____ is a bankrupt.

Dated : _____.

                                                 _____,
                                                 Bankruptcy Judge.

Form No. 12.   Order for First Meeting of Creditors and Related Orders, Combined With Notice Thereof and of Automatic Stay

[Caption, other than designation, as in Form No. 1]

ORDER FOR FIRST MEETING OF CREDITORS AND FIXING TIMES FOR FILING OBJECTIONS TO DISCHARGE AND FOR FILING COMPLAINT TO DETERMINE DISCHARGEABILITY OF CERTAIN DEBTS, COMBINED WITH NOTICE THEREOF AND OF AUTOMATIC STAY

To the bankrupt, his creditors, and other parties in interest:

_____ of *_____, having been adjudged a bankrupt on a petition filed by [*or* against] him on _____ _____, it is ordered, and notice is hereby given, that:

1. The first meeting of creditors shall be held at_____, on _____ _____, at ____ o'clock ___.m.

*State post-office address.

2. The bankrupt shall appear in person [*or, if the bankrupt is a partnership*, by a general partner, *or, if the bankrupt is a corporation*, by it president *or other executive officer*] before the court at that time and place for the purpose of being examined.

3. _____ is fixed as the last day for the filing of objections to the discharge of the bankrupt.

4. _____ is fixed as the last day for the filing of a complaint to determine the dischargeability of any debt pursuant to § 17c(2) of the Bankruptcy Act.

You are further notified that:

The meeting may be continued or adjourned from time to time by order made in open court, without further written notice to creditors.

At the meeting the creditors may file their claims, elect a trustee, elect a committee of creditors, examine the bankrupt as permitted by the court, and transact such other business as may properly come before the meeting.

As a result of this bankruptcy, certain acts and proceedings against the bankrupt and his property are stayed as provided in Bankruptcy Rules 401 and 601.

If no objection to the discharge of the bankrupt is filed on or before the last day fixed therefor as stated in subparagraph 3 above, the bankrupt will be granted his discharge. If no complaint to determine the dischargeability of a debt under clause (2), (4), or (8) of § 17a of the Bankruptcy Act is filed within the time fixed therefor as stated in subparagraph 4 above, the debt may be discharged.

In order to have his claim allowed so that he may share in any distribution from the estate, a creditor must file a claim, whether or not he is included in the list of creditors filed by the bankrupt. Claims which are not filed within 6 months after the above date set for the first meeting of creditors will not be allowed, except as otherwise provided by law. A claim may be filed in the office of the undersigned bankruptcy judge on an official form prescribed for a proof of claim.

[*If a no-asset or nominal asset case, the following paragraph may be used in lieu of the preceding paragraph.*] It appears from the schedules of the bankrupt that there are no assets from which any dividend can be paid to creditors. It is unnecessary for any creditor to file his claim at this time in order to share in any distribution from the estate. If it subsequently appears that there are assets from which a dividend may be paid, creditors will be so notified and given an opportunity to file their claims.

Unless the court extends the time, any objection to the report of exempt property must be filed within 15 days after the report has been filed.

Dated: _____.

_____,
Bankruptcy Judge.

Form No. 13.   General Power of Attorney

[Caption, other than designation, as in Form No. 1]

GENERAL POWER OF ATTORNEY

To _____ of * _____, and _____
_____ of * _____:

The undersigned claimant hereby authorizes you, or any one of
you, as attorney in fact for the undersigned and with full power of
substitution, to vote on any question that may be lawfully submitted
to creditors of the bankrupt in the above-entitled case; [*if appropriate*]
to vote for a trustee of the estate of the bankrupt and for a committee of creditors; to receive dividends; and in general to perform any
act not constituting the practice of law for the undersigned in all
matters arising in this case.

Dated: _____.

                                Signed: _____
             [*If appropriate*] By _____
                                    as _____
                                Address: _____,
                                         _____

[*If executed by an individual*] Acknowledged before me on _____
_____.

[*If executed on behalf of a partnership*] Acknowledged before me
on _____, by _____, who says that he is a
member of the partnership named above and is authorized to execute
this power of attorney in its behalf.

[*If executed on behalf of a corporation*] Acknowledged before me
on _____, by _____, who says that he
is _____ of the corporation named above and is authorized
to execute this power of attorney in its behalf.

                                _____,
                                _____.
                                [*Official character*]

Form No. 14.   Special Power of Attorney

[Caption, other than designation, as in Form No. 1]

SPECIAL POWER OF ATTORNEY

To _____ of * _____, and _____
_____ of * _____:

The undersigned claimant hereby authorizes you, or any one of you,
as attorney in fact for the undersigned [*if desired:* and with full
power of substitution,] to attend the first meeting of creditors of the

*State post-office address.

bankrupt or any adjournment thereof, and to vote in my behalf on any question that may be lawfully submitted to creditors at such meeting or adjourned meeting, and for a trustee or trustees of the estate of the bankrupt.

Dated: _____.

Signed: _____

[If appropriate] By _____

as _____

Address: _____,

_____

[If executed by an individual] Acknowledged before me on _____ _____.

[If executed on behalf of a partnership] Acknowledged before me on _____, by _____, who says that he is a member of the partnership named above and is authorized to execute this power of attorney in its behalf.

[If executed on behalf of a corporation] Acknowledged before me on _____, by _____, who says that he is _____ of the corporation named above and is authorized to execute this power of attorney in its behalf.

_____,

_____.

[Official character]

Form No. 15.   Proof of Claim

[Caption, other than designation, as in Form No. 1]

PROOF OF CLAIM

1. [If claimant is an individual claiming for himself] The undersigned, who is the claimant herein, resides at *_____.

[If claimant is a partnership claiming through a member] The undersigned, who resides at*_____, is a member of _____, a partnership, composed of the undersigned and _____, of *_____, and doing business at *_____, and is authorized to make this proof of claim on behalf of the partnership.

[If claimant is a corporation claiming through an authorized officer] The undersigned, who resides at *_____, is the _____ of _____, a corporation organized under the laws of _____ and doing business at *_____, and is authorized to make this proof of claim on behalf of the corporation.

[If claim is made by agent] The undersigned, who resides at *_____, is the agent of _____, of *_____, and is authorized to make this proof of claim on behalf of the claimant.

*State post-office address.

2. The bankrupt was, at the time of the filing of the petition initiating this case, and still is indebted [*or* liable] to the claimant, in the sum of $_____.

3. The consideration for this debt [*or* ground of liability] is as follows:

_____
_____.

4. [*If the claim is founded* on writing] The writing on which this claim is founded (or a duplicate thereof) is attached hereto [*or* cannot be attached for the reason set forth in the statement attached hereto].

5. [*If appropriate*] This claim is founded on an open account, which became [*or* will become] due on _____, as shown by the itemized statement attached hereto. Unless it is attached hereto or its absence is explained in an attached statement, no note or other negotiable instrument has been received for the account or any part of it.

6. No judgment has been rendered on the claim except _____
_____
_____.

7. The amount of all payments on this claim has been credited and deducted for the purpose of making this proof of claim.

8. This claim is not subject to any setoff or counter-claim except
_____
_____.

9. No security interest is held for this claim except_____
_____.

[*If security interest in property of the debtor is claimed*] The undersigned claims the security interest under the writing referred to in paragraph 4 hereof [*or* under a separate writing which (or a duplicate of which) is attached hereto, *or* under a separate writing which cannot be attached hereto for the reason set forth in the statement attached hereto]. Evidence of perfection of such security interest is also attached hereto.

10. This claim is a general unsecured claim, except to the extent that the security interest, if any, described in paragraph 9 is sufficient to satisfy the claim. [*If priority is claimed, state the amount and basis thereof.*]_____
_____
_____.

Dated :_____.

Signed :_____.

Penalty for Presenting Fraudulent Claim.—Fine of not more than $5,000 or imprisonment for not more than 5 years or both—Title 18, U.S.C., § 152.

Form No: 16.   Proof of Claim for Wages, Salary, or Commissions

[Caption, other than designation, as in Form No. 1]

PROOF OF CLAIM FOR WAGES, SALARY, OR COMMISSIONS

1. The bankrupt owes the claimant $_____
computed as follows:

    (a) wages, salary, or commissions for services
performed from_____
to _____,
at the following rate or rates of compensation____
_____ $_____

    [if appropriate] (b) allowances and benefits,
such as vacation and severance pay *[specify]*
_____
_____ $_____
    Total amount claimed_____ $_____

2. The claimant demands priority to the extent permitted by § 64a (2)
of the Bankruptcy Act.

3. The claimant has received no payment, no security, and no check
or other evidence of this debt except as follows:_____
_____

Dated :_____.

                      Signed :_____,
                                      Claimant.

              Social Security Number :_____
                         Address :_____,
                               _____

Penalty for Presenting Fraudulent Claim.—Fine of not more than
$5,000 or imprisonment for not more than 5 years or both—Title 18,
U.S.C., § 152.

Form No. 16A.   Proof of Multiple Claims for Wages, Salary,
or Commissions

[Caption, other than designation, as in Form No. 1]

PROOF OF MULTIPLE CLAIMS FOR WAGES, SALARY, OR COMMISSIONS

1. The undersigned, whose address is *_____,
is the agent of the claimants listed in the statement appended to this
proof of claim and is authorized to make this proof of claim on their
behalf.

2. The bankrupt owes the claimants $_____, computed as
indicated in the appended statement.

    *State post-office address.

3. The claimants demand priority to the extent permitted by § 64a (2) of the Bankruptcy Act.

4. The claimants have received no payment, no security, and no check or other evidence of this debt except as follows: _____
_____
_____
_____

Dated: _____.

Signed: _____.

Penalty for Presenting Fraudulent Claim.—Fine of not more than $5,000 or imprisonment for not more than 5 years or both—Title 18, U.S.C., § 152.

STATEMENT OF WAGE CLAIMS

Names, Addresses, & Soc. Security Numbers	Dates services rendered, rates of pay, & fringe benefits	Amounts claimed
---------------------	---------------------	--------------------
---------------------	---------------------	--------------------
---------------------	---------------------	--------------------
---------------------	---------------------	--------------------

Form No. 17. Order Approving Election of Trustee or Appointing Trustee and Fixing the Amount of His Bond

[*Caption, other than designation, as in Form No. 1*]

ORDER APPROVING ELECTION OF TRUSTEE OR APPOINTING TRUSTEE AND FIXING THE AMOUNT OF HIS BOND

(1) _____, of *_____, is hereby approved as the elected [*or* is hereby appointed] trustee of the estate of the above-named bankrupt.

(2) The amount of the bond of the trustee is fixed at $_____.

Dated: _____.

_____,

Bankruptcy Judge.

Form No. 18. Notice to Trustee of His Election or Appointment and of Time Fixed for Filing a Complaint Objecting to Discharge of Bankrupt

[*Caption, other than designation, as in Form No. 1*]

NOTICE TO TRUSTEE OF ELECTION OR APPOINTMENT AND OF TIME FIXED FOR FILING A COMPLAINT OBJECTING TO DISCHARGE OF BANKRUPT

To _____, of *_____:

You are hereby notified of your election [*or* appointment] as trustee of the estate of the above-named bankrupt. The amount of your bond

*State post-office address.

has been fixed at $_____. You are required to notify the under-
signed forthwith of your acceptance or rejection of the office.

You are further notified that _____ has been fixed
as the last day for the filing by you or any other party in interest of
a complaint objecting to the discharge of the bankrupt.

Dated: _____.

                              --------------------,
                                   Bankruptcy Judge.

Form No. 19.   Bond of Trustee or Receiver

[Caption, other than designation, as in Form No. 1]

BOND OF TRUSTEE [OR RECEIVER]

We, _____, of *_____, as principal,
and _____ of *_____, as surety, bind
ourselves to the United States in the sum of $_____ for the faith-
ful performance by the undersigned principal of his official duties
as trustee [*or* receiver] of the estate of the above-named bankrupt.

Dated: _____.

                              --------------------,
                              --------------------.

Form No. 20.   Order Approving Trustee's Bond

[Caption, other than designation, as in Form No. 1]

ORDER APPROVING TRUSTEE'S BOND

The bond filed by _____ of *_____
as trustee of the estate of the above-named bankrupt is hereby
approved.

Dated: _____.

                              --------------------,
                                   Bankruptcy Judge.

Form No. 21.   Order That No Trustee Be Appointed

[Caption, other than designation, as in Form No. 1]

ORDER THAT NO TRUSTEE BE APPOINTED

1. The bankrupt having been examined and the creditors not having
elected a trustee; and

2. The court having determined that there is no property in the
estate other than that which can be claimed as exempt, and that no
other circumstances indicate the need for a trustee;

*State post-office address.

It is ordered that, until further order of the court, no trustee shall be appointed.

Dated: _____.

_____,
Bankruptcy Judge.

Form No. 22. Report of Exempt Property

[Caption, other than designation, as in Form No. 1]

REPORT OF EXEMPT PROPERTY

The following property is set apart as provided under the Bankruptcy Act as exemptions allowed by law:

The following property claimed as exempt is not set apart for the reasons indicated:

Dated:. _____.

_____,
Trustee.

[*The report should describe the items of property set apart as exempt, should state the estimated value of each, the amount of money, if any, claimed and allowed, and should contain references to the statutes creating the exemptions.*]

Form No. 23. Order Approving Report of Exemptions

[Caption, other than designation, as in Form No. 1]

ORDER APPROVING REPORT OF EXEMPTIONS

It is ordered that the report of property, set apart as exempt to the bankrupt, a copy of which is attached hereto [*or* which was filed on _____], is approved and the claim of the bankrupt to his exemptions is allowed, except as follows:

Dated: _____.

_____,
Bankruptcy Judge.

Form No. 24. Discharge of Bankrupt

[Caption, other than designation, as in Form No. 1]

DISCHARGE OF BANKRUPT

It appearing that the person named above has filed a petition commencing a case under the Act on _____, was duly adjudged a bankrupt and that no complaint objecting to the discharge of the bankrupt was filed within the time fixed by the court [*or* that a complaint objecting to discharge of the bankrupt was filed and, after due notice and hearing, was not sustained]; it is ordered that

1. The above-named bankrupt is released from all dischargeable debts.

2. Any judgment heretofore or hereafter obtained in any court other than this court is null and void as a determination of the personal liability of the bankrupt with respect to any of the following:

(a) debts dischargeable under § 17 a and b of the Bankruptcy Act;

(b) unless heretofore or hereafter determined by order of this court to be nondischargeable, debts alleged to be excepted from discharge under clauses (2) and (4) of § 17a of the Act;

(c) unless heretofore or hereafter determined by order of this court to be nondischargeable, debts alleged to be excepted from discharge under clause (8) of § 17a of the Act, except those debts on which there was an action pending on the date when the petition was filed as specified above in which a right to jury trial existed and a party has either made a timely demand therefor or has submitted to this court a signed statement of intention to make such a demand;

(d) debts determined by this court to be discharged under § 17c(3) of the Act.

3. All creditors whose debts are discharged by this order and all creditors whose judgments are declared null and void by paragraph 2 above are enjoined from instituting or continuing any action or employing any process to collect such debts as personal liabilities of the above-named bankrupt.

Dated: _____.

-------------------------,
Bankruptcy Judge.

Form No. 25.   Caption for Adversary Proceeding

United States District Court
for the _____ District of _____

In re _____, *Bankrupt*

_____, **PLAINTIFF**   Bankruptcy No. _____

                    v.

_____, **DEFENDANT**

COMPLAINT [*or other designation*]

Form No. 26.   Summons and Notice of Trial
of Adversary Proceeding

[Caption, other than designation, as in Form No. 25]

SUMMONS AND NOTICE OF TRIAL

To the above-named defendant:

You are hereby summoned and required to serve upon _____
_____, plaintiff's attorney, whose address is _____,
a motion or an answer [1] to the complaint which is herewith served
upon you, on or before _____, and to file the motion or
answer with this court not later than the second business day thereafter. If you fail to do so, judgment by default will be taken against
you for the relief demanded in the complaint.

You are hereby notified that trial of the proceeding commenced
by this complaint has been set for _____, at ____ o'clock __.m.,
in _____.

_____,
Bankruptcy Judge.

By: _____
Address: _____,
_____

Date of issuance: _____.

---

[1] If you make a motion, as you may in accordance with Bankruptcy Rule 712, that rule
governs the time within which your answer must be served.

Form No. 27.   Subpoena to Witness

[Caption, other than designation, as in Form No. 1 or No. 25]

SUBPOENA TO WITNESS

To _____:

You are hereby commanded to appear at _____, on
_____, at ____ o'clock __.m., to testify in the above-entitled
case [*or* adversary proceeding *or* contested matter] [*add if appropriate*] and to bring with you _____
_____
_____.

Dated: _____.

_____,
Bankruptcy Judge.

Form No. 28.   Notice of Appeal to a District Court From a Judgment or Order of a Referee Entered in Adversary Proceeding

United States District Court for the _____ District of _____

In re _____, *Bankrupt*

_____, PLAINTIFF   Bankruptcy No. _____

           v.

_____, DEFENDANT

NOTICE OF APPEAL TO DISTRICT COURT

_____, the plaintiff [*or* defendant *or other party*] appeals to the district court from the judgment [*or* order] of the referee entered in this case on _____, [*here described the judgment or order appealed from*] _____

_____.

The parties to the judgment [*or* order] appealed from and the names and addresses of their respective attorneys are as follows:

_____

_____.

Dated: _____.

                    Signed: _____,
                              Attorney for Appellant.
                    Address: _____,
                              _____.

Form No. 29.   Order and   Notice for Final Meeting of Creditors

[*Caption, other than designation, as in Form No. 1*]

ORDER FOR FINAL MEETING OF CREDITORS AND NOTICE OF FILING OF FINAL ACCOUNT[S] OF TRUSTEE [AND RECEIVER] AND OF FINAL MEETING OF CREDITORS [AND OF HEARING ON ABANDONMENT OF PROPERTY BY THE TRUSTEE]

To the creditors:

The final report[s] and account[s] of the trustee [*if appropriate:* and of the receiver] in this case having been filed,

It is ordered, and notice is hereby given, that the final meeting of creditors will be held at _____, _____, on _____, at ____ o'clock __.m., for the purpose [*as appropriate*] of examining and passing on the report[s] and account[s], acting on applications for allowances, and transacting such other business as may properly come before the meeting. Attendance by creditors is welcomed but not required.

The following applications for allowances have been filed:

Applicants	Commissions or fees	Expenses
-- *Receiver*	$-----------	$-----------
-- *Trustee*	-----------	-----------
-- *Attorney for bankrupt*	-----------	-----------
-- *Attorney for receiver*	-----------	-----------
-- *Attorney for trustee*	-----------	-----------
-- *Attorney for petitioning creditors*	-----------	-----------

Creditors may be heard before the allowances are determined.

The account of the trustee shows total receipts of $------------, and total disbursements of $------------. The balance on hand is $------------.

In addition to expenses of administration as may be allowed by the court, liens and priority claims totaling $------------, must be paid in advance of any dividend to general creditors.

Claims of general creditors totaling $------------ have been allowed.

[*If appropriate*] the trustee's application to abandon the following property will be heard and acted upon at the meeting:

--.

The bankrupt has [not] been discharged.

Dated: ------------.

-------------------------,
Bankruptcy Judge.

Form No. 30.   Report of Trustee in No-Asset Case

[*Caption, other than designation, as in Form No.1*]

REPORT OF TRUSTEE IN NO-ASSET CASE

To -------------------, Bankruptcy Judge:

-------------------, of *-------------------, trustee of the estate of the above-named bankrupt, reports that he has neither received any property nor paid any money on account of this estate; that he has made diligent inquiry into the whereabouts of property belonging to the estate; and that there are no assets in the estate over and above the exemptions claimed by, and by him set aside to, the bankrupt.

Wherefore he prays that this report be approved, and that he be discharged from office.

Dated: ----------.

Signed: -----------------------.
Trustee.

*State post-office address.

Form No. 11–F1. Original Petition Under Chapter XI

United States District Court
for the .... District of ....

In re

...., } Bankruptcy No. ....

*Debtor [include here all names
used by debtor within last 6 years]*

ORIGINAL PETITION UNDER CHAPTER XI

1. Petitioner's post-office address is ....

2. Petitioner has resided [*or* has had his domicile *or* has had his principal place of business *or* if a partnership, or corporation, has had its principal assets] within this district for the preceding 6 months [*or* for a longer portion of the preceding 6 months than in any other district].

3. No other case under the Bankruptcy Act initiated on a petition by or against petitioner is now pending.

4. Petitioner is qualified to file this petition and is entitled to the benefits of Chapter XI of the Act.

5. Petitioner is insolvent [*or* unable to pay his debts as they mature].

6. A copy of petitioner's proposed plan is attached [*or* petitioner intends to file a plan pursuant to Chapter XI of the Act].

7. [*If petitioner is a corporation*] Exhibit "A" is attached to and made part of this petition.

Wherefore petitioner prays for relief in accordance with Chapter XI of the Act.

Signed: ....,

Attorney for Petitioner.

Address: ....,

....
[*Petitioner signs if not represented by attorney.*]

..................................,

Petitioner.

State of .... }

} *ss.*

County of .... }

I, ..., the petitioner named in the foregoing petition, do hereby swear that the statements contained therein are true according to the best of my knowledge, information, and belief.

..................................,

Petitioner.

Subscribed and sworn to before me on ....

..................................,

....
[*Official character.*]

[*Unless the petition is accompanied by a list of all the debtor's creditors and their addresses, the petition must be accompanied by a schedule of his property, a statement of his affairs, and a statement of executory contracts, pursuant to Rule 11–11. These statements shall be submitted on official forms and verified under oath.*]

Exhibit A

[If petitioner is a corporation, this Exhibit A shall be completed and attached to the petition pursuant to paragraph 7 thereof.]

[Caption, other than designation, as in Form No. 11–F1.]

FOR COURT USE ONLY

....
Date Petition Filed.

....
Case Number.

....
Bankruptcy Judge.

1. Petitioner's employer's identification number is ....•

2. If any of the petitioner's securities are registered under section 12 of the Securities and Exchange Act of 1934, SEC file number is ....

3. The following financial data is the latest available information and refers to petitioner's condition on ....

a. Total assets: $ ....

b. Liabilities:

Approximate number of holders

Secured debt, excluding that listed below $ ....
Debt securities held by more than 100
  holders: .... $ ....
     Secured .... $ ....
     Unsecured .... $ ....
Other liabilities, excluding contingent or
  unliquidated claims .... $ ....
Number of shares of common stock ....
Comments, if any: ....

4. Brief description of petitioner's business: ....
....

5. The name of any person who directly or indirectly owns, controls, or holds, with power to vote, 25% or more of the voting securities of petitioner is ....

6. The names of all corporations 25% or more of the outstanding voting securities of which are directly or indirectly owned, controlled, or held, with power to vote, by petitioner are ....
....

Form No. 11–F2.   Chapter XI Petition in Pending Case

[Caption, other than designation, as in Form No. 11–F1.]

CHAPTER XI PETITION IN PENDING CASE

1. Petitioner's post-office address is ....
....

2. Petitioner is the bankrupt or debtor in Bankruptcy Case No. ...., pending in this court.

3. Petitioner is qualified to file this petition and is entitled to the benefits of Chapter XI of the Bankruptcy Act.

4. Petitioner is insolvent [*or* unable to pay his debts as they mature.]

5. A copy of petitioner's proposed plan is attached [*or* petitioner intends to file a plan pursuant to Chapter XI of the Act.]

6. [*If petitioner is a corporation*] Exhibit "A" is attached to and made part of this petition.

Wherefore, petitioner prays for relief in accordance with Chapter XI of the Act.

Signed: ....,

Attorney for Petitioner.

Address: ....,

....

[*Petitioner signs if not represented by attorney.*]

.............................,

Petitioner.

State of .... ⎫
⎬ **ss.**
County of .... ⎭

I, ..., the petitioner named in the foregoing petition, do hereby swear that the statements contained therein are true according to the best of my knowledge, information, and belief.

.............................,

Petitioner.

Subscribed and sworn to before me on ....

.............................,

....

[*Official character.*]

[*Unless the schedules and statements have already been filed in the bankruptcy case they must be filed with this petition or within 15 days thereafter as provided in Rule 11–11. These statements shall be on official forms and verified under oath.*]

Exhibit A

[*Exhibit "A" as in Form No. 11–F1.*]

Form No. 11–F3.   Verification on Behalf of a Corporation

[*Form No. 4 of the Bankruptcy Forms is applicable and should be used.*]

Form No. 11–F4.   Verification on Behalf of a Partnership

[*Form No. 5 of the Bankruptcy Forms is applicable and should be used.*]

Form No. 11–F5.   Schedules

[*Form No. 6 of the Bankruptcy Forms is applicable and should be used. The word "bankrupt" wherever used in Form No. 6 should be changed to "debtor."*]

Form No. 11–F6.   Statement of Affairs for Debtor Not Engaged in Business

[*Form No. 7 of the Bankruptcy Forms is applicable and should be used. The word "bankrupt" wherever used in Form No. 7 should be changed to "debtor."*]

Form No. 11–F7.   Statement of Affairs for Debtor Engaged in Business

[*Form No. 8 of the Bankruptcy Forms is applicable and should be used. The word "bankrupt" wherever used in Form No. 8 should be changed to "debtor."*]

Form No. 11–F8.   Order Appointing Receiver or Disbursing Agent and Fixing the Amount of His Bond

[*Caption, other than designation, as in Form No. 11–F1.*]

ORDER APPOINTING RECEIVER [OR DISBURSING AGENT] AND
FIXING THE AMOUNT OF HIS BOND

1. . . . ., of *. . . . .
is hereby appointed receiver of the estate [or disbursing agent for the estate] of the
above-named debtor.

2. The amount of the bond of the receiver [or disbursing agent] is fixed at
$. . . . .
Dated: . . . .

. . . .,

Bankruptcy Judge.

Form No. 11–F9. Notice to Receiver or Disbursing Agent of His Appointment

[Caption, other than designation, as in Form No. 11–F1.]

NOTICE TO RECEIVER [OR DISBURSING AGENT] OF HIS
APPOINTMENT

To . . . ., of *. . . . .
. . . .

You are hereby notified of your appointment as receiver of the estate [or disbursing
agent for the estate] of the above-named debtor. The amount of your bond has been
fixed at $ . . . .

[The following paragraph is applicable to receiver only.]

You are required to notify the undersigned forthwith of your acceptance or rejection of the office of receiver.
Dated: . . . .

. . . .,

Bankruptcy Judge.

Form No. 11–F10. Bond of Receiver or Disbursing Agent

[Caption, other than designation, as in Form No. 11–F1.]

BOND OF RECEIVER [OR DISBURSING AGENT]

We, ...
of *. . . . ., as principal, and . . . .
. . . .
of *. . . . . , as surety, bind ourselves to the United States
in the sum of $ . . . . for the faithful performance by the undersigned principal
of his official duties as receiver of the estate [or disbursing agent for the estate] of
the above-named debtor.
Dated: . . . .

. . . .,
. . . .

Form No. 11–F11. Order Approving Receiver's or Disbursing Agent's Bond

[Caption, other than designation, as in Form No. 11–F1.]

*State post-office address.

ORDER APPROVING RECEIVER'S [OR DISBURSING
AGENT'S] BOND

The bond filed by .... of* .... as
receiver of the estate [or disbursing agent for the estate] of the above-named debtor
is hereby approved.
Dated: ....

................................,

Bankruptcy Judge.

Form No. 11–F12. Certificate of Retention of Debtor in Possession

[*Caption, other than designation, as in Form No. 11–F1.*]

CERTIFICATE OF RETENTION OF DEBTOR IN POSSESSION

I hereby certify that the above-named debtor continues in possession of his [its]
estate as debtor in possession, no trustee in bankruptcy or receiver having been appointed or qualified.
Dated: ....

................................,

Bankruptcy Judge.

Form No. 11–F13. Order for First Meeting of Creditors and Related Orders, Combined With Notice Thereof and of Automatic Stay

[*Caption, other than designation, as in Form No. 11–F1.*]

ORDER FOR FIRST MEETING OF CREDITORS COMBINED WITH
NOTICE THEREOF AND OF AUTOMATIC STAY

To the debtor, his creditors, and other parties in interest:

....

of* ...., having filed a petition on ....
stating that he desires to effect a plan under Chapter XI of the Bankruptcy Act, it
is ordered, and notice is hereby given, that:

1. The first meeting of creditors shall be held at ....,
on .... at .... o'clock .... m.;

2. The debtor shall appear in person [or, *if the debtor is a partnership*, by a general partner, or, *if the debtor is a corporation*, by its president or other executive
officer] before the court at that time and place for the purpose of being examined;

3. The hearing on confirmation of the plan shall be held at a date to be later fixed
[or at a date to be fixed at the first meeting or at ....
on .... at .... or immediately following the conclusion of the first meeting].

4. Creditors may file written objections to confirmation at any time prior to confirmation [or .... is fixed as the last day for the filing of objections to confirmation, or objections to confirmation may be filed by a date to be later
fixed.]

You are further notified that:

The meeting may be continued or adjourned from time to time by order made in
open court, without further written notice to creditors.

At the meeting the creditors may file their claims and acceptances of the plan, elect
a standby trustee, elect a committee of creditors, examine the debtor as permitted by
the court, and transact such other business as may properly come before the meeting.

The filing of the petition by the debtor above named operates as a stay of the commencement or continuation of any court or other proceeding against the debtor, of

*State post-office address.

the enforcement of any judgment against him, of any act or the commencement or continuation of any court proceeding to enforce any lien on the property of the debtor, and of any court proceeding commenced for the purpose of rehabilitation of the debtor or the liquidation of his estate, as provided by Rule 11–44.

In order to have his claim allowed so that he may share in any distribution under a confirmed plan, a creditor must file a claim, whether or not he is included in the schedule of creditors filed by the debtor. Claims which are not filed before confirmation of the plan will not be allowed except as otherwise provided by law. A claim may be filed in the office of the undersigned bankruptcy judge on an official form prescribed for a proof of claim.

[*If appropriate*] .... of* ....
has been appointed receiver of the estate of the above-named debtor.
Dated: ....

.................................,
Bankruptcy Judge.

Form No. 11–F14. Proof of Claim

[*Form No. 15 of the Bankruptcy Forms is applicable and should be used. The word "bankrupt" wherever used in Form No. 15 should be changed to "debtor."*]

Form No. 11–F15. Proof of Claim for Wages, Salary, or Commissions

[*Form No. 16 of the Bankruptcy Forms is applicable and should be used. The word "bankrupt" wherever used in Form No. 16 should be changed to "debtor."*]

Form No. 11–F15A. Proof of Multiple Claims for Wages, Salary, or Commissions

[*Form No. 16A of the Bankruptcy Forms is applicable and should be used. The word "bankrupt" wherever used in Form No. 16A should be changed to "debtor."*]

Form No. 11–F16. Power of Attorney

[*Caption, other than designation, as in Form No. 11–F1.*]

POWER OF ATTORNEY

To .... of* ...., and ....
.... of* ....:
The undersigned claimant hereby authorizes you, or any one of you, as attorney in fact. for the undersigned and with full power of substitution, to receive distributions and in general to perform any act not constituting the practice of law for the undersigned in all matters arising in this case.
Dated: ....

Signed: ....
By: ....
[*If appropriate*] as ....
Address: ....
....

[*If executed by an individual*] Acknowledged before me on ....
[*If executed on behalf of a partnership*] Acknowledged before me on ....
.... , by ...., who says that he is a member of the partnership named above and is authorized to execute this power of attorney in its behalf.

*State post-office address.

[*If executed on behalf of a corporation*] Acknowledged before me on . . . .
. . . ., by . . . ., who says that he is . . . .
. . . . of the corporation named above and is authorized to execute this
power of attorney in its behalf.

. . . . ,

. . . .
[*Official character.*]

Form No. 11–F17.   Order Fixing Time To Reject Modification of Plan Prior to Confirmation, Combined With Notice Thereof

[*Caption, other than designation, as in Form No. 11–F1.*]

ORDER FIXING TIME TO REJECT MODIFICATION OF PLAN PRIOR
TO CONFIRMATION, COMBINED WITH NOTICE THEREOF

To the debtor, his creditors and other parties in interest:

The debtor having filed a modification of his plan on . . . .,
it is ordered, and notice is hereby given, that:

1. . . . . is fixed as the last day for filing a written rejection of the modification.

2. A copy [*or* a summary] of the modification is attached hereto. Any creditor who
has accepted the plan and who fails to file a written rejection of the modification
within the time above specified shall be deemed to have accepted the plan as modified.

Dated: . . . .•

. . . . ,
Bankruptcy Judge.

Form No. 11–F18.   Order Confirming Plan

[*Caption, other than designation, as in Form No. 11–F1.*]

ORDER CONFIRMING PLAN

The debtor's plan filed on . . . ., [*if appropriate*, as modified
by a modification filed on . . . .,] having been transmitted to
creditors; and

The deposit required by Chapter XI of the Bankruptcy Act having been made; and

It having been determined after hearing on notice:

1. That the plan has been accepted in writing by the creditors whose acceptance is
required by law [*or* by all creditors affected thereby]; and

2. That the plan has been proposed and its acceptance procured in good faith, and
not by any means, promises, or acts forbidden by law [*and, if the plan is accepted by
less than all affected creditors*, the provisions of Chapter XI of the Act have been
complied with, the plan is for the best interests of the creditors and is feasible, the
debtor has not been guilty of any of the acts or failed to perform any of the duties
which would be a bar to the discharge of a bankrupt];

It is ordered that:

A. The debtor's plan filed on . . . ., a copy of which is
attached hereto, is confirmed.

B. Except as otherwise provided or permitted by the plan or this order:

(1) The above-named debtor is released from all dischargeable debts;

(2) Any judgment heretofore or hereafter obtained in any court order than this
court is null and void as a determination of the personal liability of the debtor with
respect to any of the following:

(a) debts dischargeable under § 17a and b of the Act;

(b) [*if the court has fixed a time for the filing of complaints under § 17c(2) of
the Act pursuant to Rule 11–48*] unless heretofore or hereafter determined by order

of this court to be nondischargeable, debts alleged to be excepted from discharge under clauses (2) and (4) of § 17a of the Act;

(c) [*if the court has fixed a time for the filing of complaints under § 17c(2) of the Act pursuant to Rule 11–48*] unless heretofore or hereafter determined by order of this court to be nondischargeable, debts alleged to be excepted from discharge under clause (8) of § 17a of the Act, except those debts on which there was an action pending on .... , the date when the first petition was filed initiating a case under the Act, in which a right to jury trial existed and a party has either made a timely demand therefor or has submitted to this court a signed statement of intention to make such a demand;

(d) debts determined by this court to be discharged under § 17c(3) of the Act.

C. All creditors whose debts are discharged by this order and all creditors having claims of a type referred to in paragraph (B)(2) above are enjoined from instituting or continuing any action or employing any process to collect such debts as personal liabilities of the above-named debtor.

Dated: ....

....,

Bankruptcy Judge.

Form No. 11–F19. Notice of Order of Confirmation of Plan and Discharge

[*Caption, other than designation, as in Form No. 11–F1.*]

NOTICE OF ORDER OF CONFIRMATION OF PLAN AND DISCHARGE

To the debtor, his creditors, and other parties in interest:

Notice is hereby given of the entry of an order of this court on .... , confirming the debtor's plan dated ...., and providing further that:

A. Except as otherwise provided or permitted by the plan or such order:

(1) The above-named debtor is released from all dischargeable debts;

(2) Any judgment theretofore or thereafter obtained in any court other than this court is null and void as a determination of the personal liability of the debtor with respect to any of the following:

(a) debts dischargeable under § 17a and b of the Bankruptcy Act;

(b) [*if the court has fixed a time for the filing of complaints under § 17c(2) of the Act pursuant to Rule 11–48*] unless theretofore or thereafter determined by order of this court to be nondischargeable, debts alleged to be excepted from discharge under clauses (2) and (4) of § 17a of the Act;

(c) [*if the court has fixed a time for the filing of complaints under § 17c(2) of the Act pursuant to Rule 11–48*] unless theretofore or thereafter determined by order of this court to be nondischargeable, debts alleged to be excepted from discharge under clause (8) of § 17a of the Act, except those debts on which there was an action pending on .... , the date when the first petition was filed initiating a case under the Act, in which a right to jury trial existed and a party has either made a timely demand therefor or has submitted to this court a signed statement of intention to make such a demand;

(d) debts determined by this court to be discharged under § 17c(3) of the Act.

B. All creditors whose debts are discharged by said order and all creditors having claims of a type referred to in paragraph (A)(2) above are enjoined from instituting or continuing any action or employing any process to collect such debts as personal liabilities of the above-named debtor.

Dated: ....

....,

Bankruptcy Judge.

B

Bankruptcy and

Insolvency Cases

Case I.   SER Corporation

The three cases in this Appendix illustrate some of the types of reports which are issued in bankruptcy and insolvency proceedings. The case of SER Corporation is an example of a report issued to the creditors' committee in a Chapter XI proceeding and describes the procedures followed by the independent accountant in auditing the records.

The case came to Jones & Company, Certified Public Accountants, in November, through the New York Credit Men's Adjustment Bureau. A meeting of the larger creditors of SER Corporation was held at the Bureau; a letter requesting the meeting and specifying the time and place had been sent from the attorney for the debtor. The attorney in this case was a specialist in bankruptcy practice and had been selected to handle a settlement under Chapter XI.

At this first meeting, the larger creditors met in closed session with the debtor, heard the debtor's problems, and then decided to form a creditors' committee and to select a committee counsel, a committee accountant, and a committee secretary. New York Credit Men's Adjustment Bureau was maintained as the secretary, and Jones & Company was selected as the accountant.

Immediately following the meeting John Jones, a partner in the firm of Jones & Company, established contact with the secretary for the committee and the attorney for the creditors. The attorney provided some general background information about the case, explaining that the company had filed under Chapter XI and that there were third parties who would be interested in financing a settlement for the debtor. The attorney also gave Jones the name of the bank which was financing the receivables and pointed out that SER Corporation had two businesses. One was the manufacture of women's jeans, on a Cherokee Indian reservation in North Carolina, and the other was the manufacture of plastic hairpins and accessory sets, hairnets, and related products, in New York City.

Jones immediately called the controller at SER Corporation, who advised him that an audit could not be begun for approximately three weeks since the books were not current and additional time was needed for SER's accountant to prepare SEC reports (10–Q's) for past periods (July 31 and October 31). Jones agreed to give them additional time and advised the creditors that there would be a delay in beginning the conduct of the audit. The creditors requested that Jones accelerate the proposed schedule, and Jones was able to begin the audit within two weeks.

As a preliminary step Jones questioned two of the creditors to see whether they had any additional information which might be helpful in his examination. Did they feel that any of the statements that had been issued to the creditors should be checked for accuracy? Did they have any information or suspicions of wrongdoing? Was SER utilizing any practices that they thought he should look into? Were there any unusual loans or abnormal transactions with other companies?

Nothing of any substance was mentioned other than the fact that SER Corporation rented property on the Cherokee Indian reservation. Jones wrote to the Department of the Interior, Bureau of Indian Affairs, to find out the facts surrounding the financing of the situation. Jones learned from his inquiry that only the Indians themselves can own property on an Indian reservation. SER's plant had been set up some ten years before with the Cherokee Indian tribe as the owners of the property and SER occupying it as a tenant. In actuality, however, SER was paying mortgage payments, interest payments, and incidental expenses, and the owners were receiving some income from SER over and above these payments.

Since it was a very complicated, structured arrangement, Jones requested and received from the Department of the Interior a copy of the original documents signed at the time the leasing of the property was finalized.

The books of SER Corporation were brought up to date as of October 31, which was the end of a quarterly period for which the company was required to report to the SEC and to its stockholders. SER's accountant was instructed not to expend any more time bringing the books up to the date of filing under Chapter XI, which is the date used for the report to the creditors. The date on which SER filed its petition was November 24 (a Monday), or twenty-four days after the end of the quarter. Jones reasoned that it would be time-saving and efficient to take a trial balance from the October 31 statements, which the accountant had completed, and to pick up interim transactions (to November 24) from working papers rather than wait until they were formalized and posted to the general ledger. Jones's papers then contained all items or entries from November 1 to November 24 in sufficient detail to answer any questions regarding transactions during that period. The working papers supplied summaries of the sales and purchases transactions, cash receipts, cash disbursements, and payroll information for November 1 through November 21—the Friday before the date of filing the petition.

SPECIAL AUDIT PROCEDURES

Cash

A bank reconciliation of cash was made, establishing the outstanding checks and verifying the cash balance. Canceled checks for the prior four months were examined at the same time. The purpose of this examination was to establish a list of the larger checks that had been issued in the preceding four months. Jones wanted to determine whether any one creditor had been paid a larger percentage of the debts owed than any other creditors had received—a practice which could be deemed preferential and would require replacement under the terms of the estate. Jones also examined the checks to see whether there had been any irregularities in disbursements, whether the signatures were proper, whether the recipients were people or firms with whom the corporation normally did business, and whether the endorsements on the checks conformed to the names of the payees. In previous audits several different types of irregularities were discovered by analyzing the canceled checks. Checks had been made out to a company, as opposed to a corporation, and endorsed in ink by the company. Further investigation indicated that the debtor had set up dummy companies and was using them as a means of extracting money from the corporation. Jones's analysis of canceled checks of SER Corporation did not reveal any irregularities.

Accounts Receivable

The accounts receivable were financed and periodically audited by a local bank. Nonetheless, Jones requested and obtained a schedule of the accounts receivable and tied this into the control figure. He also aged the receivables so that an allowance for the doubtful accounts could be established. He was able to obtain and use an aging schedule that had been prepared by the bank. When the aging schedule was tied in with the control figure, there were only minor differences in the balances, so that an allowance for the doubtful accounts could be established based on the aging schedule.

The receivables were not confirmed. There were so many of them that Jones did not think the time involved was justifiable. Also, the bank, having had a pledge of the receivables and securities, was doing this periodically. Jones discussed the confirmation procedures and there was mutual satisfaction that all receivables were valid. Jones did spot-check the proofs of delivery against invoices to verify that the shipments recorded were actually received. If the bank had not confirmed the receivables periodically, Jones would have made a partial confirmation. On other audits, he had found, however, that confirmation delays an audit and, under the time pressure that is usually present, sufficient answers can be obtained by other means for the report to the creditors' committee. Jones decided to rely instead on the proofs of delivery. He determined in the course of the examination that all shipments conformed to the sales invoices.

Inventories

The inventory, Jones could see, would be another problem, particularly as to the plastic products manufactured in New York City. There were many small items of very little value. In order to value them, Jones obtained a price list that the debtor had prepared for its customers, and then examined the sales invoices to determine whether SER Corporation was actually using the price list. The comparison showed that sales were being made for less than the prices listed. The markoff was fairly consistent at about 25 per cent.

Jones's staff accountant prepared from the sales invoices a schedule showing for each product the quantities sold, the actual sales price, and the original selling price. This schedule was used to substantiate the fact that the debtor was selling at about 25 per cent off the list price. A considerable number of invoices were examined and the results were very close to the 25 per cent estimate.

In addition to this information, Jones obtained some cost records from SER Corporation's files. They were of only limited value since each of the items purchased went through a manufacturing process which made it difficult to establish an actual cost for each finished product. The plastic items, for example, went through an extrusion process and the expenditures for labor, use of machinery, and other costs could not be reliably pinpointed. By starting with the selling prices of the finished items and deducting what he felt would be a normal markup, Jones was able to back into a fair cost that was in conjunction with the debtor's cost records.

The costs of fabric for manufacturing the women's jeans were more easily determined. The inventory at the plant in North Carolina was examined by an experienced senior accountant. Jones then obtained the cost records kept by SER Corporation and compared them with other clients' costs in the same industry. The cutting tickets which indicated the exact yardage of fabric used were compared with the purchase documents for the fabric. The labor records, showing how much time was spent on each job, were compared with SER's records. Using a previous inventory taken by the debtor, SER's cost records, and his own investigation, Jones was able to establish a cost for the manufacture of the jeans. As a supporting document, he obtained from SER a letter indicating what the company felt were the true markups on the plastic items. The debtor's response substantiated the information he had gathered. The debtor also advised Jones that the inventories would bring only about a 10 per cent markup under a forced emergency-sale situation. The regular markup was about 25 per cent.

Fixed Assets

The Small Business Administration (SBA) had loaned SER Corporation money against machinery, equipment, furniture, and fixtures. Jones knew that a copy of the Financing Statement required under the Uniform Commercial Code would be on file at the state capital in Albany (N.Y.), but before requesting a photocopy from the official file he inquired and was able to obtain a copy from one of the creditors. The Financing Statement gave Jones a good description of all of the fixed assets, since the SBA documents itemized the fixed assets and listed the serial number of each. Jones was also able to determine the actual loan value, how the loan was to be repaid, and all the terms concerning the SBA loan secured by machinery and equipment. This information was compared with various entries for the SBA loan in the debtor's records, and with the recent tax returns filed by SER Corporation. The senior accountant, while in North Carolina, had made a general examination of some of the fixed assets, which provided at least a surface verification. No additional itemization seemed necessary.

Other Assets

To complete the listing of assets, Jones obtained a schedule of insurance from the insurance broker, and determined the amount of unexpired insurance. The corporation's rent deposit, he thought, could be verified by examining the lease. Jones was unable to obtain the lease before the report was completed, but in checking the books he was able to find records of the actual payments made to the landlord.

The facilities in New York were partially subleased, and SER Corporation deposited the payments from the subtenants into a savings account. Jones obtained the savings account passbook and ascertained that the deposits had actually been made. He then obtained copies of the subleases to see that the subtenants had actually paid the required amounts.

In the arrangement concluded with the Cherokee Indian tribe, which involved almost half a million dollars, SER Corporation had agreed to set up a manufacturing facility on the reservation and to construct a building to house the facility. SER then leased the building from the owners for a period of 25 years with an option for an additional 25 years. The title to the building was given to the Cherokee tribe, as was ownership of the machinery placed on the property. The property was "purchased" by SER Corporation with funds borrowed from the Cherokees. However, the books did not show any liability to the Cherokees for the money that had been advanced to the firm. The previous accountant had set up the land and buildings as an asset of the corporation, with detailed footnotes, and presented it this way in the report to the SEC. Even though the previous accountant had offered this disclosure, Jones felt the procedure was improper: SER Corporation did not own the property and therefore had no right to depreciation on it. Jones was of the opinion that the liability should be placed on the books— more particularly now because the books would be open to examination by the creditors. Jones wanted them to see the actual assets and liabilities. He therefore removed the land and building from the accounts, set up a deferred charge on the leasehold, and set up the liability.

Investment in Subsidiary

In the course of the audit, Jones found that SER Corporation had invested in a subsidiary, but the investment no longer appeared on the books. In response to an inquiry, SER indicated that the subsidiary had been liquidated and all the assets had been disposed of. A request was sent to the debtor's bank asking for confirmation of the liquidation of the subsidiary, which had been in default on a loan. The confirmation Jones received from the bank indicated that the cash balance of the subsidiary was zero, and stated the amount that had been due to the bank on the loan. The bank had liquidated the loan, all assets were sold, and the amount received from the sale did not equal the indebtedness. Since the subsidiary still owed money and there was of course no equity left for SER Corporation, the investment was worthless.

Taxes Payable and Receivable

Jones showed in his report (Schedule A–1) a detailed schedule of federal, state, city, and local taxes payable, and the dates on which the taxes were due. This breakdown was prepared with extreme care because the tax information as reported in the books had to be substantiable in any examination of the tax returns filed. Also, the debtor had to have this information available for verifying the claims filed by the governmental agencies.

In the normal course of developing the payroll tax figures, Jones verified them quarter by quarter. He examined the payroll tax records for the previous twelve months and extracted for his workpapers the basic data appearing on each return. Each payment due was checked against the taxes that were paid because sometimes a client will skip an interim period. The accountant may be lulled into thinking that if the last two periods in the year are paid, certainly the earlier ones were paid, which is not always true.

Jones scanned the tax files of SER Corporation to determine whether there were any letters from the various governmental agencies which would alert him to additional unrecorded liabilities. He conferred with the debtor's own accountant and obtained copies of the federal, state, and city corporate income tax returns for the preceding three years to see whether there were any refunds due. He verified the returns against the records to determine that the information on the tax returns was correct and that the required payments had been made.

On refunds due currently, even though the loss period was not a full year, he took whatever losses existed and set up a refund based on the loss existing at the date of filing. Jones usually assumed that the profits for the balance of the year would not overcome the loss. SER Corporation could not file a refund until the year end, but, as in previous bankruptcy cases, Jones had the debtor's attorney discuss this refund with the Internal Revenue agent at the time of settlement. On the supposition that the loss would not be overcome, they worked out an arrangement whereby the taxes due would be offset by any refunds that might become due later.

Often, all of a corporation's losses are not completely canceled by refunds and there is a potential asset in a carryover loss. Jones felt that the value to the debtor was normally about 10 or 15 per cent of the loss. This was based on the supposition that a purchaser of a corporation with a loss would pay approximately that amount for a loss carryover spread over five years. Since there are so many problems with using a loss carryover, an outsider will rarely pay any more than 10 or 15 per cent. The debtor corporation may not be able to overcome some of its losses, and even if it does, the maximum federal benefit that is available is 48 per cent. Although Jones did not place the possible refund from the carryover on the balance sheet, he explained to the creditors that there might be some value in the tax carryover.

Accounts Payable

Jones normally had the debtor prepare a schedule of accounts payable. In a Chapter XI proceeding, there is an advantage to this procedure in that the debtor must file with the court a complete list of creditors. But sometimes the debtor asked for a delay and either prepared the schedule while the audit was underway or requested the accountant to prepare the schedule for the debtor's use in court.

Jones did not ordinarily confirm accounts payable because of time restrictions. Since the amount of money involved was substantial and he was not satisfied that other available information would substantiate the amounts, he did confirm them for SER Corporation. The form he used was different from the preprinted form used in most audits because Jones was not the accountant for the debtor. His confirmation was in the form of a letter stating that he had been retained by the creditors' committee and that the debtor had filed under Chapter XI on a given date. In addition to the standard information requested in a confirmation, Jones asked whether any returns were made within the last four months that might have resulted in preferential treatment, whether any unusual credits were granted in the last four months, and whether any unusual extensions of time for payments were made. Jones also examined some original invoices to substantiate the list of creditors, and compared receiving documents with invoices to determine that the merchandise had actually been received. He also verified the amounts on the list with the secretary of the creditors' committee, who had received either statements or notations as to the amounts of the claims from the people who served on the committee and who were the larger creditors. Differences between control accounts and the schedule of accounts payable are not unusual. In this case they were not major and Jones adjusted the control amount to the schedule total. One freight payable amount was substantial and a separate schedule of the freight payable was included in the report (Schedule A–2).

Accruals

Up to the date the petition was filed, Jones accrued all payroll taxes, even the federal unemployment insurance tax which was not payable until the end of the year. He accrued the cost of labor, in the normal manner of accruals, right up to the date of the report. Payrolls paid after filing under Chapter XI were indicated as having been paid. Even though this debt existed prior to the filing, Jones knew that the courts normally will authorize it because employees will walk off their jobs if they are not paid.

Jones examined the employee contracts and the accrued vacation pay, particularly the provisions for accrued salaries in the union contract. On non-union salaried office employees who were entitled to, for example, two weeks' vacation with pay, Jones accrued the proper amount up to the date of filing under Chapter XI.

Notes Payable

The SBA loan, as discussed previously, was confirmed and the books were examined to see that the amounts of the loan and of the payments were entered correctly. Following good auditing procedure, Jones made sure that the report indicated the amount of the original loan, the terms of the loan in general, and the payments made on it within the last year. Jones confirmed the loan with the bank. He also examined the records to see that the actual amounts had been advanced by the bank, and satisfied himself that these amounts had been deposited in the corporate account.

The same procedure was followed for a loan made by an officer.

Jones examined the bank statement indicating the deposit and requested proof from the officer that the money was actually advanced to the corporation. This step was taken to be sure that the officer had not taken cash sales or other business funds and deposited them as though they were a loan from himself. Jones examined the savings account passbook if the officer withdrew the money from a savings account, or the canceled checks if the cash had been drawn from his own checking account. In this case, an amount of $20,000 due to this officer had been on the books of SER Corporation for many years, and the officer could not readily find his personal records dating back that far. In checking the reports of the accountants in the past, Jones found that they had shown this liability to the officer. Jones was satisfied on that basis. If there had been fairly recent loans, Jones would have examined each loan thoroughly. Creditors are always interested in knowing whether money advanced by an officer came from his personal resources and they usually ask why he invested his own money in the business.

Since the procedures for auditing notes payable to creditors are basically the same as the procedures for accounts payable, Jones combined these two accounts and showed one total for each creditor.

Schedules were made for notes payable to various individuals on equipment, or other types of loans, and Jones attempted to verify them. Monthly payments were traced to the payment book. Jones ascertained that the money had actually been received in the amounts stated.

Owners' Equity

The equity section in every accountant's report indicates the stockholding values, retained earnings or deficit, and any capital surplus accounts. Jones did not verify these accounts beyond comparing the account balances with the amounts shown on the tax returns. However, if treasury stock had been shown on the balance sheet, further steps would have been necessary. The problem with treasury stock is that a corporation cannot buy back its own stock unless it has a surplus. It must be substantiated that there was a surplus at the time the treasury stock was purchased.

Payroll

The payroll for the prior 60 days was analyzed week by week in order to determine the amount that was being paid to employees, and especially to officers, on a weekly basis. The detailed lists of people on the payroll were reviewed. Jones looked especially for familiar or repeated family names, and selected a few names at random for identification and verification, to be sure there was no payroll padding. He also observed the manner of distribution of paychecks.

For his analysis of the payroll for the preceding year, Jones examined a month at the beginning of the year, a month in the middle, and a month at the end. He scanned the payroll for unusual names or amounts, but he was primarily interested in comparing the amount of payroll for the current month with the amounts for prior months. The percentages of the prior period were in line with the current audited period, so Jones was reassured that no material padding had occurred in the preceding period.

The payroll records were also tied in with the wages and salaries reported on the federal tax returns filed with the Internal Revenue Service.

AUDITORS' REPORT

TO

CREDITORS' COMMITTEE

OF

SER CORPORATION

AT

NOVEMBER 24, 1975

SER CORPORATION

CONTENTS

Creditors' Committee of
The SER Corporation
205 Apple Avenue
Bronx, New York 10476

Pursuant to our engagement, we have reviewed the books and
records of SER Corporation, for the period commencing May 1, 1975,
and ending November 24, 1975, and for such prior periods as we
considered necessary under the circumstances.

Since we did not apply the generally accepted auditing procedures
of observing inventories and independently confirming assets and
liabilities, we are unable to express an opinion on the accompanying
financial statements.

JONES & COMPANY
Certified Public Accountants

New York, New York
February 19, 1976

GENERAL COMMENTS

1. SER Corporation maintains New York offices at 205 Apple Avenue, Bronx, New
York, paying a rental of $50,000 per annum until June 30, 1976, and $55,000 thereafter
until June 30, 1979. The corporation has subleased portions of the premises to two
tenants until June 30, 1979, at total annual rentals from $73,250 to $76,000, under terms
of said subleases. The subtenants have deposited with the corporation $10,000 and
$9,341.72 respectively, which sums have been deposited in special security bank accounts.

2. In May, 1974, the corporation expanded its business of manufacturing about 300
items in the hair accessory field to include the manufacturing and sale of jeans (trousers).
    This latter field of manufacturing proved a distinct failure and in the Spring of 1975
the corporation discontinued this operation.
    On the financial statement for the year ended April 30, 1975, a net loss of $175,305
was indicated for the trousers operation.

SER CORPORATION

STATEMENT OF FINANCIAL CONDITION

November 24, 1975

(Unaudited)

Assets

Current Assets:			
Cash in Bank and On Hand		$ 1,814	
Accounts Receivable	$198,943		
Less: Allowance for Doubtful Accounts	16,000		
	182,943		
Less: Partially Secured Liabilities (deducted contra):			
Manufacturers Trust Co.	182,943		
Inventory (Note 1)		649,522	
Total Current Assets			$ 651,336

Fixed Assets:	Cost	Accumulated Depreciation	Book Value	
Machinery and Equipment	$261,687	$153,778	$107,909	
Leasehold Improvements	10,257	2,719	7,538	
	$271,944	$156,497	$115,447	
Less: Fully Secured Liabilities (deducted contra):				
SBA		$64,918		
Chase Manhattan Bank		4,259	69,177	
			46,270	
Less: Partially Secured Liabilities (deducted contra):				
Eastern Band of Cherokee Indians			46,270	
Equity in Fixed Assets				—
Deferred Charge—Leasehold (Note 2)				453,758
Other Assets:				
Unexpired Insurance			3,925	
Tools and Dies			6,000	
Rent Deposit (New York)			9,166	
Miscellaneous Receivable (Tak-Sing of Hong Kong)			4,986	
Tenants' Security (Cash in Bank)		19,341		
Less: Security Payable (deducted contra)		19,341	—	
Total Other Assets				24,077
Total Assets				$1,129,171

Note—The letter of transmittal and Notes attached are an integral part of this report.

Liabilities and Stockholders' Equity

Liabilities Having Priority:			
Taxes Payable (Schedule A-1)		$ 26,463	
Labor Accrued (Paid on 12/2/75)		14,600	
Vacation Pay Accrued		3,500	
Total Liabilities Having Priority			$ 44,563
Fully Secured Liabilities:			
SBA (Schedule A-3)	$ 64,918		
Chase Manhattan Bank (Schedule A-3)	4,259		
	69,177		
Less: Fixed Assets (deducted contra)	69,177	—	
Security Payable	19,341		
Less: Other Assets (deducted contra)	19,341	—	
Partially Secured Liabilities:			
Manufacturers Hanover Trust Co.—Notes Payable	48,000		
Advances on Accounts Receivable	187,770		
Total Due	235,770		
Less: Accounts Receivable (deducted contra)	182,943	52,827	
Eastern Band of Cherokee Indians (Schedule A-3 and Note 2)	453,758		
Less: Fixed Assets (deducted contra)	46,270	407,488	
Unsecured Liabilities:			
Accounts Payable	366,842		
Freight Payable (Schedule A-2)	17,470		
Trade Acceptances Payable (Schedule A-3)	2,840		
Advanced by Jobber (Harbour Road)	12,411		
Notes Payable—Johnson County Industries (Schedule A-3)	6,928		
Due to Officers (Prior to 1970)	20,000		
Sundry Expenses	662	427,153	
Total Unsecured Liabilities			887,468
Total Liabilities			932,031
Contingent Liabilities (Note 3)			—
Stockholders' Equity (Exhibit C)			197,140
Total Liabilities and Stockholders' Equity			$1,129,171

APPENDIX B

SER CORPORATION

COMPARATIVE INCOME STATEMENTS

Prior Fiscal Year and Current Year to Date of Filing

(Unaudited)

	May 1–November 24, 1975 (Seven Months)	% of Sales	May 1, 1974–April 30, 1975	% of Sales
Net Sales	$745,651	100.0%	$2,092,708	100.0%
Cost of Goods Sold:				
Inventory—Beginning	$ 731,898		$ 803,226	
Purchases—Net	355,862		1,098,127	
Direct Labor	163,775		494,488	
Manufacturing Overhead (Schedule B-1)	46,703		108,863	
Total Cost Available	1,298,238		2,504,704	
Less: Inventory—Ending	649,522		731,898	
Cost of Goods Sold		648,716	87.0	1,772,806	84.8
Gross Profit on Sales		96,935	13.0	319,902	15.2
Other Income:				
Contracting Income	$102,029			
Less: Labor and Material	88,823			
Net Income from Contracting	13,206		—	
Rent Income (New York)	43,575		70,040	
Miscellaneous Sales Income	7,316	64,097	8.5	1,927	71,967	3.4
Total Income		161,032	21.5	391,869	18.6
Operating Expenses:				
Officers' Salaries (Schedule B-4)	61,918		110,679	
Selling Expenses (Schedule B-2)	100,458		183,905	
General and Administrative (Schedule B-3)	124,412		227,171	
Total Operating Expenses		286,788	38.4	521,755	24.9
Operating Loss		(125,756)	(16.9)	(129,886)	(6.3)
Other Deductions:				
Taxes (Payroll and Other)	27,650		56,496	
Bad Debts Written Off	30,823		9,251	
Interest	19,375		44,332	
Depreciation and Amortization	15,855		23,050	
Total Other Deductions		93,703	12.5	133,129	6.4
Net Loss from Operations		$(219,459)	(29.4)%	$(263,015)	(12.7)%

Note—The letter of transmittal and Notes attached are an integral part of this report.

Exhibit C

SER CORPORATION

STOCKHOLDERS' EQUITY STATEMENT

November 24, 1975

Capital Stock	$ 54,000	
Paid-In Surplus	742,775	
	796,775	
Less: Treasury Stock	32,428	
Total Capital Stock and Paid-In Surplus		$764,347
Less: Deficit—May 1, 1975	(361,975)	
Net Loss—Exhibit B	(219,459)	
Loss on Canadian Subsidiary (Note 3)	(44,678)	
Deferred Credit Prior Year	58,905	
Retained Earnings (Deficit)		(567,207)
Stockholders' Equity		$197,140

Note—The letter of transmittal and Notes attached are an integral part of this report.

SER CORPORATION

NOTES TO STATEMENT OF FINANCIAL CONDITION

Note 1. Inventory: $649,522

Since no current inventory was made available to us, we proceeded to establish an inventory amount as follows:

(a) We sampled many sales at random from the months of May, June, and October, 1975. These actual sales totalled $37,345. (b) According to a published sales catalog that SER issues, these sample sales would have totalled $43,200 if these items had not been sold at mark-down prices. (c) Using the historical gross profit of 25 per cent, the cost of these marked-down sales would have been $32,400. (d) Applying these figures, we arrived at a gross profit of 13 per cent on actual sales as follows:

Sales at catalog sales prices	$43,200	Sales made at actual prices	$37,345
Cost	32,400	Cost	32,400
Gross Profit	10,800	Gross Profit	4,945
Percentage	25%	Percentage	13%

(e) We then applied the 13 per cent gross profit to the total sales of $745,651. The gross profit of $96,935 indicates the cost of goods sold was $648,716. Deducting the cost of goods sold from the total cost of goods available for sale leaves an inventory of $649,522. (The items are shown in detail in Exhibit B, above).

Note 2. Due to Eastern Band of Cherokee Indians: $453,758

On September 1, 1975, the Corporation was indebted to the Eastern Band of Cherokee Indians (hereinafter known as "Eastern Band") for an amount of $465,188. Three equal monthly payments of $3,810 were made in September, October, and November, 1975, leaving a balance of $453,758 at statement date. The above amount conforms with Modification Form No. 1 from the United States Department of the Interior, Bureau of Indian Affairs.

This liability arises out of an agreement made between the Corporation and the Eastern Band, dated June 1, 1966, whereby the Eastern Band loaned the Corporation $600,000.

Under the terms of the arrangement, the Corporation agreed to operate a manufacturing facility which was constructed by the Eastern Band, and, in connection therewith, leased such facility and machinery and equipment for a period of 25 years with an option to renew for an additional 25 years.

On June 1, 1966, the Corporation transferred its title to said machinery and equipment to the Eastern Band. The Corporation agreed to maintain such machinery and equipment and to replace obsolete and destroyed machinery and equipment (title of replacements to vest in the Eastern Band).

This liability of $600,000 was never shown on the books of account as such. However, an amount of $350,000 was deposited and the credit was shown as a deferred credit, being the difference between the building cost of $250,000 (title vests in the Eastern Band) and the $600,000.

The Corporation adopted a policy of amortizing this deferred credit (less future costs applicable to the first fifteen years of the lease) and accordingly reduced rent expenses recorded thereunder. At April 30, 1975, the deferred credit amounted to $58,905.

Since the financial statements issued by the Corporation did not indicate any liability due to the Eastern Band, we are reflecting the present liability of $453,758 and setting up a corresponding asset of "Deferred Charge—Leasehold."

The present repayment of this loan, which is being charged to rent, totals $3,810 per month until the loan is repaid.

The asset "Deferred Charge—Leasehold" is then reduced by each monthly payment. The liability is correspondingly reduced by each monthly payment.

At this time, we are also transferring the deferred credit of $58,905 to the Retained Earnings account since we are reflecting the entire liability.

Note 3. Contingent Liabilities
A. NAD Manufacturing Corporation

Nad Manufacturing Corporation is a wholly owned subsidiary located at 5235 Mary Street, Montreal, Canada.

The books of SER Corporation show an investment in this subsidiary of $3,701 and an amount due from NAD (current account) of $40,977 at November 24, 1975. This latter amount stems from intercompany transfers. On April 30, 1974, this current account showed a balance due from NAD of $39,281, so there was no material change between May 1, 1974, and November 24, 1975.

On January 19, 1976, NAD owed the Bank of Montreal $21,130 on open notes which were guaranteed by SER. Further, on January 19, 1976, the bank made a formal demand for payment by January 22, 1976. If payment was not made by that date, the bank was to take possession of the premises, sell the inventory, and collect the accounts receivable to satisfy its loan. The bank also informed SER that it would be held responsible for any deficiency.

Payment was not made. The bank took possession and the plant was closed. At the present writing the deficiency is unknown.

B. Smith Fabrics

It is our understanding that Smith Fabrics is bringing suit against SER for $30,000 for goods sold and delivered. The outcome of this suit, at the present time, is unknown. The books and records reflect a liability of only $9,506.

Schedule A-1

SER CORPORATION

TAXES PAYABLE

November 24, 1975

Federal:		
FICA and Withholding (4th Quarter)	$ 8,178	
Unemployment (Balance 1975)	200	
Total Federal		$ 8,378
New York State:		
Withholding (4th Quarter)	10,625	
Disability (1975)	50	
Franchise (1975)	270	
Unemployment (4th quarter, 1975—Estimate)	65	
Total New York State		11,010
New York City:		
Withholding (4th Quarter)	2,675	
Franchise (1975)	215	
Total New York City		2,890
North Carolina:		
Unemployment (4th quarter, Estimate)	1,800	
Withholding (4th Quarter, Estimate)	1,885	
Corporation Tax (Balance 1975)	500	
Total North Carolina		4,185
Total Taxes		$26,463

SER CORPORATION

FREIGHT PAYABLE

November 24, 1975

ABC Freight Forwarding 201 Eleventh Ave. New York, N.Y. 10001	$ 301.09
Associated Air Freight 167–17 146th Ave. Jamaica, N. Y. 11434	104.87
Baltimore–NY Express 1100 No. Macon St. Baltimore, Md. 21205	127.56
Boss-Linco Lines, Inc. P.O. Box 489 Buffalo, N. Y. 14240	111.68
Bronx & Westchester Express 2301–29 Story Ave. Bronx, N. Y. 10473	105.50
Central Motor Lines P. O. Box 1848 Charlotte, N. C. 28201	279.69
W. T. Cowan 820 S. Oldham St. Baltimore, Md. 21224	387.66
Consolidated Freightways P. O. Box 4488 Portland, Ore. 97208	412.56
Consolidated Air Freight P. O. Box 3011 Portland, Ore. 97208	328.50
Dale Deliveries 176 Perry Street New York, N. Y. 10012	1,068.90
Other Creditors	14,242.00
Total Freight Payable	$17,470.01

SER CORPORATION

NOTES AND TRADE ACCEPTANCES PAYABLE

November 24, 1975

Notes Payable—Johnson County Industries

5/1/75	Balance		$ 9,125.26	
5/75	Repaid	$ 434.99		
6/75	Repaid	437.17		
7/75	Repaid	880.90		
10/75	Repaid	443.70	2,196.76	
11/24/75	Balance Due			$ 6,928.50

Notes Payable—Chase Manhattan Bank

5/1/75	Balance		$ 4,950.16	
5/75	Repaid	$ 115.12		
7/75	Repaid	230.24		
9/75	Repaid	230.24		
10/75	Repaid	115.23	690.83	
11/24/75	Balance Due			$ 4,259.33

Trade Acceptances Payable

2/26/76	Due		$ 1,420.00	
3/26/76	Due		1,420.00	
11/24/75	Balance Due			$ 2,840.00

Notes Payable—Small Business Administration

7/75	Due		$ 67,600.00	
9/75	Repaid	$1,341.00		
10/75	Repaid	1,341.00	2,682.00	
11/24/75	Balance Due			$ 64,918.00

Due Eastern Band of Cherokee Indians

9/1/75	Balance		$465,188.00	
9/75–11/75	Repaid		11,430.00	
11/24/75	Balance Due			$453,758.00

SER CORPORATION

MANUFACTURING OVERHEAD

November 24, 1975

	May 1– November 24, 1975	May 1, 1974– April 30, 1975
Indirect Labor	$18,173	$ 43,243
Rent	11,227	22,619
Light, Heat, and Power	3,802	8,814
Repairs and Maintenance	1,414	5,725
Factory Expenses	4,390	17,588
Equipment Rental	7,697	10,874
Total	$46,703	$108,863

SER CORPORATION

SELLING EXPENSES

November 24, 1975

	May 1– November 24, 1975	May 1, 1974– April 30, 1975
Freight Out	$ 27,739	$ 42,757
Sales Salaries	15,823	25,910
Shipping Salaries	7,350	8,705
Shipping Supplies	6,229	843
Sundry Shipping	1,011	2,215
Advertising	4,072	3,397
Commissions	15,641	55,948
Travel	5,454	11,128
Auto Expense	7,059	14,532
Selling Expenses (Salesmen)	9,496	16,277
Shows	475	2,043
Dues and Subscriptions	109	150
Total	$100,458	$183,905

SER CORPORATION

GENERAL AND ADMINISTRATIVE EXPENSES

November 24, 1975

	May 1– November 24, 1975	May 1, 1974– April 30, 1975
Rent	$ 24,999	$ 48,486
Office Salaries	38,092	60,907
Warehouse Salaries	9,027	16,536
Supervisory Salaries	7,040	11,396
Insurance	11,003	18,565
Repairs and Maintenance	2,263	
Office Expenses	2,880	17,658
Telephone	11,222	18,963
Hospitalization	908	2,240
Electricity	1,647	6,039
Truck Rental	1,175	3,528
Professional	4,916	11,587
Credits and Collections	370	2,058
Postage, Stationery, Printing	3,895	
Sundry	4,975	9,208
Total	$124,412	$227,171

SER CORPORATION

OFFICERS' SALARIES

November 24, 1975

	May 1– November 24, 1975	May 1, 1974– April 30, 1975
Leo Smith	$16,648	$ 30,200
Robert Hammond	16,648	30,200
Thomas Fields	16,648	30,201
T. A. Porter	11,974	20,079
Total	$61,918	$110,680

SER CORPORATION

COMPARISON OF MONTHLY GROSS SALES, PURCHASES,
DIRECT LABOR, AND PAYMENTS TO MERCHANDISE
CREDITORS

January, 1973–November, 1975

	1973	1974	1975
Gross Sales			
January	$ 170,278	$ 129,090	$ 177,054
February	126,035	187,836	180,934
March	166,449	166,504	159,023
April	108,050	152,368	185,102
May	126,313	149,622	173,657
June	130,611	190,680	133,083
July	128,320	173,742	87,371
August	122,428	158,227	127,652
September	135,040	201,464	122,257
October	185,048	219,747	113,531
November	150,052	185,697	(25,250)
December	161,727	180,988	
Total	$1,710,351	$2,095,965	$1,434,414
Percentage to Sales	1,000%	1,000%	1,000%
Purchases and Freight In			
January	$ 37,674	$ 92,830	$ 113,474
February	75,463	43,800	107,606
March	29,135	94,084	44,088
April	93,943	93,596	51,222
May	39,331	70,488	77,845
June	30,290	97,777	49,562
July	37,968	68,492	57,434
August	37,868	90,042	53,767
September	107,372	169,433	42,041
October	59,554	79,886	46,474
November	75,835	108,769	39,529
December	24,172	89,874	
Total	$ 648,605	$1,099,071	$ 683,042
Percentage to Sales	379%	525%	476%

Special Schedule 1

	1973	1974	1975
Direct Labor			
January	$ 41,190	$ 36,342	$ 37,371
February	34,347	29,312	25,968
March	33,644	28,173	45,480
April	28,879	40,150	42,761
May	34,454	32,919	21,556
June	16,019	32,199	26,109
July	28,912	42,374	20,551
August	27,110	35,526	19,300
September	25,174	36,371	23,209
October	35,140	44,958	19,632
November	31,002	37,420	28,952
December	31,022	46,268	
Total	$366,893	$ 442,012	$310,889
Percentage to Sales	214%	212%	216%
Payments to Merchandise Creditors			
January	$ 65,327	$ 77,585	$100,482
February	76,683	68,728	63,848
March	51,839	86,363	95,077
April	89,287	48,404	69,840
May	91,241	101,141	92,362
June	73,122	76,002	47,199
July	61,102	77,768	73,420
August	70,572	94,518	59,330
September	65,852	86,918	43,600
October	85,953	99,023	43,013
November	83,170	91,844	4,267
December	83,727	112,747	
Total	$897,875	$1,021,041	$692,438
Percentage to Sales	525%	488%	482%

SER CORPORATION

CHECKS ISSUED IN EXCESS OF $2,000

July 24–November 24, 1975

Payee	Date		Amount	Account
Manufacturers Trust Co.	Aug.	1	$ 2,719.71	Interest
Tom Jones		24	4,568.86	a/c Pay
Manufacturers Trust Co.		24	48,000.00	Note
Eastern Band of Cherokee Indians		4	2,325.00	Rent
E. I. Davis		1	2,454.00	a/c Pay
Sam Smith		31	4,160.66	Rent
Tom Jones	Sept.	1	3,417.66	a/c Pay
Manufacturers Trust Co.		5	2,222.00	Interest
Tom Jones		26	2,651.00	a/c Pay
Manufacturers Trust Co.		25	41,300.00	Note
Eastern Band of Cherokee Indians			2,325.00	Rent
Tim Brown		18	2,000.00	a/c Pay
Sam Smith		23	4,166.00	Rent
Manufacturers Trust Co.	Oct.	2	2,239.00	Interest
Tom Jones		12	2,893.00	a/c Pay
Eastern Band of Cherokee Indians		12	3,810.00	Rent
Manufacturers Trust Co.	Nov.	1	2,384.00	Interest
Sam Smith	Oct.	27	4,166.00	Rent
Eastern Band of Cherokee Indians		27	3,810.00	Rent
Schuster Naval		17	5,476.00	a/c Pay

Case II.   CDE Corporation, YZ Inc., and GB Industries, Ltd.

The SER Corporation case is an example of an audit by an independent accountant for the creditors' committee of a debtor corporation that filed a petition under Chapter XI of the Bankruptcy Act. The accountant was appointed by the committee to perform the audit. This second case is an example of a report issued for a business that was able to reach an informal arrangement with creditors by subordinating their claims and deferring payment. Also included is an interim report prepared by the accountant for three months and nine months.

The accountant's opinion is qualified due to uncertainty regarding the ability of the debtor to make timely payments under the extension agreement and to continue as a going concern. The extension agreement was not reached until March 7, 1975; however, the financial statements for the year ending November 30, 1974, have been revised to reflect this arrangement.

In a situation involving an extension of credit or some other type of arrangement with creditors, the creditors usually require an independent accountant to prepare financial statements quarterly, or even monthly, setting forth the results of operations. The interim statements issued by the accountant for the third quarter of the fiscal year are presented here. Generally, these statements are prepared by the independent accountant without an audit and it is therefore necessary to issue a disclaimer of opinion.

———

CDE CORPORATION

YZ INC.

AND

GB INDUSTRIES, LTD.

REPORT ON EXAMINATION OF COMBINED FINANCIAL STATEMENTS

(RESTATED)

Year Ended November 30, 1974

———

CDE Corporation
YZ, Inc.
GB Industries, Ltd.
New York, New York

We have examined the accompanying combined balance sheet (Restated, Note 1) of CDE Corporation, YZ Inc., and GB Industries, Ltd., as of November 30, 1974, and the related statement of combined operations and retained earnings for the year then ended. Our examination was made in accordance with generally accepted auditing standards, and accordingly included such tests of the accounting records and such other auditing procedures as we considered necessary in the circumstances.

As discussed in Note 1 to the financial statements, certain creditors have agreed to subordinate their claims and allow the Companies to defer payment of debts. Management believes that the extension agreement with creditors will enable the Companies to obtain future credit on normal terms and continue as a going concern.

In our opinion, subject to the effects, if any, on the financial statements of the ultimate resolution of the matter discussed in the preceding paragraph, financial statements referred to above present fairly the combined financial position of CDE Corporation, YZ Inc., and GB Industries, Ltd., at November 30, 1974, and the combined results of their operations for the year then ended, in conformity with generally accepted accounting principles applicable to a going concern applied on a basis consistent with that of the preceding year.

JONES & COMPANY
Certified Public Accountants

New York, New York
February 6, 1975
(March 7, 1975, as to Note 1)

CDE CORPORATION, YZ INC., AND GB INDUSTRIES, LTD.

COMBINED BALANCE SHEET
(RESTATED, NOTE 1)

November 30, 1974

Assets

Current Assets:	
Cash	$ 185,640
Accounts Receivable (less provision for estimated uncollectible amounts and for allowance for sales discounts of $91,142; Note 2)	1,016,649
Notes Receivable	23,090
Inventories—At Cost (which approximates first-in, first-out method) or Market, whichever is lower (Note 4)	1,507,198
Income Tax Refund Receivable	11,490
Prepaid Expenses	34,878
Total Current Assets	2,778,945
Fixed Assets—At Cost:	
Machinery, Equipment, Furniture, and Fixtures (less accumulated depreciation of $198,232)	156,020
	$2,934,965

Liabilities and Shareholders' Investment

Current Liabilities:		
Notes Payable—Bank (Note 2)		$ 856,400
Accounts Payable and Accrued Expenses		420,368
Federal Income Taxes		103,477
Total Current Liabilities		1,380,245
Accounts Payable Deferred (Note 1)		910,000
Commitments and Contingent Liabilities (Notes 3 and 5)		—
Shareholders' Investment (Note 1):		
Capital Stock	$ 19,630	
Retained Earnings	625,090	644,720
		$2,934,965

See Notes to financial statements.

CDE CORPORATION, YZ INC., AND GB INDUSTRIES, LTD.

STATEMENT OF COMBINED OPERATIONS AND RETAINED EARNINGS

Year Ended November 30, 1974

Net Sales		$6,409,446
Cost of Products Sold (Note 6)		5,254,626
		1,154,820
Selling, Administrative, and General Expenses (Note 6)		998,220
		156,600
Taxes on Income:		
Federal	$60,700	
State	8,700	69,400
Earnings Before Extraordinary Items		87,200
Extraordinary Items:		
Reduction in federal and state income taxes applicable to utilization of loss carryforward applicable to prior years	7,300	
Capitalization of machinery, equipment, furniture, and fixtures (Note 7)	9,277	16,577
Net Earnings		103,777
Retained Earnings, December 1, 1973		521,313
Retained Earnings, November 30, 1974		$ 625,090

See Notes to financial statements.

CDE CORPORATION, YZ INC., AND GB INDUSTRIES, LTD.

NOTES TO COMBINED FINANCIAL STATEMENTS

Year Ended November 30, 1974

Note 1. Subsequent Events

Inventories at the end of the year were substantially higher than those of the preceding year (Note 4). An orderly reduction of such inventories is required in order to realize funds to pay creditors.

It is recognized that continuity of the business of the Companies depends upon the maintenance of adequate credit arrangements and the orderly realization of inventories. Under an agreement dated March 6, 1975, certain creditors have agreed to subordinate their claims as of December 28, 1974, and allow the Companies to defer payment of debts as described below. Management believes that the extension agreement with creditors will enable the Companies to obtain future credit on normal terms and to realize the excess inventories in an orderly fashion, but this can only be proved by the passage of time.

Financial statements previously issued have been restated retroactively to give effect to payment terms which are as follows:

	July 31	December 31
1975	20%	15%
1976	20	20
1977	25	

The agreement with creditors, among other matters, prohibits the Companies from paying dividends or other distributions, redeeming capital stock, and pledging or mortgaging any assets or property (without the written consent of the Creditors' Committee). The agreement shall be deemed breached and the claims of the deferring creditors reinstated in full if the Companies are in default of any of the terms or provisions of the agreement, including the reduction of net worth below $300,000.

Note 2. Assigned Accounts Receivable

The Companies have revolving credit agreements with a bank. These are collateralized by assignment of substantially all of the Companies' accounts receivable as of November 30, 1974.

At November 30, 1974, there was approximately $100,000 included in accounts receivable due from certain customers for shipments made during the past fiscal year. Extended payment dates were granted whereby these past-due balances would be payable during the period March 1, 1975, to July 31, 1975.

Note 3. Notes Receivable

The Companies are contingently liable for $33,575 of notes receivable discounted with a bank.

Note 4. Inventories

	November 30, 1974			November 30, 1973		
	Swimming Pools	Pool Tables	Total	Swimming Pools	Pool Tables	Total
Raw Materials	$256,560	$375,425	$ 631,985	$169,155	$478,048	$ 647,203
Finished Goods	364,026	511,187	875,213	172,266	257,304	429,570
	$620,586	$886,612	$1,507,198	$341,421	$735,352	$1,076,773

Finished goods include swimming pool units which are complete except for production of certain components, normally done just prior to shipment.

Note 5. Leases

At November 30, 1974, the Companies were obligated under three leases with annual rentals aggregating $156,798 plus certain other expenses. One lease expires in 1976 and the other two in 1978.

Note 6. Depreciation Expense

Depreciation expense, which is calculated principally by using the straight-line method, totalled $54,533.

Note 7. Extraordinary Items

An Internal Revenue Service examination in 1974 resulted in capitalization of machinery, equipment, furniture, and fixtures in the amount of $23,291. The cost of the items capitalized had been charged to repairs and maintenance in the 1971, 1972, and 1973 fiscal years. Depreciation in these years, calculated retroactively, totalled $4,414. Applicable taxes were $9,600.

———

CDE CORPORATION

YZ INC.

AND

GB INDUSTRIES, LTD.

COMBINED FINANCIAL STATEMENTS

Three Months and Nine Months Ended August 31, 1975

(Unaudited)

———

CDE Corporation
YZ Inc.
GB Industries, Ltd.
New York, New York

The accompanying combined balance sheet of CDE Corporation, YZ Inc., and GB Industries, Ltd., as of August 31, 1975, and the related combined statement of operations and retained earnings for the three months and nine months then ended were not audited by us, and accordingly we do not express an opinion on them.

Inventories, as shown in the combined unaudited balance sheet and explained in Note 3 to the financial statements, were determined by the Companies through subtraction of the standard cost of products shipped during the period from the total of beginning inventories and all production costs for the period. The amounts of inventories so determined can be proved only by the performance and evaluation of a physical inventory, which have not been done since November 30, 1974.

These interim financial statements do not necessarily include all disclosures that might be required for a fair presentation.

JONES & COMPANY
Certified Public Accountants

New York, New York
October 21, 1975

CDE CORPORATION, YZ INC., AND GB INDUSTRIES, LTD.

COMBINED BALANCE SHEET

August 31, 1974 and 1975

(Unaudited)

	August 31, 1975	August 31, 1974
Assets		
Current Assets:		
Cash	$ —	$ 22,262
Accounts Receivable (less allowances for estimated uncollectible amounts and sales discounts of $151,941 and $121,362, respectively; Note 2)	988,589	683,581
Inventories (Notes 2 and 3)	1,500,496	1,360,011
Prepaid Expenses	25,813	13,645
Total Current Assets	2,514,898	2,079,499
Property and Equipment—At Cost:		
Machinery, equipment, furniture, and fixtures (less accumulated depreciation of $227,420 and $185,654, respectively)	155,454	109,124
	$2,670,352	$2,188,623
Liabilities and Shareholders' Investment		
Current Liabilities:		
Notes Payable—Bank (Note 2)	$ 701,277	$ 381,700
Accounts Payable and Accrued Expenses	580,453	1,228,020
Cash Overdraft, Net	57,374	—
Federal Income Taxes	172,773	1,632
Total Current Liabilities	1,511,877	1,611,352
Accounts Payable Deferred (Note 1)	472,198	—
Commitments and Contingent Liabilities (Note 4)	—	—
Shareholders' Investment (Note 1):		
Capital Stock	19,630	19,630
Retained Earnings	666,647	557,641
	686,277	577,271
	$2,670,352	$2,188,623

See Notes to combined financial statements.

CDE CORPORATION, YZ INC., AND GB INDUSTRIES, LTD.

COMBINED STATEMENT OF OPERATIONS AND RETAINED EARNINGS

For Three Months and Nine Months Ended August 31, 1974 and 1975

(Unaudited)

	Three Months Ended August 31		Nine Months Ended August 31	
	1975	1974	1975	1974
Net Sales	$1,451,619	$1,707,393	$4,369,634	$5,200,253
Cost of Products Sold (Notes 3 and 5)	1,203,319	1,405,563	3,533,108	4,349,425
	248,300	301,830	836,526	850,828
Selling, Administrative, and General				
Expenses (exclusive of interest; Note 5)	210,397	273,740	627,394	737,376
Interest Expense	33,930	14,427	82,216	49,915
	244,327	288,167	709,610	787,291
Net Income Before Income Taxes	3,973	13,663	126,916	63,537
Taxes on Income (less tax benefits of carryback loss; Note 6):				
Federal	15,563	7,700	74,089	23,700
State	717	500	11,270	3,500
	16,280	8,200	85,359	27,200
Net Income (Loss)	(12,307)	5,463	41,557	36,337
Retained Earnings, Beginning of Period	678,954	552,178	625,090	521,304
Retained Earnings, End of Period	$ 666,647	$ 557,641	$ 666,647	$ 557,641

See Notes to combined financial statements.

CDE CORPORATION, YZ INC., AND GB INDUSTRIES, LTD.

NOTES TO COMBINED FINANCIAL STATEMENTS

Three Months and Nine Months Ended August 31,1975

(Unaudited)

Note 1. Agreement With Creditors

Under an agreement dated March 6, 1975, certain creditors have agreed to subordinate their claims as of December 28, 1974, and allow the Companies to defer payment of debts as described below. Management believes that the extension agreement with creditors will enable the Companies to obtain future credit on normal terms and to realize the excess inventories in an orderly fashion, but this can only be proved by the passage of time.

The initial payment representing 20 per cent of the deferred payments was made July 31, 1975. The remaining payment terms expressed as percentages of the total deferred amounts are as follows:

	July 31	December 31
1975		15%
1976	20%	20
1977	25	

The agreement with creditors, among other matters, prohibits the Companies from paying dividends or other distributions, redeeming capital stock, and pledging or mortgaging any assets (without the written consent of the Creditors' Committee). The agreement shall be deemed breached and the claims of the deferred creditors reinstated in full and immediately become due and payable if the Companies are in default of any of the terms or provisions of the agreement, including the reduction of net worth below $300,000.

Note 2. Notes Payable—Bank

The Companies have revolving credit agreements with a bank. These are collateralized by assignment of the Companies' accounts receivable and the pledge of inventories.

Note 3. Inventories

Inventories were determined by subtracting the standard cost of products shipped during the period from the total of beginning inventories and all production costs for the period. A summary of the inventories is as follows:

	Swimming Pools	Pool Tables	Total
August 31, 1975	$1,024,778	$475,718	$1,500,496
August 31, 1974	535,639	824,372	1,360,011

Note 4. Leases

At August 31, 1975, the Companies were obligated under two leases with expiration dates of 1978 and 1990. The annual payments on these leases are $4,548 and $169,280, respectively, plus certain other expenses.

Note 5. Depreciation Expense

Depreciation expense, calculated principally by using the straight-line method, totalled $29,188 and $29,823, respectively, for the three-month and nine-month periods.

Note 6. Income Taxes

Since the Companies file separate tax returns, the taxable income of one company in the group may not be reduced by the losses of another. No relationship necessarily exists between combined income and federal income taxes.

Loss carrybacks of YZ Inc. and GB Industries, Ltd., for the nine-month period ended August 31, 1975, were reflected in the financial statements for the three-month and nine-month periods ended August 31, 1975, and resulted in an $81,335 reduction in federal tax expense and an $11,273 reduction in state tax expense.

Case III.   ABC Corporation

This case contains an example of a report issued by the accountant for a small manufacturing company which was in bankruptcy at the time the audit report was issued, but not during the period covered by the report. An opinion is disclaimed due to the uncertainties regarding the ability of the debtor to work out an arrangement with its creditors under the provisions of Chapter XI of the Bankruptcy Act.

The two accounts of this company which presented the major problems for the independent accountant were Inventories and Investments. The inventories were reduced to about 45 per cent of their normal price, yet there was considerable doubt as to whether this was a reasonable value. This adjusted value represented the amount which management considered reasonable, provided sufficient working capital was available to continue operations with a normal marketing program.

———

ABC CORPORATION

REPORT ON EXAMINATION OF FINANCIAL STATEMENTS

Year Ended February 28, 1975

———

Board of Directors
ABC Corporation
1175 Adams Street
Brooklyn, New York 11236

We have examined the accompanying balance sheet of ABC Corporation as of February 28, 1975, and the related statement of loss and deficit and additional paid-in capital for the year then ended. Our examination was made in accordance with generally accepted auditing standards, and accordingly included such tests of the accounting records and such other auditing procedures as we considered necessary in the circumstances.

On April 1, 1975, the Company filed a voluntary petition under Chapter XI of the Federal Bankruptcy Act. The accompanying financial statements do not give effect to any adjustments resulting from future court-approved actions of the Referee in Bankruptcy as to the nature and extent of the Company's operations or to any adjustments which would be part of a plan of arrangement with creditors or would result from a sale of all or part of the Company's assets.

We were present to observe the Company's taking of its annual physical inventory and satisfied ourselves as to the quantities on hand. As explained in Note 1, inventories have been substantially reduced to an amount estimated by management to be realizable value. While we are of the opinion that the amount that can be reasonably expected to be realized upon final disposition of the inventories is less than cost, we were unable to satisfy ourselves that the inventories, as adjusted, are stated at realizable value.

We are unable to evaluate the investment in XYZ, Inc. (see Note 2) inasmuch as there was no available objective evidence as to the market or underlying book values of the investment.

Because of uncertainties regarding the future actions of the Referee in Bankruptcy, and because of our inability to satisfy ourselves as to the amounts that may be realized on inventories and investment in XYZ, Inc., all referred to in the preceding paragraphs, we are unable to and do not express an opinion on the accompanying financial statements.

JONES & COMPANY
Certified Public Accountants

New York, New York
July 22, 1975

ABC CORPORATION

BALANCE SHEET

February 28, 1975

Assets

Current Assets:		
Cash		$ 20,018
Accounts Receivable:		
Trade Accounts Receivable	$ 187,071	
Accounts Receivable (hospitals, awaiting grants)	31,525	
	218,596	
Less: Allowance for Doubtful Accounts and		
Sales Allowances	15,223	203,373
Inventory at Estimated Realizable Values (Note 1):		
Raw Materials	87,694	
Work in Process and Finished Goods	99,093	186,787
Manufacturing Supplies		4,000
Total Current Assets		414,178
Investments:		
Investment in XYZ, Inc. (Note 2)	81,250	
Cash Surrender Value of Life Insurance (net of		
$26,656 policy loan)	2,132	83,382
Machinery, Equipment, and Fixtures (less		
accumulated depreciation of $142,117; Note 3)		236,130
Other Assets (including unamortized debt expense		
of $39,600)		52,434
		$786,124

See Notes to financial statements.

Liabilities and Stockholders' Investment

Current Liabilities:		
Notes Payable		$ 28,000
Trade Accounts Payable		197,539
Estimated Costs To Complete Government Contracts		35,000
Salaries and Wages Including Taxes Withheld and Payable		21,504
Accrued Interest		29,546
Miscellaneous Accrued Expenses		3,015
Total Current Liabilities		314,604
Long-Term Liabilities:		
6% Convertible Subordinated Notes (Notes 4 and 5):		
Due November 1, 1977	$ 95,000	
Due October 15, 1978	50,000	
Due April 15, 1980	400,000	545,000
Stockholders' Investment (deficiency in assets) (Notes 4 and 5):		
Capital Stock (par value $1 per share; authorized, 600,000 shares; issued and outstanding, 246,183 shares)	246,183	
Additional Paid-In Capital	894,833	
(Deficit)	(1,214,496)	(73,480)
		$786,124

ABC CORPORATION

STATEMENT OF NET LOSS AND DEFICIT

Year Ended February 28, 1975

Net Sales			$ 601,564
Cost of Goods Sold (Note 1)			825,889
Gross Loss			224,325
Selling Expenses:			
Salaries and Commissions		$ 42,769	
Advertising		14,649	
Shows, Conferences, and Travel		10,145	
General Sales Expense		16,692	
		84,255	
General and Administrative Expenses:			
Officers' Salaries	$42,417		
Office Salaries	23,825		
Payroll	17,859		
Insurance	10,752		
Professional Services	38,978		
Provision for Doubtful Accounts			
Receivable	13,199		
Telephone	12,119		
Office Expense	6,471		
Amortization of Debt Expense	8,400		
State and Local Taxes	3,948		
Other (including interest of $34,225)	52,670	230,638	314,893
Net Loss			539,218
Deficit, March 1, 1974			675,278
Deficit, February 28, 1975			$1,214,496

See Notes to financial statements.

ABC CORPORATION

STATEMENT OF ADDITIONAL PAID-IN CAPITAL

Year Ended February 28, 1975

Balance, March 1, 1974	$886,533
Additions:	
Excess of principal amount of Convertible Subordinated Notes over par value of 900 shares of capital stock issued in exchange	4,100
Excess of fair market value over par value of 700 shares of capital stock issued in exchange for patent	4,200
Balance, February 28, 1975	$894,833

See Notes to financial statements.

ABC CORPORATION

NOTES TO FINANCIAL STATEMENTS

Note 1. Inventories

Inventories are stated at estimated realizable value, determined in the following manner, which is less than cost:

Raw materials were priced at invoice cost. Work in process was priced at raw material cost plus direct labor at standard cost and burden at 100 per cent of direct labor. Finished goods were generally priced at the lower of 60 per cent of catalog price or lowest actual selling price. Such methods resulted in an aggregate inventory of approximately $437,000. The amount so determined was then reduced to $186,787, in an attempt by management to state the inventories at estimated realizable value, taking into consideration discontinuation of certain products, obsolescence, spoilage, and other factors.

Management is of the opinion that the inventories, as stated at $186,787, are realistic, provided that sufficient working capital is available to continue operations and to allow for a normal marketing program.

Note 2. Investment

During the year ended February 28, 1973, the Company exchanged 16,250 shares of its capital stock for 4,250 shares (3.3 per cent of total shares outstanding) of XYZ, Inc. The investment in XYZ, Inc. is stated at the estimated fair market value of the Company's capital stock issued in the exchange as determined by the Board of Directors.

Note 3. Machinery, Equipment and Fixtures

Such assets are stated at cost less accumulated depreciation, the basis applicable in the case of a continuing business. Accordingly, such basis does not purport to represent realizable value, which may be more or less than the carrying amount.

Depreciation expense for the year ended February 28, 1975, amounted to $49,849.

Note 4. Capital Stock Reserved

As of February 28, 1975, 220,169 shares of capital stock were reserved as follows:

	Date Granted	Expiration Date	Option Price	No. of Shares
Under restricted stock options granted to officers and employees; exercisable two years after date of grant to the extent of 33-1/3 per cent each year for three years	9/14/70 9/14/70 6/20/71 10/ 9/71	9/14/75 9/14/75 6/20/76 10/ 9/76	$ 9.00 10.50 7.50 7.50	33,333 33,333 2,000 1,000
Options granted to others exercisable at any time within five years from date of grant	2/14/71 11/ 1/72 10/16/73	2/14/76 11/ 1/77 10/15/78	9.00 6.75 7.50	13,333 5,000 2,500
Options granted to others; exercisable at any time after November 18, 1974	11/18/72	11/18/77	7.00	6,000
				96,499

Capital stock reserved for issuance to holders of 6 per cent Convertible Subordinated Notes, due November 1, 1977, convertible at the option of the holders at the rate of 180 shares of capital stock for each $1,000 of indebtedness 17,100

Capital stock reserved for issuance to holders of 6 per cent Convertible Subordinated Notes, due October 15, 1978, convertible at the option of the holders at the rate of 133.4 shares of capital stock for each $1,000 of indebtedness 6,670

Capital stock reserved for issuance to holders of 6 per cent Convertible Subordinated Notes, due March 31, 1979; convertible at the option of the holders at the rate of 222 shares of capital stock for each $1,000 of indebtedness until October 31, 1976, and thereafter at the rate of 167 shares of capital stock for each $1,000 of principal (see Note 5) 88,800

Capital stock reserved for issuance to underwriter in connection with issuance of 6 per cent Convertible Subordinated Notes due April 15, 1979 (see Note 5) 11,100

220,169

Note 5. Long-Term Debt

In April, 1974, the Company issued Convertible Subordinated Notes payable in the amount of $400,000, with interest at 6 per cent per annum, which mature five years from date of issuance. The net cash proceeds amounted to $352,000 after deducting underwriters' and other fees of $48,000. The latter amount is being amortized over five years.

The underwriter was granted an option to purchase an additional $50,000 of Convertible Subordinated Notes at par. The option expires in April, 1979.

All of the above notes, including those covered by the aforementioned option, are convertible at the rate of 222 shares of capital stock per $1,000 of principal until October 31, 1976, and thereafter at the rate of 167 shares of capital stock per $1,000 of principal.

Under the terms of the underlying agreements, the notes became due and payable on April 1, 1975, upon the filing of a voluntary petition under Chapter XI of the Federal Bankruptcy Act. The notes are shown in the accompanying balance sheet as long-term, in accordance with the original maturity dates.

Note 6. Tax Carryforward

Based upon returns as filed for the years ended February 28, 1968, and prior, the Company has a net operating loss carryforward of approximately $624,000 which, together with the tax loss for the year ended February 28, 1975, may be offset against future earnings of the Company.

Note 7. Lease Agreement

The company leases property used in its operations under a lease expiring September, 1977, at an annual rental of $21,200.

Glossary

Adjudication. An order, whether by decree or operation of law, declaring that a petitioner is bankrupt.

Arrangement. An agreement between a debtor and its creditors, subject to court approval, wherein the debtor normally remains in business but secures an extension of time for payment, or a reduction in amount, or both, of all or part of its unsecured debts. Also used to refer to the proceedings under Chapter XI of the Bankruptcy Act.

Assignment. A remedy available through the state courts for a company in an insolvent condition. The debtor voluntarily transfers title to assets to an assignee who then liquidates them and distributes the proceeds among the creditors.

Bankruptcy. The proceedings initiated voluntarily by a debtor or involuntarily by creditors and involving the filing of a petition in a federal court under the Bankruptcy Act when the debtor is unable to pay obligations due or to reach an agreement out of court with creditors.

Bankruptcy Act. A federal statute enacted July 2, 1898, and amended more than ninety times, which provides the basis for the present federal bankruptcy system.

Bankruptcy Court. The United States District Court of trial jurisdiction. Also used to describe the proceedings held under a federal bankruptcy referee. Unless the district judge or judges direct otherwise, the responsibility for all cases filed under Chapters I to VII, Chapter XI, and Chapter XIII of the Bankruptcy Act rests with the referee.

Bankruptcy judge. The referee of the court of bankruptcy where a bankruptcy case is pending.

Business bankrupt. A bankrupt whose financial problems result from some type of business activity.

Chapter X proceeding. An action taken under Chapter X of the Bankruptcy Act. Used mostly by large corporations with complex debt structures and with widely held public securities.

Chapter XI proceeding. An action taken under Chapter XI of the Bankruptcy Act. Used mostly by businesses for the purpose of working out an arrangement, with court approval, for creditors to agree to accept partial payment in satisfaction of their claims and/or an extension of the time for repayment. The agreement must be approved by the majority of creditors in number and amount. The provisions of Chapter XI apply only to unsecured creditors.

Committee case. A bankruptcy situation that is referred to an unofficial creditors' committee to effect a voluntary agreement, out of court, between the debtor and its creditors.

Composition (informal). An out-of-court agreement between a debtor and its creditors which provides for an extension of time for payment or for full satisfaction of claims by partial payment, now or at some future date.

Confirmation of arrangement. An official acceptance by the court of a plan of arrangement which makes the plan binding upon the debtor and creditors. Before an application for confirmation by the court is filed, the plan must be accepted in writing by a majority in number and amount of those creditors filing claims.

Date of bankruptcy. Date when a petition in bankruptcy is filed with the Bankruptcy Court.

Discharge. An order entered in a bankruptcy proceeding which releases the debtor from all of its provable debts existing after non-exempt assets are distributed, providing the debts are not excepted by the Bankruptcy Act.

Estate. The non-exempted assets of a bankrupt which are available for payment of administrative expenses and creditors' claims.

Executory contract. A contract in which something must be performed wholly or in part to complete the original agreement. Unexpired leases or purchase commitments are examples of executory contracts typically found in bankruptcy cases.

Exempt assets. Property which is prohibited from becoming a part of an estate by federal or state laws. The bankrupt maintains possession of the assets.

Insolvency. 1. In the equity sense, the inability of the debtor to pay obligations as they mature. 2. In the bankruptcy sense, a condition where the liabilities of the debtor exceed the fair valuation of the assets.

Insolvency proceedings. Action undertaken in a state court under the state insolvency laws.

Involuntary petition (bankruptcy). A petition filed by creditors alleging that a debtor has committed an act of bankruptcy.

Irregularities. Any transactions which are not in the ordinary course of business. Especially includes those transactions which resulted in the apparent dissipation of the debtor's assets in a manner other than by loss in the ordinary course of business.

Non-business bankrupt. A bankrupt whose financial difficulties are unrelated to any type of business operations.

Petition. A document filed in a court of bankruptcy, initiating proceedings under the Bankruptcy Act.

Plan of reorganization. A plan formulated in Chapter X proceedings under the supervision of the court. After the court's approval, it is circulated among creditors for their acceptance. The plan may affect secured creditors and stockholders as well as unsecured creditors' interests.

Priority creditor. A creditor whose claim is among those which are paid first, after the secured claims and administrative expenses have been paid.

Receiver. An individual appointed by the bankruptcy court to receive and preserve the property of the bankrupt. The receiver is often appointed for an interim period to look after the assets until a trustee can be elected or appointed.

Referee. A federal official appointed for a six-year term to preside over bankruptcy proceedings. See also *Bankruptcy judge.*

Reorganization. A designation for the proceedings under Chapter X, which applies to large corporations with complex debt structure and publicly held securities.

Schedules. The lists of debts and assets which the debtor is required to file with a petition in bankruptcy or shortly thereafter.

Secured creditor. A creditor whose claim against a debtor is secured by collateral. The property pledged as security may be used to satisfy the debt in the event the creditor defaults.

Seller's lien. A lien which a seller of goods has at common law for the unpaid portion of the purchase price of the goods in his or her possession.

Statement of affairs. A report filed with a petition under Chapter XI and consisting of answers to twenty-one questions concerning the debtor's past operations. Also used to refer to a statement of a debtor's financial condition as of a certain date, based on the assumption that the business will be liquidated. The statement consists of an analysis of the debtor's financial position and the status of the creditors with respect to the debtor's assets.

Trustee. An official elected by the creditors at a meeting before the referee to liquidate the estate of the bankrupt. If the creditors fail to elect a trustee, the referee will make the appointment. In a Chapter X proceeding, the term "trustee" is used to refer to one or more disinterested officials who may be appointed by the court to supervise a reorganization. If the liabilities of the debtor exceed $250,000, it is mandatory that a trustee or trustees be appointed.

Turnover order. An order by a district judge directing that property or proceeds from sale of property be turned over to a trustee or receiver as part of a bankruptcy estate.

Unsecured creditor. A creditor whose claim is not secured by any collateral. The term is generally used in bankruptcy and insolvency proceedings to refer to unsecured claims which do not receive priority under the Bankruptcy Act or under state laws.

Voluntary petition (bankruptcy). A petition filed by a debtor of his or her own free will, initiating proceedings under the Bankruptcy Act. All petitions filed under Chapter XI are voluntary.

Bibliography

Abramson, Leslie W. (Editor). *Basic Bankruptcy: Alternatives, Proceedings and Discharges.* Ann Arbor, Mich.: Institute of Continuing Legal Education, 1971.

"Accountant's Role in a Bankruptcy Case" (Statement in Quotes), *The Journal of Accountancy,* Vol. 115 (June 1963), pp. 59–62.

Administration of the Bankruptcy Act, Report of the Attorney General's Committee on Bankruptcy Administration. Washington, D. C.: Government Printing Office, 1941.

Administrative Office of the U. S. Courts. *Tables of Bankruptcy Statistics.* Washington, D. C.: Government Printing Office, 1972.

Altman, Edward I. "Bankrupt Firms' Equity Securities as an Investment Alternative," *Financial Analysts Journal,* Vol. 25 (July–August 1969), pp. 129–33.

———. *Corporate Bankruptcy in America.* Lexington, Mass.: D. C. Heath and Co., 1971.

———. "Corporate Bankruptcy Prediction and Its Implications for Commercial Loan Evaluation," *The Journal of Commercial Bank Lending,* Vol. 53 (December 1970), pp. 8–22.

———. "Financial Ratios, Discriminant Analysis and the Prediction of Corporate Bankruptcy," *The Journal of Finance,* Vol. 23 (September 1968), pp. 589–609.

"Ambiguities of Section 17(a) of the Bankruptcy Act of 1966," *Texas Tech Law Review,* Vol. 3 (Fall 1971), pp. 135–42.

"Amendments to the Bankruptcy Act—An Attempt To Remedy Discharge Abuses," *Michigan Law Review,* Vol. 69 (June 1971), pp. 1347–67.

American Institute of Certified Public Accountants, *Accounting Principles.* Chicago: Commerce Clearing House, Inc., 1972.

American Jurisprudence, With 1971 Annual Cumulative Supplement, Second Edition. Rochester, N. Y.: The Lawyers Cooperative Publishing Co., 1963.

Armour, P. H. "Practical Aspects of a Members' Voluntary Liquidation," *Accountants' Magazine* (Scot.), Vol. 69 (February 1965), pp. 130–35.

Arthur Young and Company. "Accountants' Role in a Bankruptcy Case . . . ," *The Journal of Accountancy,* Vol. 115 (June 1963), pp. 59–63.

Ashe, George. "The Corporate Entity in Bankruptcy: Subordination—Consolidation—Mergers," *The American Bankruptcy Law Journal*, Vol. 46 (Fall 1972), pp. 291–304.

————. "Reclamation Under UCC—An Exercise in Futility; Defrauded Seller v. Trustee in Bankruptcy," *Journal of the National Conference of Referees in Bankruptcy*, Vol. 43 (July 1969), pp. 78–83.

————. "Rehabilitation Under Chapter XI: Fact or Fiction?," *Commercial Law Journal*, Vol. 72 (September 1967), pp. 259–64.

————. "Subordination of Claims—Equitable Principles Applied in Bankruptcy," *Commercial Law Journal*, Vol. 72 (April 1967), pp. 91–95.

Bailey, Henry J. "UCC Cases: Group No. 10," *The Practical Lawyer*, Vol. 15 (May 1969), pp. 85–92.

"Bankruptcies Drop in Number," *Credit and Financial Management*, Vol. 73 (September 1971), pp. 32–33.

"Bankruptcies on the Rise" (A Longer Look), *Credit and Financial Management*, Vol. 69 (May 1967), pp. 14–15, 38.

"Bankruptcy—Bankrupt Cannot Resort to Small Debts to Invoke Requirement of Three Petitioning Creditors," *Texas Law Review*, Vol. 50 (January 1972), pp. 375–81.

"Bankruptcy—Bankrupt Retains Accrued Vacation Pay," *West Virginia Law Review*, Vol. 73 (September 1971), pp. 302–9.

"Bankruptcy: Corporate Reorganization Criteria for Choice Between Chapters X and XI of Bankruptcy Act," *Minnesota Law Review*, Vol. 41 (January 1957), pp. 215–19.

"Bankruptcy—Creditors' Rights—A Bona Fide Purchaser-Plus Test for Statutory Liens in Bankruptcy," *North Carolina Law Review*, Vol. 50 (December 1971), pp. 90–103.

"Bankruptcy—Discharge of Taxes—No Discharge of 'Stale' Taxes in Bankruptcy When Taxpayer Has Consented to Extension of Statute of Limitations on Assessment and Internal Revenue Service Has Not Issued a Statutory Notice of Deficiency," *Creighton Law Review*, Vol. 4 (1971), pp. 349–72.

"Bankruptcy: Effect of the 1970 Bankruptcy Act Amendments on the Discharge That Never Was," *Wisconsin Law Review* (1971), pp. 1174–89.

"Bankruptcy: Equitable Subordination of Unconscionable Claims," *Southern California Law Review*, Vol. 40 (1967), pp. 165–75.

"Bankruptcy—New Approach to Dischargeability," *West Virginia Law Review*, Vol. 73 (September 1971), pp. 309–18.

"Bankruptcy—Preferences—Secured Transactions—Security Interest in

After-Acquired Property Is Voidable Preference if Received Within Four Months of Bankruptcy," *Michigan Law Review*, Vol. 65 (March 1967), pp. 1004–13.

"Bankruptcy—Pressure as a Defense—Fraudulent Preferences," *Alberta Law Review*, Vol. 8 (1970), pp. 154–60.

"Bankruptcy—Priorities—Internal Revenue Code Provision Making Withheld Taxes a Trust for Government Held Not to Supercede Bankruptcy Act Priorities Which Give All Costs of Administration Pro Rata First Priority," *Loyola University Law Journal*, Vol. 1 (Summer 1970), pp. 359–71.

"Bankruptcy Law—A Survey of Recent Fifth Circuit Decisions," *Houston Law Review*, Vol. 8 (November 1970), pp. 322–41.

Bankruptcy Legislation 1967, Hearing Before a Special Subcommittee of the Senate Committee on the Judiciary, 90th Congress, 1st Session, Washington, D. C.: Government Printing Office, 1967.

"Bankruptcy Schedules and Their Importance," *Decalogue Journal*, Vol. 14 (June–July 1964), p. 17.

"Bankruptcy—Tax Discharge—Tax Priority," *Southwestern Law Journal*, Vol. 25 (May 1971), pp. 326–30.

"Bankruptcy—Tax Liens—A Government Lien Securing Taxes Legally Due and Owing More Than Three Years Prior to Bankruptcy Does Not Attach to Property Acquired Subsequent to Discharge in Bankruptcy," *Texas Law Review*, Vol. 49 (March 1971), pp. 554–62.

"Bankruptcy—The Nature and Scope of the Dischargeability Amendment to the Bankruptcy Act," *Houston Law Review*, Vol. 8 (May 1971), pp. 991–97.

"Bankruptcy Trap Snaps Shut on Inept Management," *Industry Week*, September 7, 1970, pp. 25–31.

Banks, Charles S. *Treatise on Bankruptcy for Accountants*. Chicago, Ill.: LaSalle Extension University, 1948.

Bateman, Hal M. "Recent Developments in Bankruptcy," *Missouri Law Review*, Vol. 32 (Winter 1967), pp. 1–28.

Beaver, William H. "Alternative Accounting Measures as Predictors of Failure," *Accounting Review*, Vol. 43 (January 1968), pp. 113–22.

———. "Financial Ratios as Predictors of Failure," in *Empirical Research in Accounting: Selected Studies 1966*. First University of Chicago Conference (May 1966), pp. 71–127.

Berger, Theodore. "Acquisitions of Financially Troubled Businesses," *TAXES—The Tax Magazine*, Vol. 50 (December 1972), pp. 809–19.

Berney, Robert E. "Effect of Corporate Loss Carryovers on Stabilization," *National Tax Journal*, Vol. 20 (June 1967), pp. 149–54.

Bernstein, David M. "The Administration of Bankruptcy Law in Canada with Special Reference to Trustees," *Commercial Law Journal*, Vol. 76 (February 1971), pp. 39–41.

———. " 'Preferences' Under the Bankruptcy Law of Canada and the Applicable Laws of the Province of Quebec," *Commercial Law Journal*, Vol. 76 (December 1971), pp. 423–27.

Beyer, Robert. "Profitability Accounting: The Challenge and the Opportunity," *The Journal of Accountancy*, Vol. 117 (June 1964), pp. 33–36.

Birkett, W. P., and R. G. Walker. "Response of the Australian Accounting Profession to Company Failure," *Abacus*, pp. 97–136.

Black, C., and B. Doherty. "Failure Stirs Investor Fears," *Electronic News*, October 12, 1970, p. 50f.

Black, John L. C. "Stockbrokerage Bankruptcies: Implementing CCS," *Cornell Law Review*, Vol. 54 (May 1969), pp. 750–62.

Blan, Lucie. "Measuring Business Morality," *Conference Board Record*, Vol. 8 (February 1971), pp. 28–31.

Blum, G. L. "Ramifications of Bankruptcy in Federal Tax Matters," *New York University Institute of Federal Taxation*, Vol. 29 (1971), pp. 937–43.

Blum, Walter J. "Corporate Reorganizations Based on Cash Flow Valuations," *The University of Chicago Law Review*, Vol. 38 (Fall 1970), pp. 173–83.

———. "Full Priority and Full Compensation in Corporate Reorganizations: A Reappraisal," *The University of Chicago Law Review*, Vol. 25 (Spring 1958), pp. 417–44.

Blum, Walter J. (Editor). *Materials on Reorganization, Recapitalization and Insolvency.* Selected and edited by Walter J. Blum and Stanley A. Kaplan, with the assistance of Louis A. Huskins. Boston: Little, Brown and Co., 1969.

Boden, Robert F. "Some Areas of Conflict Between the Uniform Commercial Code and the Federal Bankruptcy Act," *New York Institute of Continuing Education*, Vol. 4 (May 1967), pp. 41–61.

Boshkoff, D. G. "The Bankrupt's Moral Obligation to Pay His Discharged Debts: A Conflict Between Contract Theory and Bankruptcy Policy," *Indiana Law Journal*, Vol. 47 (Fall 1971), pp. 36–69.

Braucher, Robert. "Reclamation of Goods from a Fraudulent Buyer," *Michigan Law Review*, Vol. 65 (May 1967), pp. 1281–98.

Brendes, Ralph C., and Lawrence H. Schwartz. "Schlockmeister's Jubilee: Bankruptcy for the Poor," *Journal of the National Conference of Referees in Bankruptcy*, Vol. 40 (July 1966), pp. 69–77.

Bretten, G. R. "Disposition of Property after Commencement of Winding-Up," *Accountant* (Eng.), April 9, 1970, pp. 514–15.

Brody, George. "Appointment of Receivers," *Journal of the National Association of Referees in Bankruptcy*, Vol. 39 (October 1965), pp. 125–27.

————. "Bankruptcy Practice Under the 1970 Dischargeability Amendments," *The Practical Lawyer*, Vol. 18 (October 1972), pp. 81–94.

————. "So-Called Dischargeability Bill—Public Law 91–467. A Milestone in Bankruptcy Legislation," *Commercial Law Journal*, Vol. 76 (January 1971), pp. 9–11.

Bronsteen, Robert. "The Accountant's Investigation of Bankrupt Irregularities," *The New York Certified Public Accountant*, Vol. 37 (December 1967), pp. 935–43.

Brooks, Gene E. "Bankruptcy Practice Guidelines and References," *Res Gestae* (Indiana State Bar Association), Vol. 14 (August 1970), pp. 12–16.

Broom, H. N., and J. G. Longenecker. *Small Business Management*. Cincinnati: Southwestern Publishing Co., 1961.

Brownstein, G. W. "Awarding Fair Fees in Bankruptcy: Recent Developments," *Connecticut Bar Journal*, Vol. 45 (March 1971), pp. 69–83.

Brudney, Victor. "The Bankruptcy Commission's Proposed Modification of the Absolute Priority Rule," *The American Bankruptcy Law Journal*, Vol. 48 (Fall 1974), pp. 305–40.

Buchanan, Norman. *The Economics of Corporate Enterprise*. New York: Henry Holt & Co., 1940.

Burchfield, Thomas H. "The Balance Sheet Test of Insolvency," *University of Pittsburgh Law Review*, Vol. 23 (October 1961), pp. 5–15.

Caldwell, Brian. "Auditor's Certificates and Statute-Barred Debts," *International Accountants Journal* (Eng.), Vol. 29 (June 1959), pp. 40–43.

Carmichael, D. R. *The Auditor's Reporting Obligation: Auditing Research Monograph No. 1*. New York: American Institute of Certified Public Accountants, 1972.

Cavitch, Zolman. *Business Organizations With Tax Planning*, Vol. 7. New York: Matthew Bender & Co., Inc., 1965.

Cerf, Alan R. *Professional Responsibility of Certified Public Accountants*. California Certified Public Accountants Foundation for Education and Research, 1970.

"Certified Public Accountants Held to Fiduciary Standards," *Journal of the National Association of Referees in Bankruptcy*, Vol. 37 (January 1963), pp. 7–10.

Chabrow, P. B. "Estates in Bankruptcy: Return Requirements, Rules Concerning Income and Deductions," *The Journal of Taxation*, Vol. 31 (December 1969), pp. 362–68.

Chambers, Edward J., and Raymond L. Gold. "Factors in Small Business Success or Failure; Prepared for the Montana State Planning Board," *The National Public Accountant*, Vol. 8 (October 1963), pp. 8–9, 33.

"Checklist—Bankruptcy," *Law Office Economics and Management*, Vol. 7 (May 1966), pp. 95–101.

Clifford, Joseph A. *Bankruptcy.* Jamaica, N. Y.: Gould Publications, 1964.

Cocanowner, David L. "Federal Restrictions of Wage Garnishments: Title III of the Consumer Credit Protection Act," *Indiana Law Journal*, Vol. 44 (Winter 1969), pp. 267–92.

"Code and the Bankruptcy Act: Three Views on Preferences and After-Acquired Property, by Sydney Krause, Homer Kipke and Charles Seligson," *New York University Law Review*, Vol. 42 (April 1967), pp. 278–300.

Codification of Auditing Standards and Procedures, Statement on Auditing Standards No. 1. New York: American Institute of Certified Public Accountants, 1973.

Cohen, Manuel. *Receivership, Bankruptcy and Reorganization.* New York: Practising Law Institute, Commercial Law and Practice Course Handbook Series Number 48, 1970.

Committee on Accounting Concepts and Standards, *Accounting and Reporting Standards for Corporate Financial Statements and Preceding Statements and Supplements.* Columbus, Ohio: American Accounting Association, 1957.

Conner, Paul. "Financial Reporting for Companies in Financial Difficulty," *Oklahoma CPA*, Vol. 7 (October 1968), pp. 21–25.

Constandse, William. "Why Companies Fail," *Business Management*, Vol. 39 (October 1970), pp. 13, 42.

Coogan, Peter F. "The Proposed Bankruptcy Act of 1973: Questions for the Non-Bankruptcy Business," *The Business Lawyer*, Vol. 29 (April 1974), pp. 729–54.

"Corporate Failures; Suddenly Last Summer," *The Economist*, October 10, 1970, p. 92f.

Countryman, Vern. "Code Security Interests in Bankruptcy," *Commercial Law Journal*, Vol. 75 (September 1970), pp. 269–80.

———. "Executory Contracts in Bankruptcy: Part I," *Minnesota Law Review*, Vol. 57 (January 1973), pp. 439–91.

———. "New Dischargeability Law," *The American Bankruptcy Law Journal*, Vol. 45 (Winter 1971), pp. 10–55.

———. "Use of State Law in Bankruptcy Cases," *New York University Law Review*, Vol. 47, Part I (June 1972), pp. 407–76; Part II (October 1972), pp. 631–73.

Countryman, Vern (Editor). *Bankruptcy Act*. Boston, Mass.: Little, Brown and Co., 1968.

"Creditors' Rights—The Exempt Status of the Cash Surrender Value of Life Insurance in North Carolina," *Wake Forest Law Review*, Vol. 7 (June 1971), p. 515.

Currie, Hector. "Exempt Property and Bankruptcy: Secured and Waiver Claims," *Louisiana Law Review*, Vol. 31 (December 1970), pp. 73–82.

Cyr, C. K. "Bankruptcy Courts in Transition Toward Debtor Rehabilitation," *Maine Law Review*, Vol. 22 (1970), pp. 333–61.

———. "The Bankruptcy Act of 1973: Back to the Drafting Board," *The American Bankruptcy Law Journal*, Vol. 48 (Winter 1974), pp. 45–73.

Davenport, William B. "Seventh Circuit Upholds UCC Floating Lien in Bankruptcy," *The Business Lawyer*, Vol. 24 (July 1969), pp. 1375–77.

Davidson, Sheldon. "Schemes and Methods Used in Perpetrating Bankruptcy Frauds," *Commercial Law Journal*, Vol. 71 (December 1966), pp. 383–87.

Diamant, L. A. "Bankruptcy and the Secured Creditor," *Los Angeles Bar Bulletin*, Vol. 45 (August 1970), pp. 416–20.

Dolphin, Robert J. *An Analysis of Economic and Personal Factors Leading to Consumer Bankruptcy*. Occasional Paper No. 15. Flint, Mich.: Michigan State University Graduate School of Business Administration, Bureau of Business and Economic Research, 1965.

Donaldson, Elvin, John Pfahl, and Peter L. Mullins. *Corporate Finance*, Fourth Edition. New York: The Ronald Press Co., 1975.

Donnelly, R. A. "Alive and Kicking; Chapters X and XI Sometimes Have a Happy Ending," *Barron's*, May 26, 1969, p. 3f.

———. "Unhappy Ending? Chapters 10 and 11 of the Bankruptcy Act Don't Always Tell the Story," *Barron's*, July 12, 1971, p. 3f.

Donnelly, Samuel, Mary Ann Donnelly, George Hirsch, and Sydney Krause. *Bankruptcy, Arrangements and Reorganizations*. New York: Practising Law Institute, 1972.

Dugan, R. F. T. "Creditors' Post-Judgment Remedies: Part I," *Alabama Law Review*, Vol. 25 (Fall 1972), pp. 175–227.

Dun and Bradstreet, Inc. *Failure Record Through 1962; A Comprehensive Failure Study, By Location, By Industry, By Age, By Size, By Cause*. New York: Dun and Bradstreet, Inc., 1963.

———. *The Business Failure Record, 1973*. New York: Dun and Bradstreet, Inc., 1974.

Dunscomb, S. Whitney, Jr. *Bankruptcy: A Study in Comparative Legislation*. New York: Columbia University Press, 1968.

Earl, David R. *Bankruptcies*. Jericho, N. Y.: Exposition Press, Inc., 1966.

Edwards, K. B. "Disposition of Property After Commencement of Winding-Up," *Accountancy* (Eng.), Vol. 81 (July 1970), pp. 536–38.

————. "Fees for Preparing a Statement of Affairs," *Accountancy* (Eng.),
Vol. 81 (August 1970), pp. 608–10.

Elliot, Milton. "What Taxes, If Any, Are Released by a Discharge in
Bankruptcy?," *The Journal of the Oklahoma Bar Association*, Vol. 40
(March 29, 1969), pp. 683–89.

Erbacher, Philip J. "Is the National Bankruptcy Act Paramount Over the
Internal Revenue Code in Federal Tax Matters?," *TAXES—The Tax
Magazine*, Vol. 48 (March 1970), pp. 153–62.

Farlinger, William A. "Bankruptcy—A Trustee Speaks Out," *Canadian
Chartered Accountant*, Vol. 93 (July 1968), pp. 29–32, 37.

————. "When Companies Crash: Atlantic Acceptance—Calamity or
Catalyst?," *Accountancy* (Eng.), Vol. 83 (January 1972), pp. 12–16.

Farrar, R. Thomas. "Appealability as of Right of Interlocutory Discovery
Orders in Bankruptcy," *University of Miami Law Review*, Vol. 23
(Winter–Spring 1969), pp. 366–84.

Feibelman, Herbert U. "Which Shall It Be—Bankruptcy, an Arrangement
or Corporate Reorganization?," *Commercial Law Journal*, Vol. 69
(January 1964), pp. 6–10.

Feigenbaum, J. Walter. "Observations Concerning Trustees in Bankruptcy and Federal Income Taxes," *Journal of the National Conference
of Referees in Bankruptcy*, Vol. 43 (July 1969), pp. 73–78.

Fishberg, Joseph. "Cost of Administration—An Economy Program,"
Journal of the National Conference of Referees in Bankruptcy, Vol. 40
(April 1966), pp. 58–60.

Fisher, Milton. "Creditors Beware," *Chicago Bar Record*, Vol. 50 (February 1969), pp. 245–49.

Flanagan, Harold T. "The Determination and Payment of Federal Taxes
in Bankruptcy," *The American Bankruptcy Law Journal*, Vol. 47 (Spring
1973), pp. 81–100.

Forman, Leon S. *Compositions, Bankruptcy, and Arrangements*. Philadelphia: The American Law Institute, 1971.

Frye, J. H., Jr. " 'Fair and Equitable' Doctrine—Are Liquidation Rights a
Realistic Standard During Corporate Reorganization?," *Catholic University Law Review*, Vol. 20 (Spring 1971), pp. 394–423.

Fullerton, Robert P. "Some Observations About Bankruptcy," *Colorado
CPA Report*, Vol. 32 (Spring 1968), pp. 7–12.

Fundamentals of Investment Banking. Sponsored by the Investment
Bankers Association of America. Englewood Cliffs, N. J.: Prentice-Hall,
Inc., 1949.

Gelb, Harold, and Irving Goldberger. "Retention Order of the Accountant in Insolvencies and Bankruptcies and Petition for Compensation,"
The New York Certified Public Accountant, Vol. 23 (October 1953), pp.
632–34.

Gendel, Martin. "Jurisdiction Problems in Bankruptcy Court Or 'Think
Before You File a Proof of Claim'," *Journal of the Beverly Hills Bar
Association*, Vol. 4 (September 1970), p. 56.

———. "What Court Has Jurisdiction in a Suit Against a Chapter X
Trustee Conducting a Business?," *The Business Lawyer*, Vol. 24
(November 1968), pp. 317–70.

Gerstenberg, Charles. *Financial Organization and Management of Business*. Englewood Cliffs, N. J.: Prentice-Hall, Inc., 1959.

Gleick, Harry S. "A Comparison of Relief Afforded by Chapters X and XI
of the Bankruptcy Act—Non-Judicial 'Workouts'," *Law Notes: Commercial Area*, Vol. 3 (October 1966), pp. 4–5.

Gordon, Herbert G. "Operation of a Business in Bankruptcy," *The
Canadian Chartered Accountant*, Vol. 76 (May 1960), pp. 454–58.

Gordon, M. J. "Toward a Theory of Financial Distress," *Journal of
Finance*, Vol. 26 (May 1971), pp. 347–56.

Grange, William J., *et al. Manual for Corporation Officers*. New York: The
Ronald Press Co., 1967.

Greene, Jack. "Secured Transactions," *The Business Lawyer*, Vol. 25
(April 1970), pp. 1179–84.

Greenfield, Robert A. *"Lines v. Frederick* (91 Sup. Ct. 113): The Effect of
Bankruptcy on a Bankrupt's Accrued Vacation Pay and Other Forms of
Deferred Compensation," *Los Angeles Bar Bulletin*, Vol. 47 (December
1971), pp. 67–73.

Greidinger, B. Bernard. "Responsibilities of Independent Accountants in
Chapter X Proceedings," *The New York Certified Public Accountant*,
Vol. 36 (April 1966), pp. 278–82.

Hadley, Donald. "Bankruptcy—Alleged Bankrupts Not Required To File
Schedules of Assets and Liabilities or Statement of Affairs Preceding
Adjudication—*Berg v. Hoppe*," *The George Washington Law Review*,
Vol. 34 (June 1966), pp. 945–49.

Hall, J. "Effect of a Winding-Up Order Upon the Income and Capital of a
Company," *Accounting Research* (Eng.), Vol. 6 (January 1955), pp. 9–16.

Hamilton, Charles. "Statutory Liens Under Section 67C of the Bankruptcy Act: Some Problems of Definition," *Tulane Law Review*, Vol. 43
(February 1969), pp. 305–30.

Hatfield, Henry, *Modern Accounting*. New York: Appleton-Century Co.,
Inc., 1909.

Hayek, E. J. *Principles of Bankruptcy in Australia*, Second Edition. Portland, Ore.: International Scholarly Book Service, Inc.

Hazelett, John M. "Need for Investigation of Business Failures" (Letters), *The Journal of Accountancy*, Vol. 118 (August 1964).

Heebe, Frederick J. R. "Corporate Reorganization Under Chapter X of the Bankruptcy Act," *Loyola Law Review*, Vol. 16 (1969–1970), pp. 27–42.

Hefferan, H. H., Jr. "The Secured Creditor Versus the Trustee in Bankruptcy," *Connecticut Bar Journal*, Vol. 45 (March 1971), pp. 84–89.

Hellerstein, Jerome R., and Victor Brudney. "Tax Problems in Bankruptcy or Insolvency Reorganization," in *Lasser's Encyclopedia of Tax Procedures*, Second Edition. Englewood Cliffs, N. J.: Prentice-Hall, Inc., 1960.

Henson, Ray. "The Interpretation of the Uniform Commercial Code: Article 9 in the Bankruptcy Courts," *University of Miami Law Review*, Vol. 22 (Fall 1967), pp. 101–20.

———. "Subordinations and Bankruptcy: Some Current Problems," *The Business Lawyer*, Vol. 21 (April 1966), pp. 763–72.

Hertzberg, Stuart. "A Survey of Chapter XI With a Side Trip Through Chapter X," *Commercial Law Journal*, Vol. 77 (March 1972), pp. 86–92, 94.

Herzog, Asa S. "Bankruptcy Law—Modern Trends," *Journal of the National Association of Referees in Bankruptcy*, Vol. 37 (October 1963), pp. 110–16.

———. "Bankruptcy Law—Modern Trends," *Journal of the National Conference of Referees in Bankruptcy*, Vol. 40 (January 1966), pp. 19–22.

———. "Bankruptcy, Arrangements and Reorganization," *Texas Certified Public Accountant*, Vol. 36 (September 1963), pp. 3–18, 40.

———. "CPA's Role in Bankruptcy Proceeding," *The Journal of Accountancy*, Vol. 117 (January 1964), pp. 59–69.

———. "Failure To Satisfactorily Explain Loss of Assets or Deficiency of Assets To Meet Liabilities," *Journal of the National Association of Referees in Bankruptcy*, Vol. 34 (October 1960), pp. 100–3.

———. "Referee in Bankruptcy—Mr., Master or Judge?," *Credit and Financial Management*, Vol. 72 (August 1970), pp. 12–14.

———, et al. *Bankruptcy Forms and Practice*, Fourth Edition. New York: Boardman, Clark and Co., Ltd., 1971.

——— (Editor). *Seminar for Referees in Bankruptcy*, Third Edition. New York: Boardman, Clark and Co., Ltd., 1965.

Hillman, William C. "Keeping Track of Creditors in Bankruptcy Chapter Proceedings," *The Practical Lawyer*, Vol. 19 (January 1973), pp. 53–58.

Hirsch, George J. *Bankruptcy*, Revised Edition. New York: Practising Law Institute, 1968.

Hogan, William E. "Games Lawyers Play With the Bankruptcy Preference Challenge to Accounts and Inventory Financing," *Cornell Law Review*, Vol. 53 (April 1968), pp. 553–74.

Holt Landmark Law Summaries. *Creditors' Rights and Bankruptcy*. New York: Holt, Rinehart and Winston, Inc., 1970.

Hoover, John Edgar. "Investigation of Fraudulent Bankruptcies by the Federal Bureau of Investigation," *The New York Certified Public Accountant*, Vol. 32 (March 1962), pp. 187–94.

Huck, Ralph. " 'Due Bills' vs. 'Trust Receipts' for Securities Purchased and Paid For But Not Delivered," *The Business Lawyer*, Vol. 23 (November 1967), pp. 163–72.

Husband, William, and James Dockeray. *Modern Corporation Finance*. Homewood, Ill.: Richard D. Irwin, Inc., 1965.

Irish, R. A. "Should We Blame the Auditing Profession?," *Chartered Accountant in Australia*, Vol. 34 (August 1963), pp. 79–96.

Ives, David A. "Floating Lien Upheld Against Trustee," *Southwestern Law Journal*, Vol. 23 (October 1969), pp. 745–50.

Jackson, Royal E. "Trends and Developments in Bankruptcy Administration," *Journal of the National Conference of Referees in Bankruptcy*, Vol. 40 (January 1966), pp. 10–12.

Jacog, Herbert. *Debtors in Court*. Chicago: Rand McNally & Co., 1966.

Johnson, Kenneth, and Jerry South. "Further Back from Whence We Started," *The Business Lawyer*, Vol. 21 (April 1966), pp. 829–33.

Joslin, G. Stanley. "Life Insurance in Bankruptcy: A Review," *Commercial Law Journal*, Vol. 76 (March 1971), pp. 59–63.

―――. "Real Property in Bankruptcy: Some Special Considerations," *Washington and Lee Law Review*, Vol. 26 (Fall 1969), pp. 209–17.

Kaiser, John, and Donald Relkin. "The Case for Out-of-Court Settlements," *Commercial Law Journal*, Vol. 69 (May 1964), pp. 123–24.

Kasner, J. A. "The F-Reorganization Enigma: What Is a 'Mere Change in Form or Place'?," *Journal of Taxation*, Vol. 29 (October 1968), pp. 210–15.

Katcher, Archie. "Image of the Bankruptcy Court," *Journal of the National Conference of Referees in Bankruptcy*, Vol. 40 (January 1966), pp. 7–9.

Katskee, Melvin. "The Calculus of Corporate Reorganization: Chapter X vs. Chapter XI and the Role of the SEC Assessed," *The American Bankruptcy Law Journal*, Vol. 45 (Spring 1971), pp. 171–94.

Kaye, Richard A. "Federal Taxes, Bankruptcy and Assignments for the Benefit of Creditors—A Comparison," *Commercial Law Journal*, Vol. 73 (March 1968), pp. 78–80.

Keeney, J. C., and R. B. Serino. "The Effect of the Organized Crime
Control Act of 1970 in Bankruptcy Proceedings," *The American
Bankruptcy Law Journal*, Vol. 46 (Winter 1972), pp. 1–38.

Kelly, James J. *Toward Increasing the Effectiveness of Creditors' Committees*. Hanover, N. H.: Dartmouth College, Amos Tuck School of
Business Administration, 1966.

Kennedy, Frank R. "The Trustee in Bankruptcy as a Secured Creditor
Under the Uniform Commercial Code," *Michigan Law Review*, Vol. 65
(May 1967), pp. 1419–40.

———. "The Proposed Bankruptcy Rules and Official Forms," *The
American Bankruptcy Law Journal*, Vol. 46 (Winter 1972), pp. 53–71.

King, John L. "Chapter X Valuation: Principles and Application," *Journal
of the National Conference of Referees in Bankruptcy*, Part I, Vol. 42
(October 1968), pp. 108–10, 125, 126; Part II, Vol. 43 (January 1969),
pp. 23–25.

King, Lawrence. "The Business Reorganization Chapter of the Proposed
Bankruptcy Code—Or Whatever Happened to Chapters X, XI, and
XII," *Commercial Law Journal*, Vol. 78 (December 1973), pp. 429–36.

———. "Creditors' Committees, Claims Arising During Pendency of
Rehabilitation Proceeding and Filing Fees: 1967 Amendments to
Bankruptcy Act," *Commercial Law Journal*, Vol. 73 (May 1968), pp.
129–32.

———. "1967 Amendment of Section 355—Time for Filing Claims in
Arrangement Proceedings," *Commercial Law Journal*, Vol. 73 (January
1968), pp. 5–7, 16.

———. "Voidable Preferences and the Uniform Commercial Code,"
Cornell Law Quarterly, Vol. 52 (Summer 1967), pp. 925–40.

Kingsmill, T. H., Jr. "Bankruptcy and the Tax Law," *Tulane Tax Institute*,
Vol. 18 (1969), p. 633.

———. "When and How Is a Bankrupt Discharged from Federal Tax
Debt?," *Journal of Taxation*, Vol. 31 (September 1969), pp. 180–83.

Kossack, Nathaniel E., and Sheldon Davidson. "Bankruptcy: Legal
Problems and Fraud Schemes," *Credit and Financial Management*, Vol.
68 (May 1966), pp. 28–32.

———. "Bankruptcy Fraud: Alliance for Enforcement," *Journal of the
National Conference of Referees in Bankruptcy*, Vol. 40 (January 1966),
pp. 12–19.

———. "Bankruptcy Fraud: The Unholy Alliance Moves In," *Credit and
Financial Management*, Vol. 68 (April 1966), pp. 20–24.

———. " 'Scam'—The Planned Bankruptcy Racket," *The New York
Certified Public Accountant*, Vol. 35 (June 1965), pp. 417–23.

Krause, Sydney. "Accountant's Role in a Liquidation Proceeding," *The
New York Certified Public Accountant*, Vol. 28 (July 1958), pp. 503–10.

Krause, Sydney. "Classic Defenses to Trustee's Claims of Voidable Preferences," *Commercial Law Journal*, Vol. 73 (April 1968), pp. 101–3.

————. "Insolvent Debtor Adjustments Under Relevant State Court Statutes as Against Proceedings Under the Bankruptcy Act," *The Business Lawyer*, Vol. 12 (January 1957), pp. 186–89.

————. "What Constitutes Insolvency," *New York University Institute of Federal Taxation*, Vol. 27 (1969), pp. 1081–93.

Krause, Sydney, and Arnold Kapiloff. "The Bankrupt Estate, Taxable Income, and the Trustee in Bankruptcy," *Fordham Law Review*, Vol. 34 (March 1966), pp. 401–18.

Landers, Jonathan. "The Dischargeability Bill," *The Journal of the Kansas Bar Association*, Vol. 40 (Spring 1971), pp. 13–17, 64–69.

Lee, J. "Title to Property—Employee Bankrupt Vacation Pay," *The American Bankruptcy Law Journal*, Vol. 45 (Winter 1971), pp. 115–19.

Leibowitz, Ephraim. "When Your Client Is in Serious Financial Difficulty," *The Practical Accountant*, Vol. 5 (March/April 1972), pp. 56–58.

"Lessons of the Penn Central Debacle," *The Journal of Finance*, Vol. 26 (May 1971), pp. 311–62.

Levin, Harris. "Accounting Aspects of Arrangement Proceedings," *The New York Certified Public Accountant*, Vol. 28 (June 1958), pp. 429–38.

Levin, J. S. "Effect of the Tax Reform Act of 1969 on Recapitalizations, Redemptions, and the Public Policy Doctrine," *Southern California Tax Institute*, Vol. 23 (1971), p. 293.

Levinthal, Louis. "The Early History of Bankruptcy Law," *University of Pennsylvania Law Review*, Vol. 66 (1917–1918), pp. 223–50.

Levitt, Louis. "Relief Available to Debtors Under the Bankruptcy Act," *Chicago Bar Record*, Vol. 49 (May 1968), pp. 342–47. *Oklahoma Bar Association Journal*, Vol. 39 (August 1968), pp. 1495–1500.

Levy, Chauncey. "Creditors' Committees and Their Responsibilities," *Commercial Law Journal*, Vol. 74 (December 1969), pp. 355–63.

Logan, Joseph P., III. "Federal Tax Liens in Bankruptcy," *Washington and Lee Law Review*, Vol. 23 (Fall 1966), pp. 370–84.

Loiseaux, Pierre R. *Cases on Creditors' Remedies*. Indianapolis: Bobbs-Merrill Co., Inc., 1966.

Loving, R., Jr. "Penn Central Bankruptcy Express," *Fortune*, Vol. 82 (August 1970), pp. 104–9f.

Lutsky, Irwin. "Tax Services in Insolvency Proceedings," *The New York Certified Public Accountant*, Vol. 38 (June 1968), pp. 433–39.

Ma, James C., and H. D. Henneg. "What It Takes To Come Out of Chapter XI," *Credit and Financial Management*, Vol. 73 (February 1972), pp. 10–12, 40.

MacBeath, Angus. "Bankruptcy and Liquidations," *Accountants' Magazine* (Scot.), Vol. 68 (July 1964), pp. 520–28.

McEachran, J. N. "Bankruptcies—The Bane of Business," *Certified General Accountant* (Canada), (November–December 1964), pp. 13–17.

Machtinger, Sidney. "Dischargeability of Taxes in Bankruptcy," *Los Angeles Bar Bulletin*, Vol. 43 (March 1968), pp. 216–18.

Mannix, Raymond R. "Analyzing the Financial Statement in a Bankruptcy Proceeding," *Commercial Law Journal*, Vol. 63 (September 1958), pp. 251–54, 257.

Marsh, Harold, Jr. "Triumphs or Tragedy? The Bankruptcy Act Amendments of 1966," *Washington Law Review*, Vol. 42 (April 1967), pp. 681–735.

Matsch, R. P. "Bankruptcy: A Study in Functional Obsolescence," *Credit and Financial Management*, Vol. 72 (April 1970), pp. 14–17.

Mautz, Robert K. "Accounting and Business Ethics," *Florida Certified Public Accountant*, Vol. 4 (May 1964), pp. 12–20.

May, David L. "What the Credit Executive Should Know About Bankruptcy," *Credit and Financial Management*, Vol. 69 (February 1967), pp. 78–80.

Meigs, Walter B., *et al. Advanced Accounting*. New York: McGraw-Hill Book Co., 1966.

Morris, C. Robert, Jr. "Bankruptcy Law Reforms: Preferences, Secret Liens and Floating Liens," *Minnesota Law Review*, Vol. 54 (March 1970), pp. 737–74.

Mulder, John E. "A Problem: Time for Filing Involuntary Petitions," *The Practical Lawyer*, Vol. 3 (May 1957), pp. 25–35.

————. "Rehabilitation of the Financially Distressed Small Business—Revisited," *The Practical Lawyer*, Vol. 11 (November 1965), pp. 39–49.

Nachman, Norman. "Developments in Commercial Bankruptcy Law," *The Business Lawyer*, Vol. 23 (April 1968), pp. 763–78.

Newman, Norman R. "UCC Brief No. 11: The Uniform Commercial Code in the Bankruptcy Environment," *The Practical Lawyer*, Vol. 15 (January 1969), pp. 67–81.

O'Neill, Bruce C. "Bankrupt's Right to Loss—Carrying Back Tax Refund: *Segal v. Rochelle*" (Recent Decisions), *Marquette Law Review*, Vol. 50 (August 1966), pp. 143–49.

Paskay, Alexander. "Congress Amends National Bankruptcy Act," *Connecticut Law Journal*, Vol. 72 (February 1967), pp. 31–34.

Paustian, Paul W., and John E. Lewis. *Small Business Instability and Failure in Alabama*. University, Alabama: Bureau of Business Research, University of Alabama, 1963.

Pearson, Roy. "The Fine Art of Failing in Business," *Personnel Journal*, Vol. 47 (March 1968), pp. 198–200.

Pennington, R. R. "Set-off in Receivership," *Accountancy* (Eng.), Vol. 77 (September 1966), pp. 611–12.

Pennington, W. J. "Embezzling: Cases and Cautions," *The Journal of Accountancy*, Vol. 118 (July 1964), pp. 47–51.

Phelan, Marilyn. "Carryover of Tax Attributes," *TAXES—The Tax Magazine*, Vol. 51 (May 1973), pp. 273–93.

———. "Tax Proceeding in Bankruptcy: Normal Safeguards Are Denied Taxpayer," *The Journal of Taxation*, Vol. 38 (June 1973), pp. 336–40.

Phelan, Robin E. "The Proposed Bankruptcy Administration (The 'FBA') —Bureaucratic Alphabet Soup Gets a Bigger Bowl," *The American Bankruptcy Law Journal*, Vol. 48 (Fall 1974), pp. 341–68.

Plumb, W. T., Jr. "Federal Priority in Insolvency: Proposals for Reform," *Michigan Law Review*, Vol. 70 (November 1971), pp. 1–108.

———. "Federal Tax Liens and Priorities in Bankruptcy—Recent Developments," *Journal of the National Conference of Referees in Bankruptcy*, Vol. 43 (April 1969), pp. 37–46; (July 1969), pp. 83–85.

Quittner, Francis. "Recent Developments Under Chapters X and XI of the Bankruptcy Act," *The Business Lawyer*, Vol. 21 (November 1965), pp. 107–15.

Quittner, Francis, Jack Stutman, and George Treister. *Insolvency Planning*. Berkeley: University of California Printing Department, 1957.

Radin, Leon I. "Some Aspects of Monthly Operating Statements in Chapter XI," *Journal of the National Conference of Referees in Bankruptcy*, Vol. 43 (July 1969), pp. 92–95; (October 1969), pp. 123–26.

Ramanauskas, Helene M. A. "How Close to Bankruptcy Are You?," *Woman CPA*, Vol. 28 (October 1966), p. 3f.

"Report of the Commission on the Bankruptcy Laws of the United States," *The Business Lawyer*, Vol. 29 (November 1973), pp. 75–116.

Ring, L. S. "How To Fail in Business Without Half Trying," *Price Waterhouse Review*, Vol. 7 (Spring 1962), pp. 30–34.

Rothenberg, Waldo. "Reliance Under Section 17 of the Bankruptcy Act," *The Business Lawyer*, Vol. 24 (July 1969), pp. 1399–1405.

Rudin, William J. "Allowances in Chapter XI Proceedings," *Journal of the National Conference of Referees in Bankruptcy*, Vol. 40 (January 1966), pp. 29–30; (July 1966), pp. 86–87.

———. "Fees and Allowances to Attorneys in Bankruptcy and Chapter XI Proceedings," *Fordham Law Review*, Vol. 34 (March 1966), pp. 387–400.

Rutberg, Sidney. *Ten Cents on the Dollar*. New York: Simon and Schuster, Inc., 1973.

Sadd, Victor, and Robert Williams. *Causes of Commercial Bankruptcies.* U. S. Department of Commerce Domestic Commerce Series–No. 69, 1932.

Salter, Leonard. "Bankruptcy Act and the Creative Imagination," *Commercial Law Journal*, Vol. 75 (July 1970), pp. 221–23.

———. "Crisis Management Under Chapter XI: A Tale of Two Cases," *Commercial Law Journal*, Vol. 72 (May 1972), pp. 153–55, 157.

———. "The Limitations of Chapter XI," *Commercial Law Journal*, Vol. 75 (January 1970), pp. 8–10.

———. "The Versatility of Chapter XI (A Case History)," *New Jersey Law Journal*, Vol. 89 (December 1966), pp. 1–6.

Savage, Charles L. (Editor). "Causes of Business Failures," *The New York Certified Public Accountant*, Vol. 34 (December 1964), p. 869.

Schrag, Philip G., and Bruce C. Ratner. "Caveat Emptor—Empty Coffer: Bankruptcy Law Has Nothing to Offer," *Columbia Law Review*, Vol. 72 (November 1972), pp. 1147–91.

Schwartz, Max. "Representing Voluntary Bankrupts," *Brooklyn Barrister*, Vol. 19 (March 1968), pp. 162–71.

———. "The Practice of Bankruptcy," *St. John's Law Review*, Vol. 43 (October 1968), pp. 208–52.

Seidman, Saul. "Chapter X or Chapter XI?," *Commercial Law Journal*, Vol. 76 (February 1971), pp. 33–38.

———. "Creditors' Voice in Election of Trustees," *Commercial Law Journal*, Vol. 75 (August 1970), pp. 238–40.

Seligson, Charles. "Creditors' Control of Bankruptcy Administration and Legislation Relating Thereto," *American Journal of Comparative Law*, Vol. 17 (1969), pp. 48–60.

———. "New Bankruptcy Rules," *Commercial Law Journal*, Vol. 76 (November 1971), pp. 383–90.

Shaeffer, Henry W. "Proceedings in Bankruptcy in Forms Pauperis," *Columbia Law Review*, Vol. 69 (November 1969), pp. 1703–22.

Shanker, Morris G. "Treatment of Executory Contracts and Leases in Bankruptcy Chapter X and XI Proceedings," *The Practical Lawyer*, Vol. 18 (April 1972), pp. 15–34.

Shapiro, H. D. "Discharging Taxes in Bankruptcy: How It Works; The Problems Involved," *The Journal of Taxation*, Vol. 35 (September 1971), pp. 168–71.

Shaw, Frank C. "Liquidations and Receiverships—Some Practical Aspects," *Accountancy* (Ireland), Vol. 2 (August 1970), pp. 19–22.

Shimm, M. C. "Impact of State Law on Bankruptcy," *Duke Law Journal*, Vol. 1971 (December 1971), pp. 879–912.

Shipley, D. "Bankruptcy and Real Estate," *The Practical Lawyer*, Vol. 17 (January 1971), p. 53.

Silberfeld, Eli S. "Recent Litigation and Legislation in Lending," *The Journal of Commercial Bank Lending*, Vol. 50 (March 1968), pp. 2–12.

————. "Legislative and Judicial Developments in 1970," *Banking Law Journal*, Vol. 88 (March 1971), pp. 205–7.

Silberfeld, E. S., and K. Silberfeld. "Chapter X (Reorganization) Courts vs. Secured Creditors: More Decisions," *The Journal of Commercial Bank Lending*, Vol. 51 (February 1969), pp. 35–39.

Simons, Harry, and Wilbert E. Karrenbrock. *Advanced Accounting— Comprehensive Volume*. Cincinnati: Southwestern Publishing Co., 1968.

Sishtla, P. V. "Financial Ratios as Detectors of Business Failure," *Management Accountant* (India), Vol. 3 (August 1968), pp. 373–78.

Sivertsen, Elmer T. "How To Prevent Credit Frauds," *Credit and Financial Management*, Vol. 69 (October 1967), pp. 30–33.

Snedecor, Estes. "Fees and Allowances in Straight Bankruptcy," *Journal of the National Conference of Referees in Bankruptcy*, Vol. 40 (January 1966), pp. 26–29.

————. "Why So Many Bankruptcies in Oregon?," *Journal of the National Conference of Referees in Bankruptcy*, Vol. 40 (January 1966), pp. 78–80.

"Specific Performance and Insolvency—A Reappraisal" (Notes), *St. John's Law Review*, Vol. 41 (April 1967), pp. 577–88.

Stanley, David T. "Brookings Institution Study of Problems of Bankruptcy," *Journal of the National Conference of Referees in Bankruptcy*, Vol. 40 (January 1966), pp. 4–6.

————. "Shedding New Light on Insolvency," *Credit and Financial Management*, Vol. 68 (July 1966), pp. 30–32.

Stanley, David T., *et al*. *Bankruptcy: Problems, Process, Reform*. Washington, D. C.: The Brookings Institution, 1971.

Starkweather, Louis P., "Corporate Failure, Recapitalizations and Readjustments." *Fundamentals of Investment Banking*. Englewood Cliffs, N. J.: Prentice-Hall, Inc., 1949.

"Statutory Trust Fund Under IRC Section 7501(a) Versus Administrative Expenses in Bankruptcy," *Maryland Law Review*, Vol. 30 (Summer 1970), pp. 283–94.

Stiglitz, Joseph E. "Some Aspects of the Pure Theory of Corporate Finance: Bankruptcies and Takeovers," *Bell Journal of Economic and Management Science*, Vol. 3 (Autumn 1972), pp. 458–82.

Strischek, Dev. "Solvency: The Concept and An Approach for the

Analysis of Long-Term Borrowers," *The Journal of Commercial Bank Lending*, Vol. 55 (February 1973), pp. 30–47.

Stutman, Jack. "What's New in Bankruptcy and What's Not So New," *The Journal of Commercial Bank Lending*, Vol. 54 (February 1972), pp. 19–27.

Stutman, Jack, *et al.* "Your Corporate Client Is in Financial Difficulty and Solicits Your Advice," *The Business Lawyer*, Vol. 28 (November 1972), pp. 253–74.

Sullivan, George. *The Boom in Going Bust.* New York: The Macmillan Co., 1968.

"Summary Jurisdiction Under Chapter XI of the Bankruptcy Act: *Collier v. Remington*," *Georgia Law Journal*, Vol. 59 (June 1971), p. 1395.

Tamari, M. "Financial Ratios as a Means of Forecasting Bankruptcy," *Management International Review*, Vol. 4 (1966), pp. 15–21.

Taylor, E. H., Jr. "Section 60c of the Bankruptcy Act: Inadequate Protection for the Running Account Creditor," *Vanderbilt Law Review*, Vol. 24 (October 1971), pp. 919–29.

Tetlow, E. "Shocking Story of Penn Central," *Director*, Vol. 24 (August 1971), pp. 210–13.

Tillinghast, David R., and Stephen D. Gardner. "Acquisitive Reorganizations and Chapters X and XI of the Bankruptcy Act," *Tax Law Review*, Vol. 26 (May 1971), pp. 663–723.

Tondel, Lyman, Jr., and Robert H. Scott, Jr. "Trustee Certificates in Reorganization Proceedings Under the Bankruptcy Act," *The Business Lawyer*, Vol. 27 (November 1971), pp. 21–47.

Travers, Nicholas. "Fight to Disaster," *Accountancy* (Eng.), Vol. 83 (April 1972), pp. 8–11, 15–17.

Treister, G. M. "Bankruptcy Jurisdiction: Is It Too Summary?," *Journal of the National Conference of Referees in Bankruptcy*, Vol. 40 (July 1966), pp. 80–85.

————. "Practicing Lawyer's Primer on the Proposed New Bankruptcy Rules," *The American Bankruptcy Law Journal*, Vol. 45 (Fall 1971), pp. 343–62.

Trost, J. Ronald. "Involuntary Bankruptcy: Pleading and Discovery Problems," *The Business Lawyer*, Vol. 22 (July 1967), pp. 1207–11.

Twinem, L. K. "Determination of Dischargeability of Debts in Bankruptcy Proceedings," *Banking Law Journal*, Vol. 88 (July 1971), pp. 591–621.

Ungerman, Jay. "Discharge: The Prime Mover in Bankruptcy," *Journal of the National Association of Referees in Bankruptcy*, Vol. 36 (April 1962), p. 62; (July 1962), p. 85.

————. "The False Financial Statement: The Plague of Our Credit

Economy," *Commercial Law Journal*, Vol. 68 (February 1963), pp. 39–40.

Ungerman, Steve Alan. "Representing a Creditor Under Chapter X of the Bankruptcy Act," *Southwestern Law Journal*, Vol. 22 (Spring 1968), pp. 306–33.

U. S. Department of Justice, *Outline of Examination, Referees in Bankruptcy*. Washington, D. C.: Government Printing Office, 1969.

Viles, Robert M. "Non-Revolutionary Bankruptcy Act Proposed by the National Bankruptcy Commission," *The Business Lawyer*, Vol. 29 (July 1974), pp. 1117–31.

Waldrip, Stuart T. "Fraudulent Financial Statements and Section 17 of the Bankruptcy Act—The Creditor's Dilemma" (Notes), *Utah Law Review* (May 1967), pp. 281–96.

Walker, Ernest. *Essentials of Financial Management*. Englewood Cliffs, N. J.: Prentice-Hall, Inc., 1965.

Walter, James. "Determination of Technical Solvency," *The Journal of Business*, Vol. 30 (January 1957), pp. 30–43.

Warner, Sherman D. "CPA Services in Insolvency Trial Proceedings," *The New York Certified Public Accountant*, Vol. 28 (April 1958), pp. 262–67.

Warren, Charles. *Bankruptcies in United States History*. Cambridge, Mass.: Harvard University Press, 1935.

Weingarten, Herbert N., and Leonard M. Salter. "The Internal Revenue Service in the Bankruptcy Court: Can Sovereign Immunity Be Eroded?," *The American Bankruptcy Law Journal*, Vol. 47 (Spring 1973), pp. 101–10.

Weinstein, Edward A. "Accountants' Examinations and Reports in Bankruptcy Proceedings," *The New York Certified Public Accountant*, Vol. 35 (January 1965), pp. 31–39.

———. "Examining a Company in Bankruptcy," *The Quarterly* (Touche, Ross, Bailey and Smart), Vol. 9 (September 1963), pp. 14–19.

Weintraub, Benjamin, and Michael J. Crames. "Critique of Chapter VII and Related Sections of the Proposed Bankruptcy Act of 1973," *The American Bankruptcy Law Journal*, Vol. 48 (Winter 1974), pp. 1–28.

Weintraub, Benjamin, and Harris Levin. "Accountants and Arrangement Proceedings," *Credit Executive* (June 1961), p. 2.

———. "Chapter VII (Reorganization) as Proposed by the Bankruptcy Commission," *Commercial Law Journal*, Vol. 79 (January 1974), pp. 15–21.

———. "Dossier of an Arrangement Proceeding Under Chapter XI: From Petition to Confirmation and Beyond," *The Federal Bar Journal*, Vol. 27 (Spring 1967), pp. 95–110.

Weintraub, Benjamin, and Harris Levin. *Practical Guide to Bankruptcy and Debtor Relief.* Englewood Cliffs, N. J.: Prentice-Hall, Inc., 1964.

Weintraub, Benjamin, Harris Levin, and Eugene Sosnoff. "Assignments for the Benefit of Creditors and Competitive Systems for Liquidation of Insolvent Estates," *Cornell Law Quarterly*, Vol. 39 (1953–1954), pp. 3–42.

Weintraub, Charles. "Loss Carryback Tax Refund—Property of the Estate of the Bankrupt Within 70a of the Bankruptcy Act," *New York Law Forum*, Vol. 12 (Summer 1966), pp. 311–18.

Weston, Fred. *Managerial Finance.* New York: Holt, Rinehart and Winston, Inc., 1962.

Whelan, John G. "Analysis of Business Failures—Some Practices Under Scrutiny," *Chartered Secretary* (Australia), Vol. 16 (May 1964), pp. 110, 113, 115.

Whelan, Roger. "Bankruptcy—A Remedy for the Financially Distressed Client," *D. C. Bar Journal*, Vol. 35 (March–April 1968), pp. 29–31, 34–39.

Whitehurst, Elmore. "How To Avoid Corporate Bankruptcy," *Texas Bar Journal*, Vol. 34 (February 22, 1971), pp. 143–46.

Williams, Donald B. "Liquidations Beware," *Accountant* (Eng.), Vol. 160 (June 21, 1969), pp. 890–91.

Willis, L. R. "Practical Aspects of Receiverships," *Accountants' Journal* (N. Z.), Vol. 44 (March 1966), pp. 258–65.

Witschey, Robert E. "Accounting Function for Small Business," *The Journal of Accountancy*, Vol. 106 (December 1958), pp. 30–39.

Yerpe, A. J. "Getting the Most from Settlements," *Credit and Financial Management*, Vol. 70 (June 1968), pp. 18–22.

Yu, S. C. "A Reexamination of the Going Concern Postulate," *International Journal of Accountancy*, Vol. 6 (Spring 1971), pp. 37–58.

Zinman, R. M., and J. J. Creedon. "Landlord's Bankruptcy: Laissez Les Lessees," *The Business Lawyer*, Vol. 26 (July 1971), p. 1391.

Bankruptcy Act Citations

Name Index

General Index

assigned, 148
audit program, 246–47, 386
factoring, 43
financial statement presentation, 233–34
financing irregularities, 233–34
offset by payables, 247
turnover, 40
Receiver
appointment, 53, 77, 87–88
defined, 435
operation of business, 87–89
responsibility for tax return, 303–6
retention of accountant, 107–8
Recessions, 25
Reorganization proceedings; see Chapter X proceedings
Reorganizations; see also Chapter XI proceedings
acquisitive, 323
continuity of business enterprise, 325
continuity of interest, 324
debt forgiveness, 298–99
defined, 435
non-taxable, 322
Section 371 (I.R.C.), 322–23
tax considerations, 322–25
Research and development costs, 43
Retained earnings
audit program, 253
debt forgiveness adjustment, 298–99
Retention of accountant; see also Audit, Fees
application for, 109, 243
authorization for, 109–10, 114
example, 117
under Chapter X, 162
by creditors' committee, 107–8, 126–27
by debtor-in-possession, 107–9
deviations from order, 119
modification of order, 119, 124
procedures
formal, 108–9
informal, 119–20
by receiver, 107–9
retainer basis, 114
example, 118–19
steps after obtaining order, 214
by trustee, 6, 107–9
Revenue, defined, 296–97

Revenue Procedure 66–34, 324
Revenue Ruling 58–600, 310, 313
Revenue Ruling 63–29, 325

Sales
audit, 222
audit program, 253
declining, 39
improper, 219–20
inadequate, 33
ratio to total assets, 41
reduced mark-ups, 39
unrecorded, 206, 221–22
Schedules
defined, 435
description of, 144–47
forms, 347–51, 377
SEC
application to change to Chapter X proceedings, 85
approval of plan of reorganization, 72
compared to creditors' committee, 187–88
may object to fees, 123–24
number of cases reviewed, 25
quasi-reorganization, 298–99
reports, 384
role of, 163–65
under proposed Act, 336
Secured claims, 201
payment under composition settlement, 65–66
provisions for, in plan of reorganization, 71–72
Secured creditors, defined, 435
Securities and Exchange Commission; see SEC
Segal v. Rochelle, 311
Seller's lien, defined, 435
Sham, 35, 217
Statement of affairs (accounting)
for creditors' committee, 190–94
defined, 435
differences from balance sheet, 274–75
example, 276–77
procedures for constructing, 275, 278–79
purpose, 271, 274
statement of deficiency to unsecured creditors, 279–80